1990

A PUNISHMENT IN SEARCH OF A CRIME

Americans Speak Out Against The Death Penalty

A PUNISHMENT IN SEARCH OF A CRIME

Americans Speak Out Against The Death Penalty

Ian Gray & Moira Stanley
For Amnesty International U.S.A.

With a Foreword by M. Kerry Kennedy

AVON BOOKS ◆ NEW YORK

A PUNISHMENT IN SEARCH OF A CRIME is an original publication of Avon Books. This work has never before appeared in book form.

AVON BOOKS
A division of
The Hearst Corporation
105 Madison Avenue
New York, New York 10016

Copyright © 1989 by Ian Gray and Moira Stanley
Foreword copyright © 1989 by M. Kerry Kennedy
Front cover painting by Mary Ann Smith
Published by arrangement with the editors
Library of Congress Catalog Card Number: 89–91919
ISBN: 0-380-75923-3

First Avon Books Trade Printing: November 1989

AVON TRADEMARK REG. U.S. PAT. OFF. AND IN OTHER COUNTRIES, MARCA REGISTRADA, HECHO EN U.S.A.

Printed in the U.S.A.

OPM 10 9 8 7 6 5 4 3 2 1

For Jack Sher

CONTENTS

x CONTENTS

A PUNISHMENT IN SEARCH OF A CRIME

Americans Speak Out Against
The Death Penalty

FOREWORD

I was eight years old when my father was murdered. It is almost impossible to describe the pain of losing a parent to a senseless murder. And in the aftermath, it is similarly impossible to quiet the confusion: "Why him? Why this? Why me?" But even as a child one thing was clear to me: I didn't want the killer, in turn, to be killed. I remember lying in bed and praying, "Please, God. Please don't take his life, too." I saw nothing that could be accomplished in the loss of one life being answered with the loss of another. And I knew, far too vividly, the anguish that would spread through another family—another set of parents, children, brothers, and sisters thrown into grief.

That was an instinctive reaction, not a tutored one. But tutored ones are not hard to find. In the past twenty years, capital punishment has been abolished and reinstated, and after more than one hundred executions under the resuscitated death penalty, the reasons to abolish it anew are as clear as ever. Abolish it because it does nothing to deter crime. Abolish it because after decades of legal tinkering it remains as random and as capricious as it was in 1972 when Justice Stewart first likened it to lightning. Abolish it because it costs us more than life imprisonment, not less. Because it exacts its toll unevenly, sending to the chair only the poor and never the rich; and those who kill whites much more often than those who kill blacks. Because it brings forth the demeaning spectacles of mobs who stand outside prisons and cheapen life by celebrating death. Because it guarantees that we'll claim innocent lives through our mistakes. Abolish capital punishment because America, alone among Western democracies, clings to its empty promise, and America is better than that.

Those opposed to the death penalty may find the argument for abolition familiar. In this book, Ian Gray and Moira Stanley provide a look at the people behind the arguments, the modern-day abolitionists who are devoting their lives to saving the lives of others. They are a varied

1

lot and a surprising one—nuns and priests, yes; and lawyers; and scholars; and politicians; and the victims of crime, as well. Their testimony takes this issue of death out of its sloganeering setting on editorial pages and helps us locate it where it actually exists, in real people's lives.

They are people like Marie Deans, who has found her way into the anti-death penalty movement after the murder of her mother-in-law fifteen years ago. She describes the all-night wait with a prisoner scheduled for execution at dawn: "Like a campfire, and the conversation between the three of us was like throwing logs on the fire to keep away the darkness and the terror."

People like Shabaka Waqlimi, who spent eleven years on death row in Florida before convincing a court he had been wrongfully convicted—a story we've seen repeated in the past year with James Richardson in Florida and Randall Dale Adams in Texas.

People like David Bruck, a South Carolina attorney, who describes the banality of the execution chamber's evil: "It's so quick and antiseptic. I suppose it would be better to say that the actual killing was incredibly disgusting, painful, gruesome, and gory to see someone electrocuted. But, to me, the truth is it was not as bad as that, and at the same time it was much worse . . . It is a completely incomprehensible miracle how a human being comes into this world—but to snuff one out is nothing."

The desire to impose the death penalty is an understandable reaction to the anger, fear, and frustration that follow a murder. Individual families, and society at large, turn to the death penalty, if not as a solution then at least as a salve. But it has become common, and politically opportune, to equate opposition to the death penalty with being "soft on crime." Opposition to the death penalty need be no such thing. Life imprisonment—real life imprisonment, without parole—answers our need to punish and our need to protect.

Though my abhorrence of capital punishment at the time of my father's murder was instinctive, I was gratified as I grew older to learn that it was shared by someone I hold in great esteem: my father. "Whenever any American's life is taken by another unnecessarily," said Robert Kennedy, "whether it is down in the name of the law or in defiance of law, by one man or a gang, in cold blood or in passion, in an attack of violence or in response to violence—whenever we tear at the fabric of life which another man has painfully and clumsily woven for himself and his children, the whole nation is degraded."

I work now in the field of international human rights. That means I am constantly forced to recall the evil of murder. It also means this: I am frequently privileged to witness responses of courage and of faith on the part of people who meet violence with non-violence. This book is full of such people, and they have lit a torch of conscience. It leaves us readers anxious to add our own little lights.

—M. KERRY KENNEDY

PREFACE

"It is the deed that teaches, not the name we give it. Murder and capital punishment are not opposites that cancel one another, but similars that breed their kind."

—George Bernard Shaw,
Man and Superman, 1903

We stared through the tinted windows of the tenth-floor offices of Amnesty International at the rush-hour traffic gridlocked at the intersection of Eighth Avenue and West 26th Street.

We were waiting for a reply from Amnesty International U.S.A. Director John G. Healey on our proposal for the production of a new book for the human rights organization. We had in mind a lavish art volume showing the beauty and tragedy in the lands where many Amnesty chapters work. The publication would feature celebrity portraits of famous Amnesty International supporters.

"Coffee table stuff is not really our style," the director said, "but I do need a book—a book on the death penalty."

We were a long way from being pro capital punishment, but we were here to help prisoners of conscience, not murderers, gangsters, and sadists. "We don't know anything about the death penalty," we protested, "and besides, you've already got a book on this subject [United States of America—The Death Penalty]."

"I want another one, maybe a little less statistical, a little more personal. Execution by government is a very important issue with Amnesty. Besides," he added, "this will give you a chance to find out about one of the more unsung parts of our mandate, to abolish the death penalty completely."

New York, December 11, 1986

We've been learning about the death penalty for the past three years. We have not tried, nor are we qualified, to write an academic work. There are volumes of learned publications on the death penalty, and it wasn't until we started our research that we found out just how many there were!

After several different approaches and a couple of false starts we eventually decided on the interview format, telling the story through the words of those whose lives had been touched by violent death itself.

Several thousand miles and many months later we've walked down death row, trod the halls of Congress, and talked with nearly fifty people in seventeen states—people who believe passionately that the death penalty in America is an evil that none of us can afford.

The more we spoke with lawyers, social workers, those involved in anti-death penalty work, church groups, civil rights groups, and perhaps more importantly with some of the relatives of murder victims, the more convinced we became that violent solutions merely produce more violence.

It is an unpleasant fact that the world's most "civilized" country kills (executes, if you prefer the euphemism) its own citizens in the name of law, order, and justice.

It is an equally unpleasant fact that there is an alarmingly high murder rate—more than 20,000 people a year—in the United States.

President Bush, in his 1988 election campaign, made much of the fact that a convicted murderer from Massachusetts killed again while on furlough from prison. This was a tragedy, as is all violent death. What President Bush failed to mention was that a murderer or any other prisoner can still kill again after being released at the end of a full prison term. If the death penalty were to be used to prevent further murders, we would have to execute the over 30,000 convicted murderers currently behind bars.

We have learned that the death penalty confuses the issue of law and order and offers revenge rather than security. An execution is, at best, a symbolic gesture of governmental power and at worst premeditated murder.

We call this book a *A Punishment in Search of a Crime* because the Supreme Court has long since outlawed branding, mutilation, and whipping, and so restricted the use of the one remaining physical punishment that a prosecutor has to search very hard indeed to find the elements that will fit the constitutional requirements for a sentence of death.

A society as powerful as the United States is quite capable of protecting itself from violent and murderous behavior without resorting to the language of the criminal, the language of death.

These interviews give a very one-sided view of the death penalty, but we conclude that retentionists have their say in the millions of tax dollars they throw at this medieval relic. They have their say, each and every time they throw the switch, drop the pellets, pour poison into a vein, or pull the trigger on an unarmed prisoner. Their actions speak louder than ever their words could.

Since 1977, the executioners' body count in the United States has already climbed into three figures. Will we have to reach the four-figure mark before we put an end to this barbaric practice?

—IAN GRAY AND MOIRA STANLEY
February 29, 1989, Los Angeles

ACKNOWLEDGMENTS

We would like to thank everyone from Amnesty International U.S.A., in particular, Jack Healey, Magdaleno Rose-Avila, Charles Fulwood, David Hinkley, James O'Dea, Jack Rendler, Lyn Bowersox, Keith Jennings, and Jean Freedberg, without whose help, support, and cooperation this project could not have been accomplished.

We would also like to thank John Batten, Keta Taylor Colby, Jane Dystel, Cedric Hendricks, Robin Farrow, Hamish MacGibbon, Lyle Poncher, Jack Sher, and of course everyone who gave us their time to make these interviews possible.

Special thanks to:

Writer and historian Watt Espy, for the rare information that he provided for our section on "Execution Methods in the United States."

Writer and director Gregory Goodell, for his computer wizardry.

Writers Franklin Zimring and Gordon Hawkins, for the use of our book title, *A Punishment in Search of a Crime,* a chapter title from their book, *Capital Punishment and the American Agenda* (Cambridge University Press).

Writer John Sandford, for an excerpt on Sacco and Vanzetti from his book *A Very Good Land to Fall With* (Black Sparrow Press).

Editor Judith Riven, for her help and encouragement.

Writer and linguist Bruce Pearson, for reading and correcting our initial transcript.

Writer and sociologist Michael Radelet, without whose editing skills and unparalleled knowledge of the death penalty in America we could never have achieved a final draft.

Perhaps the most valuable additions to this book were made by individuals whose formal interviews are not reproduced in the pages that follow. We especially learned a great deal from our talks with Abdul Aziz, Tim Caine, C. Budd Colby, Jerry Gorman, Jimmy Lohman, Margot Kidder, Camilla Mashore, Paul Mones, Bill Pelke, Neal

Walker, and Lois Williamson. These people not only gave us important background information, but in many instances, steered us in the direction of those who had been particularly instrumental in shaping their views on the subject.

INTRODUCTION

"The great masses of the people will more easily fall victim to a great lie than to a small one."

—Adolf Hitler, *Mein Kampf*

The United States of America is the most successful nation in history and the self-proclaimed leader of the civilized world.

American ideals, values, and way of life are second to none. It is the richest democracy on earth, sharing special bonds of community and human values with other democratically governed peoples. It is also the only industrialized Western democracy that continues to execute its citizens.

This contrast in human rights between the "leader of the free world" and its European allies was illustrated a few years ago when the State Department was informed by West Germany, a country that forty-five years ago practiced genocide as a national policy, that the request for extradition of a terrorist to the United States wouldn't be granted unless America would promise not to impose the death penalty on him.

The United States complied.

It is ironic that Germany refused to send this man to join the more than 2,000 souls languishing in various death rows in America. One can speculate that the Germans have learned the painful lesson of legalized homicide. In the early thirties Germany was an abolitionist country until a certain former house painter reintroduced capital punishment.

It is also noteworthy that the subject of the extradition from Germany was a terrorist. If getting tough with terrorists was the answer,

11

one would imagine that the State of Israel, which, for more than two decades has had continual domestic terror within its borders (not unlike the United Kingdom, Italy, and Germany), would have had a plethora of executions. In practice, it has employed the executioner only once in its history, in 1962 when Adolph Eichmann was hanged.

It is no coincidence that the list of actively executing regimes closely corresponds to that of politically repressive countries. The negative correlation between execution policy and governmental respect for human rights throughout the world can be demonstrated over and over again.

For some years, South Africa has had one of the highest rates of judicial execution in the world. It has also had a very high death rate for detainees in police custody. The political regime responsible for this extensive use of capital punishment has also severely curtailed civil and political rights by discriminatory and repressive legislation.

In Uganda under President Idi Amin, between 1971 and 1978, estimates of the number killed by security forces range from 50,000 to 300,000. In many African countries the use of summary executions is not so much an open disregard for human rights as the principal method for expressing it.

In South America, Brazil abolished the death penalty as long ago as 1882, but reintroduced it in 1969 under military rule. In Argentina, during the seventies, under the junta, while no one was actually sentenced to death by military tribunal, that country was considered to be a leading practitioner of extrajudicial or extralegal executions, with thousands of people disappearing.

The People's Republic of China is only one of many Asian governments utilizing the death penalty, both as a method of maintaining law and order and for punishing a wide range of political offenses. Capital offenses include provoking dissension, conducting counterrevolutionary propaganda and agitation, and spreading rumors.

In the Soviet Union, the list of offenses punishable by death in all fifteen Union Republics until recently included actions disrupting the work of corrective labor institutions, making or passing counterfeit money or securities, stealing state property, and taking a bribe; eighteen in all.

(On March 15, 1989, the USSR Supreme Soviet reduced the number of death punishable offenses to six: treason, espionage, terrorist acts, sabotage, intentional homicide under aggravating circumstances, and rape of minors. Furthermore, women are exempt from the death penalty, as are men under the age of eighteen or over sixty at the time of the crime.)

In the Middle East, the only state without an execution in the last decade is Israel. Egypt, Libya, and Syria have very poor human rights records. Those of Iran and Iraq are atrocious.

These are just a few examples from the 129 countries and territories that join the United States in retaining and using the death penalty.

Debates here in the United States over capital punishment have often failed to recognize its possible international consequences. Even the limited use of the death penalty in the United States reinforces its practice in retentionist countries, where it may be applied even more indiscriminately and arbitrarily than in the United States.

America's continued use of execution leaves open the possibility that American citizens abroad could fall victim to the discretionary use of the death penalty (a tourist convicted of "spying"?), a weapon the United States holds to be legitimate punishment, and against which it has no moral defense.

If the United States were to abolish the death penalty it could take the moral high ground and condemn state killing under *all* circumstances, thereby giving added protection to its citizens world wide. Instead it endangers their lives by joining in the same practices as the countries whose standards of civil rights it abhors.

Statistics can be misleading, but there is a set of figures on which both abolitionists and retentionists agree. This is the one that shows public opinion overwhelmingly in support of death as a form of punishment for murder, or at any rate heinous murder.

Why is it that Americans, of all people, endorse this barbaric practice?

Could it be, as philosopher, author, and leading expert on the death penalty Professor Hugo Adam Bedau so succinctly puts it, that the death penalty is "an important legal threat, abstractly desirable as part of society's permanent bulwark against crime"? or as Professor Franklin Zimring, author of *Capital Punishment and the American Agenda,* states: "The average American, who says he's for the death penalty, means he likes to have the possibility there, in the same sense he likes to have missiles in silos aimed at the Russians . . . that doesn't mean he wants to push the button now."

If we take the positive view, it is to humanity's credit that it has come so far in the last two centuries—two hundred years that witnessed slavery, punishment by torture, and the use of the scaffold for stealing a loaf of bread. But we are still shackled by history to the gallows, to the ritual nature of the murder trial, and the incantatory power of the death sentence. It is our past that causes us to be out of step with the present.

What is now called public opinion was once "the mob." One such mob is described in chilling detail by Charles Dickens in his *Tale of Two Cities:* " . . . the sort of interest with which this man [accused of murder] was stared and breathed at was not the sort that elevated humanity. Had he stood in peril of a less horrible sentence [hanging, drawing, and quartering]—had there been a chance of any one of its savage details being spared—by just so much would he have lost in his fascination . . . Whatever gloss the various spectators put upon the interest, according to their several arts and powers of self-deceit, the interest was, at the root of it, ogreish. . . ."

The ogreish aspects of modern-day executions are veiled in the legal apparatus and ritual that attends "lawful" killings.

In his book *Death Row Chaplain,* the Reverend Byron Eshelman opens: "Only the ritual of an execution makes it possible to endure. Without it, the condemned man could not give the expected measure of cooperation to the etiquette of dying. Without it, we who must preside by their deaths could not face the morning of each new execution day."

Without ritual there would be no death penalty, just murder. Of course, with the ritual it remains nothing more than a primitive human sacrifice.

In 1972, the U.S. Supreme Court, ruling in *Furman v. Georgia,* put a halt to executions. Such was the climate that Professor Bedau predicted: "We will not see another execution in this nation, in this century." It seemed that the death penalty was to become a thing of the past, that the electric chairs, gas chambers, and gallows would only exist in wax museums, along with thumbscrews and branding irons; a part of the grim and grisly historical catalogue of man's inhumanity to man.

So what happened?

The 1972 *Furman* decision infuriated many states, who regarded it as a direct attack on their sovereignty. They wasted no time in tapping the reservoir of fear among the voting public to lash back at the Supreme Court. In Georgia, Lester Maddox called *Furman* a "mandate for rapists and murderers." Other states, particularly in the South, were quick to hitch their fate to the death wagon. Traditionally sensitive to federal interference, they began drafting new death penalty laws to skirt three of the five assenting votes of the Supreme Court Justices.

Four years after *Furman,* their new laws were tested in *Gregg.* By a vote of seven to two, the U.S. Supreme Court passed the buck back to the states and in effect gave permission to polish up the electrodes, sharpen the needles, and oil the hinges of execution chambers across the land. Gary Gilmore was the first to go in 1977; by 1989 we were well into executing our second hundred.

Death penalty advocates in California soon smelled blood, and picked up on the "law and order" issue as a sure-fire vote getter. In the most prosperous state in the Union, the public's justified concern with crime was exploited in a massive and successful campaign of fear against the reelection of Chief Justice Rose Bird and two other members of the California Supreme Court.

We have yet to see how much cyanide will fill the newly renovated death chamber of San Quentin.

Retentionists sometimes claim capital punishment is a deterrent, but the claim of deterrence is a mantle that vengeance wears with ease. If capital punishment saved lives, you would have less chance of being murdered in Florida, where the executioner is a friend, than in Michigan, which deported the executioner in 1847. However, the reverse is true.

How realistic are the fears of being murdered and will the death penalty allay them? The U.S. Department of Justice's publication—*Capital Punishment, 1984*—gave the following sobering statistics. For the ten-year period 1975 to 1985, 204,000 people in the United States were known to be victims of murder or non-negligent manslaughter (0.85 percent of the population).

For these crimes, there were 198,000 arrests. Two thousand, three hundred, and eighty-four persons entered prison under sentence of death (although many were quickly reversed on appeal) and thirty-two were executed.

According to the Department of Justice's *Sourcebook of Criminal Statistics, 1986,* approximately 72 percent of the murders and non-negligent manslaughters known to the police are cleared by an arrest. This is the highest arrest rate for any type of crime. Only 14 percent of the burglaries reported to police are cleared by arrest. For all violent crimes, the clearance rate is 47.6 percent, and for property crimes it is 17.8 percent.

It would appear that the reason for such a high arrest rate for murder is that it is, for the most part, an unpremeditated crime—the mark of a bungler. With a 72 percent chance of getting caught, the logical conclusion is that the threat of execution would deter a would-be killer.

It clearly does not.

The Justice Department figures do not include the many missing who have been murdered. Premeditated murder frequently includes the disappearance of the body, and by definition, there are no statistics on this. We also see from the Justice Department statistics that a tiny .016

percent of those convicted for murder and 1.5 percent of those sentenced to death were actually executed.

Between the time that the above figures were published and today, the number of condemned has more than doubled. It continues to climb rapidly. Surely, if the death penalty is a deterrent, the murder figure would be lower. One must draw the conclusion that capital punishment laws are in reality society's answer to "garbage disposal."

One of the more forceful arguments voiced by those who seek to retain the death penalty is that the relatives of the victims feel cheated when a loved one has been murdered and the perpetrator receives a custodial sentence. New York's Mayor Edward I. Koch put it more bluntly. "When the killer lives, the victim dies twice."

These families all have the right to justice, but the death penalty fails to achieve that goal.

In practice, very, very few murderers are executed. A few "lucky" families are vindicated and may feel that justice has been served. The remainder may well ask, "Why hasn't the man who killed my loved one been executed? Was the life of my family member less worthy? I want my pound of flesh. John Doe got his, where is mine?"

The lives of their loved ones have been devalued by a system that seldom fulfills its lethal promise. A promise which merely leaves another set of bereaved relatives. If the "eye for an eye" principle was adopted, there would be over 20,000 executions a year. If all the sentences were carried out on death row, there would be over 2,000 dead. De facto capital punishment would require a massive and unprecedented escalation of killings, unparalleled in democratic history. Further, this kind of vengeance would not bring back the loved one. It only serves to keep the wound of grief open. Those who ask abolitionists, "How would you feel if someone killed your mother?" need to ask themselves how they would feel if the killer was their son.

Everyone loses under a system that is conducted like some dreadful lottery. We play a ghoulish game of chance, with the dice heavily loaded against the poor and minorities. Voltaire said that it was necessary to hang an admiral once in a while *"pour décourager les autres"* (to discourage others). He understood the merit of an arbitrary act but he never presumed to call it justice.

Executions are, at best, sops to Cerberus. Like unjust wars, they provide a focal point of hatred and solve nothing. Indeed, society's violent reaction to violence may well aggravate the very real problem of serious crime. It teaches people that killing people is okay.

And the death penalty states do react. They warehouse human beings, including children and the insane, for death, keep them in limbo, waiting for execution or commutation. Death row is not a sentence, it is a torture chamber. It is the home of the living dead, somewhere in the Twilight Zone.

The truth of the Eighth Amendment is self-evident—this kind of retaliation by society is both "cruel" and "unusual."

We believe that abolition of capital punishment in the United States is not merely another bleeding heart cause looking for social salvation; it is a vital building block on the path toward the total civilization to which humanity has always aspired.

EXECUTION METHODS IN THE UNITED STATES

"When we abolished the punishment for treason that you should be hanged, and then cut down while still alive, and then disemboweled while still alive and then quartered, we did not abolish that punishment because we sympathized with traitors, but because we took the view that it was a punishment no longer consistent with our self-respect."

—Lord Chancellor Gardiner,
    debating for the abolition of the death penalty,
    House of Lords, 1965

In the little over two centuries that America has been an independent nation and in the little under two centuries that the United States was a British colony, some 16,000 citizens are known to have died at the hands of the executioner. The earliest recorded was in 1608.

This figure, however, is a conservative one, since it represents only *confirmed* legal executions and does *not* include undocumented executions. Nor does it include the thousands of lynchings that were epidemic during the nineteenth century.

God only knows the true figure.

The United States has employed just about every method of execution that can be dreamed up. We've sawed people in half, beheaded them, burned them, drowned them, crushed them with rocks, tied them to anthills, buried them alive, and almost every way in fact except perhaps boiling them in oil.

There are, however, five methods of killing that have endured as legal sanctions in the United States. These are shooting, hanging, electrocution, gassing, and lethal injection. We've hanged people for all of our history, but we only began injecting them with poison in the 1980s.

BANG...YOU'RE DEAD!

"'Shoot, if you must this old gray head, but spare your country's flag,' she said."
—John Greenleaf Whittier, 1807–1892

Two states, Idaho and Utah, still allow for execution by shooting (both states also authorize lethal injection), but during the colonial period it was widely used throughout the land. Most Indian tribal executions in the nineteenth century were by shooting. The military also shot convicted soldiers.

The first recorded execution by firing squad in this country was in 1608. The victim was George Kendall, one of the original councilors for the colony of Virginia.

Utah will always be remembered as the site of the 1977 execution of Gary Gilmore, the subject of Norman Mailer's book, *The Executioner's Song*, and the first casualty after the 1972 Supreme Court *(Furman v. Georgia)* ruling against execution. Even though Americans will continue to kill each other extra-judicially with guns (more than 8,000 people a year), it is unlikely this nation will ever witness another death by firing squad.

The concept, however, has been successfully exported throughout the world. Death by firing squad has been embraced with unbridled enthusiasm and exceeds every other method of execution by far. The list of countries that employ it is awesome and includes Afghanistan, Albania, Argentina, Angola, Bahrain, Bangladesh, Benin, Bolivia, Bulgaria, Burundi, Cameroon, Central African Republic, Chad, Chile, China, Comoros, Congo, Cuba, Egypt, Equatorial Guinea, Ethiopia, Gabon, Ghana, Guatemala, Guinea, Guinea-Bissau, Hungary, India, Indonesia, Iran, Iraq, Ivory Coast, Jordan, Kampuchea, Korea, Kuwait, Lebanon, Liberia, Libya, Madagascar, Mali, Mauritania, Morocco, Mozambique, Nepal, Nigeria, Paraguay, Peru, Poland, Rumania, Rwanda, Sierra Leone, Somalia, Sudan, Suriname, Syria,

Taiwan, Thailand, Uganda, United Arab Emirates, Vietnam, Yemen, Zaire.

For many of these Third World and Eastern Bloc countries, some of which previously beheaded and stoned their citizens to death, shooting as a means of execution represents an attempt to appear "modern."

In addition to the "humanity" of the firing squad, the ready availability of firearms and those trained in their use (military and police), combined with lack of a fixed apparatus such as a gallows, gas chamber or electric chair makes the whole procedure far more simple, and relatively cheap.

Our image of death by firing squad has been formed by Hollywood films of the thirties, and the tally of executing countries listed above is proof of the universal influence of the motion picture industry.

The typical scenario of such a movie goes as follows:

A handsome man with a pencil-thin mustache stands before a firing squad. The dawn light casts his pale shadow on a white stucco wall. He bravely refuses a blindfold and enjoys a last cigarette.

It is time.

The Captain of the Guard gives the command.

There is a blast of musket fire.

The prisoner sinks to his knees, a thin trickle of blood seeps from his lower lip.

He is no more.

The reality is a little different.

After the Nüremberg Trials, dozens of condemned war criminals in Germany and Austria were sentenced to death by this method. It turned out to be inefficient and messy. So many executions were botched, that the authorities quickly stopped the practice and the remainder of the condemned were hanged.

A large-caliber revolver placed in the mouth of the victim, as they do in China, would have done the job perfectly, but this method had a major flaw. The image is not acceptable. Too much blood.

What is "acceptable" is the procedure for execution by shooting in the United States.

The victim is bound to a chair by leather straps in front of an oval-shaped canvas wall. A doctor, using a stethoscope, locates the heart and pins a cloth target directly over it. The victim is given the choice of a hood.

Twenty feet away in an enclosure, five sharpshooters stand, each with a .30-caliber rifle. The yard captain issues a single round to each member of the firing party. One receives a blank.

(The famous "blank round" is mandated so that none of the marksmen will know if he was the one who fired the fatal shot. Of course anyone who has ever fired a blank and a live round cannot fail to recognize the enormous difference in the recoil of the two types of ammunition. However the significance of this regulation should not be underestimated. If killing this person is such a good idea, why would we need a blank round? The answer is simple. It is the deep-down human knowledge that execution is wrong that places the blank in one of the rifles.)

Each man places his weapon through a slot in the canvas and fires in unison. Four bullets pump into the heart.

Some marksmen have been known to "cheat" and have aimed away from their target. In Utah on September 10, 1951, all four members of the firing party hit the prisoner, Elisio J. Mares, on the right-hand side. He slowly bled to death.

At the 1977 shooting of Gary Gilmore his executioners were less squeamish, and all four bullets pierced the heart. Notwithstanding, Gilmore lived for a full two minutes.

Time for a last cigarette?

THE DROP

"The prospect of hanging concentrates the mind wonderfully."

—Dr. Samuel Johnson, 1709–1784

In early history, hanging was only used as a mark of indignity on the lifeless bodies of criminals. As a form of execution it does not appear in the Mosaic Code, but under Persian rule gallows were certainly used.

It came to England via Germany. Henry I (1068–1135) was the first to decree that all thieves should be hanged, and it became the fully established punishment for murderers by the time of Henry II.

Hanging has received many euphemistic nicknames over the centuries, including: the drop; the morning drop; dancing at [the Old] Bailey's ballroom; topping; getting topped; launching him into eternity; taking a leap in the dark; the dance of death. Of the executioner: the crap merchant; the sheriff's journeyman and the topsman. And of the gallows: the wooden legged mare.

The early colonists brought "the drop" across the Atlantic and it was retained in the majority of American states after the achievement of independence.

In the 1900s twenty-seven jurisdictions opted for electrocution as a more humane method of killing than hanging: Alabama, Arkansas, Connecticut, the District of Columbia, Florida, Georgia, Illinois, Indiana, Kentucky, Louisiana, Massachusetts, Mississippi, Nebraska, New Jersey, New Mexico, New York, North Carolina, Ohio, Oklahoma, Pennsylvania, South Carolina, South Dakota, Tennessee, Texas, Vermont, Virginia, and West Virginia. At the present time only Washington, Delaware, and Montana have hanging as a form of execution, although Washington and Montana provide the victim with a choice of lethal injection, and Delaware allows those convicted before June 13, 1986, to opt for hanging. There has not been an official hanging in the United States since James Latham and George York were sent through the trap in Kansas on June 22, 1965.

Years of practice had gone into perfecting the technique of hanging. To be *hanged by the neck until he be dead* meant that the victim would stand on a trapdoor, a noose placed around his neck, with the knot positioned tightly behind the left ear. The legs were bound together to prevent kicking; the face was covered by a hood, so that witnesses would not see the grimaces, and the hands were tied behind the back. Then the hangman would signal for the trapdoor to be opened so the body would drop. The trapdoor is actually sprung open by cutting a string. Sometimes there are three men in a booth on the platform, each of whom cuts a string at the hangman's signal, only one of which actually springs the trapdoor, not dissimilar to the firing squad's "blank round."

In a "clean hanging" the body drops about six to eight feet before the rope takes the strain. If all goes perfectly, the first three cervical vertebrae are fractured or dislocated when the knot strikes behind the left ear, instantly rendering the prisoner unconscious.

If the "right" number of bones are broken in the neck, the bones collapse on the spinal cord, cutting off oxygen to the brain and paralyzing the rest of the body. Brain death follows rapidly, in about seventeen seconds.

An average job means the victim thrashes at the end of the rope for a few minutes. Wheezing can be heard. The stench can be awful since the victim empties his bowels, urinates, and frequently ejaculates at the same time. The resulting odors mixed with overwhelming perspiration can be sickening.

At the end, the dying man shudders violently and after some final jerking and twitching there is quiet.

Former San Quentin Warden Clinton Duffy, who witnessed sixty hangings, described the following types of executions as being botched or "dirty." "The condemned strangled slowly, which could take as long as a quarter of an hour. The wheezing is extremely loud, like the hysterical squealing of a dying pig. The victim may bob up and down like a yo-yo. It may even be necessary for a guard to hold onto his legs so his violent churnings do not break the rope. A poorly placed knot occasionally gouges out a chunk of the face and head. There have been cases where the head has been completely ripped off."

In order to understand the "mechanics" of the practice, we have reproduced excerpts from the testimony given to the Royal Commission on Capital Punishment in 1950, of Albert Pierrepoint, the official executioner for Great Britain, who hanged, in his own words, "some hundreds." His other occupation is given as "licensee." In Great Britain, a licensee is a man who runs a pub, and a first-rate licensee is a man who can "pull a pint with a good head." By all accounts a pint of ale pulled by Mr. Pierrepoint would be expertly poured. The Pierrepoint family were "hereditary" executioners from 1901 to 1956. Mr. Albert Pierrepoint now lives in Southport, England.

At one stage during his testimony before the Royal Commission, when asked if he ever discussed his work, Pierrepoint says, "No—it is sacred to me, really." Hopefully his expertise was so great that he never subjected a condemned man to the kind of horror described by Warden Duffy.

At the beginning of his book, entitled *Executioner Pierrepoint: An Autobiography,* Pierrepoint writes:

"I operated on behalf of the state, what I am convinced was the most humane and the most dignified method of meting out death to a delinquent—however justified or unjustified the allotment of death may be—and on behalf of humanity I trained other nations to adopt the British system of execution . . . I do not now believe that any one of the hundreds of executions I carried out has in any way acted as a deterrent against future murder. Capital punishment in my view, achieved nothing except revenge."

And, at the end of the book, he says:

"I have come to the conclusion that executions solve nothing, and are only an antiquated relic of a primitive desire for revenge which takes the easy way and hands over the responsibility for revenge to other people."

Below are some excerpts from Mr. Pierrepoint's testimony before the Royal Commission on Capital Punishment, November 2, 1950:

Q: We are very grateful to you for coming, Mr. Pierrepoint. How long have you been an executioner?

P: About 20 years.

Q: How did you become appointed? What put the idea into your head, and what did you do in order to secure the appointment?

P: It is in the family, really, I am the third in our family to hold the position—my father, my uncle and myself.

Q: It seems a sort of hereditary job?

P: It seems like it.

Q: How long before your appointment did you serve as an assistant executioner?

P: About nine years.

Q: When you are an assistant executioner what are your actual duties?

P: It is really not much, but it is always handy to be there in case the executioner is sick or anything like that. The assistant executioner straps the legs of the prisoner on the drop itself. He does not play a big part really; it is just experience he is there for.

Q: You say you were an assistant executioner for nine years, so I suppose you attended quite a number of executions as assistant executioner?

P: Probably about 40.

Q: How many executions have you attended as executioner?

P: Some hundreds.

Q: Then you are in a very good position to express an opinion on this question: do you consider that the method of execution by hanging as followed in this country is as humane and quick as any method of capital punishment could be?

P: Yes, I think it is quick, certain and humane. I think it is the fastest and quickest in the world bar nothing. It is quicker than shooting and cleaner.

Q: Have you had any awkward moments?

P: No, I have only seen one in all my career.

Q: What happened?

P: He was rough. It was unfortunate; he was not an Englishman, he was a spy and kicked up rough.

Q: He went for you?

P: Not only me, he went for everybody.

Q: That is the only case is it?

P: I have had probably three more, like a faint at the last minute, or something like that, but it has not been anything to speak about.

Q: Can you think of any improvements which you would like to suggest?

P: On the English method, no. I could not suggest anything to improve it. I think it is perfect and foolproof, that is, provided an experienced man is doing the job.

Q: Would you just tell us, so that we may have it on record, exactly what you do from the moment you arrive at a prison in order to carry out an execution until the end of the operation?

P: We have to report at the prison before 4 o'clock in the afternoon the previous day. On arriving at the prison we are shown to our rooms. Shortly afterwards we are shown the execution chamber and we prepare. We have a dummy execution, a rehearsal, on that afternoon when we arrive. Then in the evening, say at 5 o'clock or 6 o'clock, we see the prisoner, probably at exercise or in his cell. Then we ask for his age, height and weight and in the evening we make out his drop. Every person has a different drop. That is all for the first day. Then in the morning at 7 o'clock you go to the execution chamber again and get all ready, make the final arrangements for the job itself. Then we finish there about half an hour before the execution is going to take place, and that is all there is to it.

Q: Do you see the prisoner without the prisoner knowing you are seeing him?

P: Definitely. We see him through a spy-hole, or we look through the window when he has his exercise.

Q: You say you have his age, height and weight. I know why you want his weight, but why do you want his age and height?

P: We have to have his age. If you get a person of say, 24 years of age, he weighs 9 stone [126 lbs]; you might get a man of 65 years of age and he weighs 9 stone, but the man of 65 has feeble muscles and the young fellow of 24 might have a strong, powerful muscular body; and we have to allow for that, so as to have it perfect and instantaneous.

Q: Do you allow for that by putting something on the drop?

P: More inches on the drop for a stronger man.

Q: A longer drop?

P: A longer drop for a muscular man; that is why we see him on the previous day.

Q: There is no formula for that? You have to trust your experience to do that—you cannot do that by mathematics?

P: No, just experience.

Q: I suppose it takes a good deal of experience to make sure of doing it right?

P: I think so myself, yes.

Q: The knot, as you showed us this morning, must always be under the angle of the left jaw?

P: Yes.

Q: That is very important, is it?

P: Very important.

Q: Why is it very important?

P: If you had the same knot on the right-hand side it comes back behind the neck, it finishes behind the neck, and throws the neck forward, which would make a strangulation. If you put it on the left-hand side it finishes up in front and throws the chin back and breaks the spinal cord.

Q: It depends on where he is standing on the trap?

P: No. I do not think so. The knot is the secret of it, really. We have to put it on the left lower jaw and if we have it on that side, when he falls it finishes under the chin and throws the chin back; but if the knot is on the right-hand side, it would finish up behind his neck and throw his neck forward, which would be strangulation. He might live on the rope a quarter of an hour then.

Q: Would you agree with those who tell us that the great majority of condemned prisoners, when their time comes, go calmly and collectedly on to the trap?

P: From my experience, I would say 99 out of every 100 go that way, and that is a big majority, is it not?

Q: I think you told us this morning that you were against blindfolding a man before you take him onto the trap?

P: Yes.

Q: Because it would make the proceedings longer?

P: It makes it a lot longer. It has been tried on three or four occasions abroad, and it has been a bad failure.

Q: Where abroad?

P: In Germany, and also in Austria. I trained the Austrians in the English method of execution.

Q: Did you execute condemned war criminals in Germany and Austria after the war?

P: Yes, after the war was finished they were all sentenced to death by shooting, but I believe after a few shootings it was stopped and they all had to be executed by hanging.

Q: Did that all go smoothly?

P: Perfect.

Q: Do you always pull the lever yourself?

P: Yes, the executioner must do, that is the executioner's job.

Q: Do you find your duties very trying, or have you got accustomed to them?

P: I am accustomed to it now.

Q: You do not turn a hair?

P: No.

Q: Have you had any experience of judging what the general opinion of ordinary people in England is about capital punishment? I imagine that people must talk to you about your duties?

P: Yes, but I refuse to speak about it. It is something I think should be secret myself. It is sacred to me, really.

Chairman: Thank you, Mr. Pierrepoint; we are very much obliged to you.

(The United Kingdom abandoned the practice of capital punishment in 1965.)

A SHOCKING WAY TO GO

"In his own grease I made him fry."
— Geoffrey Chaucer, 1340?–1400,
Prologue from *The Wyves Tale of Bathe*

The following is an excerpt from a speech made to Harvard Law School, Class of 1931, by Senior Associate Justice William J. Brennan, Jr., on September 5, 1986.

"The calculated killing of a human being by the state involves, by its very nature, an absolute denial of the executed person's humanity and thus violates the command of the eighth amendment."

Brennan adds,

"In his *Furman* dissent, Chief Justice Burger distinguished capital punishment from 'a punishment such as burning at the stake that everyone would find ineffably repugnant to all civilized standards.' In my view, this is not an argument; this is simply the view of a single judge. Think about it: burning at the stake *is* capital punishment. It is simply one way of graphically describing one particular method of execution. Why did the Chief Justice think it different? Death by electrocution could be described in equally graphic terms. As I described in a dissent in a case called *Glass v. Louisiana* in 1985, the flesh does burn when the electric chair is used, just as it might burn at the stake. *Furman* might have been characterized not as a case about the death penalty, but rather as a case about death by electrocution, which might be fairly described as 'frying in a chair.' How would 'frying in a chair' be distinguished from burning at the stake?"

The year was 1890 and America was preparing to enter the twentieth century in a welter of wealth and prosperity. Science was the new religion and electricity the Messiah. The industrial revolution was all but won. Maybe the "enlightenment" talked of by founding fathers Franklin and Jefferson was about to become a reality.

Public opinion was changing from a frontier society to that of a great industrial nation. The time was also ripe for this modern society to embrace new technology in the area of execution.

After a particularly graphic description in the newspapers of a hanging, where the victim had dangled on the end of a rope for over fifteen minutes before finally choking to death, there was an outcry deeming this method of slaying as barbaric. A new and humane method was sought. Lethal injection was suggested as a more modern method, but it was electricity that was to win the day.

In the late 1880s, Thomas Edison and George Westinghouse were in vicious competition over business profits connected with the domination of the electrical power industry. Edison was faced with Westinghouse's superior AC system over his cumbersome and expensive DC system, and he decided to send a young engineer, Harold P. Brown, around the country staging shows to demonstrate the effectiveness of this new shocking system (or shocking new system).

The public were treated to bizarre, circuslike sideshows during which stray dogs, cats, horses, and even an orangutan were electrocuted to demonstrate the ghastly effectiveness of the new discovery.

A special commission decided that the concept of the electric chair as a means of humane execution was feasible, despite the fact that the poor orangutan caught fire. The supposition, one assumes, was that human beings, having less hair, were less likely to be combustible!

With the single exception of the light bulb, invented in 1879, the electric chair was to predate virtually every other electrical appliance —toasters and blenders, juicers and kettles, irons and hairdryers, and all the other labor-saving appliances that we take for granted. Exactly who designed the apparatus is not known; it has even been suggested that it was a dentist. However, three people are given credit: Dr. Alphonse D. Rockwell, Dr. A. E. Kennelly, and Harold P. Brown. Who knows whether any of those gentlemen were dentists?

The first person to be put to death by this method was William Kemmler, electrocuted on August 6, 1890, at Auburn Prison in New York State.

There were those, Kemmler's lawyers in particular, who failed to recognize the advantages of massive doses of electricity over rope, and they attacked the validity of this method as a violation of the Eighth Amendment. They argued that electrocution constituted "cruel and unusual punishment," even though *The New York Times* described the new "Electrical Execution Law" as a means to ensure "euthanasia by electricity."

The decision was sustained first by the state appellate courts and eventually by the U.S. Supreme Court, which concluded: "It is in easy reach of the electrical science at this day to so generate and apply to the person of the convict, a current of electricity of such known and sufficient force as certainly to produce instantaneous and therefore painless death."

The Justices could hardly have been more wrong. The following is an extract from a reporter for the *New World* newspaper who witnessed this landmark execution:

> *The first execution by electrocution has been a horror. Doctors say the victim did not suffer. Only his Maker knows if that be true. To the eye, it looked as though he were in convulsive agony. The current had been passing through his body for 15 seconds when the electrode at the head was removed. Suddenly the breast heaved. There was a straining at the straps which bound him. A purplish foam covered the lips and was spattered over the leather head band. The man was alive.*
>
> *Warden, physician, guards . . . everybody lost their wits. There was a startled cry for the current to be turned on again . . . the rigor of death came on the instant. An odor of burning flesh and singed hair filled the room. For a moment, a blue flame played about the base of the victim's spine. This time the electricity flowed four minutes.*
>
> *Kemmler was dead. Part of his brain had been baked hard. Some of the blood in his head had been turned to charcoal.*

This was a far call from "euthanasia by electricity" or the Supreme Court's optimistic prediction of a "painless death." The poor man had fared little better than the orangutan.

Notwithstanding, the invention took off like wildfire and soon was adopted all over America.

The chair itself is a simple construction, usually built of hardwood. It generally has two legs in back and a heavier single leg in front. Apart from the adjustable headrest, it has binding leather straps. The chair itself is not electrified; it is simply where the victim sits while the current runs in his head and out his leg. It has adjustable brass electrodes. The machine consists of a stationary engine and alternating dynamo capable of generating a substantial current at a pressure of over 2,000 volts. The voltmeter, ammeter, and switchboard controlling the current are located in another room.

Because it is quite a simple contraption, Louisiana and Mississippi have, in the past, used portable chairs. The convicted man was saved the agony of lingering on death row and was dispatched with alacrity as the mobile "Old Smokey" was brought into an adjoining cell or even into the courtroom itself and hooked up to a powerline leading to the generators in a truck outside.

In 1946, Louisiana prisoner Willie Francis was only half electrocuted when the state's portable electric chair fouled up. Sympathetic lawyers came forward and stopped the state from trying again. But the U.S. Supreme Court divided 4-1-4 in deciding whether or not they, too, should be sympathetic. With a split vote, Louisiana got a second chance. This time the portable chair worked. Willie Francis was unlucky. But the screw-up had given him another year of life.

In the more sedate versions of this instrument of death, the prisoner's head, chest, arms, and legs are secured by broad leather straps. One electrode, thoroughly moistened with salt solution, is affixed to the prisoner's shaven head by the means of a "death cap," another to the calf of one leg. Both are molded to secure good contact.

A tight mask is placed over the face to hide any facial contortions and to keep the eyes from popping out of their sockets.

The application of the current is usually as follows: The executioner pulls the switch and contact is made through the head cap, grounded through the leg. The first jolt is a robust 2,000 volts or more, for about three seconds. This is cut back to 1,000 volts to prevent "unseemly burning of the body," although a huge blister invariably runs up the leg and chest area. The procedure is usually repeated as a precautionary measure. "Ideally" an electrocution is a three-minute drill.

The effect of this operation is supposed to be painless and instantaneous death. Robert G. Elliott, New York's one-time official executioner who carried out over 300 sentences, believed that the initial charge "shatters the person's nervous system instantaneously and beyond recall." Dr. Amos O. Squire, who attended many electrocutions at Sing Sing, believed that the electric chair was more humane and less painful than hanging.

However, from the very beginning opinions differed as to the humanity of "Thunderbolt."

Dr. E. A. Spitska witnessed the first electrocution and pronounced the execution a "failure."

The New York Globe reported that "manufactured lightning to take the place of the hangman's rope for dispatching of condemned murderers cannot be said to be satisfactory."

Nikola Tesla (1856–1943), the inventor of AC current, pointed out that "electrocution is not necessarily instantaneous. Alternating current may pass through the body in such a way that the functions of vital organs are momentarily preserved, with the result the victim may retain consciousness and experience great pain."

In 1989 this method of inflicting death has been retained by fourteen death penalty states: Alabama, Connecticut, Florida, Georgia, Indiana, Kentucky, Louisiana, Nebraska, Ohio, Pennsylvania, South Carolina, Tennessee, Vermont and Virginia, and the story seems to have changed little.

An eyewitness report describes the process of death in the electric chair. "The *crunch,* the mounting whine and snarl of the generator. The man's lips peel back, the throat strains for a last desperate cry, the body arches against the restraining straps as the generator whines and snarls again, the features purple, steam and smoke rise from the bald spots on head and leg while the sick-sweet smell of burned flesh permeates the little room."

Executioners have their anxious moments. Prisoners have been known to try to blow a fuse in the apparatus by swallowing quantities of metal. Albert Fish, a frail, elderly man convicted of murder and cannibalism, actually succeeded in 1936 in short-circuiting New York's first attempt to dispatch him, allegedly because of the number of needles which he had inserted into his body near his genitals as part of his sadomasochism.

The electrocution of William Vandiver in Indiana on October 16, 1985, was reported to have taken seventeen minutes, requiring five charges of electricity.

In Alabama on April 22, 1983, the first electrical charge burned through the electrode on John Louis Evans's leg. The electrode fell off; the prison guards repaired it after doctors determined he was not dead. During the second charge, eyewitnesses saw smoke and flame erupting from his left temple and leg, but the man was still alive. Following this second jolt, Evans's lawyer, Russell Canan, demanded by telephone that Governor George C. Wallace grant clemency and immediately halt the proceedings. Wallace, who had a few days earlier turned down such a request, communicated another rejection through an aide. It took three separate jolts of 1,900 volts, over a fourteen-minute period, before Mr. Evans was officially pronounced dead.

Leaving aside the aspects of physical pain and taking the assumption that the victim felt nothing, the question of mental anguish has not even been touched upon.

In his book *Condemned to Die: Life Under Sentence of Death,* criminologist Robert Johnson made a series of taped interviews of men on death row in Alabama in 1978 and recorded the tremendous mental stress that living under the threat of electrocution, and the fear of being burned to death, placed on the prisoners of death row.

In later interviews with the same inmates Johnson found a loss of mental acuteness, confusion, and evidence of some psychosis in 70 percent of the cases. The waiting had driven them mad.

Alpha Otis Stephens cut his wrists in an attempted suicide two hours before being sent to the chair. The first two-minute charge failed to kill him in Georgia in December 1984, and he struggled for breath for eight minutes before a second charge was applied.

A report states: "His body slumped when the current stopped . . . but shortly afterward witnesses saw him struggle to breathe. In the six minutes allowed for the body to cool before doctors could examine it, Mr. Stephens took about 23 breaths." The second charge was applied 10 minutes later after two doctors had determined that he was still alive.

A prison spokesman described it this way: "When the physician noticed he was still breathing, we hit him with a second jolt. It's standard procedure."

Witnesses always report that there is a smell of burning flesh. An official in Virginia's death row said he put Vaseline in his nostrils to keep out the stench and that death chamber employees soaked their clothes for days afterwards to get rid of the smell.

A French scientist concluded after extensive research that "In every case of electrocution . . . death inevitably supervenes but it may be [a] very long and, above all, excruciatingly painful [death] . . . The space of time before death supervenes varies according to the subject. Some have a greater physiological resistance than others. I do not believe that anyone killed by electrocution dies instantly, no matter how weak the subject may be. In certain cases death will not have come about even though the point of contact of the electrode with the body shows distinct burns. Thus, in particular cases, the condemned person may be alive and even conscious for several minutes without it being possible for a doctor to say whether the victim is dead or not."

Since William Kemmler thousands of men and women in the United States have been "fried"—and there seems to be no end.

We submit that this method of execution is a form of torture and is a direct violation of the Eighth Amendment's prohibition against cruel and unusual punishment.

THE LAST GASP

"When the people realized that the showers were in fact gas chambers, they started to make the most horrible wail."

—Nazi concentration camp survivor (anonymous)

Arizona, California, Colorado, Maryland, Mississippi, Missouri, and North Carolina currently mandate the gas chamber as their means of execution. Four persons have been gassed to death since 1977: in Nevada, Jesse Bishop in 1979 (Nevada now uses lethal injection); in Mississippi, Jimmy Lee Gray in 1983; Edward Earl Johnson in 1987; and Connie Ray Evans in 1987 (Mississippi switched to lethal injection for those convicted after July 1, 1988). It is California's San Quentin Prison, home of a chamber with two identical, painted metal chairs, that has become most synonymous with execution by gas.

There is little doubt in any informed person's mind that before long, more human life will once again be snuffed out, like candles in a vacuum, in the surgical green, octagonal chamber a short elevator ride from California's death row. Death row Chaplain Byron Eshelman describes it thus:

"The gas chamber at San Quentin is irrevocable. On this earth there is no undoing what it has done. It waits impartially to embrace all the condemned who come down the elevator from death row. It takes them all, the devout and the atheist, those who are resigned and those who fight to the last breath of life."

Originally the idea of execution by lethal gas, variously called prussic acid, hydrocyanic gas, hydrogen cyanide and cyanide gas, was conceived in an effort to provide a more "humane" method of execution than electrocution. It was developed for civilian use by Major D. A. Turner of the U.S. Army Medical Corps.

Prussic acid was first used against men in gas shells during World War I but was later banned in warfare under the Geneva Convention. Its toxic action is due to the inhibition of the normal oxidative processes in the tissues, resulting in a form of asphyxia with attending paralysis of the heart and respiratory organs. Inhalation of the gas produces, in rapid succession, giddiness, headache, palpitation, acute chest pains followed by labored respiration, loss of consciousness, and death, according to the *Encyclopaedia Britannica*.

The first criminal to be executed in this way was in Nevada on February 8, 1924. He was Gee Jon, a Chinese, convicted of a Tong gang killing.

The procedure for execution by gas is as follows: Underneath the chair is a bowl. A pound of cyanide is measured into a gauze bag, which is then hung from a hook beneath the chair and poised over the bowl, connected by a lever to the outside.

The condemned man has a stethoscope attached to his chest which can be monitored by a doctor outside. After the chamber is sealed, the sulphuric acid is released into the bowl, via a tube, and the executioner drops the lever which lowers the sodium cyanide into the acid.

The poisonous gas is produced when the sulphuric acid comes into contact with the pellets of sodium cyanide, causing a chemical reaction which produces cyanide gas.

The fumes rise from beneath the chair, which has a perforated seat. The doctor listens to the cessation of the heartbeat through a long stethoscope. Soon the victim is pronounced dead.

Finally, the lethal mixture is sucked out of the chamber by a fan and the corpse is sprayed with liquid ammonia to neutralize any traces of hydrocyanic gas.

The warden of San Quentin from 1942 to 1954, Clinton Duffy, described the process as follows:

"In a matter of seconds the prisoner is unconscious. At first there is evidence of extreme horror, pain and strangling. The eyes pop. The skin turns purple and the victim begins to drool. It is a horrible sight. Witnesses faint. It is finally as though he has gone to sleep. The body, however, is not disfigured or mutilated in any way."

The whole process is known to inmates as "The Big Sleep" or "The Time Machine."

In *Murder USA,* John Godwin wrote: "The condemned man can hold out for as long as he can hold his breath. To the extent that the victim is advised to take deep breaths to pull the gas down into his lungs, he has to aid in his own destruction, which is a crime against human decency."

The victims are advised to breathe deeply as soon as they smell the odor of rotten eggs, but since man's instinct is to live, he will gasp, wheeze, and struggle for air. Survivors of Nazi concentration camps reported that bodies of the strongest were always the furthest away from the source of the Cyclon B gas when the corpses were removed from the gas chambers.

Asphyxiation is slow. The skin turns purple, the eyes bulge, the prisoner drools, and a swollen tongue hangs out. He may scream, choke, and thrash about. It has been known for a victim to break an arm free, severing the skin, so that blood spurts over the window through which witnesses view the proceedings.

Caryl Chessman, twelve years on death row, had outlived more than a hundred men before he too was taken to the chamber in 1960. His end was described as, "dying hard, gasping, drooling, rolling his head."

In Mississippi, Jimmy Lee Gray was reported to have had convulsions for eight minutes and to have struck his head repeatedly on the pole behind him. It was also alleged that he did not appear to be dead when deputies asked witnesses to leave.

Little wonder the use of gas was outlawed by the Geneva Convention.

JUST A LITTLE PRICK

"The cowards weapon, poison."
—Phineas Fletcher, 1582–1650

At about the same time the criminal justice system adopted the electric chair, in the late 1880s, it rejected lethal injection. It was believed the electric chair would be more humane.

Almost a century later, the euphemistic concept of lethal injection has been enthusiastically "rediscovered" as a humane answer and a "nice" way of killing people.

Lethal injection compounds the act of execution with the hypocrisy of making people believe that it is, at worst, a mercy killing and at best painless euthanasia. This hypocrisy was well illustrated by Governor Dolph Briscoe of Texas in 1977 when he said, at the signing into law of the state's bill on this new form of execution, "I think and I hope this will provide some dignity with death."

Lurking in the back of the governor's mind may have been the image of a benevolent sandman giving merciful relief to an incurably sick child; a little prick in the arm and then "night-night." But the reality is still the same.

It remains the killing in cold blood of a helpless prisoner.

Lethal injection may have been a late bloomer, but in less than a decade it became the most authorized form of execution in the United

States. Oklahoma was the first to adopt it in 1977. Texas, Idaho, and New Mexico quickly followed suit.

It is now the method of choice of Arkansas, Delaware, Idaho, Illinois, Mississippi, Montana, Nevada, New Jersey, New Mexico, North Carolina, Oklahoma, Oregon, South Dakota, Texas, Utah, Washington, and Wyoming. All these states are now able to provide "death with dignity."

In the infectious wave of enthusiasm that swept across the continent, legislation was drafted at a speed only marginally slower than the "fast-acting barbiturate" prescribed to the condemned. Montana and Washington states, which had not executed anyone for forty and twenty years respectively, were quick to pass the new "humane" method into law.

Amnesty International's *United States of America—The Death Penalty* describes the procedure:

> *Execution by this method involves the continuous intravenous injection of a lethal quantity of a short-acting barbiturate in combination with a chemical paralytic agent. In Texas, a combination of three drugs is used (sodium thiopental, pancuronium bromide and potassium chloride), each of which is fatal when administered in sufficient quantities but one of which is used to render the subject unconscious before the fatal dose takes effect. The solution is administered by medically trained technicians from behind a wall through which four intravenous lines run into the death chamber.*

One of the more frightening aspects of this method of slaying is the alliance between the execution process and the medical profession. An uneasy relationship certainly, but the apparatus of drugs and needles has undeniably evolved from the operating theater and not the dungeon.

Lethal injection is a strange hybrid; the bastard child of torture and medicine.

That the American Medical Association did not reject lethal injection out of hand says as much about the AMA as it does for capital punishment. The Hippocratic Oath is completely unambiguous: "[I] will give no deadly drug to any, though it may be asked of me, nor will I counsel such."

In testimony before the Royal Commission on Capital Punishment on February 3, 1950, the chairman of the British Medical Association, Dr. R. G. Gordon, affirmed the Hippocratic Oath with the following statement:

"In the opinion of the Association, no medical practitioner should be asked to take part in bringing about the death of a convicted murderer. The Association would be most strongly opposed to any proposal to introduce, in place of judicial hanging, a method of execution which would require the services of a medical practitioner, either in carrying out the actual process of killing or instructing others in the technique of the process."

The AMA states that a physician should not become an executioner, but they provide no guidelines for *counsel* or "instructing others in the technique of the process." And there is no doubt that their apparatus— needles, tubes, barbiturates, gurneys and white coats—has been scandalously hijacked by the executioners.

To get a historical perspective on lethal injection, we have to cross the Atlantic and go back forty years to the United Kingdom where, as mentioned above, His Majesty's Government appointed a Commission to study every aspect of capital punishment. The report is the most thorough investigation into the subject that has ever been undertaken. The penalty for murder in Britain at the time was death by hanging.

The chairman, Sir Ernest Gowers, called for examination of three anesthetists: Drs. W. Alexander Low, Francis Evans, and Geoffrey Organe, in order to pursue the subject of lethal injection, because not all members of the Commission accepted the conclusion that "hanging is expeditious and humane." In giving their evidence on December 6, 1951, the doctors discussed the technical difficulties of injection and referred to their hospital practice.

Dr. Low: "We go and see the patient the night before. Even if the patient had quite nice veins [the night before], as my colleague has said, because of fear [of injection], next morning the 'very nice' veins have shrivelled down to the size of a bit of cotton."

The anesthetists shocked the Commission when later in their testimony they suggested a veterinary surgeon as the best for the job. "He is the real expert with a needle and vein," stated Dr. Organe.

Commission member Sir William Jones responded in kind. "I think the chairman put it to you that hanging was considered by a good many people to be a barbarous way of execution. Which would you consider the most barbarous way?—Hanging, or sending for the man who kills the dog to kill the man?"

Dr. Evans: "If we were to tie a rope around the neck of a dog, take it to the stairway and drop it over the banisters, this would be cruelty. Therefore you send for the veterinary surgeon and you can stand and see it [the lethal injection] done."

Having dealt with the problems of vein sizes and vets, they went on to consider the question of potential violence from a prisoner about to get his "jab." When strapping the prisoner to a gurney was suggested, the doctors unanimously agreed, "We three, at any rate, have ruled that one out."

Dr. Low's solution was "stick and carrot," or to be more precise, "carrot and stick." He felt that lethal injection should be offered as an *alternative* to hanging, stating that the prisoner may think twice about "cutting up rough" if he knew the hangman is waiting in the wings.

Since one would assume, as has later been proved in the U.S., that the condemned man will always choose injection over hanging, the idea of a hangman hanging around as a deterrent (presumably losing his skills through lack of practice) brings up the subject of deterrence.

Dr. Evans testified: "I must admit that personally the fact that I was going to lose my life would not worry me to all that extent, but the method by which I was going to be passed on into the next stage of existence would worry me considerably. If I were contemplating a murder, the knowledge that I was risking death by hanging would be a much greater deterrent to me than if I knew my punishment would be death by intravenous injection."

So would boiling in oil! But the doctor brings up a valid point. Is the loss of life the deterrent, or the method? Do murderers give enough thought to the consequences of their act so that *any* punishment can be a deterrent?

At the end of the inquiry, a negative verdict on lethal injection was recorded, but the Commission unanimously recommended that "the question should be periodically examined, especially in the light of the progress made in the science of anaesthetics."

Britain abandoned capital punishment in 1965, and so regardless of any improvement in the "science of anaesthetics" there has been no occasion to consider lethal injection further.

Back in America, and twenty-six years later, the 1976 Supreme Court decision in *Gregg* allowed the states to renew executions. Sixteen states introduced lethal injection, hoping, one must assume, that the new "humane" method would neutralize opposition to execution.

In the six years after the first execution by lethal injection in Texas in December 1982, about one third of all American executions have been by this method. Most of these have been in Texas, but North Carolina, Nevada, Utah, and Missouri have also made use of their execution gurneys.

In 1989 lethal injection seems no less sordid than the chair or the gas chamber. It has turned out to be just another way of killing people.

Lethal injection is a sham, an impostor and a failure.

We could turn to history for one solution that combines deterrence and "dignity with death," exemplified by the likes of Sir Walter Raleigh, Charles I, and the countless other victims of capital punishment —the reintroduction of the headsman. Of course the condemned man would have to cooperate, but perhaps he could take a leaf from the book of sixteenth-century martyr Sir Thomas More who, on mounting the scaffold, best summed up that brief journey into eternity.

"I pray you, Master Lieutenant, see me safe up, and for my coming down let me shift for myself."

Now that's dignity.

THE HIGH COST OF DEATH

"Up and down the city road,
In and out the Eagle,
That's the way the Money goes
—Pop goes the weasel!"

—W.R. Mandale, 19th Century

There has been a debate surrounding the death penalty for as long as the punishment has existed. The arguments, for and against, have nearly always stemmed from two points of view: (1) The moral viewpoint, emphasizing sanctity of life over the payment of a life with a life; and (2) the law and order view, emphasizing the need for a strong deterrent over the notion that violence begets violence.

In the early years of America's history, executions were designed as graphic warnings that certain crimes would be dealt with by death. Execution, in public, followed swiftly on the heels of conviction, normally the next day and rarely more than a week later.

At the turn of the century most states had moved their killings behind closed doors, although Kentucky continued until as late as 1936 to hang its wrongdoers in public.

During the twentieth century the move toward due process continued, resulting in a greater length of time between sentence and execution. Even as late as the 1920s the average time spent on death row was still under eight months.

The execution of two innocent immigrants in 1927, the world-famous Sacco and Vanzetti affair *(see interview with Sara Ehrmann)* planted the entire issue of capital punishment onto the front pages of

41

the nation's newspapers and planted the potential for injustice in the minds of the American public. There was a liberal backlash, and prisoners' defense funds sprang up in every state, bringing with them the entire fabric of the legal process.

Constitutional law was more and more the issue now. Circuit courts, courts of appeal, state supreme courts, and in the end the Supreme Court itself were theaters where the game of life and death was played. Tenure on death row was becoming longer and longer, and by the time that Caryl Chessman was executed for kidnapping/assault on May 2, 1960, he had spent twelve years on death row.

Over the last fifteen years, while the issue of "law and order" has become a major political stepping stone to power for zealous politicians, all the old arguments have been dragged out of the closet to demonstrate, once again, the wisdom and goodness of capital punishment. But a new issue has surfaced in recent years and reflects, quite accurately, the value we place upon money in the eighties. It concerns the cost of keeping men in prison as opposed to simply killing them.

The idea of killing someone because it's too expensive to keep him or her alive speaks volumes about the society in which we live, but since it is a subject that is frequently brought up, we thought we should address it.

The most common popular argument, often given on TV audience-participation shows such as those of Geraldo Rivera, Oprah Winfrey, Phil Donahue, and Morton Downey Jr., goes something like this: "Why should society have to feed and clothe this murderer for the rest of his stinking life? His victim is six feet deep and he just lounges around in a nice warm cell, watching TV and using up honest citizens' hard-earned tax dollars. Hang the bastard! Fry the bastard!"

We have visited death row. There isn't much lounging around; it would be more accurate to describe it as a mind-numbing lethargy. You boil in the summer and freeze in the winter while the specter of death weaves its way through each and every cell. But if the death lobby wants to address the question of cost, they are on dangerous fiscal ground.

This short chapter is gleaned from hundreds of documents and briefs. We have sifted through thousands upon thousands of pages of evidence—and these from just a handful of states.

In the 1982 New York gubernatorial race, Mario Cuomo promised that he would veto any death penalty law enacted by the legislature. He defeated outspoken proponent of capital punishment Lewis Lehrman, who had made the death penalty a central issue to his campaign. While Cuomo opposes the death penalty on moral grounds, he cited a New

York study demonstrating that it would cost $660,000 to jail a man for forty years but $1.8 million to execute him.

In California it has been estimated that the minimum cost, just for the trial phase of a capital case, is a half million dollars. It doesn't end there. According to a report in *The Wall Street Journal* on October 15, 1986, entitled "Price of Executions Is Just Too High," only 10 percent of the prosecutions are successful, and thus it costs the citizens of California $4.5 million to sentence just *one* person to death.

Arkansas found out about the cost of executions in 1971 when fiscal minded public officials commuted fifteen death sentences to life imprisonment, saving the state $1.5 million.

The Kansas legislature learned the true cost of the death penalty in 1987. Prior to that, for eight years, the legislature had had its death penalty bills vetoed by the governor. The electorate sent the state's senior official packing and voted in a pro-death penalty governor. After looking at the costs, the legislature voted against reintroducing executions. The price tag would have been $10 million for the first year alone and a $50 million tag before the first execution in 1990.

Oregon estimates its costs per case at $700,000.

The Ohio Public Defender's Office cites costs of at least $1 million per execution.

Texas, the leading executing state, has by some estimates spent over $183 million in its pursuit of the death penalty. This averages out to over $6 million per death.

One county in Georgia spent seven times its entire annual budget for criminal prosecutions on just one death penalty case.

Florida's first post-1972 execution was of John Spenkelink, in May 1979. It has been estimated that the execution cost the state $5 million and the murder rate *rose* in the months that followed.

In a study published on July 10, 1988, the Miami *Herald* estimated that Florida taxpayers had spent over $57 million on executions since 1973, or $3,178,623 per execution. They also figured that the cost of life imprisonment was $515,964. Hence, by executing rather than sentencing an inmate to life imprisonment, the cost is about $2.66 million per case. The difference would, of course, be even more remarkable if we had a prison system in which inmates could work to help victims and to pay for their own upkeep.

These figures may appear mind-numbing at first sight, but anyone who has had the misfortune to get involved in the legal process will know, from personal experience, the high cost of law, let alone justice. In our interview with Michael Millman, the director of the California Appellate Project, he estimated the number of legal hours for the defense, for the appellate stage alone, at 1,000 hours of lawyer time.

This did not include either paralegal and investigative hours or the time spent by the prosecution. Some death penalty briefs and transcripts run into 50,000 pages—the *Encyclopaedia Britannica* only runs to 35,000 pages.

The dean of Santa Clara Law School, Professor Gerald F. Uelmen, made some interesting points about costs of the death penalty in an article for the *Los Angeles Times* in 1983. He pointed out that in California each side has twenty-six peremptory challenges during the course of jury selection. It costs $4,000 a day to operate a trial court, so jury selection alone can add as much as $200,000 simply because the death penalty is being sought.

When one looks at these figures closely, the very high sums of money involved in capital cases start to have some perspective.

There are cost-cutting alternatives, but they raise some chilling prospects. One of these would be to simply put the clock back a century or so, forget all this appeals business, and just get on with it. "Hang the bastard! Fry the bastard!"

Since no serious legal mind is suggesting this, and no Supreme Court would ever approve it, there is the very cynical approach of making the number of capital cases pursued far more narrow. That is to say, zero in on a few well-chosen cases and throw all the resources of the DA's office into, for example, just three cases a year instead of the over three dozen a year that the states with large death row populations prosecute annually.

However, as Dean Uelmen points out in his article, if the death penalty is so selectively used, a serious issue of proportionality arises. How can we justify the imposition of the death penalty against one defendant if another, accused of a similar crime in a neighboring county, escapes the death penalty because there is not enough money in the budget? As in any system of capital punishment, once we decide we will determine who lives and who dies, we run into the problem of where to draw the line.

How else can we economize? Cut the Public Defender's budget? This is already being done in some places, and at first glance it seems the simplest of all solutions. Court-appointed lawyers have always been notoriously badly paid and overworked. It could, again cynically, be argued that the net result is ideal. The defendant gets death and the state saves money.

In practice, as Dean Uelmen writes, it doesn't work quite like that. Under the United States Constitution a defendant has a *constitutional* right to a competent lawyer, and since the highest standard of competence is required in a trial for life (at least in theory), this could prove very costly in the long run. It has proved very costly in the past. The

$4.6 million price tag for the retrial of Juan Corona is a sobering reminder of how expensive incompetent counsel can be [Corona killed 25 migrant workers in the seventies, was tried and convicted; was retried and reconvicted in 1982].

The Wall Street Journal concurs with the dean and adds a chilling reminder about the execution of the innocent. "Nor can costs be significantly lowered. Because of the Supreme Court's rulings, there is no way to streamline this elaborate process. Any attempt to do so would deny a defendant the protections guaranteed under the Constitution and increases the possibility of sending innocent people to their death. . . . Like it or not, the Supreme Court has made it abundantly clear that shortcuts to justice are legally unacceptable."

The article goes on to say that New York and California could save $75 million and $125 million respectively by not having the death penalty. This does not include the running of death rows, which are known to cost at least four times as much per man as the normal prison population.

All the experts we talked with during our interviews estimated that a death penalty case costs a minimum of a million dollars and usually more. With over 2,000 inmates on death row, the financial costs of the death penalty must have exceeded $2 billion since 1972. The social and moral costs are incalculable.

Two billion dollars is still a sizable sum, even by today's inflated prices, and represents the real price of electing politicians who hitch a political ride on this facile, muck-raking, and dead-end policy.

We would agree with Ronald Reagan's Attorney General, Edwin Meese, when he complained bitterly at the waste of taxpayers' money (the employment of a special prosecutor to investigate his behavior) in July of 1988. We believe, perhaps cynically, that Mr. Meese was more worried about his possible prosecution than our money, but it was nice to see that he recognized that the cash came from somewhere. Edwin Meese has caused, directly and indirectly, more than any other individual during the eighties, millions and millions of tax dollars to be squandered on death penalty prosecutions. Whatever benefits the death penalty may have (and we believe there are none), are these benefits really worth the hassle and expense?

We have some recommendations for the former Attorney General, who in his waning months in office, faced with censure from all directions, at last recognized the need for fiscal restraint by prosecutors.

These are just a few suggestions for a man who is so worried about the cost of keeping murderers in jail. This is what he could do with the money he saved.

How about justice? They could give $10,000 to each of the relatives of the estimated 222,000 victims of homicide over the last ten years.

How about security? They could employ another 4,000 police officers.

How about social reform? The creation of job programs, old people's homes, drug rehabilitation centers, housing for the homeless.

The list of real needs is endless.

We would like to conclude with the words of Special Appeals Court Judge Alan Wilner of Maryland: "The cost of pursuing this largely fruitless course has become so high that public attention should be directed to the reality of the situation."

AMERICAN GOTHIC

"Civil government does not consist in executions. It is the nature of compassion to associate with misfortune. In taking up this subject, I seek no recompense—I fear no consequences. Fortified with that proud integrity that disdains to triumph or to yield, I will advocate the rights of man."

—Thomas Paine, *The Rights of Man*, 1791–1792

Thirty miles north of Florida's panhandle and fifteen miles west of the Georgia state line lies the tiny township of Headland, Alabama. Charming colonial-style houses stand uniformly on the tree-lined Main Street of this classic Southern town, a community that still conjures up images from the South's rural past.

Watt Espy is the director of the Capital Punishment Research Project; his home, and project headquarters, lies on the outskirts of Headland, in a turn-of-the-century single-story frame house, complete with porch and swing.

Inside these headquarters, 200 eight-by-ten-inch black and white photos, the faces of the dead, some smiling, others grim, hundreds of them, line the walls staring into the living room. These are some of the faces of the men and women who have been killed by judicial execution in this country, executions that go back 160 years before Independence, to the colony of Virginia. The photos are just a part of Mr. Espy's somewhat macabre collection.

To the casual observer, chaos reigns. Office files are stacked in piles against yellowing walls. File cabinets are crammed, but the informa-

*tion contained in them is scrupulously accurate, the entire project
beyond academic or historical reproach.*

*Mr. Espy himself is a walking encyclopedia and is no stranger to the
media. Reporters as far away as Germany have written about his
somewhat unusual collection, which grew from a hobby, seventeen
years ago, into this country's most serious resource of death penalty
material.*

*The director is a man in his mid fifties, pale, heavy set but not
overweight. We set the tape recorder down and just let Mr. Espy talk.
This native Alabamian chain smoked his way through a pack of More
brand cigarettes while recounting the bizarre history of capital punishment in ringing Southern tones with such flair and richness that the
images sprang to life.*

Headland, Alabama
Monday, February 15, 1988, Noon

Watt Espy

To date I have confirmed, through my research, 15,759 men,
women and children killed by judicial-execution. These figures predate
independence and go back to Colonial times. They do not include summary executions (lynchings).

The earliest execution that I have confirmed was of George Kendall,
in 1608, one of the original councillors for the colony of Virginia.
Kendall was very unpopular among his fellow council members and
another man William Reed, who had been sentenced to be hanged for
threatening and blaspheming the President of the Colony, told the
council, "If you will spare my life I will tell you about a plot by
Kendall to betray us to the Spanish." The council pardoned Reed, with
the provision that he testify against Kendall and *also* serve as executioner. Kendall was shot and so the first confirmed execution in this
country was by shooting.

Going back in time, we have had any number of judicial burnings in
this country; it was a common practice until the nineteenth century.
The last burnings that have been confirmed both took place in South

Carolina. There were two separate occurrences in 1825. Burning was generally reserved for slaves; most slaves were hanged but slave women were frequently burned and also those convicted of arson would frequently be burned.

The most bizarre execution that I have encountered was in New Orleans, during the days when the French were the colonial masters. There was a mutiny on Cat Island and the commander, a sadist and an awful man, was murdered and the mutineers, three soldiers and a guide, escaped. They fled to Georgia but on the way were overtaken in Alabama by a band of Choctaw Indians, friendly to the French, who carried them back to New Orleans. The guide and two of the soldiers were broken on the wheel, but the French governor decreed that the third soldier, a Swiss mercenary, be executed by being placed in a wooden box and sawed in two. That was a form of execution in Switzerland. There were a number of Swiss mercenaries in Louisiana, and they served as executioners.

During the period of the Salem witchcraft trials an old man was accused—his wife had already been hanged as a witch. His name was Giles Corey and he refused to plead guilty, because if he had pleaded guilty his estate would have been confiscated. The judgement of the court was that he be "pressed" until he confessed. He was placed on a stone floor and a board or something was placed over him and weights were placed on the boards. He was supposed to have been ninety years old according to some accounts. So he was pressed to death.

Many were gibbeted alive, in other words, hanged in a gibbet, an iron cage in the shape of a man, and just left in it, without food or sustenance or water, and the birds would literally eat the flesh, while the victims were still alive. The bodies were left in the gibbet, even when they were just skeletal remains.

It was also a very frequent thing to quarter a person after he or she had been hanged. The various quarters were placed in parts of the jurisdiction and the head on a pole to serve as a warning to others who might transgress similarly.

In 1812 there was a slave revolt in Pointe Coupee Parish, Louisiana. Most of them were killed but sixteen of them were captured. They were taken to New Orleans and tried. They were decapitated in the public square. Their heads were placed on pikes up and down the Mississippi River to serve as a warning to other slaves.

Before the Civil War there were a large number of slave executions, but very few slave lynchings. That just didn't occur. They were tried and executed, and there's a reason for that. The legislatures were made up of large land owners and slave owners, so they wrote it into law that if a slave was executed, the state or county had to compensate the owner for the loss of his property. If a slave was lynched there was no compensation.

There was a prominent planter here, in Alabama, named Porter Bibb. He was a very wealthy man. He had a fourteen-year-old son who had gotten into an altercation with a slave boy about the same age, who killed the son. When the neighbors found out about it, they wanted to lynch the young slave. They showed up at Bibb's home and the old man met them on the front door step with a shotgun. He said, "I'll kill the first one of you that comes in here. I've already lost my son, don't make me lose my nigger without any compensation. We'll try him and hang him and the state will have to pay me." And that's what they did.

There was a case in the state of Missouri. This was not an execution, but the story illustrates a point. A master, mortally wounded by his slave, as he lay dying called his best friend, who was also the executor of his estate, and told him, "I know I am dying. It's a mortal wound and I am greatly encumbered with debt, but I have got to leave my wife and children as well off as I can. If my slave is executed, they will only get partial compensation (they got one half of the assessed value). I want you to take him to New Orleans, sell him, get the full amount and give it to my wife and children." Which his friend did.

In the earlier days, the Mosaic-code was the basis for many of the capital laws of this country. Where sodomy or bestiality was the offense, the law almost invariably provided that the animal be executed in front of the person who committed the act. It read something like:

"Thy mare lover, thy sow lover, thy bitch lover, shall all be knocked on the head before Thee, and put to death. Then Thou shall be hanged by the neck until Thou be dead." So we have provided for the execution of animals in this country even though they were, one could say, passive partners in the crime.

In the earlier days they had very little money for law enforcement. The county jails were very crude, shacks really. The cost of maintaining them was high. So, if you didn't want to kill somebody, it was easier to cut a hand off or mutilate or brand them. There was a case I just recorded down in Florida where a woman slave had her ears nailed to a post and cut off.

Here in the United States we have done practically everything that was done in Europe, for the simple reason that our heritage was so versatile.

Historically, right through to the present day, the death penalty has been largely a political tool. George Stinney Jr., a fourteen-year-old kid, was electrocuted in South Carolina in 1944. He was a young black boy who had raped and murdered two little white girls. There's no question as to the innocence or guilt—he did it. But here's the question: Is it morally right to execute a fourteen-year-old kid?

At the time they had the most liberal governor in South Carolina since the Civil War, Olin D. Johnston, and the clemency decision was square in his lap. He was running for United States Senate against Cotton Ed Smith, who had been a member of the Senate for 30 years and was a fixture and the biggest demagogue and bigot of the classical old Southern school as you can imagine. Well had Johnston granted clemency it would have ruined him politically. I guess he felt like his political career was more important than the life of a fourteen-year-old black kid because he let the execution proceed.

We have used the death penalty almost genocidally against blacks, especially here in the South. I have had the opportunity to research slave executions based on the record of compensation for owners of executed slaves in the Southern states. Now this is not all of them by any means, a lot of the records have been lost. In the states of Virginia, Alabama and Louisiana blacks account for 85% of all executions through history. In the other slave holdin' states the percentages run over 60% and I haven't even had the chance to research all the executions in those jurisdictions. So it's been used almost in a genocidal fashion and still is.

Death by hanging has been the predominant method of execution. It was used in every jurisdiction where we have the death penalty and accounts for far more executions than any other single method.

There was a famous executioner named Philip Hanna. As a very young man he had witnessed a hanging that was horribly bungled, as so many of them were.

Hanna made his own study of what it would take to break a man's neck. He studied weights and everything and he became an unofficial hangman. He even had his own gallows which he would take with him. Now one might think he was a real sadist but that was not his motive. He wouldn't take any pay for it. He did it strictly from the point of view that if you are going to do it, let's do it properly, let's do it in a humane way. The only pay he would take was a fifth of whisky, which he and the sheriff would drink after the execution.

Then there was Robert G. Elliott. He was more famous than Philip Hanna. He was an electrocutioner at Sing Sing Prison. In time he became the official executioner for the states of New York, Massachusetts, Connecticut and New Jersey, maybe Pennsylvania too. He executed Richard Hauptmann, he executed Sacco and Vanzetti. In his later years he became an opponent of the death penalty because of a case where he really thought the man was innocent. He died in the early 1940's. On one occasion his home was literally bombed. You know people in this country love executions—but they hate executioners.

The electric chair was considered modern when it replaced hangings but there have been some bad botches, people being burned instead of electrocuted.

Two states, Louisiana and Mississippi, even used a portable electric chair. They carried it in a truck, with its own generator. When a man was to be electrocuted the portable generator would pull in and they'd set the chair in the jail or the court house and electrocute there. I have some pictures of it in operation.

Gas was designed as an even more humane way than either hanging or electrocution. The original plan was to execute the prisoner while in his cell, while he was asleep, so he would know nothing about what was coming down. But that was determined to be completely impractical and could not be done without jeopardizing other inmates in the prison and the prison personnel.

There was a case in Arizona where a man was executed by gas and his widow bent over and kissed him on the lips as he lay in his coffin and she got violently ill from the after effects of the gas.

There is nothing they can do once the pellets have fallen. When Burton Abbot was executed in California, just at the time the lever was pulled that dropped the pellets into the acid the phone rang and it was Governor Goodwyn J. Knight granting a stay of execution. Well, of course, they couldn't open the doors of the gas chamber without killing all the witnesses and the prison officials and everybody else present and so they just had to let him die.

It is not a pleasant death. It is just awful. What literally happens is, as you breathe the gas in, it burns the linings of your nose, your throat, your lungs, your esophagus—everything. It literally burns you out from the inside. It is not an easy death.

It is somewhat ironical that this country, with all of its raving and ranting about human rights all over the world and all of that, gave Adolf Hitler the means of economically exterminating large groups of people. We were the first country to experiment with cyanide gas, which is something of course that Himmler adopted in the various camps of death. We were the first ones to use gas as a means of execution in a sealed chamber and, of course, that is what the Nazis did, they herded them into shower rooms that spewed out gas instead of water.

The latest method of execution is lethal injection. Stephen Morin was one of the first to die by this means in Texas on the 13th of March, 1985, and they had a hard time locating a vein strong enough to take the catheter. They had to prod him with needles for forty minutes or more before they found a vein that was strong enough to take the catheter—and it is a thick needle. Now can you imagine the agony of being strapped down and held immobile while somebody sticks needles into you for forty minutes?

Every time we have gone from one method of execution to another in this country it has invariably been for alleged humanitarian reasons, but I think we missed the boat completely in arguing what is supposed to be a humanitarian way of killing. In fact there is no such thing as a *humanitarian* way of premeditating and setting out to kill another human being.

EYE OF THE BEHOLDER

"On horror's head horrors accumulate..."
—William Shakespeare, *Othello*

The Carmel Highlands stretch east from Pebble Beach westward to the Carmel Valley. It is a near paradise on earth of rolling hills and pine-filled canyons, home to Clint Eastwood, Kim Novak, and Howard and Isobelle Brodie.

A dirt road clings to the hillside and climbs steeply to a structure of timber and glass set on a hill; their home, straight from the pages of Architectural Digest, *has a breathtaking view of the Monterey peninsula where eagles hang, motionless, in the clear blue sky and the sound of sea otters drifts through the pure sea air.*

Howard Brodie stands tall at 6 feet 1 inch. He is distinguished, slim, with a white mustache and white receding hair. His face is virtually unlined, even serene. An unusual quality in any adult, but in a seventy-three-year-old man who has witnessed more horror in a single day than most people see in a lifetime, it is quite remarkable.

He is an artist/reporter whose illustrations have been published by among others Life *and* Look *magazines and have been seen on CBS television for almost three decades.*

As a sketch artist who has covered four wars, from World War II through Korea to the French Indochina conflict that was to become the tragedy of Vietnam, Howard Brodie has captured, in his poignant drawings, the pain and courage of his fellow human beings for almost half a century.

Howard Brodie

I was born in California, in Oakland, seventy-three years ago I think. Age to me has no meaning, so many young people are older than I am. The static mind to me is the old mind and really the way I feel is there are so many old young people and old old people and young young people and young old people.

I have sketched the four wars, the major trials of our time, famous and infamous people.

What made you interested in capital punishment?

I became friends with the late warden of San Quentin, Clinton Duffy, and he took me around the prison. I remember walking up the steps of the old gallows; it was deserted but I had the real feel of what it must be like. Then he took me down to see the gas chamber and he said something that I remember to this day: "When anybody comes in here and wants to see *the* gas chamber, I correct them. I say, this is *your* gas chamber." He was the warden and he didn't want to have anything to do with killing another human being and he was in utter pain whenever there was a scheduled execution.

We know that you have sketched more than one execution. Can you tell us about the first one?

I was with *YANK* magazine in Belgium at that time. During the Battle of the Bulge, the war was very intense and I recall being at a press camp and hearing correspondents say that they had just got word of a pending execution. Our troops had just caught three Germans who had been posing as GIs and they were going to execute them.

It was a freezing morning and I jumped into a Jeep with other correspondents. The mucus in our noses froze; our ears stung. I say that because the condemned men were not given warm clothes to die in. The correspondents and I drove to an MP post near the front. I'll just try to recreate that experience.

(Mr. Brodie put his forehead into his hands, closed his eyes.)

There was silence for a time. Then a chaplain came out of a little headquarters building, volunteered his name and hometown, and told us that a neighboring German woman had been singing to these doomed men.

Shortly thereafter an MP beckoned to me and pointed. I followed his direction down behind the building. Looking, I saw a number of military policemen and they were dressed warmly in field jackets. Interspersed between the MPs in a file were these three Germans, dressed in just fatigues on this bitter cold morning. The breath of all these men was hoary. I walked to the side of them and we went down to, I guess it was a concrete farm building maybe forty feet long. Behind it were embedded three stakes.

These three young enemies were tied, their hands behind them, to the stakes. The two men on the side stakes were almost cringing, but the man in the center stake held his head erect, rigidly erect, as he was being tied, an amazing example of courage. When the blindfolds were offered to the men, he refused it. But all the men's eyes were covered with the black blindfolds, regardless of their choice.

White target disks were pinned over their hearts. I moved from the stakes to behind the firing squad. One blank cartridge had been issued to the MPs on the firing squad to assuage any guilt. Sort of amazing to me at that time because I didn't think seasoned soldiers would think one way or the other about taking a life.

I didn't like my position so I walked down to the side of the stakes, at a safe distance. At this moment the triggers were being squeezed by the firing squad. The man at the center stake, the one who was rigidly erect, said: "Long live the Fuehrer, Adolf Hitler."

The shots rang out and I could just feel the impact and hear the bullets thud onto the chest of the man closest to me. Blood spewed out of his mouth.

You know, just before the shots fired, regardless of what the Germans had done, I wanted to cry out. I had been in war but I had never seen men deliberately killed and it seared me. It was very dehumanizing. I wanted to shout, but managed to muffle my impulse.

Blood spewed out of all their mouths, they quivered, and then there was silence. This was broken by the shuffle of feet of several GIs. They carried white sacks into which they slid these three young men. The sacks just became saturated with blood. It was very dramatic for me, and I walked almost in silence to the Jeep with a *Stars and Stripes* correspondent and went with him to the correspondent's billet, which was just a few kilometers away. We had a hotel there, two or three stories high, and I walked up the stairs with him to his second-floor room.

I went to the window because I heard planes and he shouted, "Get down, get down!" I dropped to the floor. The window blew in and you could hear the blast and more bombs coming. We got out into the hallway and the ceiling blew up and a beam crashed. We could hardly see each other in the dust, but we went down the stairs and there was a GI lying wounded. Outside, there was a dead correspondent on the steps and there were dead civilians on the sidewalk. A dismembered leg, I remember that vividly; a priest giving last rites. Yet, if I can make this point, this was a relatively chance death, and it literally had no meaning to me. I was still numbed from seeing the designed deaths of those young men on the stakes.

I came across the remains of eleven hundred people burned alive. I am talking about the Holocaust. I was one of the early GIs to come across them and the bodies were still smoking. They had been herded from a concentration camp, but my memory of the executions is still far more horrendous to me than the horrors of war, as horrible as war is.

Would you mind describing your experience witnessing an execution in the United States?

There was this young man in Florida. I witnessed his execution. It was just pitiful.

Who was that?

His name was Spenkelink. *(John Spenkelink, executed May 25, 1979).* He was quite a talented young artist. His father was an alcoholic, if my recollection serves me. His father committed suicide and the boy found him, when he was twelve, and he turned to crime two years later. Now I am sure there are many children whose parents may have committed suicide who go on in life, but I am trying to tell you about the contributing cause.

He had walked away from a minimum-security prison, in California, and crossing the country, picked up a hitchhiker, who happened to be another con, who at gunpoint raped and robbed him. John shot him. Florida offered him second degree to plead guilty, but he wouldn't take it.

I went to Starke Prison in Florida with several other reporters. We were guided into a charming room with venetian blinds. I associate the color with beige-pink. They all took seats. I stood. We waited for the blinds to go up. We wanted to see what was going on and we knew the time was coming. There were sounds of cups beating on the sides of the prison walls and prisoners called from the adjacent buildings in sympathy for Spenkelink.

We must have been waiting at least ten minutes. We knew something was going on behind the blinds, but what, we didn't know.

Now-days, as I understand, reporters can witness the whole preparation, but when I was there the guards took about eleven or twelve minutes to get him strapped in the chair behind the closed blinds. As I understand it he was in agony all during that period, great agony.

As I say, we were in this pinky-beige little room, like in a theater, then the blinds came up and all I could see were his eyes. He had a towel, a sort of a strap coming across the lower part of his head. He was strapped to the chair and there was a strange piece of folded rubber, his mask, on top of his head. The only thing you could see was his eyes. I will show you in my sketch. But those eyes were the most haunting I have ever seen on any human in my life and they sort of rode the room. He was unable to speak. Ghastly eyes, just ghastly. I am not a religious man but, my God, the only thing I can associate with this was Christ on the Cross or something like that. It was incredible, these haunting eyes.

There were several persons around him. I don't know what they were doing, I guess one was a doctor. I didn't know who they were, but they were not the executioners. Then I looked in the corner of this chamber. The executioners were there and I saw them. Two humans, chest high, in this little rectangular opening to the left and high in the rear. But then, when I looked again, I saw they had slipped on black gowns and black hoods. The hoods had eye slits. They reminded me of medieval ax men. Then some other man came up to Spenkelink and dropped the rubber mask totally over his head. The executioners bent down: 2,400 volts jolted across Spenkelink. It seemed to me that a portion of his skin below his knee, his right pant leg was pulled up so that his knee was exposed, seemed to split. His hands changed color, fading to an ashen value at the tips.

And then it was over or so I thought. The doctor lifted up the long mask slightly so he could see John's chest, put a stethoscope to his heart, and said, "No"! He signaled. The executioners bent down again. Spenkelink shuddered a second time.

The doctor came forward again and examined his heart. Looked at the warden and said, "No"! This was after about six minutes, I think, besides the eleven minutes or so preparing him. And they jolted him again.

The doctor came up for the third time, examined his heart, took a little flashlight, pulled up the mask and looked into his eyes, and said, "Yes, he's dead."

It seemed to me Spenkelink was like packaged meat; cellophaned, packaged meat in a supermarket. That is why the execution was so horrible. It was such a hygienic sort of a setting with a pink-beige little room, and then to see the venetian blinds being drawn and this agonizing human with his eyes and the men in black, it boggles my mind. I mean, how can we do this? Repeat the killing.

(After the few minutes that Mr. Brodie took to recover from the reliving of this episode, he showed us some of his sketches.)

This is Gary Gilmore. He had been starving and he made a suicide attempt. Remember, these sketches are not posed portraits. This was done in a flash from life. The executions were sketched from memory afterwards.

Some years before the John Spenkelink execution weren't you present in the San Quentin gas chamber at the execution of Aaron Mitchell?

Yes. The San Quentin one was moving. I had decided, at that time, that the public should see an execution. So, on my own, I wasn't representing CBS or a paper or magazine, I just decided, as a human being, to go the State Department of Corrections and, lo and behold, they said they would allow me to do this and they made me an official state witness. Now the warden at the time was Larry Wilson, he was the one who okayed it.

Witnesses met at San Quentin, there were some eleven of us or so, aside from the press. We were guided into this room, I remember there was a big sign—"No Smoking." It was a totally green room with five windows of the octagonal gas chamber emerging from the forward wall. The other three were in the rear of that.

Through the wall came a piercing cry. I was about four feet from a window. Two guards came into the gas chamber, half dragging a slumped Aaron Mitchell. Aaron was dresed in a new white shirt with long sleeves, these covered a suicide slash from the night before. They quickly strapped him to the chair. He turned to look around to see who was watching in the windows, and as he turned he said four words loud and clear for all of us to hear: "I AM Jesus Christ." That's all he said.

The pellets were dropped and he immediately dropped forward, his arms and chest were strapped. I remember thinking death by gas is really immediate, it must have been as soon as the pellets were dropped. Then I was just astonished because he moved slowly back to the upright position *(Mr. Brodie enacted it, rising like a dreadful half-dead, half-alive corpse)* and happened to look directly at the window into which I was facing, and I could hardly believe my eyes. His mouth was constantly moving, constantly moving, he wasn't saying words or anything, but just constantly moving, bubbles of saliva were on his mouth. You could see his heart beating, beating, beating, there was a stethoscope attached to it which came out of the chamber and into our room at the end of which was a doctor. Aaron sat like that, chest heaving, mouth constantly moving, peering out of that window.

Now I am talking about minute after minute and I just burned his image into me because this was incredible to believe that anyone gassed could be sitting that way and breathing, with lips moving. His hands, his fingers gripped his thumbs, just clenched. That was the total scene. Heaving chest, clenched fist with thumbs inside, mouth constantly moving, heartbeat. And this went on—I can't say exactly, but I would say several minutes. Then he raised his head higher and higher and looked up at the end. Then he finally slumped. I believe the official time was eleven minutes, half of which he was sitting up, looking at us.

I remember the guard saying, "Oh, he's not feeling anything." My God, how do we know? How do we know when a man clenches his hands that way, the chest heaving, sitting erect, eyes open?

As an artist and reporter, can you summarize for us how you feel the death penalty affects society?

You know, when people see me coming, they often say, "Where's the trouble?" Because I am usually assigned to major criminal trials, sometimes wars, but I feel less a human whenever I witness an execution. I can't believe that we sane human beings can do this to another mad human being. It doesn't mean for a moment that I am easy on criminals but I still know they are fellow human beings.

I've covered the killing fields of World War II, Korea, French Indo-China, and Vietnam. I have seen the horrors of the Nazis, known of atrocities in other wars, but I must say that executions constitute the most dehumanizing experiences I have ever had in my life.

THE QUALITY OF MERCY

"The quality of mercy is not strain'd.
It droppeth as the gentle rain from heaven
Upon the place beneath:
It is twice blest;
It blesseth him that gives, and him that takes."
                —William Shakespeare, *The Merchant of Venice*

We knew a little about the tragedy that had befallen Norman Felton's family. Betsy, his youngest daughter, her husband, David, and their nine-month-old daughter Jessica, had been brutally murdered in 1982 in Detroit, Michigan. But nothing could have prepared us for the two hours we spent talking with Norman Felton during which he recounted the savage murders of his family, slain in a manner so heinous that the mind purged the visions of unspeakable horror as fast as they were recounted.

Norman Felton is a Hollywood writer, director, and producer. His best known works, "The Man from U.N.C.L.E." and "Dr. Kildare," are icons of the television industry. A youthful seventy-four years old, he still retains a faint English accent that has survived an adult life working in the United States. Norman lives with his wife Aline in Malibu, California.

Norman Felton started directing plays in college. He eventually came to Hollywood and achieved further successes. Aline and Norman had three children: John, who is married and lives in France; Julie, also married, and living in Los Angeles; the youngest was Betsy.

Norman Felton is a truly extraordinary human being and his own

*story is, within the fearful parameters placed upon him, a tale of love
and of hope for the future.*

*The interview was extremely charged emotionally, for us as well as
for him.*

Beverly Hills, California
Friday, November 13, 1987, 11:30 a.m.

Norman Felton

We had three children. Betsy was our youngest daughter; her real
name was Aline, which is also my wife's name, but the family called
her Betsy. She met a young man at college, David Berkley, and they
got married. Betsy graduated with honors, and decided to go into law.
David was a science major, and determined to do cancer research.

At this point we had two young people who were really ready to step
out and do something in the world. The whole family felt the same
way.

David got a grant at Wayne State University in Detroit. Betsy
enrolled in law school at the Catholic University of Detroit and shortly
thereafter became pregnant and gave birth to a baby girl, Jessica.

Betsy did well in her law studies, in spite of the fact she had a baby
and they still remember her at the school carrying little Jessica down to
the law library.

The last time we saw our daughter was in the summer of 1982, when
she and David got away from school for a couple of weeks and came to
stay with us. Then on Friday night, December 20, Aline and I got a
call from Betsy to say she had just finished her finals and was on top of
the world. Aline said to me, "I've never heard her more excited." She
had offers to go with quite a few law firms and also from a judge as a
clerk.

They had always spent Christmas with us, but this Christmas they
were going to take Jessica to David's folks in Bethesda, Maryland. On
Sunday night, this was the 22nd of December, we had a call from
David's father, he said, "Did they come to you? Because they haven't
come to us and I called them last night, Saturday, and there was no

answer, and all this morning there was no answer." I said, "No they're not here." I was concerned too. He said, "Well, I'll check around and call the apartment superintendent in Detroit." This was late in the evening.

About midnight he called back. He said, "I must tell you. . . . Betsy and the baby have been found stabbed to death in the apartment and David has disappeared."

Before I left for Detroit the next morning, I got a call from the homicide division in Detroit to say that they had found David. A man had been found on Saturday, half frozen, about two blocks from the apartment, but there was no identification on him so he was taken to the morgue—Dead On Arrival. . . . unknown. When the police and the homicide people found Betsy and the baby stabbed to death, they also found that the baby's name was Jessica. One of the detectives then discovered that a man, unknown, in the morgue, had also been stabbed and was wearing a T-shirt with "JESSICA'S DADDY" on it. And they then, you know.

When I arrived in Detroit I met with the homicide detectives and with Burton Berkley, David's father, and they told us what happened to David. He had gone to the labs to feed his research animals. On his way back to the apartment he was accosted by who knows, one, two, three men. He, like Betsy and Jessica, had multiple stab wounds. His wallet, with identification, was missing. The police concluded the murderer(s) must have taken his wallet and keys and, knowing where he lived, had gone to the apartment, opened the apartment, and killed Betsy and the baby. And that's all they knew.

The whole apartment was ransacked. We went there, both David's father and myself. They did not want us to go into the bedroom. The homicide man found it hard to ask me at the end of the day, "Did she have an outside lover?" She didn't have an outside lover, of course. Imagine that? But that and questions of all kinds . . . to try to find some clue. The fingerprint people could not find any fingerprints. The police were in the place for a long time and made a thorough search.

The only things I thought were missing were an old black and white TV and some Christmas presents we'd sent. Betsy had said she put them under their little Christmas tree.

At the end of the day we were back in the homicide headquarters and there were cameras outside from several television stations, because it was such a terrible crime and the newspeople, you know, took advantage of it. Of course, when they found out that I was from Hollywood, a television producer, this made it even more news-worthy. The homicide people said they'd been trying to keep them away, but there was ABC and CBS and so on, and they all had camera crews. I asked

the investigators, "What do you think? Is it a good idea?" and they said
it was. They had no leads and any activity could result in somebody
coming forward and so they brought two crews in. One of them started
talking to Burton Berkley, the room was not much bigger than this one
[10 × 15 feet], and the other reporter started talking to me, asking me
questions about the family and so on and I heard Burton say . . . he
used very strong language and cursed whoever did it, I couldn't blame
him, adding: "I believe in the death penalty, always have, always will,
and if ever there was a case for the death penalty, this is it. These three
wonderful people stabbed to death, stabbed . . ." I can't even repeat the
terms that he used to describe the bestiality; his voice was pitched
pretty loud. Now the crew talking with me were looking in his direction, and I thought, "I don't want him speaking for me too." I stopped
them taping me and told them that I would like to comment on what
Mr. Berkley had just said, about the death penalty. Well—that got their
attention back to me. I said, "Our family has never believed in the
death penalty and I can't say at this moment, although I'm torn by
what has happened to my daughter, David, and baby Jessica, that I can
change the way I feel. Because if what I feel has any meaning, then am
I going to change my beliefs because somebody in my family is murdered? It would make it a ridiculous farce." And the TV people said,
"Why do you feel that way?" And I replied, "I just feel that way" . . . I
just . . . I don't remember what else I said . . . not much else.

I'm not a religious person. I grew up in the Episcopal Church in
England, my parents' church. When I went to church or Sunday
School I asked many questions and don't remember getting satisfactory
answers. So I never did become involved with religion later on. My
wife and I had certain beliefs on how to live and how to treat other
people, and hoped that we would be treated likewise. We sometimes
talked about crime and the terrible things that were happening. I remember telling Aline about one time in England being near a prison,
Wandsworth Prison, where people had gathered outside—wanting to
experience a hanging, an execution, and how repulsive that was. As a
family we didn't really talk much about the death penalty, but I knew,
and my wife Aline knew, that we did not believe that killing people
was an answer to murder, or any other crime for that matter. If somebody was involved in a crime, no matter how awful, it would be better
to find out why this horrible thing happened, and try not to have those
conditions happen again. Just killing that person wasn't the answer.
Later I recall someone telling me a story about mad dogs. How, at one
time, we used to kill mad dogs—then a scientist in France said, "Why
kill the dogs? Let's find out what caused the dog to be mad," and how
that led to scientific findings of great benefit to humanity.

Now with the murders in our very own family, comes a test of what we believed.

I went back to the hotel and called my wife. One of the first things I remember saying, after telling about what was happening in the investigation, was, "You know how we feel about the death penalty," and I told her what was said in the squad room about it. And she replied, "What you said. . . ."

(At this point Mr. Felton found it difficult to speak). . . . Now this is very interesting, I haven't broken down for a year I guess. Once in a while something I say . . . it's hard . . . excuse me for a moment.

(He then continued) But Aline was wonderful . . . Here she was. . . . she was wonderful. She didn't come to Detroit with me. For many reasons, I persuaded her to stay in California. She had a mother who was almost ninety and her great-grandchild had just been murdered, so Aline stayed with her. My daughter, Julie, was also at home. It was hard. I knew just how hard it was for her to be there and not with me. She was marvelous to be able to say to me what she said, "I agree."

Then I told her that I thought something needed to be done about the apartment and the things in it. There was a Unitarian church on the corner that had a day-care center. Betsy had said she wanted to send Jessica there. I thought I would call them and ask if they would like to look at the apartment and take what was left. So I did, and the man in charge said, "I'll get my people together and we'll go there, don't worry about it."

Later in my life this proved to be a very important thing to do because it led to us supporting the day-care center. We started the "Jessica Fund." We have been there and seen children. We are still in contact with them—It has been a positive act for us.

Finally, after many more talks with the homicide people and having to go to identify the bodies—that was the most difficult part of my being in Detroit—I went back home.

The investigation continued and finally the killers, Timothy Smith, Willie Talley and Jackie Shepherd ended up in court, three years after the murders.

It turned out the murderers were all related, either half brothers or brothers; it was a complex family. The question of witchcraft came up because one of the killers, Timothy Smith, said in court that the murders happened because they were on drugs and the mother, Jackie Shepherd's mother, was a witch, and she had something to do with making them do this thing.

The murders occurred because they were crazed on drugs and wanted money to pay for more drugs. I will tell you later about one of them, Jackie, and his background, because I think it's important.

So, after three years, we were back in Detroit. Our son John had flown over from France to give us support. Everyday, TV and the press were waiting outside the courtroom to question and challenge our position on the death penalty.

The trial was all over in five days. The jury was only out two hours, to the amazement of the prosecutor. Verdicts of murder in the first degree. All three were convicted. I think they each were found guilty of three counts of murder and two of armed robbery. About a month later, the judge passed sentence on them: imprisonment for life without parole. I was not present at that time. Burton, who lives in Maryland, was closer to Detroit, so he went there. He read a statement about how he felt the men should be given the death penalty.

The judge was also very much for the death penalty. He made a speech in which he said—well, he got quite poetic—he said he regretted he could not sentence Jackie Shepherd "to ride the lightning into the hereafter," and to Talley he said, "The only sentence that would be fair would be to take the only thing you have—a short drop would do it."

They don't have the death penalty in Michigan.

That's right, but at that time there was a big effort being made to restore it to their statutory arsenal. The claimed it was a deterrent. The principal newspaper in Detroit was for the death penalty and the press again called me for a statement. I could only tell them the way I felt, and how my family felt. "It comes from the heart," I told them. "I don't have information to give you about the death penalty as to a deterrent. I only speak from my heart." After I said this, I thought I should do something to find out more about the death penalty and what those who had studied it discovered. "Maybe I'm wrong about it," I thought. Deep down I didn't think so, but I really needed to reinforce my feelings.

After the trial was over I went to the library, got all the information on capital punishment I could from various sources, and I became convinced from what I was reading that it did not appear to have a deterrent effect. In states that had the death penalty the crime rate was no different than in states that did not.

You found revenge was not the answer, how did you deal with your grief?

I want to tell you about a group called Parents of Murdered Children. My wife and I have attended meetings, and there are usually about twelve or fifteen or twenty people who have lost children through murder.

At meetings each one would tell about what happened, and each time they would tell what happened to them, they relived it and in a way it helped. When you talk about something and don't keep it deep inside, it can be a release. Many felt that whoever it was who did the terrible thing to their loved one should be strung up, killed, executed —whatever. Frequently prosecutors would send people to Parents of Murdered Children's monthly meetings to speak on behalf of bringing back the death penalty. We didn't see that it helped anybody to hear that message. At the third meeting I attended I spoke about positive action and the way Aline and I felt about directing one's energies to something that can have a healing effect. I talked about the death penalty and how retribution does not appear to enter into the healing process, that it only keeps the wound open.

It was dark when we left that meeting, and two nervous people came up to us and said, "We are not for the death penalty but we have never wanted to say it here, because we thought that it would be something that the rest wouldn't like, and when you spoke up it gave us a feeling that we too should speak the way we feel next time." Many people, many friends and even strangers have heard of our beliefs. There are a lot of people, good people, who feel that the death penalty is the only way to deal with murder. There is so much crime and I think they are frustrated and believe the death penalty will wipe everything out. Get rid of the problem. But it doesn't work that way.

After the trial I went to the court and asked how I could get a copy of the transcript of the trial. They got one for me. At the same time I was also able to get some information from the Wayne County Adult Probation Service—it's called a Presentence Investigation Report, and I was quite interested in it.

(The following was extremely difficult for Mr. Felton)

Here was a dreadful group of murders. . . . I mean . . . they were stabbed. . . . one murderer in his twenties . . . the others thirties . . . The baby was stabbed. It was testified in court that my daughter pleaded for her. . . . for the life of the baby . . . she was raped and then they killed the baby in front of her . . . before they killed her. . . . and I can't think of much worse than that . . .

But then, when I later thought about it. . . .

(Long pause)

I think there are people . . . perhaps who are close to me . . . who would not like me to say what I'm going to say. . . .

(Mr. Felton looks through his papers)

They were under the influence of drugs, seeking more drugs . . . they all had a record of drugs.

. . . .Just one instance I later found. . . . he . . . he . . . Jackie was 32 years old when this happened. He was born in Cleveland in 1954. When he was seven months old he was taken from his mother and put in a foster home. He went from foster home to foster home. *(At this point, Mr. Felton is very upset, but continues)* until age sixteen . . . no longer any foster homes. . . . he was. . . . he was turned out. He worked in McDonald's. . . . he was laid off. Worked in an auto place . . . was laid off. He was on drugs before he was out of the foster homes. And what did he have in his life? No help. . . . But I mean these people, there are thousands in this country who have no reason to want to live. They walk the streets. They can't get jobs. And here's a case . . . What would he want to live for? . . . Who cares? Inhumanity had become the norm for this boy. No one cared about him, so why should he care about anyone else? Now somebody might very well say, "Well you like him then, you think he should be let out?" No, I don't think he should be let out. It was a horrific crime. But I think it's terrible that the circumstances should allow something like this to happen. We don't do enough to prevent these crimes.

I've not talked to anybody about this before . . . this situation. But when I read in this report about one of the murderers I can understand. . . . and to kill the man I don't think helps.

We aren't going to change the society overnight, but to pin it right down, the death penalty is certainly not the answer to stopping crime . . . murders. To keep a person alive and find out why he did the crime and then work towards helping change conditions. . . . offers society a better chance in the future than capital punishment. . . . That's it. That's about what I feel, as simple as that.

They didn't get the death penalty on the ballot in Michigan, by the way.

LIVING IN BABYLON

"Indeed I tremble for my country when I reflect
that God is just."

—Thomas Jefferson,
Notes on The State of Virginia, 1785

*Everyone said there is no one quite like Marie Deans; a one-woman
coalition for the state of Virginia. She is in her forties, long-limbed
and slender. Her hair is dark and curly, flecked with gray, her eyes
dauntless, heavy-lidded.*

*She laughs off the harassments she has had to endure since becom-
ing the director of the Virginia Coalition on Jails and Prisons and
founder of Murder Victims' Families for Reconciliation, including obscene telephone calls and well-stuffed body bags dumped in her yard.*

*As the daughter-in-law of a murder victim, she understands the pain
brought about by violence. She once said, "Perhaps it would surprise
you to know that every time I am about to meet a man, woman, or
child on death row for the first time, I am thrown back into Penny's
[Marie's mother-in-law] murder, and that I identify so strongly with
the victims and their families that I spend days calling on God to help
me remember that the man or woman I am about to meet is my brother
or sister. I am thankful that God has answered every one of those
prayers."*

*When asked why she goes on doing this kind of work, she answered,
"There are many reasons. I have the need to understand why we are so
good at passing on violence and so poor at passing on love."*

It is true, there is no one quite like Marie Deans.

Marie Deans

We understand your mother-in-law was a murder victim. Would you mind telling us about it?

When I was thirty-two and pregnant my mother-in-law, Penny, was murdered. This was the worst year of my life. I was really close to my father-in-law and my mother-in-law. Jabo, my father-in-law, had died just a year before Penny was killed. After he died, Penny was very depressed until she found out that I was pregnant and then it was like a new life for her, a new life for all of us. First we did a lot of shopping and talking and planning for the baby, then she went to North Carolina to tell all my father-in-law's family.

She came home early because she missed us. We were living in South Carolina. Somewhere along the road this guy saw her and followed her all the way home. The guy came into the house and there was a struggle and he shot her twice. A neighbor called the police and my brother-in-law called us. Just before we got to the house, cops had arrived and there were already reporters there. They told us Penny had been shot.

(Marie was very emotional at this time)

We wanted to see Penny, but the cops told us we couldn't go into the house but that paramedics were with her. We waited for a while and then realized that my husband's younger sister didn't know what had happened, so we left to get her, and on our way back we passed an ambulance with no lights on.

When we got back to Penny's house, we asked the police if she was in that ambulance and they said, "Yes, she's been taken to the hospital for an autopsy." And that's how we found out she was dead.

What a terrible story. Did you hold your abolitionist views at that time?

We were opposed to the death penalty, or perhaps a better way to put it is that we had not been for it. Somewhere along the line during the investigation someone asked us if this was going to change our minds. It was the first time we had really even thought about the idea that this man could get the death penalty.

They were trying to bring back the death penalty in South Carolina at the time, so we tried to get some information from the prosecutor, and they just kept telling us that was not our responsibility. We even talked to our minister and he told us the same thing. So we decided we would oppose any effort to sentence the man to death.

About that time I started hemorrhaging.

Did you lose the baby?

No. The "baby" is my fifteen-year-old treasure, Robert.

Did they catch the murderer?

Yes. The man had escaped from a prison in Maine. During the escape he had killed a woman and taken her car. I believe it was my hemorrhaging and the possibility of losing our baby that triggered my husband's going to the prosecutor and telling him we'd fight extradition. He'd got a life sentence in Maine, there is no death penalty there. So they never did extradite him back to South Carolina. He is still in prison in Maine.

His sister turned him in. She called down to South Carolina, I didn't talk to her, but she was utterly distraught about what had happened. She wanted to know about us and if we were all right.

We found out that the guy had been in prison three times before, each time for progressively more violent attacks on women. His family and his attorneys had asked for treatment for him and he had gotten no treatment whatsoever. He was just warehoused and released over and over again. I really felt like Penny had paid for our society's inability to face its problems and deal with them effectively. We are more interested in satisfying our emotional needs than we are in finding real solutions to our problems.

How did you get involved with jails and prisons?

I joined Amnesty in 1973. I made one trip to see Rose Styron and some others from Amnesty. Then a man in South Carolina [J. C. Shaw] dropped his appeals and the Alston Wilkes Society (a prison reform organization in South Carolina) called me and asked if I would come out and talk to him. I called the Commissioner of Corrections and made the arrangements to see this inmate.

I never felt so inept in all my life. I didn't know what to say to the prisoner. I didn't know what happened to him; I didn't know what his crime was. All I knew was that he had dropped his appeals primarily from remorse, because he felt the victim's family would be helped by his death. Nevertheless, I returned to visit him again.

J. C. had been mute during his trial, before his trial and for a long time after his trial. But one day, he suddenly started talking. I asked if he knew why I was there and he said, "No, not really," and I said, "I am here just because I don't want you to die, I don't want you to be executed." He asked me why and I said, "I don't know, your life is sacred that's all I know. I don't have any good reasons except that." So he asked me if I would come back to see him, and I did. Between me, a priest, and another friend, we were able to persuade him to pick up his appeal. Then he asked me if I would see another guy on the row who was sitting crouched up in his cell, in the corner of his bunk, and not talking to anybody. So I went to see him, and the next thing I knew I was visiting all the men on the South Carolina death row and working with their attorneys.

Why were you so concerned about vicious murderers?

From the moment Penny was killed, I never understood it. Why she was killed. I came to the conclusion that we would not find out why unless we talked to the people who had done these things and find out from them. Of course they can't tell you why. You have to dig a lot deeper than that. I learned the answers to my "whys" through working with J. C. Shaw and others on death row. But they killed Shaw in 1985.

Tell us about him.

He had asked me to be with him at the end and I went; however, I left before the execution.

I was trying to get J. C. to pick up his appeals. He had said to me several times, "Stop, you are torturing me," so when he was sitting in the death house, I asked him about that, and he said, "Oh no, no, these have been the best years of my life, the best years, because I changed, I came back to God. I really would not have wanted to die back then."

How long was he on death row?

Five years after he picked up his appeals. All told, he was there about seven years.

J. C. Shaw was my first client, my first contact with death row. J. C. was real shy and he would come up when I was doing general visits and would just stand beside me.

It is strange to hear that. J. C. Shaw was always portrayed as the older psychotic, dangerous killer, drug addict, sadistic ex-military policeman.

He was certainly in a psychotic state when he killed. His family could not believe the change in him. J. C. could not believe it either. He had been on Lithium as a youngster, but when he was in the Army, he stopped taking it. He had been diagnosed as a schizophrenic. He had gone to the military hospital two or three times pleading that he be committed. The last time they were having a hot dog party in the backyard and they told him to come back the next day. That was just an afternoon before the murders happened.

He would tell me, "I have lived this crime," and he named a number that was over a thousand, I think. The warden said that was the exact number of days since the murders. He had relived the murders every night since he had committed the crimes.

He told me that going to the electric chair was not a problem for him. The problem for him was what it was doing to his family and his loved ones. So we cried together, and he told me, "I don't want you here if you are afraid you may come to hate these people." I don't think it would have happened, but I was afraid it might.

By the time J. C. Shaw was executed I had moved to Virginia.

Have you been harassed because of your work?

You know the intimidation has been pretty good here in Virginia. I walked out of my house one time and found a body bag, well stuffed, on my doorstep. They painted the outline of a dead body where I parked my car. Came home from work one day and there was this "dead body" I was supposed to park over. People continue to send hate mail and make threatening phone calls.

Who are they?

I don't know who they are. I don't know. They stay anonymous. I suppose because they are as full of fear as they are of hatred.

We read about a case in Virginia where a representative, during a debate, advocated letting condemned men bleed to death so their organs could be used for transplants.

That's true. When that kind of debate can go on in our legislature, we are in more trouble than we want to admit.

I know David Bruck *[see David Bruck interview]* has told you something about being in the execution chamber. I haven't been in the chamber itself. But I have been in the death house with eight people now who have been killed and a number who have gotten stays at the last minute. I have seen two men go crazy right before my eyes in the death house. I have seen us kill Morris Mason, a man-child with a sixty-two IQ who was diagnosed by the state of Virginia as a paranoid schizophrenic [executed June 25, 1985]. Morris said to me before I left, "You tell Roger Coleman [a death row inmate who is a very good basketball player] that when I get through here, I am going to come back and show him that I can play basketball as good as he can." Morris knew he was going to the electric chair but he didn't know he wasn't coming back—that he was going to die. He didn't know what that was. I mean he even asked one of the guards what he should wear to his funeral! And we killed him like we killed all those other people . . . like Richard Whitley, who was seriously brain-damaged.

I have this intellectual concept of God. I believe that God is life and love, and those things that move toward life are good things and godly things and sacred things, and those things that move toward unnatural death are evil, in my mind. Joe Ingle *[see Joseph Ingle interview]* calls the death chambers the "Vortex of Evil" and you feel that when you are in the death house because it is so banal, it is incredibly banal.

There is a ritual, you see, and the American people need ritual. If you deal with something straight up you don't need a ritual. In the death house, ritual is the engine that drives the death machine and it encompasses the most absurd things.

There is a chef at the state penitentiary, who generally wears work clothes but when he serves the last meal in the death house, he wears a suit, a chef's hat, and pulls on white gloves! Even if he's serving french fries. I have to tell the guys not to ask for french fries because every piece of food has to be inspected in front of the execution squad. They go through the french fries in case there is a razor blade or the like. So finally when they get their food, it's cold.

Now Richard Whitley wanted ice tea and he wanted tea for everybody, so they brought a jug of ice tea. I am sitting near the bars close to Richard and they put the jug down and it says on the side "Cider Vinegar" and without thinking I said, "Oh my God. 'And our Lord thirsted and they gave him vinegar.' "

Before I left Richard, when the execution squad said, "Marie, you have to go now," Richard had hung onto me. As long as I was there, he was okay, but as soon as I began to leave, he started shaking and he said, "I can't make it without you," and I said, "Yes, you can, you can make it." Then I said, "Where is God, Richard?" and he raised his hand and he pulled his hand in a downward movement between the two of us. And I said, "Yes, I can feel Him, I know that God is with us, here, and when I go out there Richard, I am going into Babylon but you are staying with God."

I just knew he would be all right. I just knew it. You know, you can feel it. People come in and out of there and you can tell who that Presence is with and who stays in the "Vortex of Evil."

Richard was all right and I did go back out into Babylon. And that's where I live. And that's where I work. And that's where I stay.

Sometimes I am afraid to tell that because Christians can be warped enough to say, "Then it's okay if we kill them because God takes them, they are delivered."

What do you think the death penalty does to the society that executes?

I honestly believe that we are steadily eroding the Constitution in order to kill people. I can see that in the cases. Justices [Thurgood]

Marshall and [William S.] Brennan see that, too. We are coming to the point in this country where we must choose between whether we want to kill people or whether we want the Constitution.

I believe we owe a duty to the American public to explain what is happening . . . what they are doing. If they choose to give up their Constitution to kill people, then they have made the same kind of conscious choice that the people in Nazi Germany made. That may sound harsh but when there is a problem and you are not doing anything to stop it, if you know the problem is there and you know it's wrong, then you are making, in my ethics, a conscious choice.

You talk of the Constitution. Which constitutional principle, in your opinion, is being violated?

Equal rights and due process protections. A lot of people say it's the Eighth Amendment because it's cruel and unusual punishment, but we have killed an awful lot of people. It may be *cruel*, but clearly, in American history, it's not *unusual*. What makes it cruel and unusual is the arbitrary manner in which we choose who will get the death sentence and who will be executed. I know that Justice Brennan believes that it is against the Constitution because of the evolving standards of the Eighth Amendment. The standards that clearly have evolved and continue to evolve are international standards of punishment. The death penalty in the United States demonstrates atrophying standards and creates an enormous tension in our Constitution.

The death penalty is something that is destroying the soul of our people. If people don't know that, it just tells me how quickly it is destroying us.

BANALITY OF EVIL

"The same man who is full of humanity toward his
fellow creatures when they are at the same time his
equals, becomes insensible to their affliction as
soon as that equality ceases."

—Alexis Henri Tocqueville,
Democracy in America, 1835

*It's a short elevator ride to the second-floor law offices of Bruck &
Blume in downtown Columbia, South Carolina. The space is white and
airy, and differs completely from the organized chaos of most capital
defense lawyers. David Bruck looks Preppy but definitely not Yuppie.
A youthful thirty-seven years, he is blue-eyed, blond-haired and soft-
spoken.*

*David Bruck was born in 1949 in Canada, though of American par-
ents, and came to the United States to go to college.*

*He graduated from Harvard and did military counseling work and
GI legal rights. As the anti-war movement was spreading in the military, he worked with a civilian group on Army bases in Tennessee and
Kentucky. It was there, as an offshoot of anti-war, anti-Vietnam activity, that he first had the idea of becoming a lawyer, and eventually
went to law school in South Carolina. He worked as a public defender
for three years, then quit the bar for a year to become a welder in
Vancouver, British Columbia, to "get a rest and do what everyone
wishes their whole lives they would have done."*

*When he returned to South Carolina he "hit" on the idea of working
against the death penalty and returned to law. He spent time in South
Africa, the most actively executing Western industrialized nation,
studying the use of the death penalty there.*

Columbia, South Carolina
Thursday, February 18, 1988, 2:30 p.m.

David Bruck

*What made you just "hit" on the idea of working in the capital
punishment area?*

Oh, I don't know. I had always been opposed to capital punishment
in a somewhat abstract kind of way, just thinking that it was such an
evil. I couldn't understand how anyone could possibly be in favor of
killing unarmed prisoners.

I already knew my way around the criminal courts, but I had no
experience at all in capital cases, or virtually none, but I decided to
become South Carolina's "expert" on death penalty defense. To my
surprise the Office of Appellate Defense was willing to hire me, on a
modest contract, to be their death penalty specialist. In fact, I had all
of three death penalty clients in 1980. Most of the cases weren't especially well known. I still work on that same basis with that Office of
Appellate Defense. It is about half my practice.

What's it like working for this system?

There is one thing about this system. I found the same thing in South
Africa. It is that *no one is ever responsible*. Responsibility is diffused.

The legislature passes the law but, of course, the legislators are not
the ones who decide who actually gets executed, that's someone else's
job. The jury passes the death sentence, but often the jurors feel sure
that there will be appeals and the sentence won't really be carried out:
if it's the wrong thing to do, someone else will stop it. Every other
actor or decision maker along the line then defers to the legislature, or
the jury, both of which were, at the time of making their decision,
deferring to *them*. The courts won't interfere because the jury heard the
evidence and they don't want to second-guess them. Anyway, say the
courts, it's the legislature that decides whether or not to have the death
penalty. The legislature never decided to give the death penalty to any

particular case, but that is neither here nor there. By the time a case gets to the appeals courts, the court assumes that if the legislators had not wanted that person to get death, they would have said, "Don't give it to X or Y." Then finally in the wee hours of the morning the death sentence gets onto the governor's desk. And he defers to everybody before him. The legislature passed the law, the jury passed the sentence, the courts have reviewed this and, therefore, thinks the governor, "Who am I to interfere?" Of course, all the time everyone was deferring to him, and to each other. Where everyone is responsible, no one is responsible. Or, at least, no one takes responsibility.

Have you ever been involved in a case where someone you represented was executed?

Yes. Terry Roach [convicted of rape/murder with co-defendant J. C. Shaw—*see Marie Deans interview*]. I had not represented him in court. My involvement with the case came at the end, and I only became directly involved in the last few weeks when an effort was made to persuade Governor Dick Riley to grant clemency. I assisted his lawyers on that. Clemency was denied during the last week or so of appeals. The attorneys found themselves in Washington on the night before the execution, waiting for the Supreme Court to act, so I served as Terry's lawyer here, at the penitentiary in Columbia, which basically meant that I was the person to keep him company while he was waiting to be killed.

His was the first, in legal lingo, "non-consenting" or "non-volunteer" execution of a person for a crime committed by a minor since 1964.

There had been one execution of a seventeen-year-old kid the preceding fall, in Texas, but that execution occurred because he had dropped his federal *Habeas* appeal, and so, in that sense, he was a "volunteer."

Terry Roach was seventeen at the time of the crime. Wasn't there also a question about his mental capacity?

Terry was at the low end of the borderline range, that is to say, one, two, three IQ points above being clinically diagnosed as mentally retarded. What that meant, as a practical matter, was that in talking to him it seemed like you were talking to a twelve or thirteen-year-old kid. He was very slow, he had a slack-jawed way of talking, he had very limited understanding of why he was being executed. I don't mean by that he didn't understand that he had been sentenced to death for committing this murder and was going to be executed for his part in the crime.

But anyone on death row has to try to come to terms with the tremendous randomness of who gets executed and who doesn't. The public may not understand it, but the people on the row know that only a handful of murderers get death while the vast majority are spared. The brighter ones recognize that it has to do with bad luck, discrimination, or incompetent representation, but people who are as mentally handicapped and as slow as Terry tend to break it down into a more childish explanation. Terry knew some of what was going on. He told a newspaper reporter on the day before he was executed that if he and his girlfriend had been murdered, the people who committed that crime would not have been executed. And that is certainly true. I mean Terry's family were mountain people, people who came from the backcountry. I think Terry perceived his execution to be the outcome of an unequal family feud, sort of a personal feud, between the prosecutor on one hand and his family on the other. His people were not influential and, unlike the families of Terry's two teenage victims, they didn't have political connections. To Terry, it was really as simple as that. It's a brutish, violent world, and the bigger battalions always win out. That was his perspective, and for that reason he felt, right to the end, that his death sentence could be arbitrarily removed.

When I went to the death house, half an hour after midnight on the morning he was to be killed, he was still hoping that the governor would change his mind. Well, there was no chance in the world that Governor Riley would change his mind. I suppose it was natural for Terry to be thinking that, but such thoughts reflect the fact that these decisions are arbitrarily changed, revised, or rescinded. He had seen that happen to people on death row over the eight years he had been there. Why not for him? There was no good reason.

How did he end up on death row?

Terry's life was that of a borderline, retarded kid who falls through the cracks. He got no help, no special training. Terry was a kid who did not grow up alongside all the other kids. He found friends among drug abusers, who are, in effect, people who artificially suppress their own maturity, who slow themselves down through drugs, so that they were at the same level as Terry.

A kid like Terry grows up always being rejected. His playmates get older, more mature, get quicker, get more impatient, and before long, they are bored with him, because Terry stayed at an eight-year-old level. So his life experience is going to be one of rejection: people not wanting him around and not liking him, thinking he's a drag. People like that then become starved for acceptance and they will do anything for it. He dulls the pain with drugs, and Terry became the classic sidekick for any psychopath whose path he happens to cross. And that's what happened. Terry was the retarded sidekick of an older, more experienced criminal, and that was his role in this crime. He was taking orders.

People say that the death penalty is a deterrent to criminal activity, that it makes potential murderers think twice. After the murder, Terry fled by taking a taxi from Columbia to his father's home in Seneca. Of course, he didn't have money to pay for the taxi so he made his "getaway" by scooting into the house. Well, the cab driver comes in after him, and Terry gets arrested for not paying the cab fare. That's how he was apprehended. This gives you a picture of his ability to calculate consequences, to plan ahead. For people to believe that the prospect of an execution three, six, or eight years down the line may have the slightest effect on someone who has that type of mental capacity, is a sad joke.

There was the whole issue about Huntington's disease?

The question of Huntington's disease has never been resolved *[Huntington's disease is a debilitating, incurable, hereditary illness that affects the nervous system; sufferers are unable to control their movements and frequently appear "drunk."]* Terry's mother is dying of Huntington's disease, and a number of his family members have been diagnosed as having it. So Terry was at risk with a 50 percent possibility of carrying the gene. At the time of his trial, a psychiatrist from the state mental hospital told the judge that as far as he knew, it was impossible for Terry to have Huntington's because a male could not inherit the gene from the mother. That is just an old wives' tale. No one knows where that came from. This was a notoriously incompetent psychiatrist who has since left the scene, but that was the information the judge had about Huntington's disease. The rest of the information was that Terry had been tested and his IQ test scores at that time ranged between 69 and 80. The psychiatrist simply seized on the 80 and said that puts him in low normal or borderline category. He described him to the judge as someone who really just wasn't too much slower than the rest of the population. But the main thing the doctor had to say was that he was not going to get any better. It was almost as if his mental condition aggravated rather than mitigated his crime.

As for the Huntington's disease, two years later when Terry got proper legal representation, a neurological evaluation was done which found abnormalities but said that it was too early to be diagnosed. Before the execution, we found a neurologist who was willing to give an examination for free, and he said that he believed that he was exhibiting early clinical signs of Huntington's and that a lot of his social and criminal history may have been the early manifestations of the disease.

Although the state would not pay for a proper neurological examination before the execution, at the autopsy they spared no expense, and the neurological report stated that there was no evidence of degenerative effects of Huntington's. That does not mean he did not have it, but they said they couldn't find the proof, so the question remains unresolved.

Could you tell us a little about his last hours?

Terry asked me to stay through the whole night and be there until he was killed. I had never thought that much about it, but when it was over, I discovered that it is the most natural thing in the world not to want to be alone when you die. It is a violent death, but it is also a death. It is a dying, and anyone should have support and reassurance when they die. Execution is such a degrading and humiliating death. The task was to block that out and make it as though it was just death, rather than a killing. Marie Deans was there, too. The two of us were there for the last few hours. The way she described it was very apt: "Like a campfire, and the conversation between the three of us was like throwing logs on the fire to keep away the darkness and terror." In the case of someone as slow and childlike as Terry, it was not that hard to do. He was very, very brave, he was limited and very slow, very concrete in his thinking, but it felt in some ways like sitting with a child who was about to have a really horrible dentist appointment. It is sort of silly to say we were trying to keep our minds off of what was happening because that was impossible, but it was like that.

It was impossible to keep his attention diverted all night. The guards arrived at about three-thirty in the morning with a safety razor to shave his head. Shaving cream and everything. I had never realized that . . . I had just filed it away in the corner of my mind that they put conducting gel on his head. But what I didn't know was that they *massage it in for over half an hour*. It's a long process. This is after the barber ritual, the sheet around his shoulders, sitting in the cell like he was having a haircut. They cut his hair off with clippers, then shaved it with disposable safety razors and aerosol shaving cream and then, when they finished that and he had a smooth shiny head, they started caressing the head with conducting gel. They would work the gel in and then put more on and work that in and, when that was worked in, they would do it some more. This goes on and on and on and all the time we were trying to make conversation.

What about the prison staff? Did it have any effect on them?

I don't know, but it must have affected them. If it didn't affect them . . . well, it must have affected them . . . but I don't know. They also shaved his leg with safety razors, then rubbed the conducting gel in, over and over again. Terry asked them at one point, "Why do you have to do this?" and the officer said, "Just to make it easier, Terry." Those were his words, "Just to make it easier, Terry."

So that was the ritual. Everything that happened made you think we ought not to be doing it. It's an ugly, very ugly ritual.

After spending five hours with him, seeing him go through the ordeal of the preparation, the actual killing part wasn't much of anything. I mean, newspaper reporters or the public or whoever gets to witness an execution should not believe that they have seen much of what was done to the person if they witnessed only the last five minutes. It's so quick and antiseptic. I suppose it would be better to say that the actual killing was incredibly disgusting, painful, gruesome, and gory to see someone electrocuted. But, to me, the truth is it was not as bad as that, and at the same time it was much worse. It was as easy as shutting a drawer or snapping one's fingers. It was fast. The process worked the way it was supposed to work [and not the way it worked with John Evans in Alabama, where they had to do it over and over again]. When it's being done "right," death appears to be instantaneous. Although one never knows. One senses that he really never knew what hit him. Unconsciousness seemed to be instantaneous.

The whole ritual in the death chamber was very fast. To me, what it said was that they take a living person, who took twenty-five years to create—and even Terry Roach, as damaged as he was, was unique, there never has been anyone like him and there never will be again, all of modern science cannot create his fingernail—and within just a few seconds they converted him into a piece of junk to be wrestled out on a stretcher and carted away. To me, the message was that human beings are junk and if you don't believe it—watch this. It is a completely incomprehensible miracle how a human being comes into this world . . . but to snuff one out is nothing. It is the easiest thing. Murderers can do it, anyone can do it. We can do it. Watch this! It was banal. That was my reaction, and it was hard to believe that there were people who knew him, who loved him, who at that moment were waiting with anguish, because he appeared to be just a piece of trash. It was dehumanizing. Not only to him. It was a ritual which denied the importance and uniqueness of any of us.

What I got out of it was that it is amazingly easy to snuff someone out. We don't know how to create a person but we sure can kill him . . . nothing to it. All of our lives are just flickering candles. Anyone of us is so fragile and frail. That's what it proved.

What do you feel is the effect on a society that condones executions?
Executions emit violence. They are violent and they emit violence.

We always have to keep in mind that executions, no matter how frequent they become, will never be anything more than symbolic human sacrifice. I say that simply because of the numbers. If we executed two percent, one out of every fifty people convicted of homicide in the United States, we would be witnessing a bloodbath which is beyond our wildest imaginations.

I went to South Africa two years ago to look at how they use the death penalty there. In December 1987, they hanged twenty-one people in one week on the gallows. In one week they had three batches of seven, all at one prison in Pretoria. There it seems a little more obvious what the effect is—although it is not really all that obvious there, either. The death penalty is used, with very few exceptions, in non-political, violent cases. It is a crime control method used fairly routinely, although only a very small percentage of homicides in South Africa are punished by death. So, in a way, the same "lottery" effect operates there. It's a flexing of muscles, a show of government strength, it's a ritual of power and powerlessness. It certainly doesn't deter many people in South Africa. They have a murder rate four times [per capita] that of the United States. Astounding! And that's in a country where the majority of the population are not allowed to have guns.

State executions release violence into the atmosphere. What effect that has, I don't know, but it can't be good.

WHO KILLED JIMMY'S MAMA?

"It would be ugly to watch people poking sticks at a caged rat. It is uglier still to watch rats poking sticks at a caged person."

—Jean Harris, convicted of murder

Scharlette Holdman has been called many things, many of them unprintable. She describes herself as a mixture of " 'ole 60's radical" and "poor white trash."

Actually, Scharlette is a lusty, chain-smoking, workaholic champion of death row inmates. Certainly outspoken, in full swing her tongue would peel the very paint from the porches and verandas of those Southern "gentlemen" who favor death as a punishment.

In Memphis, she majored in anthropology and joined the civil rights movement. Scharlette had worked as state director for the American Civil Liberties Union in Hawaii, New Orleans, and Miami, before taking the position of director of the Florida Clearinghouse on Criminal Justice.

Scharlette had the unmitigated gall to use every legal means in her power to delay executions for years. Having no law degree herself, she recruits attorneys and shares her hard-earned experience with them. Not infrequently she saves men from death row entirely.

In her role as director of the Florida Clearinghouse, and later roles as well, she was a thorn in the flesh of first Governor [now Senator] Bob Graham and then Governor Robert Martinez, men who sign death warrants with an unrestrained zeal and sense of righteousness.

Scharlette lives in Tallahassee and has a son and a daughter.

Tallahassee, Florida
Thursday, May 26, 1988, 9:15 a.m.

Scharlette Holdman

*Why do you think that you are the most infamous/famous, loved/
hated abolitionist in the country?*

(Laughs) If what you say is true . . . and it may be, it is because the
nature of public protests and guerrilla theater we stage in Florida.

I'm a Southerner and came up through the ranks of the South in
Memphis during the civil rights movement. I learned about the value
of symbolism and resistance from my own family members, who
were very active in "massive resistance"—that's what opposition to
integration was called in the South. Citizens' councils engaged in an
active policy of resistance to equal rights for black people and I was
party to hearing, every night at dinnertime, how white people with
power and money, motivated by fear, were resisting the movement.
My father was very involved and obsessed with the changes that
were coming. So I learned what the system responded to and how
frightening public opposition to racism was for the South. There was
nothing that shook Southern white family foundations more than in
1968 when the garbage strikers in Memphis put their fingers on the
pulse of white racism. They wore these wonderful armbands that
said, "I AM A MAN." That drove white men across the South crazy,
because their whole notion was that black people weren't men and
for black people to say, "I AM A MAN" meant that all those other
rights and privileges flowed to them. It scared white men across the
South horribly—just four simple words. "I am a man." Very effective. Done by powerless people, with no money, no standing in the
majority community, and yet they shook the foundation of the South.
They shook racism.

That effectiveness taught me that we could make a big difference,
even if we were powerless, and didn't have any money. If you are
powerless you can't buy an ad in *The New York Times* or control the
electronic media. They are not going to run our public service announcements against the death penalty along with the Cancer Society's

announcements, so we have to compel attention to the injustice. Powerless people have always had "going to the streets" as a forum when their message was true. Powerless people can say, in as stark terms as possible, just what was the nature of the debate. I have always defined the nature of the debate as division, so my strategy is confrontation rather than reconciliation. I believe there is no reconciliation with powerful, white, wealthy men who decide which poor, black, or white trash person is to be killed in a bizarre state-orchestrated ritual. How to present this, how to make the community look at this? By 1978, the death penalty was confined to legal debate. No one actually talked about the reality, so we tried to point out that each person is involved —each of us individually is responsible.

We have been told by more than one source that John Spenkelink (first execution in Florida after the moratorium) was beaten up prior to electrocution. How are the men treated on the row now?

The enquiry that was held after John was executed was a several-day affair. They took testimony down at the prison and I sat in for a couple of days of it. The guards, prison officials, and government witnesses described the actual execution in "guard language," this really artificial language that they use in order to sound official and impersonal. For example, one guard testified: ". . . and then we 'escorted' the prisoner to the chamber." Now when I was growing up, an "escort" was well . . . *(Laughs)* . . . someone who took you to a dance. One guard testified that he was one of the escort death squad that put the calipers on the prisoner; calipers are those metal rod claw things. They put them on the prisoner so he can't kick or have any flexibility in case he wants to fight back. One prison official identified himself as "something . . . something . . . Program Coordinator for Region Three." Well, his *program* was *escorting* John from one cell fifteen feet away from the electric chair, into the electric chair, and putting the chest strap on.

It is really much more gross than people can imagine. Guards are an isolated group of men who have extraordinary power, who hate and fear black people and inmates. Guards have the power to decide how many pieces of toilet paper to give prisoners, how many embraces prisoners are going to get from their mothers or their wives or their children, or how many hours outside of the cell prisoners will spend each week—whether it will be two hours or three or none at all. It is a significant, decision-making power that the guards have over the people on death row and that absolute power distorts everyone. I know of no guard or prison person who has been able to hang onto that position and come out of it a decent, caring, rational, fair human being. Brutal people do that job and people who weren't brutal, get brutal. Killing affects guards the same as killing affects the people on death row and the rest of us. It hurts us individually and collectively. The closer we are to the killing, the greater the injury.

What aspect of your work affects you more than any other?

Certainly there are two issues that move me more than any other. One is when I am working on a case where race is involved and I talk to these incredible women, the mothers, who have had children who have grown up to be put on death row. Women who maybe had their first baby at thirteen or fourteen years old, who worked in the fields picking tobacco or scrubbing white people's floors, trying to feed their children, trying to keep a roof over their heads. Many of them unable to.

I'll tell you about some cases, but I have to use pseudonyms.

You know Jimmy Franklin's mama was trying to make it from Macon, Georgia, to Miami, where she had heard there were better jobs. An older sister, working as a maid, had sent her bus money. She got on the Greyhound bus. She was thirty years old, had a new baby, Violet, and Jimmy with her. She died on the bus, in Albany, Georgia. Jimmy was seven years old, holding Violet, his mama dead in the back of the bus. He remembers he wouldn't let the white people take Violet and going to the front of the bus, scared, to say that his mama had died.

It was not just that Jimmy's mama had died. Jimmy's mama died, I know as well as I know which way the Mississippi runs, that she died at thirty because she was a black woman in the South. She had no prenatal care, she had high blood pressure because all she got to eat was beans, had worked herself to the bone in the fields and was trying to raise two kids she couldn't feed.

Jimmy is now on death row.

But who killed Jimmy's mama?

There are so many stories like that. They always move me because of the eloquence with which the stories are told, the tragedy, the family's struggle for a better life, my familiarity with racism in the South. People pretend racism isn't the issue—after all, this is 1988.

Then there is a whole other area that wells up the same kind of motivation and that is for the people on death row who are mentally retarded.

A month ago we put on a lengthy evidentiary hearing in a case where the client, Larry White, is retarded. He has been in and out of mental institutions since 1958. Larry has a sister, Gloria. They were migrant workers; fruit pickers. They started out in Virginia, came down the eastern migrant trail to end up in a shack in central Florida. I was talking to Gloria before the hearing, and found it was hard for her to say "mental retardation" about someone she loves. It is frequently a prohibited word in a family, especially a very poor family. It is a word that only has negative connotations for them. A word that many of them have been teased with all their lives. The lawyers were going to be using this word a lot in court so I wanted to prepare Gloria for it, so she wouldn't be hurt by it, and also to get her to understand that she was supposed to tell the truth about this cloud that had hung over the whole family all their lives. Another sister had said that Gloria was "different" too, like Larry. She might even be slower than Larry. She never could pick fruit because they couldn't teach her the difference between big and little and shades of color. I said at one point, "Gloria, were you ever able to learn to read and write?" She said, "Well, I can't read," and I said, "Well, can you write?" and she said, "No, but I can count." I asked her if Larry was like that too, and she said, "Yeah, he's 'different' too, we are both 'different.'" I asked her if she used the word "different" because she meant mentally retarded and mentally retarded is an ugly word. She said, "Yeah, I don't like that word."

You know, here's this family trying to protect themselves from this debilitating status that we know how to deal with. Mentally retarded people can be rehabilitated. Mentally retarded people can lead meaningful lives. These folks in his family never even came close to being considered for any program other than something that would separate them out. I guess it hurts because they struggle so hard.

What about the relatives of victims?

Beauford White was executed in August 1987, after his jury had unanimously recommended life imprisonment. Two years before the execution, his mother was murdered in Liberty City. She was sitting on her front porch and there was a gun battle between rival gangs and a stray bullet shot and killed Beauford's mama. So Beauford was a victim, too. His kids lost their grandmother and I didn't see anybody, other than us, talking to Beauford about the pain he felt when his mama was murdered.

Black and poor people are the victims of violent crime every day and I'm not just talking about the institutional violence we inflict on folks every day across this country. I'm talking about one on one, homicide and assault. The people that we deal with and their families are those people who suffer the disproportionate share of violence. Our society only cares about the victim when the status of the victim is that of the majority.

What motivates you to carry on this uphill battle?

For the most part my motivation comes from the mothers of those people on death row. In the long run I think their stories are the most compelling of all because the injury that we have inflicted on these women is not equalled. They have managed to survive and they have managed to put one foot in front of the next, even though their children have ended up on death row. They know who is at the other end of that piece of fabric—the mothers of men who were lynched.

There was a wonderful woman I was talking to just north of town. She had her first baby when she was thirteen and picked tobacco. I asked her to tell me some things about her life. She talked about growing up in those near slavery places. I asked her how she was paid and she said, "Off the envelope." I asked what that meant and she told me her bosses gave her and the other tobacco workers an envelope every Friday. When I asked what was in the envelope she said, "Nothing." On the back of this envelope the bosses would write numbers that would tell the workers why they didn't get any money. Her children told me that the amount on the back was what the bosses deducted and the numbers showed *what they still owed and what she still had to work off*. She did get five chips a year to go into Quincy, a nearby town, to see a medical doctor. One year she had to use up all her chips because her son, Johnny, had fallen into a fire and gotten real badly burned, so she had no more chips left. Then Johnny got polio when he was six years old and the "Strawboss" would not give her extra chips to take Johnny to the doctor. Instead, she caught and dried a turtle and sprinkled it on his body. He swelled up and his leg dried up and is crippled now. Johnny is on death row.

These are the women whose children we are killing.

I am a woman and I share being a woman with them. The blessing to me is that because I have two children, it creates a permanent link between me and them.

A Pilgrim's Progress

"Remember, what you do to these men, you do to God."

—Mother Theresa, on Death Row
at San Quentin, 1987

She says her nun's habit "went out with the guitar," a reference to the fact that at one time she followed in the footsteps of Dominique, the "Singing Nun"; she now prefers slacks, blouses, and pullovers.

Sister Helen Prejean is a petite woman, with fire in her eyes and love in her heart. Glasses set in a round, smiling face perch on the end of her nose. Although in her mid-forties, she has that ageless look of one who has dedicated herself to the welfare of others.

A do-gooder in the best possible sense of the word, her life represents the most appealing part of the Christian religion—the unquestioning, non-judgmental love of her fellow human beings. Sister Helen has given her heart, not only to the men on death row of Louisiana's Angola Prison, but also to the relatives of murder victims. She talks about the human wreckage that inhabits the underclass, the "other" America.

New Orleans, Louisiana
Friday, February 5, 1988, 6:30 p.m.

Sister Helen Prejean

I am a Roman Catholic Sister, born in Baton Rouge. I'm a native of Louisiana, lived here all my life.

When I became a Sister of St. Joseph I moved to New Orleans where, until the time I was about forty, I worked in middle-class suburbs. But then in 1980 our religious community called us together to face the new challenges of the eighties.

Our Sisters from Latin America were coming up to our meetings and telling us of the tremendous struggle for justice going on among the poor and how we in the United States needed to be part of that struggle.

These meetings were a big turning point in my life. I was always saying these idealistic things like, "Well, if the poor have God, they have everything." It was because I didn't know what they were suffering. I was living in a bubble.

For me, this conversion was integral to the Gospel of Jesus—to stand on the side of the poor and to be with them in their struggle. This work was to lead me into a black inner-city project, St. Thomas, here in New Orleans, where there is violence and frustration and struggle for human dignity.

I saw in St. Thomas an incredible juxtaposition of good and evil.

I saw mamas with faith, humor, and love trying to raise their children, juxtaposed with drugs dealt in the open; people in arguments, shooting and killing each other over a pair of sunglasses. Sometimes when we'd walk to church on Sunday morning there was blood on the sidewalks from people who'd been killed the night before.

What got you into death penalty work?

A friend who worked at a place called the Louisiana Coalition on Jails and Prisons saw me one day, and asked, "Helen, you wanna be a pen pal to somebody on death row?" I said, "Sure."

The friend gave me the name of a prisoner, Elmo Pat Sonnier, and I began to write to him and he wrote back to me. I found out that he hadn't had anyone visit him in six months. All of the men on death row are poor. It's hard for families to visit Angola Prison, which is at the end of nowhere in Louisiana.

Was he Catholic?

Yes. He had been an altar boy and everything. He was Cajun. You know the Cajuns in Louisiana, in Saint Martinville. I had just presumed that he would be black, but he wasn't. Anyway, I began visiting with him.

Our conditions on death row in Louisiana are incredibly bad. Prisoners are kept in a six-foot by eight-foot cell twenty-three out of twenty-four hours a day.

How many are there on death row?

Forty-three men. They are let out one hour a day to take a shower and visit with the other guys on the tier. There are twelve guys on one tier. They are supposed to be able to get out several times a week for exercise, but you know with rain and such it doesn't always work out. Well, the guys just lose energy, they just begin to get so numb that many of them don't bother with exercise.

Can you tell us about your first visit?

You could hear Pat coming by the sound of the chains on his legs. He had a belt around his waist and his hands were handcuffed to that. They locked me in a room and put Pat in this very small cubicle with a screen between us. But he was all showered and had combed his hair. He was so glad just to see a human being, someone who'd come specially to talk to him. I was a bit nervous, you know. What am I gonna say to this guy for two hours? I hadn't had any experience with this you understand, except *(laughs)* one time in the sixties, you remember the Singing Nun, Dominique and all that. I had been brought into the city jail to play my guitar. I mean I only knew a few chords and was totally without understanding of what I was doing.

So here I am going into the death house. I go in through the visitors' place, and they frisk me. I get my pass, I go in, and a guard walks with me down a special place to where the death row is.

You were in civvies?

Oh, yes. The habit went out with the guitar. The guards call out, "Woman in the hall" because there was also a CCR [Contained Cell Restricted] where other inmates were, and they were ordering them to clear the halls. They bring me through and they kept shutting gates behind us. Clang . . . Clang . . . Clang. I rounded a corner and there on a green wall was a green metal door with bars and above it in bright red stenciled letters it said: DEATH ROW. That was where the guys were kept in their cells. In the cell there is a metal bunk with a mattress, a toilet bowl and basin, metal of course, a stainless-steel kind of mirror, a desk in the wall, and a locker under the bed. That's it.

Tell us a little about Pat.

Well, he started telling me a little bit about himself, about being Cajun. About what his mama used to cook, about how he was out on his own by the time he was sixteen, workin' on an oil rig. You know Louisiana's big on oil. He was what you call a "roustabout," one of the young guys who do the gump work, whatever's needed. He forged his mother's signature, he was only sixteen, out there with the big guys on the oil rigs. Very, very dangerous work.

Anyway he was just as happy as could be to have somebody see him. You know, one of the things that had happened once before was that he had announced somebody was coming to see him, told all the guards and everybody on the tier, and then he had sat on his bunk all day and that person didn't come.

Why was he sentenced to death?

Two teenage kids in a little town in New Iberia, Louisiana, Loretta Bourque and David LeBlanc, were shot in the back of the head. Loretta had been raped by at least one man. It must have been a horrific ordeal. I mean it was just senseless and terribly cruel. Pat and his younger brother Eddie were found guilty. Pat got death; Eddie, two life terms.

Have you ever witnessed an execution?

Yes, three.

Could you tell us about one?

There was Willie Celestine, executed in July 1987. I was his spiritual adviser.

It's as if you can't believe it is really happening, but at the same time it is all so horribly real. Willie's family was there the day he was to die. They were trying to laugh and joke and make out like everything was going to be okay. His sister told him, "You're going to get a stay." Shortly after that the family were told they must leave. His mama gave him a short quick kiss and quickly left. All the family was crying as they got into the prison van. Later, at the funeral, Willie's mama told me that if she had put her arms around him, boy, no guard could have pried them loose.

Willie ordered his last meal, "crawfish étouffée" because, as he said, "They kept asking me what I want." He ate some of it, but not much. Who can eat six hours away from being electrocuted? He made some phone calls, collect; who would the telephone company bill otherwise? He called some old friends, the Watson brothers. He'd played basketball with them. He tried to talk to his ex-wife but her new husband wouldn't allow the call.

At about 10:30 p.m. a guard they call "Slick" came into the cell with three other guards. He shaved Willie's head, even his eyebrows. Then he cut off the left pant at the knee and shaved around his ankle. They put a diaper and a clean white T-shirt on him and Willie's body was prepared for execution.

At midnight six guards came into the cell and led him to the death chamber. I was allowed to follow and be a witness. I had told him I'd be there for him to see one loving face as he died.

In the end he asked forgiveness from the victim's family.

The family of the victim was at the execution?

Yes. The state of Louisiana allows family members to witness executions. Willie said to them, "I'm very, very sorry." Then he spoke a few words of love to his family and friends and said, "Well, I guess that's about it."

He walked to the chair, sat in it, and told me that he loved me. He watched as they strapped him in, his arms, his legs. The executioner then put a cap on his head and inserted a huge electrode into it. Then they put a mask over his face (to spare the witnesses). They pulled the switch, his whole body jerked. They pulled it two more times.

That was the end of Willie Celestine.

Is it usual for the families of victims to attend executions here in Louisiana?

Yes it is. Lloyd LeBlanc and Godfrey Bourque witnessed Pat's execution. Lloyd is an interesting man; he says he believes in capital punishment but not for vengeance. Pat asked for his forgiveness just before he was executed and Lloyd nodded to him, forgave him. The Bourques took a much harder line and were very upset with the Church. They felt that we had sided with the killers because our bishop had conducted Pat's funeral mass.

I can understand that resentment. I think that it's very important that in our efforts to save all human life that we do not forget the terrible suffering of the families of victims.

You were with another man who was executed, Robert Willie, back in December 1984. Did a family member witness his execution?

Yes—Vernon Harvey. He's pretty well known in Louisiana for his very pro-death penalty views. He and his wife sat in the front row for Willie's execution.

Bizarre!

His fifteen-year-old daughter Elizabeth and friends broke open a bottle of Bourbon and danced outside the prison gates. It was in *Life* magazine, a two-page spread.

Later Vernon told the press that Willie died too quickly. That we should have staked him to an anthill, like they did in the Old West.

An eye for an eye?

Well, I read in the newspaper that he said the execution wouldn't help him heal, that no medicine, doctor, or psychiatrist can take away the pain. So, I guess it didn't work. But I must tell you about the Harveys and me.

After Robert's execution, as I was leaving the prison, Vernon Harvey said to me, "What are you doing with that scum? You ought to be helping victims' families." I felt like I was betraying them; like I was adding to their grief. They had lost a daughter in the most heinous way you can imagine, and here I was, a naive, bleeding heart nun adding to their grief.

I am, perhaps, the most vocal opponent of capital punishment in Louisiana. You know, every time I led a public demonstration, the Harveys were there to confront us with their signs and they would always say to me, "What about the victims?"

About two years after Willie's death, our group sponsored a seminar on the death penalty. It wasn't a big event and proponents of the death penalty almost never came to these kind of events. Well, I looked across the room and there were the Harveys.

I averted my eyes and all day I avoided them. At the end of the day, as everyone was leaving, Elizabeth Harvey was standing by the door. She said, "You haven't looked at us all day. When are you coming to see us?"

I was stunned. I told her that if they wanted me to come and visit, I would be glad to come. I knew how rough it was for anyone trying to organize victims' rights groups, but I hadn't realized how lonely they must be in their sorrow.

I had found out that Vernon liked apple pie. I baked one and took it over to their house. He was recovering from hip surgery and was real glad to get the pie.

Later in the month our group staged a march across the state, the Harveys were there to meet us. At one point during the rally we gave the microphone to Elizabeth, who said to the group, "Congress had just cut funds to victims' families. Will you help write letters for us?" The crowd applauded. Within a week we drew up a petition to our congressmen and I sent a copy to the Harveys, promising support.

They invited me to a Parents of Murdered Children meeting. Believe me, I took a big breath before entering that meeting. When I walked in Vernon looked across the room and shouted, "Hey, look, she's coming around." I was nervous, but I sat next to the Harveys and felt safer. I learned a lot at that meeting, and I made a decision at that moment to establish an advocacy group for victims of violent crime.

In June, this year, a Mennonite volunteer will come to Louisiana to work full time for victims. A first for us.

Did that mend any bridges?

If you mean by that are the Harveys any less vocal on capital punishment, I'm afraid the answer is no. About a year after the victims' meeting there was another execution scheduled at Angola. I was there with some other nuns. The Harveys were there, too. They attend every Louisiana execution and celebrate what they say is justice being carried out. I walked over to where they were sitting and said, "How's the hip, Vernon?" He nodded, "Comin' along," then he pointed to his signs. "Hey, look at our new posters." One of them read: "Tell them about Jesus, then put them in the electric chair."

Some of the nuns had formed a small circle about forty feet away. They held candles and were praying. A couple seated nearby had had a daughter murdered. The felon had got life and they were bitter about that. They drive over a hundred miles to join the Harveys at the penitentiary to stand for executions. The woman said to me, "Have you read the Bible, the part where God says, 'Whosoever doth shed blood shall have his blood shed?' " I told her I was familiar with the passage and she told me to go away and leave them alone. I said, "I'm sorry about your daughter." As I left, I heard Elizabeth Harvey say to her about me, "She's all right, she doesn't try to change us."

After the execution Vernon drove over to where I was standing. He gave me his arguments on the death penalty, which I almost know by heart. I countered by saying, "Now Vernon. . . ." I told them that I had gotten a small grant for victims and that soon we would get a person working full time. I touched his arm and told him to take care of the hip. He said something teasing and everyone laughed, including Elizabeth in the back seat, who chimed in and poked her father in the back of the head affectionately.

They drove off and I stood there all alone. The guards standing at the front gate must have been puzzled. They know the Harveys and they know me. I thought to myself that seeing us like that, they might have almost thought we were friends.

That's an amazing story. How is the victims' rights project coming along?

We are not going to do it under the name "Pilgrimage for Life." We are going to do it through another route because an anti-death penalty group is too problematic for victims, but the Church must stand on both sides of the Cross. It must stand behind everyone who is hurting, and that includes death row inmates and victims' families.

Human beings are not disposable waste. Christ's whole teaching is of redemption, so who are we to say human life is irredeemable? But by the same token we need to be very much aware of the victims and to be for the healing action of their families. People don't know how to deal with victims' families' pain, especially in the United States. We avoid death and pain.

Can you tell us about the families of the accused?

I went to visit Pat Sonnier's mama, sister, and aunt. They are shattered people. The mother has limited mental and emotional abilities. Her husband had been an alcoholic. She'd always been a victim, I think. So, the kids were moved from one place to the other. Pat had changed schools eight times by the time he was fourteen and he dropped out after that. She loved her children, of course, but there was no way she was able to appear before the court or pardon board to plead for her son's life.

A pardon board hearing is a horrendous ordeal. You sit in red chairs if you want the person to die, blue chairs if you want them to live. Just to keep things very organized and very clear. Very efficient. One of the officials, Mr. Phelps, in charge of Public Corrections, said about executions, "Now don't get me wrong, Sister, but it's almost like we want it to go clinically, we don't want a lot of emotion." Like clean, organized and well coordinated. Everybody cooperating.

Robert Willie's mama did appear before the pardon board and she said three words and burst into tears. It had been a struggle. I mean her whole life was really. . . . You know, the kid as he was growing up, she had so many struggles of her own, he had gotten involved with drugs, and she couldn't control him because she was struggling so hard with her own life. So, at his pardon board hearing she said three words, burst into tears, and left the room.

You know, everybody on death row whom I have been involved with, their prime concern, and I am sure in some way I play that kind of role. I am a source of unconditional love, a woman who loves them, who maybe helps to serve in some way.

The fact that someone who is a nun visits and cares about what happens to them really seems to help. They would say, "Thank you, Sister." It's like somebody "respectable" helping give dignity to their life. You know, Robert Lee Willie's mother was in a grocery store just three days before he died and she heard people saying, "That Robert Willie's gonna fry," and others sayin', "Yeah, that son of a bitch. He needs fryin'." And she just left the store in tears.

How do you think the death penalty affects society as a whole?

When we are having a vigil before an execution, there are also pro-death penalty rallies that bring out the worst in people. They yell violent, obscene things at us.

The guards . . . I could tell you all kinds of stories about the guards. There was a captain, a guard captain on death row. One day, on a visit, he pulled me aside and said, "Sister I am not going to be able to keep doing this, I can't sleep at night, I am dreaming about executions. I know the inmates have done terrible things but they are kids inside their bodies and to kill them is wrong." You can imagine when we are waiting for people to die, guards pulling me aside and saying, "I don't want to do this, but it goes with the job!" Later he was moved from death row and then, about a year after that, I learned that he had quit Angola altogether.

Other guards are as hard as nails. Willie Celestine one time got a stay of execution six hours before his death and his mama and his family were in there. His mama burst into tears. Well, she and I were hugging each other, I was crying with her, because I had never walked out of the death house with anybody alive. I had only been in there when people die. And she was sayin', "Thank you Jesus, you saved my son." I happened to look over at a guard and his face was hard as nails, like, "That son of a bitch is gonna live." So, I guess they've got to psyche themselves to participate in this process.

Prison guards do a dry run of an execution before it happens. They will get a guard the size and build of the inmate and put him in the chair and test the straps and try to break away, and it's like they gear up for this. But the warden, he was known as "Cowboy," he talked like a cowboy, looked like a cowboy, he had a picture of himself dressed like a cowboy—he once said to me, "Sister, you have to understand that nobody's doin' hand springs over this." But they carry it out.

I believe there is a dehumanizing thing that goes on with the state dealing death. You see the people yelling, "Fry the bastard!" Young people in Florida attend executions and do cheers, chants.

That's why they stopped public executions in this country. Twenty thousand people attended the last public execution in Kentucky in 1936 and it was a picnic, it was a circus.

THE TAPESTRY OF DEATH

"There isn't, I submit, a single admissible argument in favor of capital punishment. Nature loves life. We believe that life should be protected and preserved. The thing that keeps one from killing is the emotion one has against it; and the greater the sanctity that the state pays to life, the greater the feeling of sanctity the individual has for life."

—Clarence Darrow, 1924

Millard Farmer's reputation precedes him.

A brilliant defense attorney, he is respected, almost revered, receiving such accolades as mentor, doyen, and even guru. He has, on at least one occasion, been likened to Clarence Darrow.

Most senior attorneys surround themselves with the palatial trimmings that a large law practice affords. Millard Farmer practices his profession in a humble shop-front office, home of the Team Defense Project, on Nassau Street in Atlanta. A Xerox machine and a curtain separate the renowned man's space in the rear from the rest of the office.

Millard Farmer is fifty-three years old, tall and angular. His gray-blue eyes are set deep in a lined face and there is humor in the mouth. The hands are expressive, with long, bony fingers, which he uses to emphasize a point, but it is when he speaks that the gauge of his character can be taken. In measured Southern tones, the resonance of his voice holds the listener spellbound and has been the undoing of many who have crossed him on the courtroom floor.

Millard Farmer

*You work in a state famous for two landmark death penalty deci-
sions. What was the political climate after* Furman v. Georgia *and*
Gregg v. Georgia? *How did you respond to it and how did the opposition respond to it?*

At first I thought that people in Georgia accepted the dictate of
Furman as ending the death penalty once and for all. But obviously
they didn't, because the politicians manned their tools and wrote a new
law. But from my perspective I thought that everybody was saying,
"Okay, it's all done, we'll live without it, we'll go on." And I think
that if the court had decided that it did mean that it was all over,
society would have accepted the dictate and would have been much the
better for it. It would have been a small but important progression of
human rights had *Furman* ended the death penalty.

Let's look, for example, at what another nation has done about this
problem—Nazi Germany—the greatest killers in the history of recorded civilization. I think we would all agree to that. After World War
II, we dictated to occupied Germany that the death penalty could not
be part of their criminal justice system. So they started functioning
without it, and functioned quite well.

How do you try a case in court? Do have any special techniques?

To explain this I would like to identify the court as a microcosm of
the community. It is a more difficult microcosm to operate in than the
community at large because of its rules and restrictions and unclear
directives, and because the people we represent are generally less powerful in that arena. So we try to move, or explode the microcosm,
move into the real world and operate in the community, and try to let
the trial take place in the community. If it can't fairly take place in the
community, meaning the little village or town where it's located, we

try to expand the community to a larger sphere. And if it can't take place in that larger sphere, being a state, we try to expand it into a country or internationally. Often it is necessary to put the community on trial.

That brings us to the question of juries?

Well, you see I think you are accepting a simplistic statement of what happens in death cases. True, the jury decides; but that's only a view for a pedestrian lawyer—a lawyer who is not astute and doesn't understand this process. There are many, many elements other than the jury that decide whether you receive the death penalty. The jury, yes. The judge, yes. The prosecutor, yes. The law enforcement officers, yes. The family of the victim, yes. It's how they perceived it. If they don't want an individual to have the death penalty, generally he doesn't get it.

The death penalty fight is today's active part of the civil rights movement. It's a part of the civil rights fight that we are trying to finish up, bringing about equality to everybody, to poor people, to black people. The death penalty visits most frequently the poor and the black. So, are you fighting the death penalty, or are you fighting the social wrongs of society? Tweedledum and Tweedledee.

You have to understand that and not get caught up in the fact that there is just one man's life on trial here. It's just as important to attack the clerk of the court who does not employ black people in the clerk's office, as it is to attack the judge going to clubs that eliminate black people from their membership. And those are the kind of things that the ordinary lawyer doesn't see that they can do, but it's absolutely necessary if you are going to provide any kind of legal representation, much less actual representation. In this work a person should protect an individual from the whole of society, rather than just from the courts.

We had heard a story that you called a judge a racist and a prosecuting attorney an adulterer. Is that true?

Well, racist without question. We have attacked the prosecutor on acts of adultery with the clerk of the court, when the clerk of the court was doing improper acts to us, yes. And the attack was not because of the adultery, the attack was because of the behavior of the one he was engaged in adultery with.

Obviously most of your clients don't have any money. How are you funded?

It's very, very, very difficult. One of the ways we are funded is that interns give and volunteer their time to help. We receive a small amount of contributions from charitable organizations to help do this work, but by and large the largest contribution is made by people making in-kind contributions of their own time and their own resources.

You get your investigators that way, too?

Well, you are lookin' at our investigators—Us! I mean we don't have a chain of command that delegates responsibility. Each person works to their fullest capability and works in whatever arena he or she can work best.

Do you receive any help from the Public Defender's Office?

We give help to the Public Defender's Office rather than getting it. We are a resource center to other lawyers. We provide assistance, legal as well as other assistance.

What sort of cases do you look for that you feel will make more of an impact?

(Laughs) That's a tough question. The truth of the matter is we don't look for a case. We *hide* from a case. What kind of cases find us? To be honest with you, you can take any case and mostly find the same things. You can find discrimination, abuse of the political process, you find they want to execute a person to obtain political gain. It is difficult to identify the cases, but the same threads weave the cloth in most every case.

Which threads are they?

Well, it's the thread of *discrimination*.

It's the thread of *"I want to be well accepted in my community so I'll do something for them that'll make them like me."* The sheriff weaves with that thread, the prosecutor weaves with it, the judge weaves with it, sometimes the jury weaves with it. Everybody up and down the line weaves with that thread.

There is a common thread of *poverty* in all cases.

There is a thread of *lack of education*.

There is the thread of *mental illness* a lot of the times on the part of the person accused.

There is the thread of *child abuse*.

There is the thread of *deprived background*.

There is the thread of *not answering to other needs at the proper time*.

There is the thread of a *small community* who is outraged by the death of somebody they care for. In other words, it's a thread that shows you that *the person killed was a status person*. Had it been, in most of our cases, that the victim had killed our client, in exactly the same circumstances, it would not have been a death penalty case. That's a thread that's in there.

Oh, there are so many threads that it certainly must be a two hundred–count piece of fabric.

Do you come across genuine cases of innocence?

Of course there are people who weren't factually involved in the crime, but you know, I think that's a dodge and a duck. You fight the death penalty on the grounds there are innocent people who are executed or will be executed, but it ducks the real issue and it ducks the real way you ought to deal with this. Guilt or innocence is not relevant as to what position one should have on this.

Why on earth do you do this kind of work?

Oh, goodness, I don't know why we do these things. I think I do it for social change. I do it hoping that things will be better. *(Laughs)* Those are the same reasons politicians say they run for office.

There must have been something—as a young man coming out of law school?

I don't know where the switch onto this road was, where the sidetrack was.

Were you part of the civil rights movement?

No.

Here in Georgia in the fifties and sixties and you weren't involved in the civil rights movement?

Nope.

Were you practicing other kinds of law then?

(Laughs) I was practicing discrimination.

Ah-hah.

I don't know when the change occurred on the calendar, much less the clock. I was in a straight, uptight law practice, in a small community, representing banks and other things. There again it wasn't all bad, there was some representation of the type of individuals and type of causes that I do now. It just wasn't doing it in what I perceive now to be a respectable way.

So you do see this whole business as being political?

The death penalty is part of the political process, it is not a part of the criminal justice system. We've got to toughen up and understand that. This social problem, or this symptom, I don't know if it can be cured with a judicial decision or legislative act. The school integration problem was cured with a judicial decision, other problems have been cured with legislative acts, and who knows how this one will be cured? We have a very crude way of dealing with problems and it will probably tail off in a very slow fashion, and who's to say whether one way of curing it is any better than another?

Do you feel that chipping away at the death penalty, by attacking, say, execution of minors and the mentally retarded, is the best way to fight it at this particular point in time?

That's the way our society deals with problems. It chips away. We erode and change in a very, very slow way. It is not going to change overnight.

It can go backwards. The Supreme Court reversed Furman.

I know, but I don't think you can say that *Furman* didn't work . . . *Furman* worked. *(Laughs)* If you asked John Henry Furman—he would say it worked tremendously well. To the many people who got relief around it, to the years that society looked at things differently. It was, at least, somewhat of a statement that five people, on that day, didn't think it was right, even though they couldn't decide, all of them, exactly how they didn't think it right. But at least there was one body of highly respected people in this country who thought it was wrong. But what it really did was threaten all the judgments, that's what it really did.

How do you feel the death penalty affects the society as a whole?

Of course it's a terrible role model. The death penalty is more a symptom of an illness than an illness per se. The illness is the two hundred threads. It's a giant cold and this is only the drippy, runny nose.

Are there any milestones in your career that stand out?

I guess the word should be "tombstones." And there are quite a few. Hopefully there will be less government-caused tombstones in the future.

BEHIND CLOSED DOORS

"As long as there are prisons it matters little who occupies them."

—George Bernard Shaw, 1903

The offices of William Leeke, retired head of Corrections for the State of South Carolina, are on the ground floor of a fine red-brick colonial building that has been restored to its prewar glory. The plaque on his door reads: "Correctional Concepts, Inc."

His hair is black and shows no signs of graying. His face is chiseled and careworn. The eyes are blue. William Leeke has the bearing of someone used to running things.

Since retiring from the Corrections Department he has taken the position as vice president for marketing and operations of Correctional Concepts, Inc., a private corporation that builds prisons. Mr. Leeke is an expert on the unique requirements of these establishments—buildings that cost more to construct than luxury hotels.

When Mr. Leeke recalled the experience of having to bear the responsibility of carrying out two executions toward the very end of his term in office, a look of pain crossed his face, as he remembered the sheer horror of cranking up the death machine.

Columbia, South Carolina.
Tuesday, February 23, 1988, 1:30 p.m.

William D. Leeke

How many prisons do you have in South Carolina?
There are a lot of prisons in South Carolina. Including the work release centers, there are about thirty prisons and three under construction. The population is about thirteen thousand inmates. South Carolina has a high incarceration rate. They don't stay that long in most cases. But sentences are getting longer and longer. South Carolina led the nation for years in their per capita incarceration rate.
Why is that?
Some people say it's the Southern mentality, the eye for an eye, tooth for a tooth, the biblical conservatives, you know, let's get even, retribution.
What kind of crimes for the most part have the inmates committed?
A number of them were, obviously, serious crimes, but a large percentage were crimes where probably in another part of the country— it's not to say that that's good, but a lot of them probably wouldn't have gone to prison in New York or Los Angeles. A lot of people appear to me to be locked up for offenses where they could have functioned in the community, under extensive probation supervision, or in a restitution center, without paying such a high cost to put them in a regular prison. But a number of groups in South Carolina, such as victims' rights groups, have come out pretty strong and harshly saying we are too soft on crime and we need to make sure inmates get a stiff sentence for certain crimes. I hope all of us are against violence, but the issue becomes how much you can afford and who should go to prison and who should not. But South Carolina, along with several other states, has been perceived as one of the "lock 'em up" states. Just lock them up.
Did you have experience with executions during your career?
South Carolina allows for execution by electrocution. That's the procedure here. I had hoped to finish my career without having to go through any executions and made it, I guess, for almost twenty-seven

years without having an execution. Then we had two, about a year apart. It was in January of 1985 [J. C. Shaw] and January 1986 [Terry Roach].

Jurors and judges make the determination of guilt or innocence and decide whether the defendant is to receive the death penalty. But then it's sort of forgotten. We are told to carry out the execution. This means, when you get right down to it, they want us to do the legalized killing for the state, and that has a pretty traumatic effect on the people who work there.

As Commissioner of Corrections, while I had the basic overall authority and responsibility, I wasn't actually required, physically, to do it myself. I delegated that responsibility, although, administratively, I was responsible for it. As we saw executions nearing, we would send our people to states where they had performed recent executions, such as Florida or Alabama. One of the ironies of the death penalty is that if it was not done properly you almost go on trial yourself, by the media and others, for messing up what is not a desirable thing to do in the first place.

In Alabama a few years ago, when they sent the electrical charges into the body [of John Evans], for some reason or another it didn't work properly and they had to keep going on and on and it became a real barbaric episode. So to ensure that the execution was properly carried out, we sent people to these states, and read all the accounts of what they went through, to ensure that it was done appropriately; again, it's a bad use of words. But if you are going to kill somebody legally for the state, you want it to be humane, I guess, if that's possible.

Can you tell us more about Roach and Shaw?

They were partners in the crime. Shaw was the first one to be executed in South Carolina in well over twenty years and Roach was the second. Roach was only seventeen years old when he committed the crime and that became an issue. Shaw was the older one. He was a military policeman out of Fort Jackson. But there were just unlimited issues like the question of Roach's age and an alleged hereditary mental disease. They were convicted of a real heinous crime and emotions were high in Columbia, South Carolina, where the crimes occurred.

And the executions?

As I said before, it had been well over twenty years since there had been an execution, so we had to take care of all the extra administrative details that this would entail.

There was the question of witnesses, whether or not anybody is going to insist on being a witness at the execution, such as a member of the victim's family, for example. South Carolina law states that a witness has to be a citizen of South Carolina. We never had a request from the victim's family to be there. I always wondered what would happen if a mother or father wanted to be there and since the law states that they have to be a "South Carolina citizen in good standing," in reality the mother or father couldn't be a witness if they lived out of South Carolina. Years ago legislation was passed that limited the number of witnesses, with the intent of avoiding the "Roman arena" atmosphere of watching somebody die. By the same token it complicated matters as we still have to ensure that the printed and electronic media have appropriate representation, as well as both the prosecution and defense.

In my opinion the media made the first execution into a hideous circus. I mean, my God, it was the first one in the state since 1962, and they carried it on television before and after the execution for literally hours. There were hundreds of people and media representatives outside the prison. Some fella was actually selling, or giving away, bumper stickers—something like "BURN BABY, BURN." It's shocking. The fact that you've got to carry out the execution is enough, but placards out there! I have forgotten exactly what they said but some nasty, catchy little thing like "Roach Is Gonna Fry," or "Roaches Don't Come Out Alive," or something. Disgusting.

(Mr. Leeke paused, a look of pain came across his face) Anyway, the deputy commissioners and myself were in the warden's office with an intercom to the death house and we were continually concerned that something would go wrong. Then the roar of the generators of the electric chair is absolutely... the first time I heard it, I could hardly believe my ears. I asked if there was anything we could do about that sound. That early in the morning itself is a problem inside the prison anyway, and by and large you worry about the reaction of the general prison population to an electrocution. I think if you took a poll, you would probably find that the prison population would vote the same way as the general public on the death penalty, but when you have Old Cell Block One, with the death house right under it, at five o'clock in the morning and that generator cranks up, it awakens people. As I recall, I told them to find some way of keeping that noise down, we didn't want anyone setting off a protest, if we could avoid it.

We rotated the officers on death row because, I won't say they become attached, but they've seen the person every day and they have seen him in one role or another, maybe a repentant. By the same token if they hate the guy, you don't want them to become so callous that they say, "It's good that the son of a bitch is gonna die." We don't want them sayin' things like that, so we started rotating them, especially after we knew we were going to start having executions.

When you say the generator was whirring, does that go on all the time?

When they start the power surge, that generator absolutely has a horrible, horrible sound. When you know what's going on—and that surge, I guess at the start, has a terribly loud noise, even over the intercom. I can't remember if the generator is cranked up in advance, I can only remember it was a loud roar and it keeps going, and then there's the three surges that go into the body. The electric chair is supposed to be automatic, once so many seconds go by, then so many more, so many more.

Prior to the electrocution, the head is shaved and the man is dressed in appropriate clothing, which in South Carolina is a blue-jean-type uniform, and then there is an order for the electrodes to be attached for the current to go into the body. The warden gives the order.

The executioners are supposed to sense the person is dead, but the problem comes when the doctor hears a residual heartbeat. He may be dead, but there is a residual heartbeat.

So the person is declared dead even though there is a residual heartbeat?

I don't know for sure, but the Evans execution in Alabama, the heart kept beating and they kept going back and doing it again. From the conversations I had, they said the person really was dead but there was a residual heartbeat. In other words, I suppose he is "brain dead" but there may still be a residual heartbeat.

However you want to say it, I guess if you are gonna kill somebody, you want him to go the way he's supposed to go. The only thing that happened in the first one in South Carolina was that the pants leg burned a little bit. They said that was basically because of the pants leg touching the current and there was that little bit of burning of the cloth. It was apparently the pant leg rather than any skin burn.

You used prison employees to carry out the executions?

Yes. Our procedure was that the identity of the individuals who performed the execution was known only to me and the deputy commissioner for operations. We would meet personally with them and inquire as to why they would be willing to do it, looking to see if they were emotionally stable, why they would want to be involved in having the responsibility of pushing the buttons that set the electrocution in progress. They would go into the death house, Capital Punishment Facility, I think we called it, to make it sound more humane, but most people still call it the "death house," dressed in ponchos, covering their heads, prior to everybody else's getting there to protect their identity. They remain in the death house chamber, where the buttons that control the electric chair are located, and are brought out after everyone else leaves, again to protect their identities.

How many are there?

There are three men. There are three large buttons that all three are required to press at the same time in order to start the flow of electricity. I guess where I really got to be concerned about the awesome responsibility of the death penalty was reading a description of the Spenkelink execution down in Florida [5/25/79] with all the allegations that were made afterwards, even to the point of exhuming the body. It was alleged that they were drugging him, giving him alcohol, beating him senseless, all that sort of thing. Allegations that the body was brutalized prior to the execution. That is when I really felt the need to send the people that were going to perform the execution to another state to see how everything was done, and hopefully avoid mistakes.

What did you find in the Spenkelink reports?

Nothing, other than I think the investigating committee found that there was not any truth to those particular allegations, as I recall. But they raised a lot of issues. As I recall in Florida, shortly prior to the execution, while you had witnesses, they had the blinds to the death chamber closed until the final moment and my position was, "Well, hell, they are not witnesses if they don't see it," they can make all kind of allegations. So we decided that the media and all the other witnesses should not only see it, but hear it. We ensured that there would be no venetian blinds to obstruct the view. The witnesses would see it all the way through from start to finish, and further, that the sound should be there too.

What effect does an execution have on those who have to carry it out?

I think that the effect on the key people that carry out the death penalty is something that the public has neither known nor cared about. You meet people who say, "Let me in there, I'll pull the switch, I'll do it." They really don't know what it is all about.

At the first execution that we had, one of our deputy commissioners, Paul Weldon, said that he wanted to take a clinical psychologist along, just in case anybody broke down or had any adverse effects or if they were unstable or whatever. Well, it was rather funny, if you can have funny periods in things like this, it turned out that the clinical psychologist just about passed out without even being in there, just listening to the sounds from the warden's office. I had the deputies go with me, go meet with the warden and the people who were going to carry it out, to let them at least see our concern for what they were going to do for the state, but the clinical psychologist, he literally just about passed out. He needed the help. But you get a feeling, even though you are not personally going back and pulling the switch, knowing that you are administratively over it, you have a feeling like you, well . . .

How did you feel?

After it's all over, you feel like you want to go wallow in mud. Because although you didn't do it personally and even though you don't want to be perceived as a total liberal or soft on crime, which everybody seems to think you are if you even say you believe there is another option, you feel like you sort of degraded yourself, and you feel so sorry for the people who had to actually carry out the execution. At the same time you have concern and compassion for the victims of violent crime, but nobody said we had to *like* to kill people. There is nothing in the law says that you have to *like* killing somebody.

In my former position, as commissioner, I really did not care to see people die legally or illegally. I have seen them die plenty of times in prison, stabbed and such, but that's the statement I used to make all the time, that you are not supposed to *like* killing people, even though it's the law of the state. If I've got people who work for me that enjoy killing people, I don't want them involved in anything like that. You can see the visible effects on the people that are doing it, especially the warden who has the responsibility in the death house, the trauma that comes.

I used to favor lethal injection, but now I am not so sure. My concern with lethal injection is that it becomes so easy to put people to sleep. It's like an animal. It will make it easier for juries to say, "Well, the death penalty is not like the guillotine or the electric chair or lethal gas, so why don't we just do it?" It becomes just too easy to make that decision to kill.

It is my belief that ultimately there is going to have to be life with no parole for certain types of offenses. Otherwise, people will never agree to the abolition of the death penalty. Although I think you have to be careful that your juries don't use that to put everybody in for life, but maybe you could have another trial to determine whether it's life with-

out parole or life with a parole consideration after twenty years or
whatever. I don't think it should be too easy to kill people in our
society because we are a democracy, and I hope we remain one, and
there should be due process of law.

*We all sympathize with the victims' families, but what of the families
of the executed men? Are we not punishing these innocent people also?*

I don't think there is any doubt about that. The last execution we
had, when his parents went down to visit him the night beforehand,
the mother of the kid became totally hysterical and we literally had
to pick her up and take her away from the prison. Ironically, the
inmate during the last three days has a telephone where he can call
and talk to the media or whomever, and he called the warden of the
prison and *apologized* for the behavior of his mother. So they get
into some kind of state, I guess when they know they are going to
die, where they are just totally different people. Can you imagine
calling the warden the night before he is going to die to apologize
for his mother's behavior! It is a horrible thing for both the victim's
family as well as the family of the person who is executed.

It seems that the whole process puts an undue burden on everyone.

I think it affects an awful lot of people. But with very few exceptions, when the victims' families are interviewed, they just say that's
the whole answer that they are glad they are executed. But there is no
question that it affects both sides all the way through. You know the
mother, father, brothers, sisters, children—there is no question but it
has a traumatic effect on their lives.

*In conclusion, what would you say that capital punishment does to a
society that condones state killing?*

My concern overall is that we can become so insensitive that we can
just start killing and not think a thing about it. We could return to the
fifties or the sixties just massively putting away dozens of people
around the country. What is the purpose of the death penalty? Is it
retribution? Is it a deterrent? I think even people who used to solidly
argue the deterrence issue are backing off and saying it is just revenge,
or retribution, simply revenge, and I have heard some prosecutors who
say, "That's it. It doesn't deter anybody but we have to show society
that we are doing something, that we have some control." But you
could do the same thing by giving them life without parole. At the
same time the prison system has to be concerned about dealing with
people who potentially will try to escape but, nevertheless, I think we
can deal with that.

We would have a much more civilized society if we could find a way
not to kill people, but that is perceived as idealistic and soft on crime

and liberal, but I think putting people in prison for the rest of their lives is not being soft on crime.

I think it was Winthrop Rockefeller, former governor of Arkansas, who used to say, when asked about the death penalty, "Philosophically I believe there shouldn't be a death penalty, but as a practical matter I don't know." Made a lot of sense to me at the time, but not anymore. My main concern is that it could become so routine that we would just start exterminating people.

WHERE THE BODIES MEET
THE ROAD

"The death penalty is the privilege of the poor."
—Clinton Duffy, Former San Quentin Warden

At the Criminal Justice Building in downtown Los Angeles a trial, for which the prosecution had demanded death, was being held on— the thirteenth floor. Wooden benches and overflowing ashtrays lined the walls of the courtroom corridors. Lawyers and clients stood in corners conspiring in urgent, whispered tones while jurors filed back and forth between the coffee shop and the courts.

Warden Lawrence Wilson had been called by the defense on behalf of Keith Fudge, a young black, convicted of first-degree murder in the shooting of rival teenage gang members. The jury was deciding if Fudge would live or die.

Wilson is a gray-haired, kindly-looking man in his late sixties who spent a lifetime in the California Corrections System and who, before his retirement, witnessed many executions. In 1967 he supervised the gassing of Aaron Mitchell. At the time of writing no one has been executed in California since.

Los Angeles, California
Tuesday, August 18, 1987, 1:30 p.m.

Warden Lawrence Wilson

Why are you here today?

To give information to the members of the jury; some details of what life is *really* like in a prison setting. And what happens to these guys who are doing these long stretches in lieu of being executed. Most jurors feel that if this guy goes into prison and is not executed, then he's going to be a burden on the prison system. That's entirely false. The guy is not a burden, and in the course of a long prison sentence most prisoners straighten themselves around. When you're doing twenty or thirty, forty or fifty years, that occurs. He contributes to the operation. You don't have to execute.

Where did you witness your first execution?

I started out my career at San Quentin. I was working in the reception center, testing and measuring inmates, classifying the new recruits and determining their fitness for job assignments, and the like. While on that assignment, I was on a list of employees called "fill-ins."

The California penal code requires six people in attendance at an execution. With ordinary cases there was often not enough public interest in the execution, so they had to tap the reserve list. I was tapped three or four times to help make up the required complement, so I witnessed executions before I administered one.

Do you feel that capital punishment is a deterrent?

I feel it fails to meet this objective and that it would be absurd to argue otherwise.

I recently heard the Attorney General of Texas—now, get this—he said, "We don't have enough public interest in executions to make it worthwhile to have this thing go on. Nobody shows up. I think we should televise these things, because it's not spreading the gospel that killing *doesn't pay, that there's the death penalty for it and you're liable to get it, just like this guy on TV.*"

I don't know whether the Attorney General was serious, but whichever it was, that message is not getting down to people who commit crimes of a capital nature—the people on the row, absolutely not.

Have you always been against the death penalty?

Yes I have, although I was indifferent for a long time. You have to understand cause and effect of punishment. When you put your hand on a hot stove, well then, surely it would be a deterrent against ever doing that again, but if when you're raising your children, you wait until the end of the year and tell them, "I'm gonna punish you now for what you did ten months ago," why the chances are that the child would run from home. That's how silly it is.

And what about the moral issues involved?

I think it's entirely wrong to kill a man just because he's killed somebody else. In part I feel this way because often there's a question of judgment as to what actually happened at the time of the murder. It might have been that he was guilty of a second-degree murder but not a first-degree murder, or it might be that they have the wrong man entirely.

After an execution, it is impossible to rectify mistakes. Life without the possibility of parole is very effective, and sometimes it's a salvation when it has been shown that that person was in fact innocent.

One of the major arguments for the death penalty is that the relatives of the murdered victims feel slighted that their loved one is dead whereas the murderer lives.

Yes, I can fully understand the way they feel, especially if the killer is back on the street the next year or so. But, when you have "life without possibility of parole," which is what we have today, the person is being punished and the inmate is given the opportunity to be constructive. So why not let this guy live out his life, contributing to the state and its operation? The inmates do all the work in the prisons. People on the payroll are supervisory and administrative.

Another point that is often mentioned by retentionists is the cost of keeping murderers in prison against the cost of execution.

Well, the per capita cost of operating that condemned row as well as the cost of the execution is about twice as much as the rest of the prison. It's very costly and time-consuming, and it ordinarily takes two officers for what one officer would do because they have to be double sure that everything is done properly. Executions are expensive.

Tell us about the executions.

The method of execution in California is by cyanide gas. The condemned inmate is brought in, put in the chair, strapped in. Cyanide pellets and a solution of acid are prepared ahead of time.

At the stated time, the warden gives the command to begin the execution. Doctors are standing by with stethoscopes on the inmate's heart, and they're monitoring his life as the execution takes place. It takes about ten, maybe twelve minutes before it's over.

Do you consider this a humane method?

It's just about as humane as anything. When I was at San Quentin there was a talk about using poison lethal injection. I think it's all inhumane. It's a really ugly way of taking a fellow's life. It's really bad . . . and it rubs off on the people who are responsible for carrying out the law.

How do you feel about taking a life?

It goes with the job. I know many states contract for this detail to be done. Non-prison people come in who are executioners. They do their job and fold up their satchel and away they go afterwards. But California law reads so that the warden is responsible and carries out the mandate of the penal code. My staff members, like the chaplain and the doctors, and I are all there, we each have a certain thing to do, and we conduct the business. We don't have hoods on or robes like some states [Florida].

Does any one execution stand out in your mind particularly?

Yes. It involved a little Mexican man named Leandress Riley. Well, the poor devil slashed his wrists. They couldn't keep his handcuffs on because his arms were slippery with blood, and we had to almost literally carry him in there, set him in the chair while he was screeching and yelling. Of course his hands were all secured but he could wriggle this one arm out because he had such a small wrist, and he was floppin' that one arm around in the chair. As soon as that cyanide pellet hit the acid and he got that first whiff, his arm dropped. That's what happens.

They say that a man is knocked out on his first breath. But the body still goes through all kinds of convulsions and gyrations trying to get oxygen—and his head goes back and forth, his tongue comes out, maybe saliva appears. Tryin' to get oxygen, I guess . . . when there's no oxygen in the room.

Is the family of the condemned allowed to be present?

There's a visiting room right outside. Yes, they are allowed to be out there.

Can they see into the chamber?

Yeah, windows are there. It's an octagon thing and bullet-proof glass that surrounds there. It's kind of a greenish color, but they can witness. I would say about one in ten would be there; not very often.

What is the general attitude toward the death penalty within the administration of the prison system?

I would think that now most prison guards support executions. Prison administrators feel differently.

I belonged to the Wardens' Association of America, and we'd talk about executions at our annual congresses, and rarely did we ever find a man that said, "I'm for the death penalty." Most all those people said was, "It's a silly way to behave, to terminate a man's life. Just let the joker be inside workin' it out, contributing to the prison rather than snuffing him out."

There was also a consensus there that the death penalty had no more deterrent effect than did life imprisonment.

So you really believe that long sentences are the answer to serious crime?

Well, you know, many things can happen in that man's life. Just think about a life sentence for a moment. That's a *long* time. It's as long as you've been around, for instance. In that time there could be so many things that could happen. This man might get turned around. There is nothing more maturing than doing a long sentence. It slows you right down. You never see any old guys coming into prison.

AMAZING GRACE

"Assassination on the scaffold is the worst form of assassination, because there it is invested with the approval of society."

—George Bernard Shaw, 1903

A clinical psychologist and ex-warden who plays the bagpipes could be a character from the pages of a Dennis Potter play, but Jim Park is not fiction. He is very real.

James W. L. Park has thirty-one years of experience with the California Department of Corrections. He has worked in nearly all aspects of adult prison operations and management. He served as statewide manager of inmate classification and placement, director of program and facilities planning, supervisor of legal affairs and policy compliance units, supervisor of research and statistics, manager of the inmate appeals unit and the accreditation unit.

His career began as a clinical psychologist performing psychological testing, evaluations, and psychotherapy. As associate warden of two prisons, he was responsible for inmate classification and treatment. He participated in the inmate disciplinary process, worked with courts and lawyers regarding inmate problems, and handled press and public relations. He estimates that he has worked directly with at least 15,000 prisoners.

This ruddy-faced, all-American civil servant traces his ancestry to Scotland. If one was to believe in reincarnation, it would not take a giant leap of the imagination to picture him wielding a Claymore at Bannock Burn in a previous lifetime. Three sets of bagpipes were hanging on the wall next to a framed photo of Mr. Park's Scottish great-grandfather.

Jim Park's interview was a revelation. When a man of fairly conservative views, National Rifle Association member and active Presbyterian, who has served his country in southern Italy as a bomber pilot, equates aspects of his duties as assistant warden at San Quentin with those of a concentration camp guard in Nazi Germany, one is forced to take notice.

Sacramento, California
Monday, February 1, 1988, 11:30 a.m.

James W. L. Park

You were present in 1967 at the execution of the last man sent to the gas chamber in California, Aaron Mitchell. Do you think he went mad on death row?

Aaron Mitchell, while in the gas chamber, yelled that he was Jesus Christ. He may have been fine at the very end, you don't know, you see. The question is whether he was faking or if his breakdown in the last hours was real. My belief is that—granted nobody will ever know —he became pretty tense and pretty anxious toward the end, but all of the "I am Jesus Christ" sort of stuff was playacting. He hoped that somehow this would bring a last-minute reprieve. Obviously you cannot prove that because he isn't here anymore, and if anybody else was involved in encouraging him to fake it, they are not going to say. But it made for a very difficult execution because you had to handle his bizarre behavior.

How did this affect the officials at the execution like yourself?

It just added to the tension. There are two reactions that I had to the execution. These are kind of delayed reactions. I find that people who function fairly calmly in tight situations have a little tape recorder in their heads that records all this stuff, then they have to work through it later.

The first reaction was that as soon as the lever went forward and they put the cyanide pellets into the acid, generating the gas, it was an *irrevocable action*. Once that happened nobody could stop the execution, in fact, you wouldn't even try because you might end up with a half dead person. So, number one, it is an irrevocable action and whatever potential that person may have will never be realized. Any possibility of redemption is gone.

The second reaction was how *task-oriented* you become. I wasn't concerned with taking Mitchell's life, I was concerned with "Was that phone on the wall going to ring? Was I going to have to answer some judge's or a governor's question?" And so I was totally focused on the task—not on the fact that a man was being killed.

It is just one of my feelings that it is bad for society *to hire people to kill other people*, because it becomes a "task-oriented" thing. I can believe, without really knowing, that most of the guards in the concentration camps were good family men. They simply had a *task* to do and they did it, and somehow it wasn't "people"—it was "units." "Today we gas so many units," you know.

In fact, in the late sixties, it looked like the floodgates were going to break in terms of executions in California. Well, we would figure it out, we could do four executions a day very comfortably and we could stretch it to six if we had to. So, you are not thinking that you're gonna *kill* four *people* a day . . . Which is outrageous. You are thinking, "Well, this is how we are going to have to do it. Two in the morning, two in the afternoon." The California gas chamber has two chairs. Both chairs have been used on occasions.

Do you feel that the process dehumanized you?

Well, now you're putting the words in my mouth. I didn't say that.

When you said "task-oriented," did you mean the real "you" gets lost?

Well, yes, I suppose the word "dehumanization" is used so much and it means so many different things. But in terms of trying to get a word that people understand, I think it's more accurate to say that it allows you to put up a curtain in your mind to wall off the implications.

Why are you against the death penalty?

I am opposed to the death penalty. I'm not avidly opposed, I can conceive of people who might be worthy of being killed. They would have to be pretty monstrous. But basically I think it's a bad procedure and I think it's bad for society to kill people. I think it's bad for society to hire people to kill criminals in cold blood.

I make that stipulation because I think the police have every right to kill offenders in the course of a violent crime or in self-defense. But when you hire people to kill in cold blood, as I said before, they become "task-oriented." I think, instead of becoming appalled at executions, with more executions there is a certain hardening of an attitude. As some of the former wardens who went through eighty or more executions did, they had to develop a certain callous attitude toward the death process.

Looking beyond the killing of a criminal, and looking at the fact that criminals are defined by the society, it seems to me that if a society gets used to having hired killers to take care of its problems, or try to take care of them, it is an easy step to start taking care of other nuisances with the same procedure. You know, in Hitler's Germany, the Nazis killed people who were simply nuisances: the mental defectives, the Gypsies, and mentally ill people. They were killed not because they committed a crime, but because they were inconvenient for a society to have around. Now *we* have a lot of people in this society who are nuisances, who are inconvenient, and I would be afraid that a society that became too comfortable with killing people would extend that charter, so to speak, to dispose of other groups.

The second reason I think that it is a bad idea for society to kill people is that it gives the illusion that you have done something about the problem. "Oh," they say, "a killer, a murderer has been executed!" and somehow people then think you have done something about the problem of murder, and you have done nothing. Statistically, you have done nothing about the problem because there is no research evidence either for or against the deterrence theory. We simply don't have any evidence. The best evidence we have is that jurisdictions that do not have the death penalty do not have a significantly different murder rate than those who do.

Many of the Southern states that have more executions also have more violence. One does not cause the other. Some of the opponents say the death penalty causes violence. It doesn't cause violence. Violence is there. But by killing people, you have not done anything to remove the cause of violence or crime. Not that I think it can be removed particularly. People are really unwilling to recognize that you have to live with certain risks in life. In an industrial society, we are going to have to live with the risk of cancer. We are also going to have to live with the risk of being a crime victim because there is no way to eliminate that risk without becoming a totalitarian state. In those cases, then the state agents get to commit the crimes of murder and torture and rape, as Amnesty International has pointed out.

You also mentioned that you realized that when the pellets were dropped at Mitchell's execution it was an irrevocable act.

It is an irrevocable act. Now I also have some religious reasons. As I read the New Testament, I don't see anywhere in there that killing bad people is a very high calling for Christians. I see an awful lot about redemption and forgiveness in the New Testament.

The first two reasons I gave for opposing the death penalty are kind of secular reasons. There is also a religious reason. However, you can use the Bible to support anything you want to support. Certainly the Old Testament is full of executions. In terms of the irrevocable thing —and this is more of a philosophical, quasi-religious thing—if you feel that people are here to develop and improve, then by executing them we have precluded any possibility of redemption or improvement. And we know from follow-ups of former death row people that at least some have found a niche in our society and have found a kind of a secular redemption, I don't know about a spiritual redemption, but at least a secular redemption and have become useful citizens.

You are called as an expert witness in the death penalty phase of trials. What do you testify about?

I was an expert witness in the courts. The judges very narrowly limit what I'm able to testify to. They don't want to hear my opinion about the death penalty, although sometimes the prosecutor tries. "You are really opposed to it, aren't you? That's why you're testifying." One prosecutor said, because I was saying that conceivably I could find somebody whose execution I would support, "Isn't it a fact that you have never found a defendant worthy of being executed?" So I said, "This is only my second trial—I don't have a track record!"

But I would say this, that in a great and powerful nation like the United States, we certainly can keep people in a safe and humane way. We have certainly demonstrated that. Now we are not keeping them particularly humanely because we have this terrible crowding problem. But we should be able to, given a proper set of priorities.

As penal reform is one of your areas, do you have any comments to make on that issue?

Well, I may be very much out of step with the times, maybe I always was, but our society, including most of its college students, is so conservative, so punitive, so punishment-oriented, and so concerned about trying to have a totally safe society. I think it is not really possible to be totally safe; it is an unreasonable goal. I think you can be reasonably safe—that's reasonable.

Two things go together: one is a lot of support for the death penalty, more now than there ever has been, and total support for locking everybody up in prison as a very expensive way to handle criminal offenders. I can't even convince my friends that we are locking up too many people in California prisons. For example, in my opinion, there are at least ten thousand prisoners, and probably more, who wouldn't have even been there fifteen years ago, because of harsher laws that

preclude probation for some fairly minor offenders. This is ballooning
the prison population. This is all due to the desire of people to live in
perfect safety. And to me, overly imprisoning people and killing people compromises the safety of people. It compromises everybody's
safety because it leads to a harsher society that is quite capable of then
extending the death penalty to other people.

I think we need to be clear too because sometimes people who are
opposed to capital punishment get very maudlin about the "poor criminal" on death row. These are not nice people. They are ordinary offenders, ordinary people, they rob, they steal, they lie, they cheat, they
hurt people, and in this case they kill people. So the issue is not
whether they are worthy of being saved or executed, the issue is that
we have a lot of unpleasant people in the world, some of whom are in
prison. We don't need to and shouldn't kill them because they are
unpleasant people.

Do you feel that gun control would help?

Well, no self-respecting criminal is going to carry some crazy Spanish automatic; they are going to carry the best guns made. So the
Saturday night special argument to me is dumb. I think guns make a
nice cause for people to jump up and down about. However, I don't
think the guns cause the society to be violent. You have got to look at
some other things.

What about justice for the family of the victim?

The most difficult cases to talk about are the heinous murders of
young children, helpless victims of some kind, and torture murders.
There's a lot of terrible things and the families of the victims have to
live with that for the rest of their lives. Of course they ask, "Do I not
deserve some kind of justice and revenge?" The only comment you can
make is that revenge is a very ancient need, but it usually does not help
the situation.

It seems to me that revenge leads to a dead end, and does not satisfy
people. There is a whole movement in grief counseling dealing with
death of various kinds. Rather than revenge, what people need is some
help in dealing with the fact that their loved one died and maybe died
in some particularly horrible way. This is much more useful than revenge. I don't think we can find any indication that revenge has ever
helped a society.

*Do you feel that this society just needs the death penalty on the
books but really does not want to carry out the actual execution?*

This society has the best of both worlds. They get all of whatever
pleasure there is in having a man sentenced to death and yet he never
gets executed. It is not because judges are liberal that we have such a
backlog on death row, even fairly conservative people who are ap-

pointed to the Supreme Court become just as concerned about putting people to death as the liberals. Conservatives are no more apt to endorse a floodgate of executions. When a judge knows that his signature is going to put this man to death, that's something they have to think very seriously about. And they do. This is why in California the death penalty takes forever, because of all these appeals, and the judges have to be totally satisfied that they are not allowing a man to be executed that was not properly handled in the court process.

"Capital punishment" is a sanitized expression, "execution" is sanitized—it's something other people do. That's why I use the word "kill" and try to personalize it. Every citizen in California is killing and it's a personal thing and yet they don't take it personally, and I think that rather few of the people that agitate for the death penalty would be willing to actually do the killing. They would have some major concerns if they had to do it. Right now it's kind of a charade.

Killing criminals does no perceptible good and has the potential for doing a great deal of harm for the citizens of a free society.

CHECKMATE

"Verily, verily, I say unto you, he that believeth in me hath everlasting life."

—John, 6:47

On February 27, 1988, Darryl Bell was presented with a cake decorated with white icing and red roses, in the main lounge of the Martin Luther School, in a gray Philadelphia suburb. Surrounded by teenage kids and counselors in the bright utilitarian room, he beamed as photographs were taken.

"Happy Tenth, Darryl! Happy Anniversary!"

The anniversary of the tenth year of his release from jail. This "hardened killer" was being photographed next to seven kids—and they really love him.

Two decades ago, Darryl faced execution. He had been head-shaved and prepped, and was a few short hours from being strapped into the electric chair. But it was not the end—he received a stay of execution and eventually his sentence was commuted. He spent so long on death row that when he was released into the general prison population, he felt like a free man.

Darryl eventually received a full pardon and now devotes his life to working with abused and underprivileged children.

Darryl Bell is a black man, born in Louisiana, December 21, 1939, and, as he told us, was born again on death row on December 27, 1963. This time he was born into Christ.

He stands 5 feet 9 inches tall and weighs in at about 180 pounds. His face is unlined except for a deep furrow across the forehead, and,

although filling a little at the waist, his body is in great physical shape.
He was dressed in gray sweats and a baseball cap.

This is his story.

There were two separate cases. Two separate charges of murder.
One occurred when a bullet from Darryl's gun ricocheted off a can of
baby food, killing a store owner. The other involved a murder during a
holdup, in which Darryl drove the getaway car.

Darryl's first trial was on November 8, 1961. His court-appointed
attorney advised him to plead guilty to murder on both charges, which
he did. Poor advice, as it turned out, since Darryl was sentenced to
death on both counts. During the proceedings, the presiding judge
repeatedly called him a ghoul.

Darryl fired his attorney. His new lawyer, Lester Schaffer, appealed
to the state Supreme Court, saying that Darryl should not have been
tried for two crimes in front of the same panel of judges. He was
granted a second trial and it began on May 23, 1963.

This time Darryl entered a not guilty plea.

The Commonwealth provided twelve witnesses. The defense pro-
vided Darryl's mother.

It made no difference; the jury found him guilty of first-degree
murder, and once again he found himself under sentence of death.

Philadelphia, Pennsylvania
Saturday, February 27, 1988, 1:30 p.m.

Darryl Bell

My name is Darryl Bell. I was born in Shreveport, Louisiana, December 21, 1939. I was raised in a Christian home. My father was very
strict. There was no drinking or smoking. My family really stressed the
need to make something of my life; however, I had other plans. I
didn't pay attention in school. After I left school, I joined the Marine
Corps and was later kicked out.

What were the circumstances?

I hit the lieutenant and they discharged me, undesirably. Not long
after I was discharged I was involved in a holdup. Shortly after that I

was involved in another holdup, which resulted in a killing. I drove the getaway car. The court sentenced me to die in both of those cases. In one case I was the actual triggerman; in the other case I simply drove the car. I received death in both cases. The sentence of death was imposed on December 9, 1961, and I stayed on death row until the spring of 1974. Actually twelve years, two months, and eight days.

After they allowed me to come off death row, I was placed in the general prison population and there I proceeded to get my GED [General Equivalency Diploma].

We understand you could not read.

Yeah, I had a problem reading. What's amazing about it is that they had assigned me to a remedial reading program when I was young and I was too proud at that time to go. So I quit school.

I had built a reputation up in school as being a tough guy and a lover with the girls, and it was beneath my dignity to go to that class, so I quit. A friend of mine helped me on a test for the Marines, and I passed.

I went into the Marines and worked in communications. I could do the theory well, but when it came down to the written exams I could only do it as long as my friend James Davis was there. He was the only one who knew I couldn't read at the time. But then they split us up and I was on my own, and that's when they discovered that I had faked the whole time and things began to really go downhill for me.

Tell us why you were discharged from the Marines.

The lieutenant called me "nigger" and I punched him, I mean I hit him hard. They put me in the brig at the Philadelphia Naval Yard and then discharged me. I had never been in trouble until then and I just went off. Boy, I was angry, but I'm not blaming the Marines for my problems.

Can you tell us about the man you shot?

I went to this store close to Christmas. I bought a basket of fruit and when I got home, some of the fruit was rotten. I took it back to the man and he said he wasn't going to exchange it. He said it wasn't that way when he gave it to me. He wouldn't exchange it or give my money back and he was nasty, he had a real degrading attitude about it. I decided at that moment that I would get my money back. I think I was having flashbacks from the way the lieutenant had treated me and that whole thing.

So I stalked him, for I guess a month, waiting for the best time.

One day I went in there, it was a morning and I knew he was alone. I asked him for food. I ordered a lot of food and he packed it in the bags, and once he had packed the food I made a motion to go into my back pocket, as if I was getting my wallet to pay him, and I said to him, "Oh, I want a turkey." So he turned around to go into the freezer and my plan was to snatch the bag and run. There were two doors, one at each end of the store, so when he turned, I grabbed the bag, and then I saw the cash register and the drawer was just barely open.

Instead of running, I reached over and pulled the drawer open, but it made a noise and he heard it. Well, he ran out from the back, and I tried to get on the other side of the center counter so he wouldn't know which door I was going out of. I heard him running and because of the change jangling in his pocket, I knew his position. I pulled the gun out of my pocket. I knew I had an exit out the door so, to freeze him, I fired over his head. He was on the other side of the counter. The bullet ricocheted off a baby food can and killed him.

That must be a one in a million chance?

I know. At the trial they said the bullet hit a can and ricocheted into a two-by-four before it hit him. The pathologist's report stated where the bullet went and where it came out. It showed that I did not shoot at him.

When the judge asked me if I had anything to say before sentence, I told him I didn't mean to kill the man, in fact, I didn't even see him when I pulled the trigger. But they sentenced me to die anyway.

But you were actually carrying a gun?

Yes. In the other case, three months later, I didn't, I just drove the getaway car. The guy who was with me had the gun. In fact, he was the one who actually did the shooting. He received a life sentence and I got death for what he did.

Just to recap. You had two death sentences, one for a ricochet bullet, one for driving a getaway car?

That's right. I received a new trial on both cases because of the way the lawyers handled things at my first trial.

The man who did the actual shooting on the second case was killed in prison for stealing cigarettes from another inmate's locker in August '64. When word of that reached my lawyer, he began to file appeals, but by then the American Civil Liberties Union had taken up my case. So the appeals went on and on and on until the United States Supreme Court stopped the penalty in 1972 *[Furman v. Georgia]*.

However, we understand it went further than that, that you were actually in the death house?

Yes, and it was close.

Days or hours?

Hours.

Your head was shaved, your leg was shaved?

Yes.

Did you feel that was it?

Oh yes. In fact, each time a man is executed, you feel it's you. You know that you are going . . . but you don't know when. You are just there waiting. No one tells you anything until the time. It's like it's a secret.

When you were on death watch was there a sense of unreality?

Well, the unreality comes from the person himself. That person begins to fantasize to escape the reality of what is, and the fantasy is unreal. That's what we all did. Fantasized. You think, "Well, maybe they are just trying to scare me. This is not going to happen. In fact, they may even take me right up to the chair." You're protecting yourself really, but the reality of it—well, there are just no words to express that.

We heard you earlier talking about chess. Did you play on death row?

I learned to play in prison. We couldn't get real chess sets, but we played by making pieces from toilet paper, wetting it and making pawns, rooks, knights, and all the other pieces. I would take a pencil and draw a board on a sheet numbered 1 to 64 and I'd call out, say, "Knight from 2 to 19." The other guy would then call back and tell me where to move his piece.

Did you think about the man you killed and his family?

Oh yes. All the time. In fact, on Father's Day especially. And when I look at these kids *(Darryl indicates the kids playing behind us)* and I learn their backgrounds, and they come here and they don't have fathers because their fathers were killed or are missing, or they don't know who their fathers are . . . you know, it stays with me all the time.

Has there ever been any contact between you and the victim's family?

No. I'm a bit nervous. I have been on Philadelphia television and radio talk show programs and they know I am on the street. They did not come to the pardon hearing.

You were put in the general prison population when the sentence was commuted to life and, as we understand it, you became quite an inspiration to the other inmates.

(Darryl smiles) That could be the word. A lot of the inmates believe and expected us [death row inmates] to come out vegetables, because of the stress you go through. When we came out we began to go to school and get involved in the exercise, the football, the handball. I mean, we were just happy to be free, so that any energy we put forth was to us a new reality. They thought those guys are crazy out there in the cold weather playin' ball. But to me it was freedom. You know, not being handcuffed everywhere you go, I felt free. I just knew somehow

that the Lord would allow me to come out of there. I just felt that somehow.

You sound like you were almost born again.

There's no almost. No, sir . . . It happened! It happened in 1963 on the row. December 27. You know the school here and the institution I worked at prior to coming here knew all about my background, and they trusted me to work with these precious children.

During the time you were in prison, which was another seventeen years, you obviously proved yourself to be the kind of person who could contribute, who could give back to society. How did you do that?

When I was released from death row, the warden gave me the job of working with the camera in the visiting room. I took pictures, I was the photographer. That was just one of the jobs I did and that allowed me to become more in tune to people. You know, I was just not used to being around people and when the people would come in, I was shy, you know. I would also be the baby sitter when families would come in to visit the husbands. I made a lot of friends in Gradeford, so that when the men's children would come and they wanted to be with their wives and girlfriends and family, I would take the kids over to the side where the camera was, and that's how I started to feel at ease around people.

The kids really helped me. They made me laugh. I was afraid to laugh and to do this and to do that, but it worked its way out. I didn't have too many suspicions about people and I guess that was because I felt so happy to be free. I didn't have time to think about the other part.

Are you married now? Do you have children?

Yeah. I have a son, Darryl Junior.

Then came the day when it looked as if you would actually get a pardon. How did you find out about that?

I filed for pardon, twice, on my own, and each year they turned me down. When they turned me down the second time, I said I wasn't going to bother anymore because of the hurt, disappointment, rejection; the whole thing. So my brother contacted a lawyer who was a legislator at the time, Robert O'Donnell, and he agreed to represent me at the pardons board. So I gave it another try and they prepared the papers, and at the hearing my mother told me, "Darryl, you're ready now." That was before the decision came down. She said, "You will make it this time."

Sure enough, Murray Reed, who was director of treatment at the time, called me to his office, out of the weave shop where I was working, and said, "I have some news for you. The institution has placed me in a position that I have to give out bad news all the time" —and then he smiles—"but in this case I have good news for you."

I tell you my expression . . . I didn't believe him first of all.

He said, "They granted you the pardon." I said, "Let me see . . . let me see . . ." and there it was. He reached over, shook my hand, and gave me a hug. I just went back to my cell. I remember walking down the corridor with my head down, I was just happy, happy, happy. I went back to my cell and closed my door, and I remember just going in and thanking the Lord.

When you first came out, what then?

Well, my first job was at a cemetery. That was the only job I could get. In order for me to come out, I needed a job, and they would not allow me to come out to look for work. So through another inmate, I got the job by word of mouth, in Forest Hills Cemetery. I worked there for a while. I was digging graves, burying people. I remember one time I was on Channel 10 and some policeman said, "That's what I call a conflict of interest!" He was just trying to be smart, but I paid no mind.

How did you get into child welfare?

After I got out of prison I worked in an auto mechanic shop, working with cars. Then I began going to school. Finished school, but during that time I worked at New Life Boys' Ranch, a juvenile facility about eight miles from here. Troubled kids.

Well, I was on Channel 69 and there I met the executive director of New Life at that time and he offered me a job—right on television. Yeah. So the next week I went there.

Did you continue your education?

I graduated from Lincoln University, May 1985. I studied human services and social work. Right after graduation my employer offered me a job as a supervisor at the unit next door. It's the Martin Luther School, Silver Springs, Pennsylvania.

I took that job, but it was too much for me with the type of children they had. That was the intensive unit and the kids were too disturbed for me. Plus the majority of them were small kids and I knew that my expertise was with the type of boys on this unit. Teenagers. So I requested a transfer to this unit.

This is a residential unit. Most of the boys have had problems. Problems at home and so forth. When we receive new kids here, we get the whole brunt of the problems they had at home without them saying anything to us. They act it out. So we try to work them into the system that we have here without saying, "Hey, get into the system." We work it out through walking the plank with them. Sometimes restriction is necessary, sometimes free time is necessary, so we do that, sometimes counseling. Whatever the case is, whatever is called for, we do it. It works, it takes time, but it works.

After all your experience, what would you say to a society that condones using the death penalty?

I think it degrades the society, for example, the United States is one of the few places that executes children. That's our most precious commodity, the children. I also feel that if we, as grown people, can't deal and cope with some of the problems that we have, then we can't expect these kids, who have so far to go, to deal with their problems. They make a mistake and we want to kill them. It just doesn't make sense to me at all.

STRANGE FRUIT

"Judge not, that ye be not judged."

—Matthew, 7:1

Nashville, Tennessee, is the home of Country and Western music and Joe Ingle.

The Reverend Joe Burton Ingle is among a handful of men and women who have received a nomination for the Nobel Peace Prize. He was nominated in both 1988 and 1989.

Joe Ingle has not yet received this singular honor, but his very nomination for the world's most prestigious human rights award is not only a clear recognition of his work in the field of prison reform and the abolition of capital punishment, but a serious indictment of the conduct of the executing states of America.

Joe Ingle is the boyish, fresh-faced, bespectacled, forty-one-year-old director of the Southern Coalition on Jails and Prisons, and has been since its founding fourteen years ago. The Southern Coalition, a non-profit group with offices in eight Southern states, advocates criminal justice reform. A major part of its resources are utilized in its work against the death penalty.

Reverend Joe Ingle, a United Church of Christ minister, is the spiritual adviser to inmates and their families, and has visited or corresponded with over 400 of the men sentenced to death in the Southern states. As we quickly discovered, Joseph Burton Ingle could never be accused of sitting on the fence, regarding execution in the United States. He is very forthright in his views.

Reverend Joseph Ingle

Congratulations on your nomination for the Nobel Peace Prize. Tell us: What can be done internationally to bring about the abolition of capital punishment in the United States?

Sending telegrams, letters and all that stuff is fine—keep sending them. But we gotta up the ante and I am advocating three things. One: I am askin' all the western European countries, starting with my friends in Sweden, to launch an economic boycott against those states in the United States that have the death penalty. If they are going to open up a Volvo plant in the United States, it shouldn't be in a state that has the death penalty. They can put it in Kansas, Minnesota, Michigan or New York. Somewhere where there is no death penalty. They ought to make a public statement. You know if we are going to boycott South Africa for their racial policies. . . . my God, we are killing our citizens too! We need to be held accountable for this.

Secondly: We need help monetarily. Not just my organization but all of us. There are two thousand people on death row and one thing we know is that they are all poor. You take every organization in the country that is working against the death penalty, add up all their budgets, and it's probably less than a million dollars. Hell, most states spend several million dollars to kill one person.

Thirdly: We have to make the American people see how totally out of step we are, as a nation, in comparison with our democratic allies. We have to speak out.

There are many corrections officers and prison officials speaking out against capital punishment. . . .

. . . They may be speaking out, they may be good men, but hell, they've killed people! How can you be against executions and still kill people? This is the politics of the death penalty, that's all it is. So don't tell me about these men. . . . I know them.

Don't you think it is a good thing that they are coming forward however late?

Who cares?

But at least some of the people you are trying to reach may listen to them, rather than you.

Oh sure, they'll listen to them. But where were they when it was time to make a decision? Now they say, "Hey, I'm against the death penalty." But what difference does it make? What honest-to-God difference does it make? I mean, Jesus said, "By your fruits you will know them," and I have seen the fruits from all the so-called progressive liberals and it stinks. It is rotten fruit. . . . as Lillian Smith wrote, "It's strange fruit."

Wasn't she referring to the bodies hanging off the trees?

Exactly. Now you must understand me here, it is not a question of bad people, or bad versus good people. We have devised a political, judicial system to murder our citizens. You minimize the horror of this whole problem when you try to say it's this governor or this warden because the primary issue here is these are individuals in a *system*. We have a *system* designed to exterminate our citizens.

To me, the parallel is with the early days of Nazi Germany. We can sit here and say, "Well, Eichmann was a bad guy and Hitler was a bad guy." Well, let's face facts, the German people participated and allowed that to happen. It is exactly what is going on in this country.

Every day American citizens are participating and allowing murder to be officially carried out in their names. Sure it is concentrated in power, no doubt about it. The warden who actually gives the order to pull the switches is more powerful than the ordinary citizen, but the guilt and the responsibility go all the way down the line. It is not just a matter of a few DAs or a few wardens who are angry and want to see people killed, it is a whole *system* in this country. That's why it is so evil.

Why do you feel the American public needs to have the death penalty?

Well, the death penalty is a confession of failure. When you say as a society that you have to kill people, then that means that you have no other way to deal with them. So it is really an admission of failure. But it is also a lie, because there *are* other ways of dealing with murder. I mean, look at all the European nations. Somehow they manage to deal with people who commit murder without executing them and it certainly hasn't sent them back into the twelfth century.

So you get down to it in the South, that's all I know about, that's my bailiwick, and you talk about the death penalty and, to me, you are talkin' about race. Race of victim is paramount in all these cases. Nine out of ten times you are going to find a white victim. Second thing you are talkin' about is class. All these people are poor. They are the refuse of our society and this is how we handle it.

There are people on death row in other states too, for example, over 200 in California. Do you think they will start to execute again in these other states where one has not occurred in over 20 years and, if so, do you feel there will be a backlash?

I appreciate what you are saying. Tom Wicker [*New York Times* columnist] and I had a discussion in 1976, and he brought up the same point. He was saying that we will kill maybe two or three people and then we will get outraged and sickened with it and stop it. And I said, "Tom, you don't know how mean this thing is. You really don't know how entrenched and how mean it is." The reality is that America, Southern Americans, Western Americans, wherever, in this country . . . well Alexis de Tocqueville described it best in *Democracy in America*. De Tocqueville had one major concern and his concern was what he called "tyranny of the masses." Tyranny of the majority is what happens in America when the majority decides to do away with a minority, and he pointed to slavery and he pointed to the American Indian. He was exactly right. Well, it's the same mindset that we bring to the death penalty. We have a minority that we are going to exterminate and it's all nice and legal, set up in the laws. Everybody is saying, "Yeah, yeah, we've got the death penalty, we gotta do it." But the process of thinking here is that psychologically we have dehumanized the men on death row. Once you think people on death row are not human, you can do anything you want to them. You can give them a number. You can send them to a place to wait for their extermination and then you can exterminate them, because they are not like you and me, they are murderers. Just so happens that not only are they murderers but they are probably poor, black, and convicted of killing a white person. They are not like us. You see, de Tocqueville was right. When the majority of the American people set up laws to implement that kind of psychology, then you have mass murder. That's what we had with the Indians. That's what we had with the slaves. And that's what we've got now. It's mass murder. It's two thousand people being exterminated for beginners. We are starting right where the Third Reich started. Look at death row, look who's there. Retarded people, minors, and all these so-called bad murderers. Did you know a third of Florida's death row is there for its first offense? First offense, and they are on death row. What's goin' on here?

Why do you think there is so much violence in the American culture?

Well, we are a very violent culture, especially when you talk about the South. Lord have mercy, we are so violent. The South have the highest per capita incarceration rate in the country, and our country ranks right up at the top of the western world. So a movie like *Rambo* is nothing out of the ordinary, it's just another day at the shop as far as we're concerned. There's a bumper sticker that you'll see that says: "GOD, GUNS, AND GUTS, THAT'S WHAT MADE AMERICA GREAT." That sums up the whole mentality.

What is the effect on a society that condones state executions?

I think that what happens is that you become a society of murderers. When that happens that leads to more and more people getting murdered. Once you have removed the barrier and allowed the state to kill people, where do you stop? Where do you stop this? Do you stop it with people who commit murder? Maybe we will just stop it there for twenty years, then open the gate a little wider and bring it back for people who commit rape, and then maybe a little wider and kill people who commit armed robbery, and the next thing you know you are killing thousands of people a year.

But again it's that whole psychological mechanism. Once you regard people as non-human, subhuman, less than you, you can do anything you want to them, and that's what we're doing. That's what we're doing!

THE KILLING MACHINE

"Michael Smith, a Christian, asked to be allowed to take his worn, beloved Bible with him to the electric chair; his request was denied because 'the Bible might catch fire, and that would be inappropriate.'"

—From a speech by Marie Deans
to the Northeast Regional Death
Penalty Conference
of the NCADP, 1987

The Reverend Knox Kreutzer was ordained as an Episcopal priest in 1953. During the fifties, he served as a death row chaplain in the District of Columbia for a period of six years.

He and his wife Isabel now live in Pacific Palisades, California. With his white beard and beatific face, one is reminded more of Noah than the naval officer he was trained to be.

Born in Wasau, Wisconsin, on April 3, 1922, Knox graduated from the United States Naval Academy, Annapolis, in 1943. His first assignment was as a gunnery officer on a light cruiser, the USS Columbia, *part of a task force consisting of eight light destroyers and four light cruisers under the overall command of Admiral "Bull" Halsey. He first saw action in the Pacific at the Battle of Cape Torokina, in October 1943, when the* Columbia *was hit by a Japanese task force in what was to become the longest night naval engagement of World War II.*

After the war Knox joined the priesthood, only to find himself, as he describes it, "part of the killing machine once more."

Pacific Palisades, California
Sunday, October 1, 1987, 1:30 p.m.

Father Knox Kreutzer

You came out of Annapolis straight into World War II?
Like any young ensign fresh out of Annapolis, I was raring to go. I remember in 1944, when cruiser division twelve took its place in the Solomon Islands to support our invasion of Guadalcanal, we steamed into Tulagi Harbor. There were great tall bluffs, palisades towering out of the sea on both sides of the entrance, and there painted on the bare rock in letters that were maybe a hundred and fifty feet high was a message. The top line read KILL . . . KILL . . . KILL, second line, KILL MORE JAPS, third line signed HALSEY. We all cheered, because we were all trained killers, parts of a powerful killing machine. But later, it made me think about the ways we had been settling differences with the Japanese.
When was that?
During the Battle of Cape Torokina, it occurred to me that there just had to be a better way to resolve our differences of opinion. After the war I'd had my share of killing and I wanted out. I went into business and found out that business was as much subject to human whimsy as war. I got really curious about whimsicality. It seemed everything was based on human whimsy. So it dawned on me where I wanted to go: theological school. The Church called this whimsicality "sin" and had studied it for centuries. In addition, theologians talked about its cure and the possibility of one world of peace. So off I went to theological school. Now what interested me there was the mystical, but the teachers at the seminary laughed it off. After seminary I studied the Beat generation, they became really mystical!
You stayed in theological school?
At the time I graduated from seminary I was in psychoanalysis and wanted to continue, so rather than return to Georgia to a parish, I took up a position that I was offered in the D.C. prison system, where I

remained for six years. Also during this time I was a member of the adjunct faculty at my seminary.

Why did you leave the prison service?

There were a number of reasons, but the legalized homicides within the judicial system were a great part of it. I mean, I was back in the front lines in a killing machine. There didn't seem much difference to me. There we were, again, settling differences by killing people. I was very glad when they abolished the death penalty in D.C.

Did you witness any executions?

Yes.

Could you describe what it was like the first time?

The death row of the D.C. jail is on the top floor, and there were several cells there. The electric chair was down the hall and was in a room that was surprisingly small, about ten by ten feet, maybe. The executioner or the guy that handles all the switches, the electrician, was in a little separate alcove with a glass window where he could see through, see the chair. At the other end of the room was the electric chair, a rather grubby-looking wooden chair. To one side there was what looks like a curtain and was in fact a one-way seeing device. On the other side was seated the news media and the witnesses, including the guy's family if they wanted to watch.

When the time came, the man, two guards, the Catholic chaplain, and I walk down the narrow passage into the execution chamber where the other officials are waiting for us: the prison doctor, the Captain of the Yard, the warden of the D.C. jail, the superintendent of the D.C. prison system, and the Catholic chaplain. He thanks the Captain of the Yard for treating him well, holds out his hand. He shakes the hand of every official and thanks them all for their kind treatment. Finally, he thanks the Director of Prisons and sits down in the electric chair and motions the guards to strap him in. He is directing his own execution! The superintendent is crying, the Captain of the Yard is crying, the prison warden is crying, the prison doctor is crying. I am staring at my prayer book, teeth clenched to prevent their chattering, terrified that I too am about to break down. The man looks up at me and sort of indicates for me not to worry. Then the guards fasten his arms and legs with leather straps. They strap one electrode around the left calf. The other, like a little brass saucer, they place on his already shaved head. Finally, they drape his head with a canvas hood.

So there is the warden, the superintendent, the captain, the two guards, the doctor, the Catholic priest, you, and the prisoner in the chair. Nine of you in this tiny 10 by 10 room?

That's right. I'm standing right next to him. The superintendent raises his hand to the man that does the levers. He throws the lever. His body jerks against the straps. This lasts for about thirty seconds, then it is repeated again for a minute or more. You could hear him sizzle and when I looked down at his leg I could see a big blister just fanning out. What you are hearing is the flesh cooking. The water in the blister is boiling. It smells like something halfway between fried pork and fried chicken, that's the way it smells. They say electrocution kills in 1/217th of a second. I hope that's true; otherwise we're just cooking them. When it's all over, the guards unstrap the body and they take the hood off, the doctor checks to see if he's dead and closes his eyes, the guards cart the body out on the stretcher, and that's it. And I am devastated, a participant in another variety of killing machine.

Many Southern states are still executing in earnest. California is oiling the gas chamber door.

Winston Churchill said that you could tell the virtue of a society by the way in which it handles its criminal offenders. He himself felt that a society which permitted the death penalty was not as highly evolved as it might be. I would also invite anyone who talks about the death penalty as an abstraction, as something they'd like for society, to witness an execution. It is a horrific experience.

Why are you against the death penalty?

Research has demonstrated beyond doubt that the death penalty is not a deterrent, it's a tit for tat kind of thing. State revenge, if you will. The fact that we have prisons and penitentiaries in every state, in every city, says something about the kind of society we have. We have a society in which killers are produced, as well as thieves, and so on. The fault is not solely in the killer. The fault is largely in the society that gave birth to him. Therefore, I think an attitude of self-searching and forgiveness is appropriate here. It is irresponsible to pin all the blame on the criminal, the killer. I think when one man kills, we have all killed.

DEATH ROW CHAPLAIN

"Any man's death diminishes me, because I am involved in mankind: and therefore never send to
know for whom the bell tolls; it tolls for thee."

—John Donne, 1572–1631

*We met with Byron Eshelman in the Criminal Justice Building in
downtown Los Angeles, at the sentencing phase of a first-degree
murder trial of a young gang member, Keith Fudge.*

*Both Byron Eshelman and Warden Larry Wilson (see Warden Wilson
interview) had been called by the defense. The judge refused to allow
either Warden Wilson or Byron Eshelman to testify before the jury. In
his view, the ghastly details of a man suffocating to death in the gas
chamber were not germane to the case.*

*Byron Eshelman is a clergyman in the United Church of Christ.
After graduating from Yale, he served as resident chaplain at Alcatraz
between 1946 and 1949. Later he became supervising chaplain for the
Department of Corrections at San Quentin Prison in California from
1951 to 1971.*

*During his twenty years at San Quentin there were ninety-two exe-
cutions in his first twelve years, but only one, Aaron Mitchell, in the
last eight.*

His book Death Row Chaplain, *published in 1962, is a powerful,
moving work expressing his views on capital punishment.*

*Now seventy-two years old, Chaplain Eshelman lives with his wife
Anne in Sonoma, California. Although afflicted with the debilitating
condition of Lou Gehrig's disease, Byron Eshelman's particular
strength of character and love of his fellow men continue to bring hope
for our society's future.*

Los Angeles, California
Tuesday, August 18, 1987, 3:00 p.m.

Chaplain Byron E. Eshelman

Did you attend many executions?

I was at the executions of approximately twenty-five inmates. A condemned man could request the presence of the Catholic chaplain, the Protestant chaplain, or no chaplain at all.

The basic ministry was to visit the men in their cells every week. I would walk down the tier and talk to anyone who wanted to talk, give them religious literature, or set them up for correspondence Bible courses in their death row quarters. They could listen to our services broadcast from the chapel over the radio line.

As a Christian, how would you address other Christians who are pro-death penalty?

It's a superstitious literalism that they take; that death required for sin is death of the body. Death, as I interpret it theologically, is the death of the egocentricity, the idolatry, the delusion of alienation, separation, and isolation that immature individuals have. When that dies, *then* you are regenerated, born again, and have a new life. But the average Christian is so superstitious and so literal, so given to primitive, simplistic interpretations.

The very nature of Christ's life was forgiveness.

Sure, but the Christian religion has a lot of backbone to it, too. "He overturned the money changers," and so on . . . but yes, basically the teaching is the God of unconditional love. Nobody can be outside the pale. Nobody can commit a crime that is unforgivable, and that's where I would stand in the Christian tradition. But in practice, of course, that's not a truism among organized Christian Churches. It's split down the middle between the fundamentalists and the mainline liberal denominations. We have just as much apartheid in the Churches on the death penalty as we do in the culture.

Which Churches are against the death penalty?

Episcopalian, Catholic, United Methodist, Presbyterians, Unitarians, United Church of Christ, Disciples of Christ, American Lutheran. All mainline churches are anti-death penalty. The Pentecostal, fundamentalist Bible-centered Churches, as they call themselves, are pro-death penalty. Falwell and that type, "the Moral Majority."

Did you ever witness an execution where a stay was granted at the eleventh hour?

Several. The most dramatic one involved two crime partners who were being executed together. One was a sophisticated jailhouse inmate. The other had never been in trouble before, never been in prison —but they both received the death penalty. The more experienced man had filed a writ with the help of some other inmates; the court considered it and gave him a stay, but the other man had not submitted any writ, so he was executed.

There was the case of Caryl Chessman. I was at his execution and he had a stay—by phone, after the pellets had been dropped. There was no way to reverse the process so he was executed, in a sense, illegally, because the judge was trying to stop it for at least thirty minutes, to give him a chance to review the final writ. As I say, the whole process is so fraught with that kind of injustice.

Do you believe that the death penalty is fraught with mistakes?

It is numbing to realize that all of the 501 persons executed to this point in history by the state of California would have grounds for retrial in light of new decisions brought forth by the courts.

What is the mental state of the men on death row?

Criminals executed in California are required to be eighteen years of age physiologically, but the law sets no minimum emotional age. I have watched men die who were still children emotionally.

These men on death row have been tagged for "warehousing." It is a grim world where human nature is considered beyond change, except for that produced by introducing cyanide gas into the body chemistry. We tell him, "We are going to kill you. It may be a year, two years, three, or even twelve years, but I am going to kill you. Meanwhile, I am going to lock you up in a small steel and concrete cage, fatten you up, and keep you there until I am ready to kill you." Enough to send anyone mad.

There were those who wanted to kill themselves but were afraid. One guy said, "Now the law will do it for me." He died almost eagerly, in the gas chamber, just eight months and fifteen days after coming to death row.

I have come to the conclusion that the legal definition of sanity is a century behind psychiatric knowledge.

Does any one execution stand out in your mind?

Well, the last one was one of the most bizarre we ever had. Aaron Mitchell, on April 12th, 1967—the only execution California has had in the last twenty-four years. There hadn't been one for four years before he was executed.

I had known Aaron and he was just a regular fella. I found him quiet, intelligent, and composed. He was baptized in 1963. Close as I was to him, I had no inkling of what was happening inside him.

The state never executes the person who committed the crime. The one who finally steps into the gas chamber is by no means the same person who entered death row years earlier. To believe so is to ignore the terrible forces that mold, strengthen, shatter a man in the surrealistic world of the condemned.

In the holding cell before his execution, Aaron became a completely different person. He was stark naked, and his left arm was a mass of dried coagulating blood. He had this stare in his eyes. He seemed like he was in a trance. When I went into the cell, I said, "How are you?" or something like that, and he said, "You're not Jesus Christ," and I said, "No, I'm not, I'm Chaplain Eshelman." He didn't pick up on that at all. He just said things to the effect that . . . in fact he just kept saying, "I am Jesus Christ, this is the blood of Jesus Christ." He kept that role up through the night and into the next day. The doctor did come in, and three psychiatrists examined him, while I was there. They held his arm up to test for catatonic tension, and as they were about to leave, Aaron said, "Can I put my arm down?" That gave them a clue that he was partly rational. If he had been only pretending to be insane, he would not have said that. The doctor said, "Put your arm any way you want." The warden was relying on the medical people to give him grounds to stop the execution, but they said it's not bona fide insanity.

Finally they wrestled Aaron down and put on a change of clothes. They wanted to wrap his arm up, but he resisted that. He said, "Why do you want me to look pretty?" He said, "You don't want to help me, you just wanna kill me." Then before he went into the gas chamber he shrieked, a blood-curdling scream, so that even the witnesses who were coming in could hear the shriek. They practically carried him into the gas chamber. After he was strapped in, he spoke real loud, "I am Jesus Christ."

What a horrific story. How would you say the gas chamber compares with, say, lethal injection, as a form of execution?

Gas is more dramatic because there is nothing over the face of the victim and you can see his or her contortions. It takes about ten minutes or so before they pronounce him dead. The assumption is that they become unconscious. They don't talk or say anything after the first thirty seconds.

We did have one inmate who tried to get loose in the gas chamber. He almost succeeded. They had to strap him down again, and he tried to get loose a second time. He had his hands out and was working around the belt on his waist when the gas hit him and he just . . . just fell passive.

Most of them go to their death in a very cooperative way and don't want to rock the boat or make a fuss. Go with a stiff upper lip. Great bravado, it's amazing how they can do it.

What would you offer as the main arguments against capital punishment?

Well, the death penalty's administrative realities are so fraught with fallibilities of human beings and it is such an irreversible penalty. On that ground alone it should never be allowed, because human beings, being as frail as they are, there are always going to be mixups and mistakes.

Aside from that, the people who are accused of these heinous crimes are victims of the callous mixture in which they've grown up. Broken homes and broken communities and neglect—they've been kicked around and brutalized. They've developed a kind of insensitivity because of the suffering that they've had, and now we want to turn around and punish them further for being what we forced them to be by our insensitivity as a society. The guilt for crime cannot rest on one person's shoulders. It's always social; the guilt spreads out through the culture and falls on all of us.

If you're gonna execute anybody you are gonna have to execute everybody, because single blame—blaming the individual criminal— isn't a realistic interpretation.

Most of these people are immature by virtue of their handicapped background and a lot of them have psychological frailties that should be thought of more as a medical problem than as a moral problem. What makes it so cruel and so basically absurd is that they want to punish these victims, punish these helpless people, punish these crippled people, these emotionally stunted people, these underdeveloped people—make them carry the burden of society.

The following is an excerpt from Death Row Chaplain *by Chaplain Eshelman:*

From Greek mythology come two concepts of love. One is in the spirit of *Agape,* the other in the spirit of *Eros. Eros*-love considers some people worthy of love, and some not. It believes that if some people are good and upright, then others are bad and hateful. If you should love the good, then you should hate the evil. In the pattern of *Eros*-love, the death penalty is entirely logical.

Agape-love is a love such as the world cannot easily comprehend. It is not a love born out of a need to improve, to save oneself, to attach oneself to the strong. One simply has love in him and carries it wherever he goes. *Agape*-love flows out to the dark places, the needy, the worthless, the lost, confused and inadequate. It makes the worthless worthy, brings strength to the weak. It knows no hopeless situations or hopeless people. It is the love of God which is shed forth on the just and the unjust, and in no fashion is merited by anyone. It is the love which the world cannot give or take away. With such love in our hearts, we could not maintain the execution chamber.

With *Eros*-love, we executed Jesus Christ, and this was the ultimate tragedy of rejection. But it was also the ultimate blessing, for it exposed the meaning of sin to mankind. The same double drama is reenacted at each execution. The victim is a helpless child of God who is as unable to understand his destiny as the rest of us. Yet through him the sins of the world are exposed again, and we are reminded that salvation is not of man.

And so on each execution day, I pray for the executioners as well as for the man whose life is to be taken. If those who conduct the executions would ask to hear my prayer, it would begin with these words:

"Oh God, have mercy on us this morning as we prepare to take the life of this man. And as we see his life yielded up in sacrifice, so prepare each of us to be likewise yielded up in Thine own season."

My prayer would not be long. It would end with words only a little different from those spoken on the Cross so long ago:

"Father, forgive us—for we know not what we do."

THE VALLEY OF THE SHADOW OF DEATH

"Thou preparest a table before me in the presence of mine enemies; thou anointest my head with oil."

—Psalm 23

Susan Cary is a forty-three-year-old attorney with short, dark, curly hair and a bright round face. We met her at her Gainesville home in Florida.

Appearances can be deceptive and at first sight one may well take Susan for a nice middle-class conservative lady, a woman who might speak at a Daughters of the American Revolution luncheon. This is not Susan Cary.

Susan Cary embodies the sheer determination and above all courage required to fight the Florida death machine and succor the forgotten prisoners of death row.

Susan Cary was born in Ohio, raised in a white, upper-middle-class environment that was politically very conservative. She was in Dallas when John F. Kennedy was shot and this, she says, had a profound effect on her thinking.

As a young woman she was expected to join organizations like the Junior League and the Country Club, but instead she joined the Peace Corps and went to West Africa.

Susan lives with her eleven-year-old daughter Bayo, and a tiny dog with boundless energy called Cricket.

Gainesville, Florida
Friday, February 2, 1988, 11:00 a.m.

Susan Cary

You were in the Peace Corps in Africa. What did you do when you returned?

I taught at an all-black school here. Florida, as you probably know, was very slow to integrate. This was in 1969 and 1970 when the U.S. Supreme Court said finally, "Do it tomorrow, it has to be done." I taught eighth-grade arithmetic in an all-black school and that was my first introduction to what segregation was like and what it had done to people. My schools in Africa were better equipped than the school that I taught here in Florida.

It was horrible, it was unbelievable. I had never experienced this. I don't know whether it was because I was naive and it had been going on under my nose all along. I'd lived before in New Mexico and maybe it had been going on under my nose there, but Florida was just a whole different atmosphere.

I had children in the eighth grade who literally could not read or write their names or add two and two. I made up Bingo games, just to teach basic addition. These children were in the eighth grade and didn't know how to use rulers. They didn't know how to measure things.

When did you decide to get into death penalty work?

In the fall of 1974. It was Friday the 13th. On that December day I read in the newspaper that a fifteen-year-old boy from Fort Pierce had been sentenced to death. I was shocked, partly because that was the age of the students that I had taught. I couldn't believe that society's answer to a fifteen-year-old child was "We are going to kill you." To me, that said much more about our society than it said about whatever this kid had done. How offensive it is that a society would sentence a *child* to death!

Florida had reinstated the death penalty in 1972 so although they weren't executing at that point, there were death sentences being imposed. But they were being held by the appellate courts until the law was tested.

When I first learned about the case, I really wanted to meet the inmate. And I did. I really was very concerned that we know who this kid was and what had brought him to that point.

Can you tell us about him?

His name was George Vasil; his parents always told us it was pronounced like window-"sill". He was fifteen, had been adopted by a family. He had a very ordinary kind of upbringing. He was white. I decided that I wanted to get to know this kid, so I drove over during the Christmas break from law school to Florida State Prison in Starke to see him.

He never looked up. He kept his head down the whole time, never made eye contact with me. He just sat and wrung his hands. Physically, he was not an attractive child at all. He had very bad acne and very pasty, pale skin, which I don't think was just from being in prison. He was very gawky, you know, that real awkward age. He wore glasses and I thought if he had braces on his teeth, he would be the perfect match for the "gawky kid" stereotype. Later I learned that his braces had been removed. As you can imagine, he didn't have any girlfriends.

He had tried to seduce a classmate on her way home from school one day. He couldn't get an erection, so she laughed at him. Things just escalated. He tried to make her stop laughing. She screamed and he put a piece of cloth, which turned out to be her underwear, over her face, and she suffocated. It was an accidental killing. There was never any allegation that it was a kinky thing or that he intended to kill her. But that's the felony murder rule, since it was done during the commission of an attempted sexual assault, he was convicted of first-degree murder.

I am not saying that what he did was okay. I don't want to be misunderstood. I want to make it clear that it is not okay. But to say that the only response that we can come up with is to kill that child is barbaric and something out of the Middle Ages.

The courts later determined that the sentence should be life, not death. But it wasn't because they said there was any problem with executing a child. That question still hasn't been resolved.

You work with the men on the row. How do you help the men facing imminent death?

I started realizing that people had a lot of needs when they were going to be executed. They know they are going to die, so I started getting in touch with the people that I thought knew about death and

dying. Elizabeth Kübler Ross and people like her deal with death, from
what we would call more natural causes, all the time. I studied her
work. I became involved because I wanted to know what was known
about dying in general, so that we could help families, especially the
children of those on death row.

*How do you differentiate that role from, say, the traditional priest or
ecclesiastical role?*

I see it more as being a supportive, compassionate person. I am not
into whether this is God's will or not, or saving souls. That is not my
role. That is left to the clergy. I am a Quaker by tradition, and Quakers
don't have clergy. I am more involved in the secular aspects of death.

For example, John Spenkelink had asked us not to cry. It was very
important to him that he be able to keep his composure. He didn't want
to cry, and he knew if people around him cried, he would. It wasn't
that we weren't to cry anywhere; that was a promise no one could
make, but he asked us simply to cry somewhere else. Well, his little
nine-year-old child just couldn't deal with it, and so she started crying.
We were in this big long room. So I took her to the other end of the
room where John couldn't see us, and let this child cling to me sobbing, "Please don't let them kill my daddy." I mean, what do you say?
"This is okay, this is the reality?" I can't imagine that most people
walking around in the street would feel that they were safer having
killed her daddy.

Have you witnessed an execution at Starke?

Yes I did. David Funchess *[executed April 22, 1986]*. I always
swore because I needed to go back to the prison, that I would not
witness a killing. It had been hinted at by a couple of other people who
were killed and I just always made it clear that that was something I
didn't think I could do. It had really wiped out a lot of people. Lawyers
have become unable to continue the work after witnessing an execution
and I didn't want that to happen to me.

I made it clear that I would come to last visits, I would stay with
them as long as I could, I would support them and make funeral arrangements—I have scattered people's ashes, I have done anything to
help them and their families before or after death, things that they felt
were important to them to get done—but that I wouldn't be a witness.

What changed your mind?

I don't think it was a change of mind, it was just that I got stronger.
David was a black man, a Vietnam veteran who had Post Traumatic
Stress Disorder and was really in terrible agony.

I first met him in the fall of 1985 and he was depressed—writing
poetry like this:

Night time is the right time
To have a Nightmare.

He couldn't sleep because of this disorder so he would sit on his bed at night and tell himself dreams to have, so that he would be able to get through the night without having a nightmare. It was incredible the torture this man was experiencing. I started going to see him, as I do when people lose in the federal courts and we know they are in danger of having a warrant signed.

This was really one time when you just know you are in the right place on the planet for another human being, and he just started talking about his life. I think I went every day for a couple of weeks, all day, and just listened as this pent-up sorrow and anguish and remorse and everything started coming out. This was in October, and by Christmas he was writing about the inner joy that has no need to be caused by anything, but just is. I mean he had really been healed, or whatever you want to call that.

Was Post Traumatic Stress Disorder recognized as a defense at that time?

No, he was tried in 1974, when nobody even knew about Post Traumatic Stress Disorder. We went to Jacksonville and started talking to his family, his sisters and those with whom he had been particularly close, and just asked them, "How was David when he came back from Vietnam?" and they started telling us the horror stories about his behavior. He was digging foxholes in the ground behind these really awful slum houses. I have pictures of where he had dug under these houses. He would come into the home and have an imaginary machine gun in front of him and scout out every room before he would feel safe even to sit down.

He was also addicted to drugs, which he had never used before he went to Vietnam. You see, he had been wounded badly in a landmine explosion, and was in terrible pain. [David Funchess had been awarded five medals for bravery in Vietnam]. Nobody ever put his weird behavior together with anything at the time of his trial, as physicians had very little understanding of PTSD. So this was not relevant to the appellate courts. Despite this very important evidence, the answer from the courts was, "You are too late." They didn't care.

If we'd had the benefit of some of the opinions that have come out now, David would have been granted relief. There is no question that the mitigating circumstances were extremely compelling. As the months went on, we knew that David would have a death warrant signed. I mean, there just wasn't any question, it was simply a question of when.

There was another lawyer in Tallahassee, Jeff Thompson [see Jeff Thompson interview] who had been my next-door neighbor during law school, another coincidence, and Jeff had been in Vietnam too and he was now counseling vets. So Jeff also started coming to see David, and the three of us got to be very close.

In the end, I saw it not as being a witness at an execution and watching killing happen. I really saw it as being present at the death of a friend.

Would you mind telling us about the execution?

It is like a medieval torture scene. First they take us in there and they have a banquet! I am not kidding. They took us into this large room, where the prison guards normally eat their meals, and there, spread before us, are sandwiches, coffee, cheese. It's like we have come to a party. I am not exaggerating, I could not believe it. Jeff and I went to another area where we had nothing at all to do with this and just sat there by ourselves. But everybody else who was there to be witnesses was having a party. They may as well have had a pig with an apple in its mouth. There was no consciousness at all that they were about to watch somebody be killed.

They then took us down a hall and drove us in a van around to the back of the prison so that we could come in the execution chamber.

Then they brought David in. Of course they shave their heads and put this oil on so that it will conduct electricity. I couldn't help thinking, "Thou anointest my head with oil." It's bizarre!

They brought him in with these handcuffs on that are specially made for the purpose. This actually exists in this country today. They have handcuffs that are especially made for the purpose of escorting someone to be killed! They have screws on the top of them, so that if the person even moves wrong, the guards escorting them can break their wrists by twisting this screw. Those things exist and they are made for that purpose. They are torture items.

They are specifically designed to break a wrist?

That is what they are designed for. When the prisoner is escorted in, the guard on either side has a hold of the screw, so that if you move wrong and they think you are going to try to resist, they break your wrist.

I kept eye contact with David the whole time so I wasn't really watching all the stuff that was going on. They strapped him very tight into the electric chair. I don't know how long it took because at this point it is not really chronological time that you are dealing with. He spoke to Jeff and me, we were sitting in the second row. You couldn't really hear but you could tell he was talking to us. He said to me, "I love you." And I said, "I love you," and kind of made a fist. He asked

Jeff, "Are you okay?" and Jeff said, "Yes." Then he said, "Thank you," to both of us and we both nodded. Then they put this awful chin strap on him that totally distorts the face. It holds your head tight to the back of the chair. I really thought they were hurting him.

Up to that point I didn't think that anything that was happening was physically painful to him. But this, I thought, really must be painful, because it just totally distorted the face. I don't know whether I said, "Are they hurting you?" or had that expression on my face. He couldn't move anything but this finger *(Susan lifted her forefinger)*, and so he just moved his finger to let us know that it was okay.

Then they put this hood over his face. I thought it would be cloth, but it's rubber. There is this round piece and it had electrodes in it, and then there is this rubber piece of solid black that covers the face and it looks like something you would see in a torture chamber. That's what it looks like. Once they did that I didn't look anymore because I couldn't keep eye contact with David. We had said that the purpose of being there was to be there with him, so I didn't watch after that. I just put my head down and was sort of meditating, or whatever you call it. I did look back after they said, you know. . . . They say:

"The sentence of the state of Florida is carried out. Exit to the rear."

The next day we went to the funeral home to take care of his body.

Is the funeral home inside the prison?

No. We use a funeral home here in Gainesville.

Doesn't there have to be an autopsy?

Yes, they do an autopsy. The funeral business in Florida is very racially segregated and people feel real strongly. There are black funeral homes and white funeral homes. But one of the black funeral homes has been very helpful to us in both black and white funerals. They come and get the body and take the body to the medical examiner, who determines that electrocution was indeed the cause of death.

So there is segregation even after death?

(Laughs) Yeah. David's family really didn't have money but they felt strongly about not having him cremated. But burial is expensive, so we compromised. Jeff lives on a farm, and we got permission to bury David on Jeff's farm. A friend, a Catholic nun, got a station wagon, and we put David's coffin in the back of the station wagon. I took some African cloth, it was in the spring, in April, so that there was honeysuckle blooming everywhere, and we just filled the back of the station wagon with honeysuckle. It was really quite beautiful. The funeral home helped us, showed us how to make a kind of pulley, because coffins are very heavy, to slide the coffin into the back of the wagon, and the nun and I drove to Tallahassee. Then we parked the station wagon. *(Laughs)* I mean, there are some humorous things—

when we stopped in Lake City to eat, we wondered what we were going to do if anyone looked inside. We just told David we'd be right back.

Anyway, Jeff had dug the grave. He wanted to do it because it helped him get rid of a lot of the stress. Some of David's family came, and others, and we buried David on the farm under this beautiful tree. It was like a funeral should be.

Is there a marker?

I believe there is. There should be one there by now because he was a veteran and the military were supposed to furnish one. They were to send a marker and a flag for the family. Talk about the irony, they wouldn't help him stay alive but they would give a flag when he was killed.

BROTHERS IN ARMS

"Slowly up silent peaks, the white edge
Of the world, trod four archangels,
Clear against the unheeding sky
Bearing, with quiet even steps, and the
Great wings furled, a little dingy
Coffin; where a child must lie."

—Rupert Brooke, 1887–1915

With the Gregg decision in 1976, the Supreme Court told the exe-cuting states that to satisfy the requirement of death, there should be a number of "safeguards" built into the capital punishment laws. The most significant of these was the clause that deals with aggravating and mitigating circumstances at the sentencing phase of the trial.

The Court concluded that in deciding which convicted murderers to sentence to death, judges must instruct jurors to consider both the aggravating and mitigating circumstances that would increase or de-crease the defendant's culpability.

In the case of David Funchess, there were certainly aggravating circumstances. The ex-Marine killed two women during the course of a December 1974 robbery. But had the jurors known all the facts, the overwhelming mitigating circumstances, in all likelihood they would have returned a different verdict.

Post Traumatic Stress Disorder (PTSD), of which David Funchess exhibited almost classic symptoms, was not medically recognized until 1980. It was only first emerging as a problem at the time of the trial in 1974.

Capital punishment is a finite act. It leaves no room for error and we have occasionally executed the innocent. It also leaves no room for future discoveries in the fields of medicine and psychology. Tomorrow's discoveries could reveal that the violence of today can be explained by medical abnormalities. Recently we have learned about PTSD. Our knowledge came too late to save David Funchess.

This is the story of David Funchess, told to us by his friend, attorney, and fellow Vietnam veteran, Jeff Thompson.

Telephone Interview
Tallahassee, April 22, 1988, 1:30 p.m.

Jeff Thompson

Could you tell us a little about David Funchess?

David's father supposedly believed that David was not his child. He behaved in a very violent way toward David. He was a strict father with the other kids, but he was both physically and psychologically cruel with David.

There was an old shed behind the house and one night his father locked him in it, in the dark, without light. He was petrified. David was terrified of spiders and he was yelling and screaming and crying. The neighbors heard him, and the next morning one of them unlocked the door and let him out. David himself identified that as the time when he finally decided that there was never going to be any help, he was just going to have to deal with whatever came at him. What was even more tragic was that he was very attentive at school, very bright, very gentle—well loved.

David had an older brother whom he was particularly close to. This older brother joined the Marine Corps and didn't actually make it to Vietnam because he was killed on the street, I believe in Jacksonville, in a fight. David was about seventeen, the murder left him devastated.

Was David exhibiting neurotic or abnormal behavior at this time?

Far from it, believe it or not. He did okay in school. He was described by neighbors, former teachers, and students as being very patriotic and wanting to go to fight for his country. He enlisted in the Marine Corps.

The philosophy at boot camp is basically to tear apart the personality until you're nothing but a raw stump of a human being and then they build you back up—as a Marine. David went through that process at a time when racism was rampant. The Marine Corps was polarized between the races.

It wasn't until a few years later when I was in the Corps that actual violence began to break out on the bases between black and whites. But the polarization was there earlier and the racial violence had apparently already begun in Vietnam.

David was only in Vietnam a week or so before he was thrust into some very heavy fighting. A few of his friends mentioned how David felt endangered by both the combat and the racism around him. During the lulls in combat there was violence going on between the whites and blacks. So there he was, into some very heavy fighting and in a situation in which there was no safety at any time, *and* he was a green recruit.

It was only after a month or two of this living hell that he was wounded and medivacced out, eventually to Japan, and it was while he was recovering that he became addicted to drugs. Between the drugs they prescribed to lessen the pain and whatever psychiatric drugs they put in him, he eventually became addicted to morphine. I assume there were psychiatric drugs, because the records we obtained showed that he was in a psychiatric ward as well as the normal wounded ward.

Once he was wounded and away from the fighting, all the emotions of the terror got hold of him and he had no way of dealing with it. He had no way of dealing with anything except to shove things down, bury things as deep as possible in his mind and not deal with them, which is a basic underlying process that commonly leads to Post Traumatic Stress Disorder.

So, they shipped him back to the United States, hooked on the morphine, and soon after, he started using whatever drugs he could. He was totally lost emotionally. He had never used any drugs before the war. He just wanted to go home and be at peace, but when he went home he exhibited extremely bizarre behavior. For instance, he would lock himself in a room, not coming out for days. He would take charcoal and draw weird pictures on the wall. He would crawl under the house for days on end [see Susan Cary interview]. Eventually the Marine Corps gave him an undesirable discharge because they couldn't cope with him.

I cannot believe that a jury, in possession of these facts, could send a man to the chair.

The jury didn't know. The way the justice system works is that there is very little money for public defender defenses. There was very little background research done into David's life. None of the neighbors were interviewed and, even more significantly, at the time of the trial Post Traumatic Stress Disorder was a new concept. It was only at David's clemency hearing that it was brought up, and even then his history and illness were not fully appreciated. We listened to the tapes of his clemency hearing and his lawyer really didn't have any grasp at all of what was going on.

It is said that there could be as many as 500,000 Vietnam vets suffering from PTSD and in need of help. About one in three homeless men in this country are veterans. They often have a wandering lifestyle, suffer from drug addiction, nightmares, and isolation.

Can you tell us about the murders?

David came home to Jacksonville and got deeper and deeper into drugs and eventually became a heroin addict, just drifting around. He never committed any violent crimes. He committed burglaries to finance his habit, and his condition continued to deteriorate over the next seven years.

He finally committed the murders seven years after he was discharged. During that time he became visually and behaviorally very different. In the tapes of the clemency hearing the state's attorney, Edward Austin, talks about this "subhuman animal." David must have, at the time, seemed very much like that. He was not violent until this incident happened.

This is the way David remembered it.

He'd been working in a bar as a gofer, cleaning up and doing odd jobs, and he had been fired for taking money out of the cash register, which is the type of thing that he did to finance his drug habit. Some weeks after he was fired, he went back. His recollection, basically, was that he was led into it by two street women with guns, and they held the place up.

The situation got out of hand and people started screaming and he had a combat flashback, flipped out and went berserk—which is very typical of PTSD. The drugs, the suppressed combat experiences, the stuff with his father, and the death of his brother all burst out in this one violent episode, which was completely atypical of his own personality. He and I talked about it quite a few times and he remembered leaping over a bar and grabbing a paring knife used for cutting lemons and limes. He remembered having his hand at one woman's throat, he remembered heading into another room . . . just a few isolated instances . . . he cut her throat.

Is throat-cutting a particular Marine combat training technique?

Yeah, various techniques of hand-to-hand combat would have been taught, but he would never talk to me about Vietnam. It was something he could not deal with at all. All the information we learned about his Vietnam experiences came to us from recollections of neighbors. Susan Cary did a tremendous job of interviewing people in the neighborhood and heard from them how David had talked once or twice soon after he got back, talked to them about how horrible it was and how heavy the fighting was.

Did the Veteran's Administration give David any help when he got back from Vietnam?

No, he never had any help at all. You have to know how to seek it out and even then the quality is very poor.

Has the VA been approached about the plight of these men, particularly the ones involved in serious crime?

They have a limited budget. Over the years they have gotten better and better on the counseling they provide, but it reaches very few and counseling is very much a hit-and-miss thing. My opinion is that only one in ten counselors is really any good.

How did David approach his death?

At the end he just kept saying that he was ready to go and that he wanted to go. Susan Cary and I helped him prepare for death. I had a gut revulsion to anyone yielding to their death, and yet during his actual execution his calmness was incredible and his focus was on reassuring those of us who were there, who were his friends and allies, that he was all right. I just respected him so much. He was more worried about us than he was about himself, and was calm and considerate to the end.

I have never been into things spiritual but the most amazing thing for me was that soon after they turned on the electricity, I felt his spirit joyfully, incredibly joyfully, swirling around the room and rising up and leaving. He had really made peace with himself and with God and was ready to move on.

I had no personal conception about whether there is anything to move on to or not, but I now realize that there is a spirit that is apart from the body. He was such a beautiful human being. It is a common tragedy. Everyone on death row is a human being and has just been hurt in one way or another. Many, through help, have actually healed by the time they get executed. David had healed and returned to his essential, inherent, beautiful self.

An Englishman Abroad

"The Queen had only one way of settling all differences great or small. 'Off with his head,' she said without even looking round."

—Lewis Carroll,
Alice's Adventures in Wonderland

A small nondescript door on Atlanta's Walton Street, with a single buzzer, marks the offices of the Southern Prisoners' Defense Committee. A single flight of very steep stairs leads to a small group of offices. The last office on the right belongs to Clive Stafford Smith, an Englishman who has dedicated his young life to fighting the death penalty.

Clive was the attorney for Edward Earl Johnson, executed in Mississippi in 1987. Johnson's gassing was the subject of a BBC documentary film entitled 14 Days in May, *that was shown on HBO (Home Box Office) in the United States. The ninety-minute movie showed Stafford Smith trying every legal step in the book to save his client. At the end of this harrowing film, his anger, sorrow, and revulsion were more than apparent when he addressed a press conference after the death of his friend, Edward Earl Johnson.*

Clive Stafford Smith, twenty-eight, is a graduate of the W. C. Fields school of office management. Every inch of floor, shelf, desk, and any other kind of space is crammed with case files, briefs, and legal volumes.

The thin-faced and bespectacled Englishman reminds one of a young Cambridge don doing academic research into an obscure Greek author.

He was born in Newmarket, England, fifty miles outside of Cambridge. He was educated at Old Buckingham Hall School and Radley College. Clive then crossed the water to Columbia Law School, where he obtained his law degree. He lives with his wife Cristiana in Atlanta.

Atlanta, Georgia
Tuesday, February 9, 1988, 2:00 p.m.

Clive Stafford Smith

Why did you come to the United States?

Well, my parents worked at Cambridge, and Radley is right outside Oxford. Both these university towns are inexpressibly tedious places, if you ask me. I was going to go to Cambridge but then I was offered a place at the University of North Carolina, Chapel Hill, where they fund you to do all kinds of exotic things in the summer, one of which was working against capital punishment with Millard Farmer. So the reason I came over here was that they very generously gave me some money to do some work that I wanted to do over the summer. I had this antipathy toward the death penalty, for whatever reasons, and there isn't much you can do in England about the death penalty.

Why were you interested particularly in capital punishment?

I don't think there's anything as comparably barbaric as consciously taking a long time about putting someone to death. There is just nothing to compare it to.

And the United States is the only Western, democratic civilization that still does it?

Well, as Gandhi said when he was asked what he thought about Western civilization, he said, "I think it would be a good idea."

Can you tell us about some of your cases?

There's Jerome Holloway, here in Georgia. Jerome has an IQ of 49, a mental age of a two-year-old. I did a test on Jerome and the same test on the two-year-old daughter of a colleague. She did much better than Jerome. He has no idea what's going on. He is thirty-one, chronologically, but mentally. . . . His case got reversed by the Georgia Supreme

Court in 1987 after he'd been on death row for a year, but they're trying to stick it on him again.

How many of your cases were victims of child abuse?

It's one of the common denominators in every case.

I represent a woman named Judy Houston in Mississippi; she was beaten by her husband for fifteen years and it's an amazing thing to me that she didn't kill anyone before she did.

You get these prosecutors whose closing argument is always, "Well, this kid had four other brothers and sisters who were also abused and they didn't commit murder." Well, that's a ridiculous argument.

There are very few on death row who weren't abused. Take, for example, one of my clients from Florida. When he was six months old, his mother swapped him for a dining room table and it just went downhill from there. When he was three years old, they started sexually abusing him. When he was fifteen years old, he was seduced by this seventy-six-year-old woman who had a relationship with him for three years, then, when he wanted to get married, she taunted him about his past, told him she would tell everyone about it. She filled him up with alcohol and stuff and he killed her.

Now that's not a very nice thing to do, obviously, but this guy is completely out of it. It's absurd to execute people like that.

Can you tell us about Edward Earl Johnson, about whom the film 14 Days in May *was made?*

Oh, that all happened by chance. Paul Hamann, who I knew from back home, wanted to do a film here. The Mississippi Department of Corrections has the most open policy, so I told him that.

He made an agreement with the state of Mississippi that he would film a period prior to whatever the next serious execution date was, which, fortunately, wasn't for two years.

I took Edward Johnson's case with three weeks to go because he had lost on his first *Habeas*.

Can you give us some background?

Okay, well, Edward was tried in 1979 for the murder of a white police officer and alleged assault on an old white lady. He is black, obviously. He was eighteen at the time. He was defended by two lawyers who had no funds, no money, did no investigation, and basically it was an open and shut case. Over the next eight years of appeals, sad to say, all the serious issues in the case were not raised, for various reasons.

In what way?

Once you don't bring up something on the first *Habeas* it becomes very difficult to bring it up the second time. This was a case with a lot of publicity, a lot of which was favorable. But, unfortunately, Mississippi wanted an execution. So, however much favorable press we got, and we got a lot, it just didn't have any effect. We had a lot of people on our side by the time we got down to the wire. The Catholic Church, all the American cardinals, intervened on Edward's behalf. Perhaps one of the reasons we lost was that I was so sure we were going to win. This was the first case I ever lost. But, the fact was, the state of Mississippi wanted their execution and the Court created absurd rules of legal esoterica to ensure that they got it.

And you lost. How did you cope with that?

Well, how does anything like that make you feel? It made Edward feel a hell of a lot worse than me, I'll tell you that.

Did you have to attend the execution?

Yeah . . . unfortunately one has to. Because in one case the guy got a stay just as he was being strapped into the chair. To watch while they killed Edward was disgusting. It was the most revolting thing I had ever seen. I don't particularly care to dwell on it.

How long had you known Edward?

Well, I knew him because I knew everyone on death row, but I had only actually taken his case about three weeks before he was killed. We didn't have any time: I had only seen him three times as his attorney before the time came to kill him. We'd been running backwards and forwards trying to get papers filed. You know, these people accuse us of delay tactics and the rest of this crap. The fact is there aren't enough hours in the day to get the stuff out in time.

You mentioned in the film 14 Days in May *that you saw an opinion on the word processor before an appeal had been filed?*

That was an outrage. You see, I really thought we were going to win. The whole case was a complete travesty. We had a good case, the hearing went very well, and I thought that it was all over but the shouting. But the next day at noon came the message, "Denied relief." I went to file the notice of appeal with the Fifth Circuit and there was this clerk, typist, or whatever, looking embarrassed and trying to stand in front of the word processor. When she moved, I could see that they were running out the opinion. And the opinion had all the same spelling mistakes as the district court opinion, so they had obviously got the district court opinion long before we did, before we even got a chance to do the appeal, which was an outrage. Of course they denied it.

Politics?

Oh, the whole death penalty is political.

Do you think that Mississippi executed Johnson in order to look as tough as Florida, Georgia, and Louisiana?

(Laughs) They can't keep up with Louisiana. In Mississippi, they

wanted their execution. It came to a point when people said, "Enough of this appeal stuff. Let's get on with it."

Of course the crass part is that they chose a guy who I think is the most decent person that I have ever represented and who was probably not guilty of the crime. To my mind, this clearly illustrates the fact that the whole justice system is screwed up. The only good thing about the American justice system is that it takes so long to execute people.

What are the conditions like on death row?

Have you been there?

Not yet . . . next week.

Where are you going?

Starke.

Oh God, what a God-forsaken place. Starke is horrible, there are some really vicious people on the staff there. Guards are unpleasant, the prison is horrible. Georgia is equally disgusting. Mississippi is actually not so bad, at least comparatively. It's not nice to be sitting anywhere where they are going to kill you, but at least the guards are decent people, or at least some of them are, and at least the people treat you with a modicum of humanity. Louisiana is probably the worst. That's where they keep people locked up in single cells and when they go outside, they have to go out alone. Play basketball, alone, with a deflated basketball. It would be laughable if it was not so cruel and barbaric. I don't say that Mississippi is a holiday camp—the conditions are horrible—but it's just the way they treat the people that makes the difference.

Let me say this. The only decent people at the execution were the guards. The media acted in a disgusting way. I mean, they were talking about what color socks Edward had on, just trivia. All they wrote about was what he had for his last meal. It made me really sick.

On the other hand, some of the guards who knew Edward were crying. You get guards crying and the "liberal" press talking about socks and food. I don't mean to write off the whole media, but I was really revolted by the bunch they sent to the execution.

Johnson seemed gentle in the documentary. Was he?

I guarantee you that if I could sit Edward, or any of my clients, down in a room with twelve jurors and just leave them there for twenty-four hours, you would never get the death penalty in any case, because they would realize that there is a human element to this guy and they wouldn't do it.

The way they do it is you have this guy in a chair, you sit him there, make him look like a criminal. You never get the human side of him. Judges and DAs say, "I am just doing my job." That was what the members of the S.S. said after World War II. They are just doing their jobs? Bull—they are killing people!

Jurors are told, "You just follow this little legal pattern and if you fill in the blanks, if you get to A, you kill him, and if you get to B, you don't kill him." Of course the instructions always get the jury to A. It's a completely dehumanized system. If you did it in a human way, you wouldn't have any death penalty because people wouldn't be prepared to do it. If people had to go down to the chicken-processing plant they would all be vegetarians.

The death penalty is *Alice in Wonderland*. The whole thing is silly. I have never heard anyone articulate a sensible reason for it. There is nothing that is actually achieved by the death penalty except it keeps a lot of judges and lawyers in business and it keeps a lot of really poor and completely defenseless people on death row.

What horrified me most, especially when I was first doing this kind of work, was these guys were utterly dependent on me, a twenty-four-year-old lawyer, for their lives, in a system where the state has all the money and we have the most meager resources.

The 1987 publication by Amnesty International on the death penalty in the United States concluded, among other things, that the death penalty was a "lottery." Do you agree?

Absolutely. You may just as well take one in twenty kids, pick him up, take him to the village square, tie him up and whip him. There is just no sanity to the whole thing. And then you look at the other side of it, of course it gets hackneyed to say it too often, but it is true, that it's a rich man's justice system.

Take the Ford Motor Company. This is the single most annoying case to me. You remember the Pinto case? These guys go about designing a car and they discover that if you are rear-ended, the car blows up and incinerates the people inside. So they make this mathematical calculation that eighteen people are going to get killed each year and it's going to cost them X dollars to pay the settlement and alternatively it is going to cost them Y dollars to fix the car. Because X is less than Y they go ahead, leave the car as it is and—eighteen people duly get incinerated.

If ever there was a case where some people should get the death penalty, that's it. Because they actually *calculated* how many people they were going to kill in the most premeditated way possible, solely for financial gain. These guys not only do not get the death penalty, they don't even get tried. They get citations from the Better Business Bureau!

That sort of stuff really makes me sick, and on the other side you get these poor guys. For example, there is Troy Dugar, a kid I represent in

Louisiana. He was sentenced to die on his sixteenth birthday. He was completely psychotic at the time of the crime.

How old was he when he committed the crime?

He was fifteen at the time of the crime, the youngest person on death row in the country and maybe the world. In 1987, on the day of his sixteenth birthday, he was sentenced to death. I don't care who talks to him, Troy is his own best advertisement . . . because he's a psychotic. His case is disgusting. I don't know how people could possibly sentence someone like that to die. Troy, a fifteen-year-old, ran away from his dad and he's alone in his mom's home with no food or drink, water or heat for four days. He's watched this cops-and-robbers movie *Dillinger* too many times and he's completely off in his fantasy world. He goes out, commits a kidnapping, and kills this poor fellow, and then he goes right on and commits an armed robbery in which he steals a quart of milk and a packet of vanilla wafer cookies, for Christ's sake.

I had a hearing the other day in Troy's case in which this was exhibit K. (*Clive holds up a cheap red plastic firetruck*). This kid still plays with plastic firetrucks, for crying out loud, and I asked the parole officer whose job it was to determine whether death was a proportionate sentence, whether he thought that kids who play with plastic firetrucks should get the death penalty? And he says "Yes"!

What world are these people in? I don't understand it. I just don't understand how people can say yes to a question like that. A bunch of barbarians, if you ask me.

[Note: At the time of writing Troy Dugar is still on death row. On December 14, 1988, the defense succeeded in having him ruled incompetent to appeal. Hence, he has not been resentenced in line with the 1988 Thompson (Thompson v. Oklahoma) *case, in which the U.S. Supreme Court more or less ruled out the death penalty for fifteen-year-olds. They hope to have Dugar removed to a mental hospital.]*

Do you feel that states that have death row populations but have not executed for some time will begin again?

Oh sure they will. I guarantee it.

Do you think that when they do, there will be an outcry against it?

No. Because the terrible thing is, when you start executing, people get immune to it.

Now, eventually, there is going to be a twist in public opinion. You can see a little of it now. People now are upset about killing children. They are upset about killing retarded people, they are even a little upset about killing for racist reasons. And that is something that is different from five years ago. We have a very narrow view of history and we tend to look at the last six months. But generally over the last century it is undeniable that these things go in cycles, and inevitably the death penalty will be abolished in the end. It's first a matter of how many poor people are sacrificed on the altar of inhumanity in the meantime.

The following is an edited account of Clive Stafford Smith's remembrance of the death of his friend Edward Earl Johnson on May 20, 1987:

Perhaps telling this final story will operate as a catharsis. But to understand his final story, first I must tell you who Edward Earl Johnson was. I could mention that he was an eighteen-year-old black kid, from a shockingly poor background, who nevertheless somehow pulled himself all the way through school and into the little world of Leake County, Mississippi, without ever getting so much as a parking ticket on his record. He was the first person I have ever represented who had absolutely no record. I could tell you that he was only eighteen when they first decided that he should be sent to Parchman to be gassed, and that he spent all his adult life in the confines of death row. I could discuss for hours his family and friends—all the wonderful people who gathered around him in those final hours before he died. I could analyze the psychiatric reports, which showed him to have a serious organic brain dysfunction, perhaps the result of his alcoholic father kicking his pregnant mother in the abdomen just before she was full term. Then, of course, as Edward's attorney, I could relate one sham court hearing after another which the American legal process offered in apology for this rank injustice.

But that would be a one-dimensional view of Edward. The more important Edward was the one who responded so incredibly to those last days of his life.

Death row at Parchman, Mississippi, has all the appearances of the death camps with which the postwar world is all too familiar. Who can enter a high-security prison without the claustrophobia of someone drowning? Yet the presence of the unseen death chamber adds an additional morbidity.

After entering through the barbed-wire fencing, and then through the heavy main door, I found fifteen of Edward's family members sitting around in a small room, usually used by guards. As I entered, I did not even notice Edward, since he fit in so normally with all the others.

Immediately before I got to the prison, I had called Jackson, and learned the details of the Fifth Circuit's decision—they had of course denied Edward's appeal, but in their misbegotten effort to hammer in a few extra nails had made a couple of very serious legal errors. Paradoxically, the court's perverse zeal had lent one more chance that Edward's life could be saved in the United States Supreme Court.

The family members were all in good spirits, nobody showing it if they thought that Edward's death might be imminent. The rock upon which they all leaned, though, was Edward himself, sitting there as calm as could be. I sat with him and explained the situation as optimistically as I could, also partly for the benefit of the family, and for myself. He just gave me a hug and smiled.

I had talked to him about his games of chess with Paul Hamann, the producer of the BBC film crew who had been at the prison for two weeks previously. Edward had beaten Paul twelve times straight, so I asked him whether he would like a game.

The family gathered round, certain that someone with various university degrees would have little trouble beating Edward—certainly, filled with misguided beneficence, I had no intention of beating him at such a time, expecting the pressure of the moment to get through to any normal human being. Edward was never just a normal human being. As if we were just playing to pass time one quiet evening, he made me look like a beginner. I admired him all the more.

Two telephone calls to Washington, D.C., and the Supreme Court still had not ruled. Each time I walked to the telephone, I had to pass half a dozen guards in the antechamber of the death row unit. Everybody avoided my eyes, ashamed.

As nine-thirty approached, the "Major" in charge of death row, needing to assert his authority more loudly than necessary, said that the family had to leave. Why, reason could not really explain—but to hide behind rigid procedures depersonalizes, and somehow obscures the absurdity of something so purposeless.

Edward's small nephew began to cry, but Edward took him in his arms and told him to stop such nonsense. The little boy calmed at once. The rest of the family and friends put on brave smiles, and said they would be praying over at the prison chapel, brightly lit a half mile away, but thankfully hidden from our windowless cell block. Perhaps it was best that they would have to go. As the final moves of the legal appeals played out, Edward might find the flow of their tears harder to stem.

A guard told me that there was a telephone call. Edward smiled at me, and I walked briskly back along the cell block, out to the telephone at the front. When I picked up the receiver there was no response. Finally, I could hear Rob's voice in the background as he came back to the phone. Seven to two, he said. Only Brennan and Marshall dissenting, as they do in every death penalty case. Justice Brennan wrote a four-page dissent on one issue we had raised. Small comfort. Somehow it would have been easier if some more of them had understood what this was all about, even in the two hours that they had considered Edward's life.

It was much further back to the cell than it was leaving it. And yet, I arrived there too soon. Edward looked at me and smiled when I said, "They turned us down, seven to two."

"So it's just the governor." I told him all the reasons why the governor ought to grant clemency—no flattery, but simple truth.

—"The governor denied." So expected, yet so harsh. How to move? How to go to tell Edward that the last heartless, shameless, *barbarian* had decreed that he should die? Probably after coffee in the Governor's mansion, with due consideration of the favorable press the next morning. Truly, truly, a sick world.

—"He turned us down." Edward seemed totally unmoved. Only Sandy [Edward's spiritual adviser] suggested that we should pray. She said some things which perhaps some can believe, and from which perhaps Edward drew strength; yet, I find it small comfort to be told that God has a purpose for this senseless, *senseless* barbarism.

In the end, after Sandy told Edward that God loved him—true, I am sure—I told Edward that Sandy and I, and many others, loved him also. He looked straight ahead, and said, "It's strange, but I feel absolutely no fear." So we sat on the bed once more, and Edward agreed with Sandy that there was still time for miracles.

What can I say? The time passed. A handwritten note came around from the next cell and another was delivered by a guard. Willie Reddix wrote that everyone in the unit was praying for him, and just thanked Edward for being such a friend. It was actually only ten minutes before Commissioner Cabana came to say that it was time to go to the isolation cell, just a few short yards closer to the gas chamber.

Why do they make up these names? "Isolation Cell." Hardly designed to make anyone feel more human about such a human tragedy, but then that is doubtless the purpose. It was just a small whitewashed room, two heavy solid steel doors, and a tiny window above a prayer bench and a simple wood cross.

It is so hard to know what to say. Paul Hamann pretended to be interested in who made the wooden cross. "Another inmate," said Cabana. Although Edward still talked about hope, Sandy read some verses from the Bible concerning how God is with us in Heaven as well as on earth.

Indeed, Cabana, who I must suspect abhorred the death process as much as anyone, tried himself to be human. I admired him for his good intentions, but again the words seemed so tactless at the time when nothing could really be appropriate:

"Edward, I have to tell you that I have a tremendous amount of respect for you," he said. "And you'll remember what you promised me? You'll put in a good word for me with the Man Upstairs?"

As each person spoke, and each statement seemed so out of place, I tried myself to think of a way to break the eternal silence which periodically seized us all. Edward looked at me, and I smiled and told him, "It ain't over till it's over."

What a strange ebb and flow between hope and the need to prepare for the seemingly inevitable. As Paul and the two others from the BBC crew prepared to leave, Paul turned away to hide his tears. Edward noticed, however, and told him, "Hey, Paul, keep your chin up." At this incredible display of courage and humanity, the tears welled in the eyes of the other BBC men.

Cabana came in and presented the strangest monologue of all. "Edward," he said, "I'm going to tell you this so you won't be surprised by anything. In a few minutes, two medical personnel will come in, and they will tape two stethoscopes to your chest. They'll also tape two EKG terminals to you. They may have to shave a little hair off to do that. They'll put them on so that they can tell when your heart stops beating. Okay? I just want you to know what they are doing."

Now, it is no reflection on Cabana, who had to try to think of something to say on an impossibly cruel stage. But I wondered then if maybe it wouldn't have been kinder to use the apology used by those whom history already has condemned, who told their Jewish victims that a shower awaited them in the gas chambers.

It was all so unreal. Edward sitting there so calmly, nodding as Cabana spoke, and everyone else just listening as if this was really something quite normal for a civilized world to do. Against reality, I just kept waiting for someone to call it to an end and tell Edward he could come home with me.

Edward turned to Cabana, and I am sure his words reminded some there of Jesus Christ: "Mr. Cabana, I just want to thank you for everything you've done for me." My mind was far from such analogies to the Bible, as I was simply astounded that a human being could really be so kind.

Edward then thanked Paul, and joked about beating him at chess. He hugged the other two BBC men, and said goodbye. As they left, he turned to Sandy, and said he had something he wanted to say to her.

"You've done a lot for me these days, but I want you to remember that you've got a lot more to do out there," he said, gesturing to where the other forty-five men waited on death row. "Don't ever give up. You've got to remember that. Don't ever give up. And tell my family not to take it too hard, okay?"

I sat there afraid of what Edward might say to me. We had tried, goodness knows we had tried. We ought, in a fair world, to have won it for him, and stopped all this hours before. But there is always something else you can do, and if I had just taken on his case earlier, if . . .

But he turned to me, and thanked me. He said we'd done everything we could have. Then he smiled, and said, "It ain't over till it's over." I managed to quell the tears before Edward could see them coming, that anyone could want to kill a man like this.

The room was hot. I used a legal pad to fan the air a little, as Edward seemed ashamed that he was sweating. It was oppressive, and much quieter, now that the BBC people were gone. I was thankful when Sandy suggested we sing something, pointing to a verse in the Bible. She led us, but neither Edward nor I knew it. But it was strengthening to hear voices, strong and calm, even if out of tune.

We sat together again for a while, and I held an arm tightly around Edward's shoulder, while Sandy gripped his hand. Edward looked straight ahead and said, "I suppose everyone wonders what a man thinks about when he is about to die." It was a question thrown out, without an answer. And then, "Well, it ain't over till it's over."

The silence descended again. I suggested another song, and Sandy asked Edward what he would like. Edward thought, for what seemed a long, long time. I remember that I had the sense that he was being put on the spot—it is so hard to choose a favorite something at the best of times, and yet to choose a song at a time like this—"Amazing Grace" suddenly came into my mind, and at the same second, Edward suggested that. I was grateful that we had a song we all knew, so that we could sing loud and long. Sandy even had the words, on a little card she had been given by another prisoner.

Somehow the words she had did not have the part about saving "a poor wretch like me." I remember feeling glad since I just did not want the word "wretch" spoken in a context in which it could be associated with Edward. So inappropriate to describe him.

Then the "medical technicians" came in, and told Edward to lift up his shirt. I'm glad Edward did not look at me at that moment. I was so angry. How could those sworn to save lives assist in this gruesome ritual? What had happened to the Hippocratic Oath?

They took heavy gray binding tape which one might use to wrap a parcel, and wrapped it twice tightly around Edward's chest. He even helped them, politely holding it for them. One of those faceless men—though his face will remain with me always—then shaved a little hair next to each of Edward's shoulders, and attached the EKG contacts.

I was grateful that Sandy had the thoughtfulness to tell Edward to put his blue shirt back on, restoring his dignity after this horrible scene. Edward just smiled, saying they had done it rather tightly, and maybe they wanted to suffocate him already.

Almost immediately, Cabana came back in, and said, "It's time."

Edward reached over and hugged Sandy. Then, childlike, he kissed her on the cheek and said goodbye.

He turned to me. I said no, I would come with him. So we put an arm around each other's shoulders and walked in there.

I was glad to be there with him. There seemed to be a dozen gray-faced guards in the small room which surrounded the gas chamber. I—and I am sure, Edward—had never before seen the gas chamber. I would that I will never see it again. No description of the roughly welded oval, something like a diver's bell with four windows for the spectators, can capture the gray evil of that sight.

I put my arms around Edward, and we hugged each other. He whispered in my ear. At first, I did not hear, and asked him to repeat it. He said, "Do you know something that I don't know?" He looked at me hopefully. For a moment I did not understand. Then it hit me—somehow, he thought I still knew something that would put a stop to all this.

It is impossible for anyone to know what to say, me least of all. I mumble something, sincere but innocuous, about him knowing more about so many things than I would ever know. I hugged him once more and said goodbye. As they strapped him into that *disgusting* chair, he looked at me. I smiled and signed thumbs up. He smiled back at me.

Then the guards told me I had to leave.

The door led outside. I felt an overwhelming nausea. But the air was so fresh and cool, and the stars so full of life. A guard motioned for me to go into the witness room.

I just felt an urge not to follow the procedure that was making it so damned easy for them. So I walked over to where Sandy was standing —and she suddenly burst into tears, letting emotions from the hours of brave encouragement flood out. As we leaned against a van, its engine still hot from bringing some person who apparently wanted to be here, she sobbed that she could not go in. I told her that of course she should not—what purpose would it serve?

Myself, I wavered. I similarly felt that there was nowhere on earth I would rather be less than in that witness room—"Observation Room," as they called it. I knew that I should be there. There was a phone. Once before an execution had been stopped because they botched it, and the lawyer was there. Who knows, in an insanely unreal world, what might happen? So I went.

Fortunately, I had a chair next to the red and black telephone, high at the back where I could not really see anything. The air conditioner was on, and a large black curtain (black, to be appropriate at least) over the windows into the chamber. I took off my glasses and held my head in my hands, unable to believe that I was really in the witness room to Edward's execution. How could this be?

Rather than miss any sound someone turned off the noisy air conditioner on the order of some official. He seemed to be the master of ceremonies for this perverse occasion, and took his job seriously, explaining the minutiae of the minutes to come. I could not listen, though others seemed rapt in attention.

There were five media people there. Three guards from the prison. The attorney for the prison, who I had met at a party in the house of a friend in Indianola, Mississippi, a year before. And others I did not know. Nobody cared to look in my direction. When they caught my eye, they turned away—ashamed, I liked to believe. Although the only ones who truly looked uncomfortable were the guards, who at least knew Edward in passing his cell.

One media person, whose name shall not be mentioned, did acknowledge my presence. He wanted an interview. Was there no human decency? Could a person be so ignorant of human emotion?

Then, boisterously to his fellow journalists, the man began to ask a series of phenomenally absurd questions as to the details of this media event. The curtain was drawn, and this semi-human was interested in the color of Edward's shoes, the cloth of his trousers . . . it was the depths of depravity.

I was drawn between a desperate need to look at Edward in case I could reassure him, and a terrible desire not to look, and not to rob him of his dignity at this most undignified moment. In the end, when he spoke, I could not but look. He said, "I guess they won't call. I guess they won't call." Only now, only now, did the reality of this horrid nightmare come to him, and I could not help him. He was strapped so that he could not see those who had chosen to watch him die.

I never looked again. I did not look at my watch. After five hours of not wanting to see time go by, I wanted every second to go faster. I could not understand, they just kept him sitting there for *eight* minutes, doing nothing. At one point, Edward said, "Please, let's get it over with." But the timetable could not be changed simply to comply with the elements of human consideration.

The telephone rang. Before a fleeting hope could cross my mind, the guard said that was the signal for it to begin. I wondered later if the sound registered with Edward through the far-from soundproof walls, and if for a second the cruel thought came to him that this was the call that was never to come. Just another sadistic coincidence in the procedures which legitimized Edward's death.

Those next seventeen minutes would be those upon which the media would dwell. The only questions they would ask would be what death was actually like. From the sound of gasping for breath, and the excited chatter of the ghouls in that ghastly room, it could not have been easy, even discounting the hours and weeks of psychological torture leading up to it. But I was far away. We can leave it to others to downplay the terror of the death of a man they will never know, and ignore the courage of a friend who goes silently to a better place.

"The prisoner is officially dead." Edward could not even die without the permission of the official procedures. I wanted to be sick.

I was in front of everyone as the door opened. The reporter tapped my shoulder for an interview, but I was too sad even to tell him of his depravity. There was an eager discussion among those who never knew Edward, but I walked as fast as I could from one locked gate to another, and waited until the lock clicked back on each. And at last I was out, heading to my car, those terrible people and that terrible place behind me.

A group of guards were laughing around their vehicle as I left to drive to the chapel. I recognized some family members as I drove up. As I got out and walked toward them, the reality set in, for them and for me. Edward's cousin screamed, his sisters started sobbing uncontrollably. And at last I could weep too. For a long, long time. No words were spoken, save for exclamations about good Edward.

A long time later everyone was beginning to decide what to do. The sadness and anger was once again building up in me, and I asked Edward's uncle if I should make a statement in behalf of the family to keep the press, already snapping at the fence, from further indecencies. He said he thought it would be a good idea. I knew it would be a catharsis for me, and I doubted I would regret next morning anything I might say.

So I drove to the finale of this strange, revolting history. The press was gathered in an auditorium near the prison exit, cameras trained upon the spot where Cabana would soon make the next official statement regarding "the prisoner," my friend. The five media witnesses were lined in their seats, smugly anticipating their opportunity to describe, in fine objectivity, their wonderful journalistic experience. It was not easy, it seemed, to separate this from a press conference after a football game.

Cabana took no pleasure from a brief official announcement. However, then the journalist from the witness room went into an eternal discourse on how easy it all seemed, and how he had noted in intimate detail the remains of Edward's last supper of shrimp, such a fine treat for such a poor black boy. Oh, how the blood boils.

There is neither the time nor the eloquence when one most needs it.

I could tell the hundred and fifty reporters just a tiny part of what I wanted the world so much to hear. How much better a person Edward was than me, and, I suspect, than most of them. How absurd taking his life was. How truly incredible and sickening it was that *anyone* would want to watch Edward die and then describe it by emphasis on a shrimp dinner.

And their question: "How does his family feel about it?" What is the point of talking?

I was grateful for the BBC crew who all cried outside. I was grateful for Tom Brennan, from the Jackson newspaper, who said he did not want to talk about it at all. I was grateful for the tears that periodically overwhelmed me, and forced me to stop the car. But, as I drove one hundred thirty miles back to Jackson in the early morning, how, oh how, could they have done this to Edward?

THE DEAN

"Stone walls do not a prison make
Nor iron bars a cage.
Minds innocent and quiet take
That for an hermitage."

—Richard Lovelace, 1618–1657

The room is a muted beige pink, light and airy. Located at the far end is a plate-glass picture window, curtained by a long venetian blind. In neat ranks, facing the aluminum slats, two rows of white high-backed chairs wait. At their feet, polished vinyl tiles gleam pristine clean. The impression is of a private screening room—the property, perhaps, of a retentive millionaire.

The blinds slowly rise. It is not a movie screen that meets the viewer's eyes but a squat oak seat. A chair in which over 200 men have already been killed, short-circuited into oblivion, since it was built in 1924.

Florida's electric chair.

It killed William Jasper Darden at 7:12 a.m. EST, Tuesday, March 15th, 1988, at Florida State Prison, Starke. Beware the Ides of March.

Execution is not an unusual occurrence in Florida. It is a fact of life in the South; so is the story of Willie Darden, a black man who paid the price for taking a white life, a life that is four times more likely to be avenged by the death penalty than its black counterpart (see Tanya Coke interview).

Diversion of electricity from the microwave ovens of Florida's homes and the lights of Disney World to destroy any human being is

*wicked enough, but it is particularly outrageous when there is evidence
that the man was innocent. Such questions were raised about Darden.*

*"If ever a man received an unfair trial, Darden did" was the opin-
ion of Supreme Court Justice Harry Blackmun of Darden's trial.*

*Willie Darden, fifty-four, had been on death row for fourteen years,
since 1974, longer than any other inmate in Florida, save one. He
always maintained his innocence. His numerous close calls with death
(he had seven death warrants signed against him) earned Willie the
title "Dean of Death Row" before he was finally put to death on his
seventh warrant.*

*The irony, injustice, and plain bloody-mindedness of the system is
that he would have been a free man today if he had agreed to cop a
plea for a long prison term. Willie would not do that. He maintained
his innocence to the very end. Some of his final words, addressed
directly to the public, were via ABC News:*

"The only thing I can say to the outside world is that Willie Darden
is innocent. I will take that innocence to the grave. I will take my
principles to the grave. I will take my dignity to the grave. I will stand
tall and I will walk with my head high. I have no guilty conscience."

This is Willie Darden's story.

*It was raining cats and dogs all afternoon on September 8, 1973, in
Lakeland, Florida. Willie Darden, driving home on a weekend furlough from prison, was having a little car trouble. In fact, he had a lot
of car trouble. Trouble with the muffler, trouble with the battery, trouble with the ignition. Finally, his green Chevy ground to a halt in front
of the house of Christine Bass. Willie got out, walked up the rain-
soaked path to the single-story frame house, rang the bell, and asked if
she would phone the garage for him. Ms. Bass remembers Willie very
well; not many black men ring white doorbells in Polk County, Florida.*

*Meanwhile, in Lakeland, a small town a few miles away, Carl and
Helen Turman, owners of a second-hand furniture store, were being
robbed. The attacker shot Carl between the eyes, killing him instantly.
Part-time employee Philip Arnold was shot in the mouth, neck, and
hip, but he survived. The assailant was described as a black man
driving a green Chevy.*

*Willie Darden's problems were not over even after he got the car
started. On the drive home he skidded into a telephone pole, only three
miles from the Turmans' place of business. This time the car, not to
mention Willie, was in serious trouble. He went to get help, but when
he returned to the scene of the accident, with a tow truck, the car was
gone. He became somewhat alarmed when he learned that no less than*

twenty deputy sheriffs had taken the vehicle. He called the Highway Patrol, and was told that they would investigate. Later that evening, at his home, Willie Darden was arrested as a suspect in the murder of Carl Turman.

The case against him was, at best, circumstantial. There were questionable eyewitness identifications and a gun, found near his wrecked car, that could not conclusively be tied to the crime.

The surviving victim, Philip Arnold, has no doubt to this day that Willie Darden was the murderer, although he made his original identification from a police photograph of Darden while lying in a hospital bed. The photo had Darden's name stamped across it, while the other photos shown to him by the police were nameless faces. Darden's name, by that time, had been plastered all over the newspapers as the suspect.

The other eyewitness was the victim's wife, Helen Turman, who, at an informal gathering, picked out Darden as the killer. Darden was the only black man in the room. A key actor in the story, who was never called at the trial, Reverend Samuel Sparks (the Turmans' minister), stated to an ABC television reporter that Mrs. Turman had told him, "All blacks look alike to me, but the lawyers say he did it and that's good enough for me."

An eyewitness to Darden's car accident had told the police that Darden had thrown something from the car. Darden maintains the object was a beer can; the police claimed that it was the murder weapon. At the scene of the accident, deputy sheriffs waded around in a ditch for hours and found nothing. Seventeen hours later, an off-duty officer returned to the scene, pulled off his boots, paddled about in six inches of muddy, dirty water, and in less than ten minutes, came up with a gun.

Nowhere in the trial could the gun be traced to Willie Darden; there were no fingerprints and the ballistic tests, while confirming similarities, failed to prove it was the murder weapon.

At his trial, Darden sat for five days in a packed courthouse, his the only black face in the room, while the prosecutor called him an "animal that should be on a leash" and said that he wished Darden was sitting there with his face blown off.

Darden's witnesses were never called, although Christine Bass drove every day to the courthouse. She was ready to testify that Darden's presence in her front yard meant he could not have been at the scene of the crime. As with so many defendants on public aid, his court-appointed lawyer failed him at every turn, and once during the trial even referred to his client as a "nigger."

The legal battle and appeals continued for fourteen years. Willie

Darden remained on death row. The only time he left was to go on the unspeakable horror of death watch, the trip to a cell located a few feet from the chamber where the electric chair sits and is tested within earshot—to make sure that it is still working.

He made this journey seven times; the last one was a one-way trip.

Toward the end of his life, Darden's lawyers came up with new evidence. Reverend Sparks, who had been called in to comfort Mrs. Turman immediately after the murder, is certain he received the call telling him of the murder at 5:15 p.m. Christine Bass could testify that at that time Willie was outside her house. The reason Reverend Sparks and Christine Bass had not spoken up before was that neither knew what the other knew. Both pieces had to be fit together to be useful to the defense. Unless these two witnesses are mistaken or are perjuring themselves, their evidence gives Willie Darden a watertight alibi.

We spoke to a lawyer, Jimmy Lohman, who took the affidavits from Reverend Sparks and Ms. Bass in February 1988.

Jimmy Lohman: Yes, I went down to meet Ms. Bass and Reverend Sparks and to see what their stories were. I took the affidavits that went before the U.S. Supreme Court.

You can't find a more sincere and credible man than Reverend Sparks. If his memory is correct, there is just no way Willie Darden did it. I mean, basically I can't say whether Willie did or didn't, but the Reverend Sparks is absolutely sure of what he is talking about. He never got any good publicity out of this. He is a fundamentalist preacher whose congregation is for the death penalty. He had several telephone threats. One caller told him, "You'd better keep quiet about that nigger or someone is going to find *your* nigger-loving body among the orange groves." I mean, Lakeland is a very pro-death penalty community. Sam Sparks is not getting anything out of this. People have asked me if he said this just for the publicity. No, he didn't want publicity off this. He did it because he felt an innocent man was going to be executed.

There is no doubt in my mind that Christine Bass is completely accurate, because she has had the same story since the day Willie Darden was arrested. It's not her memory that we are talking about. She said the same thing fourteen years ago that she's saying right now.

What time did the police say the shooting took place?

They never really fixed the time of the shooting. They jacked around with that. At the very beginning, they put it at 5:30 p.m. Then Willie filed a notice saying he had an alibi. You have to notify the state that you are going to use an alibi as a defense. When Christine Bass could place Willie at five-thirty, the state dropped five-thirty as the time of the crime, and they moved it to later. The bizarre thing is that the only thing we have seen is one police report from an officer who says he got called at 6:31 p.m. and showed up at the scene at 6:34 p.m. But that is a meaningless piece of paper because by the time the guy got there, there were already police cars all over the place and the body was gone, so there is no telling when the murder actually happened. If it happened at 5:30 p.m., Willie didn't do it.

It seems clear that whether Willie Darden committed the crime or not, reasonable doubt exists.

I can't imagine, just can't imagine Willie Darden being executed. Physically, I mean. He is so vital, strong, and vibrant that the notion of him being subjugated in that manner is inconceivable to me. I absolutely can't imagine it. I cannot imagine that proud man being escorted down there. In a way it's a spiritual thing, too; I can't spiritually conceive that it could happen to him.

We made an appointment to see Willie Darden at his death row residence at the Florida State Prison, Starke.

It's a winding forty-mile drive from the university town of Gainesville to Florida's death row.

STATE PRISON—great iron letters, set in an arch on concrete posts announce the presence of Starke, home of the electric chair. The scene is surprisingly peaceful; pastoral even, with cows grazing in meadows, creeks running through wooded areas, and trees shading neat wooden houses that line the perfectly straight roadway. Every fifty or sixty yards small palm trees maybe nine or ten feet high squat like silent sentinels.

But Starke's pale green towers, each manned with machine guns, soon bring one back to reality as they loom over the prison.

Visitors are announced by using a telephone set in one of the towers; just dial 142. To the right of the tower inmates can be seen hanging out of the upper windows of one of the many cell blocks, yelling and cat-calling to each other. Thirty seconds later a disembodied speaker phone voice gives instructions to proceed toward the gate. The gate stands before a moat of polished stainless-steel, concertina barbed wire. It runs for 200 yards to the left and to the right. The door sign reads: DO NOT TOUCH. It slides open. Beyond the moat a series of gates open and close behind us. We enter a world of untouchable gates that seem to operate on the "airlock" principle. Each time you go into a holding area, the door in front and behind you closes.

In the main reception area hands are stamped, nightclub style, metal detectors are satisfied (jackets with zippers and even shoes with metal tips have to be removed), identities are checked, and matches are confiscated. We are escorted through the last of the lock devices into the main lobby. It has all the appearance of a sterile, highly polished, sanitized hospital, were it not for the bars painted incongruously in "Miami Vice" hues of pink and beige. Footsteps ring down the polished hallways, accentuated by the total absence of any soft material. A man, handcuffed, sits in a tiny holding cell, all alone in the vast hall, giving a Kafkaesque feel to the whole thing.

    Through another corridor, then to the interview room: a small, glassed-in closet with three chairs and a desk. We recognize Willie Darden through the pane chatting with guards as they unshackle his manacled hands from a chain belt, handcuff him, and open the door. The room seems even smaller as he enters.

    Although not a large man, Willie Darden is muscular and stocky, fifty-four years old, stands about 5 feet 10 inches, and weighs around 220 pounds. He wears a peach T-shirt and a filigree cross on a heavy gold chain around his neck. His hair is receding, and there is a small tuft of hair under his bottom lip which shows signs of gray. His skin is smooth, unwrinkled, and ebony black. His eyes are piercing, intelligent, and direct.

    We shake hands as well as one can with a man in handcuffs. As if he was entertaining guests in his home, which we soon realize he is, he sits down opposite us, motions us to do the same, and smiles. For almost two hours we become acquainted with Willie Darden, a man of great inner strength. He is eloquent, fiery, with a good sense of humor. Nevertheless, he is a man fighting for his life. He gestures with cat-like grace, holding an unlit cigar in immobilized hands, wearing the shiny steel cuffs as if they were jewelry.

Florida State Prison at Starke
Thursday, February 11, 1988, 10:30 a.m.

Willie Jasper Darden, Jr.

    I was born on a farm in North Carolina, and went to high school in Green County.

How old are you now?

Fifty-four.

What kind of home life did you have?

I had a beautiful home life as far as love and compassion. Things that could not be substantiated materially. A beautiful grandmother, a beautiful grandfather, I loved them both very dearly. Mother died when I was aged two, and my father died in '86 while I was on the death watch. I was on death watch in October '86 and he died on the same day I got the stay, which was a Monday night, the 21st.

Did he know you had the stay?

Yes, he knew I had the stay. I think that's what killed him. It was the excitement. The excitement was too much for him. He died in the chair, watching the TV, and he had a heart attack.

How long have you been on death row and how many stays have you had?

Fourteen years. I have been in prison since '68 and on death row since January 1974. Of course, death row started for me September 8, 1973, which was the day of my arrest. I have had six death warrants filed against me.

Do you think the kind of media attention you are getting is helping the case?

Well, it couldn't hurt. These people are trying to kill me and there's no reason for that. There's no justification for what they have tried to do to me over the years.

You must be angry.

Yes, I am angry and frustrated. I am frustrated with the system, a system that has allowed this to happen to me. There are so many things that were not done that should have been done and there were so many things that were done that shouldn't have been done.

How do you cope with the waiting?

You know, I don't think I can answer that question because I don't know myself. You know what gives me strength? I am a human being and I don't like what they have done to me, therefore, I will fight to the very end.

Have you accepted the fact that you might go to the electric chair?

There is no one in the world who knows this possibility better than I because I came within seven hours of facin' death in '85. I have been on death watch six times.

What exactly does that mean?

They normally come to your cell and get you out. They bring you into the same office like you see over there (*he points to the colonel's office adjacent to the interview room*) and they tell you that the governor has signed a death warrant on you. At this point you don't go back to death row. You go to a different location, the back of the building that they call "Q" Wing. This is where people go when they have a death warrant signed against them. You are only about twenty-five feet away from the electric chair. Only a door separatin' you and the room they murder you in, you know.

How long before your date does this happen?

Well, it depends on what date they set the warrant for. Whether they give you thirty days, or they may sign the warrant today and they say the execution is scheduled, for, say, March 8, but the warrant don't run out until perhaps March 15. That gives them the extra time in case of an appeal, you see. This is what happens every time.

They always leave that little space in between the scheduled execution and the expiration of the warrant, so if you get a stay they can appeal it, hoping that it will be lifted so they can proceed with the execution. Believe me, they have all areas planned out so where they will have the possibility. They always want to keep the possibility open.

What would you say to Governor Robert Martinez, man to man, if you were sitting across the table from him?

I would have nothing to say to him. I have nothing against him really, personally, I mean he's just like Governor Bob Graham before him, you know. They use capital punishment as a political football. He is gonna kill anybody he can kill, and killing Willie Darden will certainly give him a good reputation. But I understand the process the governor is usin' in order to try to kill me. I understand my enemies a lot better than my enemies understand me. I understand them well.

Over the years have you made friends on the row?

Believe me, guys here on death row are closer than most families on the outside. We live and breathe each other. You see, death row is a very unique environment. It has instilled in me a deep consciousness of death that I could not have obtained from any other place on earth to such a large degree. Twenty-four hours a day I am looking at death in its face. I know that any day could possibly be my last. What makes me angry and frustrated is that I ask myself, "Why am I here? What am I doing on death row? For what reason is the system trying to kill me?"

Take the scenario that Willie Darden's sentence is commuted and he's out. What goals do you have? Could you contribute something to society?

Contribute! Y'all better believe that. *(Laughs)* You know I got a letter from a friend of mine the other day, who is a writer for *The Washington Post,* and he said, "Willie, when you get out—and you will get out because we ain't gonna stop fightin'; you have got peoples all around the world who know you are innocent." He said, "I want you to do me one favor. My students," he teaches at a college. "They have asked me to ask you to speak to them." He said, "I had other people at other universities want you to speak to them, because no one can tell them more about racism, injustice, and capital punishment than you. You are a unique person." Of course, I'm not—but I am a straightforward honest person and I speak from my heart. I am not sayin' I'm a saint by a long shot. I've done my wrong, but that's in the past.

The state of Florida says it needs the death penalty to protect itself.

I would say capital punishment is a tool that no system in the world should be allowed to use. We are human beings and we are not infallible. If there is even the slightest possibility that there could be an innocent person executed—and I am a living proof that that can happen—that alone should be enough to outlaw capital punishment forever because why would any system teach us, you, me, that killing is wrong by killing people who have killed? The system puts itself in a position where it is no better and perhaps, in some instances, much worse than the person it is trying to destroy. We are supposed to be rational, thinking human beings; anyone who advocates capital punishment cannot be rational.

Do you do any writing?

That's all I do. I got about twelve hundred letters that need to be out right now. That's all I do seven days a week, sometimes from five o'clock in the morning until eleven o'clock at night. I don't even have time to write poetry any more.

So you write poetry, too?

Yeah. Somebody gave me the title of "Poet of Death Row." I don't think I deserve that title.

We heard you have been called the Dean of Death Row?

I don't deserve that title, either. I am just a person fighting against a wrong that has been done to him, and I just hope that in my fight, with the strength that I show, that some of it will rub off on my fellow inmates and give them a reason to maintain the same kind of strength, the same kind of dignity that I have. So you see, my fight is not my fight alone. My fight is every human being's fight who has a decent conscience. It's your fight, everybody's fight, throughout the world, because what I am fighting against is injustice.

Any decent, thinking person will know and will realize that racism plays a big part in who gets the death sentence. It was these ills that stopped me from receiving justice right from the beginning. I would not be here, I would not have even gone to trial, because all they had to do was investigate. They refused to do so. America is not everything people overseas think it should be. It's a good country. I love it, but I don't like its ways.

Do you think you will get a new trial?

I don't know, I have no faith, no belief, no confidence in the justice system in America. All I have going for myself is hope. We got a stay and I don't know what is going to happen, whether the court is going to end up granting our petition.

Could you tell us a little about the trial?

Even the prosecutor himself during the course of the trial proved nothing to the jury, and I am gonna show you that racism is to a large degree responsible for my being here. Racism is so thick down there that you can almost cut it with a knife, you can feel it. I was sitting in the courtroom for five days, the jury was all white, the prosecutor was white, my attorney was white, everybody was white including the officers in the courtroom, and the courtroom was full.

The *only* black face in the courtroom was mine.

I knew when I walked into that courtroom that first day that it don't make no difference how much evidence that I had that I was gonna be found guilty. Because you see the hatred on those people's faces and in their eyes.

Now this was how it was. As the jury was selected and the prosecutor was making the opening statements, he told the jury, "In a minute we are going to show that the victim in this case, Mr. Carl Turman, is a white man." Now you know he is talkin' to twelve white people. Then he said, "Now the record is also going to show that the defendant is a black man." He went further than that when he asked them, "Can you look at me and tell me if you can look at Willie Darden and try him as if he was a white man?" This was in the record.

Then throughout the trial he would continually call me all kind of animalistic names, saying that I should have been the one that got my head blown off and all of that, and that I should be sitting there with no head. I am gonna tell you the kind of atmosphere that he made was a much more powerful atmosphere, as far as racism is concerned, than it already was. When he would get up to question a witness the jury was almost at the end of their chairs, looking at him, watching him, hanging on every word that he said and every word the witness said, but when my attorney, who by the way was more an attorney for the state than for me, was questioning a witness, they sat back in their chairs, they would look at the ceiling, they would look all over the place and pay no attention whatsoever. It was like saying, I don't care what you have to say. Then I would catch them lookin' at me and when I would catch their eye, they would look away. Not one person on the jury looked me in the face.

*Obviously you have been strong enough to overcome what must be a
very difficult way of life in terms of the waiting. Have the other inmates
here fared as well?*

I have had friends here on death row who have come here with
perfectly solid minds. Capable of creative thinking, and logical thinking, and I have watched those same men over the years begin to go
downhill, downhill. Their minds have become entangled, next thing I
know they are talkin' this unknown talk, crazy talk, they are walkin'
around like zombies. I have seen this happen to quite a few. And the
sad thing is that there is nothin' that I can do about it. I talk to them
but. . . . I try to tell each inmate you never let your situation and your
condition in life cause you to become less of a person than you were.

*How do you think being on death row has affected your family and
friends?*

It has been devastating. That is another reason why I must keep
strong because it is not only for myself, it is for all of them. When I
am on death watch, I have to go through all kinds of changes. If I get
on the phone they just start listening to my voice and they start cryin',
so I have to give them comfort, you know. When you're not on death
watch you can have visitors once a week, but you know my family
lives quite a few miles away from here so they can't get to visit much,
unfortunately. We are not rich. On death watch they can visit a total of
twelve hours per week.

Your life is now in the hands of the U.S. Supreme Court?

Right. And we have to find out whether or not they want to hear our
petition because they could reject it. Because this stay, right here, does
not mean one doggone thing really, except that I am still alive. It
doesn't say the Court is going to entertain my petition, it doesn't say
that I am going to get a new trial, it doesn't say I'm going to get
justice.

You see, right now, I don't know what direction my life is gonna
take, it can change overnight. But you see I don't worry about that. I
don't worry about the death warrants, I don't worry about being on the
death watch, I don't worry about the fact that I might be executed. I
will worry about death when I get to it. In the meantime I am going to
continue to live my life to the fullest of its capacity.

Are you a religious man?

No. I am a Christian.

*The Reverend Joe Ingle, director of the Southern Coalition on Jails
and Prisons, was with Willie Jasper Darden in the final hours before
the state of Florida carried out the execution, on March 15, 1988. This*

is his account (originally reported in the Spring 1988 edition of the Southern Coalition on Jails and Prisons Report, *the quarterly newsletter of the SCJP).*

Joe Ingle: As the evening of March 14 unwound at the Florida State Prison, we heard from court after court that Willie's appeals had been denied, yet we all maintained hope until the U.S. Supreme Court ruled, shortly after midnight, that the execution would proceed. Willie had seven brief hours to live.

I gave Willie two Jamaican cigars and we smoked, talked, reminisced, and went through his voluminous correspondence. The early morning light began to peep through the darkness. Soon they would come to prepare him for killing.

At 5:30 in the morning I knelt outside his cell and we shared a final prayer. The guard arrived with a gray briefcase. We both knew inside the unobtrusive briefcase were the tools to shear his head and leg so the electricity could pass unimpeded through his body. I told him I would see him later. And I left him to be barbered for killing.

Willie had composed a statement for the press and his friends, which I read to them in a cow pasture outside the prison. I then joined the witnesses and media in the administration building. We were led to a large room which served as a cafeteria. It was approximately 6:00 a.m. We were treated to breakfast by the state of Florida.

The breakfast ritual struck me as the ultimate in insanity and I felt I was already embedded deep in lunacy itself with the macabre events surrounding the state killing of a human being. The media representatives and official witnesses, about thirty people, went through the breakfast line ordering their meals. I was without appetite. My exhaustion, the adrenaline rushing through me from drinking Willie's strong instant coffee, and my own anger left me a silent spectator, lingering on the fringes of this bizarre morning ritual as the state kindly provides for those gathered to do their duty.

I gazed about, benumbed, seeking to comprehend the events which encased me, and I noticed the room was dominated by two huge flags, hung next to each other, about fourteen feet up the high-ceilinged room. The flags were of the United States of America and the state of Florida. They were, in all their glory, a reminder that they represented governments embarked in the process of exterminating their citizens. The Florida flag, white background with red, crisscrossed bars, held the state seal encircled in the middle. Beneath the seal the state motto proclaimed: "In God We Trust."

At 6:45 a.m. we filed out of the room, down the hall corridor, and outside to where two white prison vans awaited to transport us to Q Wing—home of the death chamber.

Inside the witness room two rows of white, straight-backed chairs faced the electric chair. They were quickly and quietly filled. I leaned against the back wall in the rear of the room, standing in clear view of the electric chair. The room was crowded, all seats taken, and I was shouldered to the far end of the wall as more people joined me in standing. Finally the outside door was shut and we waited.

At 7:00 a.m. the door swung open in the rear of the death chamber and Willie Darden stepped across the threshold into the vortex of the killing machinery. He was manacled at his ankles, his hands cuffed to a chain around his waist, he moved slowly with erect posture and head proudly held high. He was led to the chair, unchained, and freed from steel bonds. He was guided into the electric chair by the firm hands of the death squad members. They began the process of cinching the leather straps around his waist, legs, and arms. They parted the right trouser leg to apply the electrode to conduct the deadly current.

As the fastening and strapping process ensued, Willie looked for me. Finding me in the corner, he nodded and gave a smile. His countenance then surveyed the official witnesses. Slowly gazing at each one individually, he looked directly into their eyes. The chief of the killing team asked Willie if he would like to make a final statement. Willie replied, "Yes."

In a slow, clear, firm voice Willie spoke from his heart and without any notes. *"I tell you I am not guilty of the charge for which I am about to be executed. I bear no guilt or ill will for any of you. I am at peace with myself, with the world, with each of you. I say to my friends and supporters around the world: I love each and every one of you. Your love and support has been a great comfort to me in my struggle for justice and freedom."*

Willie looked at me, holding me fast with his gaze. I had removed my Committee of Southern Churchmen symbol I wear around my neck. I held the symbol—a Cross over the world with equal marks within the circle of the world meaning all are equal in the world under the cross—in my clenched fist before my face. Willie and I looked into each other's eyes, the gold symbol uniting us in life and unto death.

The guards tilted Willie's shaved head back against the chair at an uncomfortable angle. With his head held back, a chin strap was fastened around his jaw; Willie winced as it was tightened. Still maintaining eye contact with me, he then did a most extraordinary thing—he winked his left eye at me, lifted his left thumb upward, as if to assure me he was all right. Then, as they dropped the black mask over his face, he waved goodbye with his left hand, even though his arm was strapped down to the infernal device. I almost lost control of myself.

After his face was covered, I returned the cross to my neck and dropped my head in prayer without ceasing. Repeatedly I prayed for strength for Willie, for acceptance of his soul, and for God to grant me some way not to lose my own soul in the next few minutes. Finally, I looked up again.

The scene which greeted me was eerily calm. Willie was strapped in the chair, two medical personnel opening his shirt to place stethoscopes on his chest to check for a heartbeat. They each leaned over Willie's body, then rose and nodded.

Willie Darden's official killing was intoned over the microphone to us all: "The sentence of the Court against Willie Darden has been carried out. He was pronounced dead at 7:12 a.m."

The state of Florida signed a seven-day death warrant on March 8, 1988.

Willie Jasper Darden was executed at Florida State Penitentiary, Starke, on the morning of Tuesday, March 15, 1988 (by hideous coincidence, Willie had given us this very date as a hypothetical execution date in the above interview).

God rest his soul.

God help us all.

TRIAL BY JURY

"I'll be the judge and I'll be the jury," said cunning
old fury,
I'll try the whole cause and condemn you to
death."

—Lewis Carroll, *Alice in Wonderland*

Professor William S. Geimer was an "Army brat." Born in Chatta-
nooga, Tennessee, he attended grade school in Japan and high school
in Germany. Naturally an Army career followed, during which he went
to law school.

The ex-soldier still has a military bearing. Ramrod straight back,
thick black hair and mustache, his handsome, aquiline features are
softened by bright, friendly eyes.

In his book-lined office at Washington and Lee University he talked
about the effect of the death penalty on jurors, a subject on which he
had made an in-depth study with Jonathan Amsterdam, son of the anti-
death penalty leader Anthony Amsterdam. Their paper is entitled "Why
Jurors Vote Life or Death: Operative Factors in Ten Florida Death
Penalty Cases."

It's the professor's opinion that the theory of "twelve just men"
being the final arbiters of impartiality is a very long way from the
truth.

Lexington, Virginia
Monday, February 22, 1988, 8:30 p.m.

Professor William S. Geimer

Can you tell us what qualifies a juror to sit on a capital case?

It goes like this. There was a basic case in 1968, *Witherspoon v. Illinois,* that discussed the selection of jurors. That case said that you may not exclude someone from sitting on a jury, where death may be a penalty, just because the person has conscientiously held scruples against the imposition of the death penalty, religious or moral, so long as they are willing to *consider any penalty* prescribed by law, including the death penalty. I think I could qualify under *Witherspoon.* Who knows when the first day will come up when I find *the* case that I change my mind and say, "Okay, well this is it."

The selection of jurors is done by asking *"Witherspoon"* questions. That's one of the reasons the death penalty costs more than not having the death penalty, because you have to bring in tons more jurors and go through this extended examination. In addition to all the other things you ask prospective jurors to try to get the right twelve to try a case, now you've got to go through this whole selection to see whether they are *Witherspoon* qualified. The way that works is that in any case, including death cases, the prosecution and the defense have a certain number of peremptory challenges. They may excuse a limited number of jurors without having to explain why. There are usually more peremptory challenges allowed in a capital case, but it's still a finite number. However, any number of jurors may be excused for "cause," if the judge agrees that there is good cause that they should not sit on a jury, like when the juror expresses reservations about the death penalty. The defense counsel will try to get the potential juror to qualify under *Witherspoon,* and the prosecution will try to get the person to indicate that he or she would never, under any circumstance, vote for the death penalty. If the juror is firmly opposed to the death penalty, the prosecution challenges for cause, and the judge either allows it or doesn't. That forms the basis of an appeal, if the person is convicted and sentenced to death. There is a whole body of law about *Witherspoon* qualifications.

But in the last five years the Supreme Court came up with a decision that said, basically, whatever the trial judge does we are not going to look at it very closely. If the trial judge decides you can't sit on the case because you are opposed to the death penalty, we are not going to look at that very closely. Then, in the 1985 *Witt* case, that changed the standard. It says that if the juror's reservations will substantially impair his or her ability to perform their function, as a juror, then they can be properly excluded. That decision increased the number of people with reservations about the death penalty who the prosecutor can exclude from capital trials.

In 1986 the Supreme Court, in *Lockhart v. McCree,* turned aside empirical evidence showing that jurors who are in favor of the death penalty are also more likely to convict in the guilt or innocence phase. They said, "Well, that's okay."

So the same jury hears both the penalty phase and the guilt or innocence phase of the trial, and people with reservations about the death penalty can be excluded from sitting on the jury in the both phases. Also it's easier now than it was five years ago to exclude anti-death penalty citizens from juries. Now you are saying that along with that there is evidence that those who favor the death penalty are more likely to bring in a guilty verdict in the initial trial?

Yeah, that's it in a nutshell.

The Court said you cannot have a mandatory death penalty for all first-degree murders, you must have individual consideration of each offender.

That is the law.

But in five Florida cases we researched, where the defendants had been executed, many jurors held the belief that anybody who is guilty of first-degree murder *must* get the death penalty.

That's not the law.

It is, however, a major causative factor that influences jurors in Florida who vote death. They believe that death ought to be mandatory for every first-degree murder, so that the penalty phase is not that important.

A second reason why jurors vote for death is a little closer to one of the statutory aggravating factors. It has to do with the manner of the killing. In a particularly gruesome killing, photographs play a great part. They really inflame the jurors. The first vote in the Spenkelink case, I believe, was 8–4 in favor of life. He was the first guy executed against his will after the 1976 decisions. [John Spenkelink, executed May 25, 1979]. Now, his jury voted life to begin with, but the foreman was in favor of death and so he kept the deliberations going, so they sent out for the pictures and finally they turned around and voted for death. So those are the two major factors for people who vote death.

I picked out pretty aggravated cases where the jury had recommended life and the judge had overridden that and sentenced the guy to death. I interviewed those jurors too, and the two operative factors that caused people to vote for life are "lingering doubt" for one; that is, we don't want to execute this guy because he might not be guilty of anything or he might not be guilty of a capital offense. The most extreme example of that, the unluckiest capital litigant I think, aside from Beauford White [executed August 28, 1987], who was executed after his jury gave a 12–0 recommendation for life, was Ernest Dobbert. Dobbert was convicted of first-degree murder, but he was really guilty only of second-degree murder. His prosecutor told me that, and a lot of his jurors told me this, and that's why they recommended life, 10–2, for the murder of his children. Nonetheless, the trial judge overrode this recommendation, and Dobbert was executed in 1984. So lingering doubt about the capital offense or about guilt at all was a primary factor.

The other major factor explaining why jurors in north Florida voted for life is "scruples," or reservations about the death penalty. In spite of the jury selection process, which supposedly excludes jurors with "scruples" against the death penalty, some of those folks get on the jury anyway. Given the recent Supreme Court decisions, however, it is going to be a lot harder for those scrupled jurors to get on.

Did you find that there was any particular judge who was most likely to overrule jury recommendations of life?

Oh sure. Jacksonville is *the* death penalty capital of *the* death penalty region of *the* death penalty state. And Judge R. Hudson Olliff is the guy. I had a very remarkable interview with him. Two of his cases were cases that I studied. *Barclay* was a race war case where I just can't imagine the jury voting life, but they did, and Olliff overruled that sentence. The dean of the law school at Florida State University got interested in the case and eventually got Barclay resentenced to life.

The other case that R. Hudson Olliff had that I studied was *Dobbert*. I asked him where the jury's recommendation on life or death fell on the scale of binding to irrelevant, and he basically said that the jury's recommendation is an excuse for weak-hearted judges who don't want to sentence people to death. He says he doesn't even want to know any more what the count is. In the *Dobbert* case, the record showed that ten of the twelve jurors recommended life. The gist of what he says is that he doesn't care about the recommendation of the jury.

Florida is, of course, only one of three states where the judge can overrule a jury's recommendation for life, but it is far and away the state where it is done most often. It has been done two or three times in Indiana, eight or ten times in Alabama, and over one hundred times in Florida.

That's the reason I chose these two override cases to compare. I figured if the guy was executed after his jury recommended life, God knows if there is any sanity to this, there would be an indication that this was an aggravated case. So, I would compare why the jurors voted one way or another.

I didn't have a lot of resources and money to go and do fifty or a hundred cases, so Jonathan Amsterdam and I only studied ten cases. But I did talk to fifty-four jurors at length. Another twelve declined. Just finding them was a problem. There were one hundred and twenty potential jurors and we managed to locate sixty some odd of them. The earliest case was *Spenkelink* in 1973, so some jurors had died and some had moved away, but we found over half. In only one case were we able to talk to three of the twelve, but in some cases we were able to talk to as many as eight. It's the kind of thing I like to do. I would rather do that than sit in the law library and think great thoughts.

We did read that there were two jurors who committed suicide. Did you find that any of the jurors you interviewed were distressed by the executions?

There was no pattern of that. The pattern, if there was a pattern, was what I would expect from insulation. That is, the jurors had been told that it was their duty to follow the law. Indirectly they were told, "It's not you," and many of them volunteered defensive comments like that, "We did the best we could," which indicated to me that they were upset about it and were giving me their defenses. A handful of them were just wrecks. I have a quote from one of Spenkelink's jurors who is still ripped to pieces by the experience, and that trial took place in 1973. But that was not the typical reaction. The typical reaction was, "We were told to do our job. We did the best we could, and here's what went on in the jury room."

Now sometimes there was a lot of animosity on both sides. Some people who were pro death would say, "We had a woman in there who committed perjury. She said that she could give death and then she couldn't." From the other side the jurors would say, "No, we believe in the death penalty in an appropriate case, but this was not the case." They didn't know *Witherspoon,* but they were virtually saying, "We were *"Witherspoon* qualified." Then there was one woman who was convinced that race was the only reason for the decision. So even years later there was still some hostility back and forth. They were still fighting the battles they fought in the jury room. But, as a group, they were not emotionally torn up, with the exception of three people. It was amazing, all these years after the trial. One woman broke down and cried, thirteen years after the trial.

What is allowed in terms of aggravating and mitigating circumstances at the sentencing phase of the trial?

The defendant, of course, may or may not elect to testify in the guilt or innocence phase. If he does not, then nothing about previous crimes that he may have been convicted of can be admitted during the first phase. Jurors hear that at the penalty phase. The state can then bring in evidence of his previous crimes. The factors in the states differ, but the most terrible one and the one that the penalty phase concentrates on is "future dangerousness," particularly in states like Texas. Even in cases where the penalty phase does not turn on future dangerousness, that kind of evidence comes in. They have a killer shrink in Texas, "Dr. Death," by the name of Grigson, who testifies [see Steve and Lisa Haberman interview below]. In Texas, the only factor that decides who gets life or death is future dangerousness. In one case, the *Barefoot* case, the American Psychiatric Association submitted a brief saying that when you try to predict future dangerousness, you are wrong two out of three times. That did not stop the Supreme Court approving it. But Dr. Grigson testifies that he is 100 percent sure that the defendant will be dangerous and violent in the future within the prison community.

Anyway, in 1980 or '81 the Supreme Court said, "You can't do that. You have to give the guy warnings that he doesn't have to talk to you if you are going to kill him with his own words given to a doctor." So now Dr. Grigson testifies to the same thing, that he is 100 percent sure that he is going to commit violent acts in the prison community, but bases his prediction on records and not talking to the defendant at all. That's the way they do things in Texas.

Were the jurors you talked to properly instructed at the trials?

I found that jurors fundamentally misunderstood that, in Florida, if you are not sentenced to death, you don't get out, no matter what, for at least twenty-five years. They just went right by that. They didn't understand that. They would say, "We had to vote for death because this guy would be out on the streets again in no time."

One of the most painful things I saw in talking with jurors is that most really tried to do the right thing. You have great sympathy when they are dragged off the street and, for eight or ten dollars a day, they have to sit and preside over someone's life. The jurors who voted for life and were overridden by the judge were often upset. It would come out that at the guilt or innocence phase of the trial, if they had doubts about whether the guy was guilty and were not convinced beyond doubt that he was guilty, they traded that off, going along with a guilty vote but agreeing that, at the penalty phase, they would vote for life. These were compassionate people who did not want to see the defendant killed, but what they had done was violate their oaths. If they had reasonable doubts about guilt, their job was to sit there until a mistrial was declared and it would be done all over again at another time. That happened in Dobbert's case. There were a lot of people who didn't think he was guilty of first-degree murder, including the prosecuting attorney, and the way they saw that was that they would vote for life after they had convicted him. Then the judge overruled them.

The prosecutors clearly play hard ball, but do they also play dirty pool?

Sure. I have had firsthand experience with a guy, who "Sixty Minutes" did a piece on, who prides himself on having been the person who has put more people on death row than anybody prosecuting. I have tried cases against him in North Carolina and he is the most unethical, unscrupulous son of a bitch I have ever come across. He's a hell of a good trial lawyer, but completely without any sense of professional responsibility. But it's a no lose proposition. If you play dirty pool as a prosecutor and if you make improper arguments to the jury, if you tell them, "Don't worry, it is not your job," or if you bring in unallowable inflammatory stuff, the penalty is simply that the case gets reversed and you get to try it all over again. You don't get disbarred. There is no real penalty. Joe Freeman Britt has been censured, he has been reprimanded a couple of times by the North Carolina Supreme Court, but there is essentially no personal penalty. As far as the defendant is concerned, they don't say, "You've lost your chance to execute him, the case is reversed and he gets sentenced to life." They just say, "The argument was improper and we are going to send it back and try him over again, and if you can try him right and send him to death row again, then fine—go ahead and do it."

What do you have in mind for your next research project?

The next place I am going, I think, is Connecticut. I've had enough of death and destruction in north Florida. I would like to see what it is about the states that feel there is the necessity to have the death penalty on the books but they don't want to execute.

Presumption of Guilt

"I never saw a man who looked
With such a wistful eye
Upon that little tent of blue
Which prisoners call the sky."

—Oscar Wilde, 1854–1900,
The Ballad of Reading Gaol

Shabaka Sundiata Waqlimi knew the drill on death row at Florida's death prison, Starke, only too well. During his thirteen years of incarceration under the name of Joseph Green Brown, he'd seen his friends sent to the electric chair, so when the guards came to measure him for his burial suit he decided to put up a fight.

He lost the fight, but he managed not only to stay out of the chair, but to prove his innocence and gain his freedom.

There are many injustices in this world, some slight, some gross, but on a scale of one to ten, what happened to Shabaka is at least an eleven, maybe more. To this day Shabaka has not received a single cent in compensation from the state of Florida.

This is his story.

Rock Hill, South Carolina,
Thursday, February 18, 1988, 11:30 a.m.

Shabaka Sundiata Waqlimi

I was born in Charleston, South Carolina, only a few miles from here. I went to school there, and in 1966 went to Orlando, Florida, where I lived most of my life.

Are you angry about what happened to you?

I am bitter, I am angry, and I am frustrated. Not only about what happened to me but—I can deal with anything that happens to me—but when those whom I love and who love me are made to suffer unjustly, I take that as a personal offense.

From your viewpoint, what happened in your case? What were you arrested for?

Murder, rape, and robbery of a white woman in Tampa in 1973. The victim, Earline Barksdale, was the wife of a very prominent attorney in Tampa. This attorney had connections straight up to Tallahassee, the state capital. I am, of course, saddened by her murder and hope that one day the killer will be brought to justice.

Nonetheless I was charged with the crimes against Ms. Barksdale.

I have always maintained, and I'm still quite sure, that my being charged and convicted was a deliberate and intentional thing, brought about by the Tampa police department and the Hillsborough County State Attorney's Office simply to frame me. They needed a murderer, and since I was young and black, in their eyes, I was perfect for the part.

The victim's husband was tight with the chief homicide detective. The leading prosecutor on the case and his assistant are [now] both sitting judges in Hillsborough County. All these people were real buddy buddies.

Anyway, I was charged with murder and I didn't have the finances to hire my own lawyer, which you have to in America—or forget about it. I went to trial, virtually alone, with a court-appointed attorney just three years out of law school. He had only tried three previous cases before a jury, and none of them was a capital case. He was up against an experienced prosecutor who had forty trials behind him, some of which were capital.

Where were you tried?

In Tampa.

What was the composition of the jury?

(*Laughs*) A very representative jury of my peers. Twelve white citizens! Average age thirty-five, maybe more.

The trial lasted four and a half or five days. The jury went out seven o'clock that Friday and came back at eleven-thirty, quarter to twelve that night, with a verdict. Guilty.

What was your defense?

Alibi . . . just about everything. The prosecution didn't have a thing. How could they? I was innocent. They didn't have prints, blood, hair or anything that could be matched to me—no physical evidence of any kind. They had this gun, a .38-caliber Smith and Wesson that belonged to me. Now the gun that killed Earline Barksdale was a .38. But the slug they took from her body was a .38 *special*. Not only were the ballistics different, the bullet wouldn't even *chamber* the gun!

What went wrong?

There was this FBI ballistics expert who was listed as a prosecution witness so my attorney didn't bother to subpoena him. He assumed that when the prosecutor called the guy, he'd prove my innocence during the cross-examination. Of course the prosecution didn't call him. Right at the end of the trial he let the FBI guy go back to some fishing holiday somewhere. So, he was gone before my attorney could call him to the stand.

That's dreadful, but surely wouldn't the judge allow a continuance?

Hey—this is Tampa, Florida. They don't allow a little thing like the truth to upset a good trial. This judge refused to recall the FBI expert.

The following Monday they set a date for the sentencing portion. I was given death for the murder, and consecutive life sentences for the rape and robbery. It was the judge's contention that if I beat the death sentence, I would never see the street as long as I was alive. I was taken to Florida State Prison, Starke. I was twenty-four years old when I went to death row; I was twenty-three when I was arrested.

What was your state of mind?

Anger. They just took me there and put me in the cell. I didn't realize I was on death row. I was so angry. You could say that for the first two years I survived primarily on my hatred. The strength I received from that hatred was from all the people that were involved. I even felt that the court-appointed attorney had something to do with it. But then I found out that he was just dumb, he did no less than he could.

Were you appointed another attorney for the appeals?

No. Under the Florida law, the same attorney handles the appeal to the Florida Supreme Court. Then in 1977 the attorney left my case and I had to find another one. During this process, I hit the books. I started to study, and from July 1977 until November of 1981, when a lawyer was found for me, I handled my own appeals. I kept myself alive with the help of Deborah Fins of the Legal Defense Fund [NAACP] in New York. We became friends. I trusted her and wanted her to handle the case, but she couldn't devote the time to it that was needed. She found an attorney, the one who eventually got me out.

If I was paying, I would not have chosen this attorney. He had just resigned as the U.S. Attorney for the state of Connecticut, had never handled a capital case. He was a prosecutor and believed in the death penalty. *(Laughs)* He had all these things going against him and, like I say, he was not a person I would choose. I wrote Debbie and said, "You must be kidding." She said, "Let him come down and talk to you, just talk to the man." He came to see me and I liked him; we had good rapport. I had one important question to ask him, though. Could he fight? And he didn't respond to it, he just sort of smiled. And I liked that; there was something in that smile.

He said, as a prosecutor, that when the transcript of my trial was given to him, he was just in awe of the injustices that he saw. So he took the case and we went through the process. He went through the filing to Tallahassee to "Barbecue Bob" Graham [governor of Florida at that time] for clemency. That failed, needless to say.

Then, in 1983, Graham signed my death warrant and I was scheduled to be killed on October 18. I think it was during this stage that Dick [Richard Blumenthal, the attorney] became a convert. It was when I was on death watch that he got a chance to actually see how the death penalty works. He was expecting a stay about three days before I got it. The judge couldn't get to my case that weekend. Dick became so enraged that I had to sit over there on death watch that he said to me, "Shabaka, I don't care what it costs me, my family, or my law firm, but I'm going to get you out of here." And he did.

We got the stay fifteen hours before I was scheduled to be killed.

What was going on in your mind at that time?

Well, you are in a cell that is located about thirty feet from the chair. You stay in that cell an average of twenty-three days. There are two ways out of that cell. One if you receive a stay of execution. The other to take that thirty-foot walk.

During the twenty-three days you are there, you are given what on death row is called the "presidential treatment." The presidential treatment means that you are subjected to the chair being tested. And knowing that the chair is being tested in your honor. You hear it. You are right next to it. It's only thirty steps away. Several times a week. Like I say, you know it's being done in your honor. Then, a week before your scheduled death, you go down to what is known as a second stage.

At the second stage you are measured for your "burial suit." And I think it was at that point, for the first time in all the years I was there I really blew my cool, because the process is like a ritual, it is so mechanical. I was being treated like I was an inanimate object. I was determined that I was not going to let this be just another ritual, so I resisted. Well, I responded very actively because, as I say, I was determined not to let this be another ritual. I am a living, breathing human being. If they wanted to measure me for a burial suit, they are not going to be doing it in this manner. Well, I responded physically, and they responded physically, and they kicked me until I shut up.

How did you manage to evolve as a man and remain sane during all those years in that kind of environment?

I realized that I had a job at hand and that the job at hand was to keep some sick people from killing me.

How did you get out?

Through the action of the Eleventh Circuit Court of Appeals in Atlanta. For my appeal my attorney cited the *Giglio v. United States* and Chief Judge [John C.] Godbold said, "Good—that's what we are interested in." That deals with the issue that the prosecutor knowingly and intentionally used false and perjured testimony. We zeroed on that issue and had enough proof to get the conviction reversed. The state of Florida had eighteen days to appeal, and they never did. The reversal came March 17, 1986, and on April 30 I was moved from death row back to Hillsborough County to await a decision as to whether I would be retried. I did eleven months waiting in the county jail in Tampa.

We were now dealing with a new state attorney, Bill James, who was elected into office by promising that he was not only interested in convicting the guilty but that he was going to make sure the innocent were not going to be caught in the web. We filed some court orders and found a lot of suppressed or unheard evidence from the 1973 trial. Like I said before, the ballistic reports from the FBI showed that the bullet that was removed from the body did not physically match the chamber of the gun that I had. We thought we had the original autopsy report, but we did not. We had the report of the medical examiner first on the scene, and this report stated that the assailants, and they used the plural, assailants, were of the blood groups AB and B+. I am A+. And the state knew this because a court order was granted in September 1973 for me to give certain tests and the blood test was one of them, as well as fingernail scraping, pubic hair, all this. They also had fixed the time of death at between 5:30 and 8:00 in the evening. Dur-

214 SHABAKA SUNDIATA WAQLIMI

ing the trial the state maintained the crime took place between noon and 1:00 p.m., since this timetable paralleled with certain witness testimony as to their whereabouts during this period. We also found the initial police investigative report on witnesses who were near the place of the murder at the same time the state said the crime was committed.

None of these things were given to us at the original trial. There were people who were supposed to be at the scene of the crime, as the prosecution had stated, who were elsewhere, actually in their places of business. And we found also statements from inmates in the jail who were coerced to testify at my trial, but who did not. Also, one real interesting fact is that the key witness who did testify at my trial, not only didn't know anything about the crime, but was taught and trained by the police and prosecution to recall details. He was taken out of the county jail daily. He was led around the scene of the crime, shown pictures of the crime and shown pictures of where the body lay inside the place.

And he was a chief witness against you?

Yes. He was taught. Anyway, evidence supporting all this was found by us, and I turned to Tom [Thomas McCoun, local counsel] and I said, "Tom, I want to say something. What I like about you white people is that you always like to write things down! Yes, man, you always write things down and they come back to haunt you."

We presented this to the state, and in their own investigation they made a polygraph test on these people and found out that what we had been saying for fourteen years was true. They had tried, convicted, condemned, and almost killed an innocent man.

So they dismissed all charges. They filed a complete dismissal.

Are they going to do anything to compensate you for all of this?

There's the irony. You see Florida, like other states, has a law. If anyone spends any time, whether it's a day, a year, whatever, in any state institution, when you are released you are given a hundred dollars, a suit of clothing, an I.D., and a ticket back to a county that you want to go to. Now, since I was released from the Hillsborough County Jail rather than the state prison I did not qualify. I didn't get a thing. In the jail I think I had about $14. I gave it all away except 75 cents to make three telephone calls. I gave away all my law books. I kept all my transcripts and I left that county jail with just the clothes on my back, my legal papers, and 75 cents in my pocket.

Seventy-five cents for fourteen years in jail?

Yeah, and I used that on the phone. I had no idea how I was going to get out of Tampa, so I called Tom, my lawyer, who is based in St. Petersburg, and asked him to come over and pick me up and take me back to St. Pete so I could get a ride to Gainesville, where I had friends.

What did you find you missed most when you were incarcerated? What did you want to do when you got free?

I always had this vision that when I got out I was gonna look up in the sky, give a prayer to the Heavenly Father, and then take a deep breath and let it out. But I did not do this because when I walked out of the door I was blinded by camera lights from the TV station out there waiting.

But you were free?

Well I, of African descent, am not a free person in this country and never was. It is not my country. When they say that I am free, I say it is because I am no longer restrained by bars, but that's as far as it goes, because they are still killing a lot of my brothers and sisters and they are doing it for the wrong reasons, and I don't think I could be free until I control my own development. I am still growing.

We heard a very tragic story about your brother.

You see, we talk about capital punishment and we talk about victims. As I said earlier, what has been done to me I can deal with, but when you touch those I love and care about, I take offense. Back in 1979 my oldest brother Willie needed a kidney transplant. He lived in Georgia, and a doctor came to Florida State Prison and examined me about a kidney match. For security reasons Florida Department of Corrections refused to allow me to go to Lyons, Georgia. So the doctor said they would transport Willie to Gainesville, which is close to the prison. Again the Florida officials denied me permission, giving security as the reason. Nine days later my brother died because he couldn't get a transplant. As far as I'm concerned, the state of Florida killed my brother as clearly as if they had put a gun to his head and pulled the trigger. If I had been in general prison population I could have given him the kidney, but because I was on death row, I was denied that.

There are victims all the way around. Society teaches that when something violent happens to us we should seek revenge, but I always ask the question about who is out there who will volunteer themselves to be a sacrificial lamb for me, so I can release fourteen years of anger and frustration? I get no volunteers. Society tells me I shouldn't act that way and I should suppress it. So I have to suppress my outrage because, you see, they have no program in society for people like myself.

Thank you, Shabaka. Anything you'd like to say in conclusion?

Do this for me. Just help abolish the death penalty.

SOCIAL CONSCIENCE

"All that is necessary for the triumph of evil is for good men to do nothing."

—Edmund Burke, 1729–1797

Michael Radelet, Ph.D., is an associate professor at the Department of Sociology, University of Florida, Gainesville. Professor Radelet completed two years of postdoctorate work in psychiatry at the University of Wisconsin and a Ph.D. in sociology at Purdue University. He has written extensively on the death penalty for many years, has appeared as an expert witness in numerous capital cases, and has worked closely with many Florida death row inmates—some of whom have been executed—and their families.

His writings include: Facing the Death Penalty: Essays on Cruel and Unusual Punishment, Miscarriages of Justice in Potentially Capital Cases *(with Hugo Adam Bedau), and* Capital Punishment in America: An Annotated Bibliography *(with Margaret Vandiver).*

After we interviewed Michael at an Amnesty International death penalty conference in San Antonio, he agreed to help us edit this book. We owe him a debt of gratitude.

San Antonio, Texas
Saturday, February 11, 1989, 11:00 a.m.

Professor Michael Radelet

Are most of your publications on the subject of the death penalty?

Actually, my training is in community mental health and in medical ethics. But so few people are doing research on the death penalty and the research is so badly needed that, over the years, I have been doing less and less medical research to the point where today probably three quarters of what I publish is in the area of the death penalty.

Do you feel the abolition movement is an extension of the civil rights movement?

Opposition to the death penalty today is a direct extension of the so-called civil rights movement. Of course the people on death row are not as oppressed as were the slaves. Most of those on death row committed horrible, vicious crimes. But the reasons why they are vicious and disproportionately black cannot be understood unless we understand the history of racism in this country and, in fact, the world.

I will be opposed to the death penalty until everybody in this country is truly born with an equal chance of dying in the electric chair. That is not true today and never has been. The idea of equal justice is a myth not only because our racist history means that blacks have a higher probability today of being raised in environments which might lead to violent behavior, but also, given similar violent behavior, blacks are treated more harshly by the criminal justice system than are other groups.

From your research are there any common denominators?

Well, every case has its own story to tell, but there are some similarities. One thing that is clear is that people do incredibly stupid things. Those who argue the death penalty is a deterrent fail to realize that 90 percent of the crimes that lead people to death row are so unplanned that any consideration of future consequences is impossible. A second common denominator is the thread of social class that is seen again and again; and the indirect effects of social class operating through the quality of the defense attorney.

Almost everyone on death row would not be there if they had played their cards right after their arrests. It is striking how many people are there for crimes similar to those for which others were sentenced to life. There is an arbitrariness with which the penalty is applied, but it is also quite systematic when the influence of race, social class, and quality of legal representation are considered.

One of the most striking things I have learned is that people are sentenced to death not so much for what they *do* but for who they *are*. And who they are becomes a function of social distance between jurors and the defendant, social distance in terms of race, in terms of poverty, in terms of whether or not the defendant is a local or an outsider, in terms of appearance, and in terms of whether or not you look right and look like one of their kids. In most cases if a juror thinks that the defendant is like them, he or she won't vote for death. If the defendant has killed people who are not like them, poor people or black people, the defendant won't be sentenced to death. But, if he kills people who could easily have been the juror's friends or neighbors, the defendant is in big trouble. If the defendant has a weird name and is from out of state, like John Spenkelink, he can be sentenced to death on a roll of the dice in Tallahassee, whereas in a different year and a different place he wouldn't have been sentenced to death. Spenkelink was sentenced to death because he was not a Floridian, he was not a good ol' boy, he had a funny name, and he was gay, or at least the victim was. In other words, it's who you are and who the victim is that counts, not the volume of blood or degree of premeditation.

One other general conclusion: this one deals not with people on death row but instead with us as a society. Support for the death penalty is based upon a tremendous amount of myth and misinformation. I see it again and again in public lectures and in classes with students; the more people learn about the death penalty, the more likely they are to oppose it.

I have had the mother of a death row inmate come and speak to a class and been swarmed by sympathetic students after the class. I have had Shabaka Waqlimi [see Shabaka Waqlimi interview] come to my classes and talk about his experiences. He was a man sentenced to death in Florida and was on death row for thirteen years before it was finally discovered that he was innocent all along. He was swamped by the students after the lecture. People wanted to get to know him and wanted to express their outrage, sympathy, and support. I still believe that people are basically good. When most learn about the horrors of the death penalty, they do react. The politicians won't. If we can educate more people and educate politicians, I am as convinced that we will eventually win as I am that the sun will rise tomorrow. Human rights is a winning issue.

Isn't it frustrating doing anti-death penalty work in Florida?
In Florida we are lucky to have a number of different people from a

220   PROFESSOR MICHAEL RADELET

number of different specialties who really work at this together. In terms of
the abolition movement in Florida, there is a high division of labor and a
tremendous amount of respect for each other in that group. That sense of
community and sense of mission is one that sustains our activities. I have
always felt that through these people and through meeting the families of
death row inmates, I have met the nicest people in the world.

*How many people on death row would you say are consistent, bru-
tal, cold-blooded murderers?*

I would have to make a computer run to find out the exact number,
but I am sure it is less than a quarter. Most of the people on death row
got caught up in something they couldn't control. Many capital crimes
involve alcohol or drug use. Very few death row inmates woke up in the
morning realizing that on that day they would kill somebody. Very few
people on death row planned their crimes twenty-four hours in advance.
Most capital crimes involve a robbery gone bad and some really stupid
blunder. They walked into a store to rob it and they didn't think that the
proprietor had a gun. The victim pulls out a gun and something goes
wrong and suddenly he or she is killed. There is no typical crime, but a
common element is that the murder was unplanned.

*The public is terrified of serial killers. You knew Ted Bundy, perhaps
the most notorious of them all. Why do you object to society ridding
itself of a man who confessed to killing several dozen people?*

If the Bundys and Night Stalkers are out on the streets, we should
feel terrorized. But they are not on the streets; they are in cages. Our
society is no safer after killing Bundy than before.

The execution of Ted Bundy may have made some people feel better,
and I saw at first hand the disgusting sight of the mob getting drunk and
chanting for his death outside the gates of Starke Prison, but it has
nothing to do with crime prevention. People brought picnic baskets.
Some shot off fireworks. They sold coffee and donuts and T-shirts. There
were thirty-five satellite dishes set up in the field. It looked like a county
fair, and had all the elements of a public execution except pickpockets. It
was the most degrading and brutal spectacle I have ever witnessed.

One of the principal reasons that they wanted Bundy dead was that
he was perceived as enjoying the taking of life, and yet here were
people in their hundreds doing just that, deriving pleasure from the
premeditated killing of another human being.

How did the other prisoners react?

It scared the pants off them, as it was supposed to. It's like little kids
pulling the wings off a fly before they crunch it. You know, in the
Orange County Jail, they have a cable system and once a week or so
they rent a movie and play it for the prisoners. During the week of the

Bundy execution the video-of-the-week was called *Faces of Death*. This movie has nothing in it but animals being slaughtered and people dying in horrible ways. It shows one guy in the electric chair with blood pouring from his eye sockets, another being beheaded, another in the gas chamber and a bunch of shootings. The jailers who showed that film had the same message that the cheering crowds had: "Squirm — we're gonna get you, too."

Governor Martinez would say that justice was done.

True. By that he means that for him, killing folks is a ticket for reelection. He will never have to worry about the Willie Hortons the way that Mike Dukakis did, because Governor Martinez can say that he killed Ted Bundy. To get at Bundy, he also killed Beauford White (in 1987), even though White's jury unanimously recommended life imprisonment.

But here is a good example of the hypocrisy of the politicians in this case. Before they realized what a popular move it would be to kill Bundy, they offered him a deal of life imprisonment. Had Ted been smart and accepted the plea bargain of life imprisonment that the state offered him ten years ago, today we would not even recognize the name Ted Bundy. We would not have heard of him again.

We saw, on television, a relative of one of Ted Bundy's victims saying that now Bundy was dead, she felt she would find some kind of peace. Doesn't it fly in the face of justice that we should worry about the murderer when the victim is dead and the relatives are grieving?

Murder is a horrible crime, and it happens twenty thousand times each year. There are over thirty thousand murderers in jail. I sympathize with the relatives of murder victims, as do all abolitionists, but we can't have a justice system that is designed simply to act as an avenging angel. I am sure that Bundy's death brought comfort to the families of some of his victims. There is comfort when the case is finally over. That same sense of finality would have come if, ten years ago, they had sentenced him to life and threw away the key. Sentencing Ted to death just kept his name in the headlines for another decade, picking at the wound's scabs, preventing healing from taking place. That's one reason why many families of homicide victims hate the death penalty. The death penalty simply aggrandizes the killer.

As it is, there are over two thousand men on death row. If we were to kill them all—and presumably our society thinks it's a good idea or they wouldn't have put them there—the United States would witness the greatest slaughter of its citizens by a Western democracy in this century and maybe even the last.

But Bundy was a mass murderer, a serial killer. Surely that kind of murderer is different? Surely society has a right to rid itself of a man like Ted Bundy?

My main opposition to the death penalty is what it does to the society. Our society kills people in cages. It is like going hunting in a zoo. In the cage they are not dangerous, but executing them is very dangerous—for us.

If we look at causes of human misery and human death, most of that misery is caused by government officials. After all, if we look at death resulting from illegal behavior, Richard Nixon, with his illegal bombing of Cambodia, killed many, many times more than Ted Bundy ever killed.

As a mass murderer Bundy isn't in the same class as Marcos, Papa Doc, Pinochet, and all our other grubby little allies and they are not in same class as the twentieth-century superstars: Adolf Hitler, Joe Stalin, and a man who is still alive and plotting more genocide, Pol Pot. So we must keep things in perspective.

It seems unreasonable that a country as mighty as the United States should feel secure by killing a mentally ill sociopath like Ted Bundy. As a Floridian I feel more threatened by some nut hunting innocent Bambis with an AK-47 than I do by a guy up in Starke in a cage.

It has happened again and again and again that governments use their power in this way. Even if we agree, for the sake of argument, that the world is a better place with Ted Bundy gone, it does not mean that we should kill him. Once we give government the power to kill any of their citizens they have consistently shown throughout history that they misuse that power and use it disproportionately on the poor and those who cannot adequately defend themselves. Once we let the government kill people, they have consistently shown they will use their nets not just to kill the Bundys, but also the poor, minorities, mentally ill, and innocent. We have to look at that system as a whole, not just on a case-by-case basis, and take it or leave it.

You mentioned that Bundy was mentally ill?

Sane people do not go round killing dozens of women, and the person that the state of Florida strapped in the electric chair was a man who was severely mentally ill. He suffered from a form of insanity which is very rarely seen and not very well understood. Our reactions to his crimes and at his execution showed pretty clearly that we are just as crazy as he was.

How did the doctors diagnose him?

The diagnosis was that he had a form of manic depression. I knew him for ten years, and I didn't understand the illness that he suffered from. Thank God it was a rare form, but the crimes were no less horrible because they were caused by mental illness. In a very real sense, Bundy was in a class by himself. When the history of the abolition of the death penalty in Florida is written, we will talk about a pre-Bundy and a post-Bundy. A month before his execution the citizens of Florida knew of one death row inmate, Ted Bundy; nobody knew two. Today, no other death row inmates are household names.

When they executed Bundy, three things happened. One is we eliminated any chance to learn more about his criminal history and really help the families he had injured. Two is we eliminated any possibility to learn about his disease, to help cure it and thereby prevent further murders by maybe recognizing the symptoms of a mass murderer before he becomes one. Three is by sentencing Ted Bundy to death, we put him on the front page of every paper in the country and his victims were degraded yet again.

The pictures of Bundy taken after his autopsy and released to the press were horrific. Bald head, scorched temples, stitches showing him after they sewed him up. Those photos were paraded all over the country. Again, we saw quite clearly that the death penalty does nothing but devalue human life.

Was Bundy horrified by what he had done?

I think the only way to understand the confessions he made in the last week of his life—and I saw him every day during that week—is to see a man who was seeking to understand himself, seeking to understand his own illness, and looking for some understanding and forgiveness. I don't mean forgiveness in the sense of being excused for what he did, but in the sense of forgiveness that moves us in the direction of reconciliation.

I was with both Willie Darden and Ted Bundy on the night before their deaths. Willie was at peace with himself, his loved ones, and with his God. He went out proclaiming his innocence and he felt support from all those around him. Ted, on the other hand, was not at peace. On his last night he still had a horrible burden that he wanted to share and express, at least insofar as he himself understood it.

So what do you feel the answer is for someone like Bundy?

Bundy should have been treated no differently than the other thousands of murderers that we come into contact with every year. They should be sent to prison for a long, long time, maybe for life. I don't think we need be making decisions now about what our children and grandchildren will be doing in the year 2030. If they want to let him out in the year 2030, that's their decision to make.

THE HALF EMPTY GLASS

"The more ancient the abuse the more sacred it is."
—Voltaire, 1694–1778

Hugo Adam Bedau, Ph.D., is the leading authority on the death penalty in the United States. Professor Bedau is the author of The Courts, the Constitution and Capital Punishment *(1977), and* Death Is Different: Studies in the Morality, Law and Politics of Capital Punishment *(1987).*

His first book, The Death Penalty in America *(now in its third edition, 1982), was the first completely comprehensive overview on the death penalty attempted by a scholar in this century. It has been updated over the years and remains one of the major sources of material for any serious student of capital punishment.*

Professor Bedau holds a Bachelor's degree from the University of Redlands, Master's degrees from Boston University and Harvard University, and a Ph.D. from Harvard. He now holds the Austin Fletcher Chair of Philosophy at Tufts University.

Professor Bedau was on a year-long sabbatical in Europe when we located him, but as luck would have it, we received a telephone call from Magdaleno Rose-Avila, the head of Amnesty's death penalty section in the United States, who was attending a conference in England. He was at the headquarters of the International Secretariat of Amnesty International in London and in the same room as Professor Bedau.

In the background the familiar sound of a British police car, Dee Daaa . . . Dee Daaa . . . Dee Daaa . . . could be heard, 4,000 miles away, as we dictated the questions over the telephone to Magdaleno, who conducted the following interview on our behalf.

Telephone Interview Atlanta/London
Wednesday, February 17, 1988, 8:30 a.m.

Professor Hugo Adam Bedau

*Your work and writing on the death penalty makes you the most
celebrated academic in this field. Did you come to it academically or
emotionally?*

I got interested in the subject thirty years ago, when I was a young
faculty member in the Department of Philosophy at Princeton. I was
teaching an introductory course in ethics and, for the first time, talking
about issues that I had never paid much attention to when I had been a
student. One of these was the problem of the death penalty.

In the spring of 1957 I suddenly became interested in the whole subject.
I can remember reading a slender little volume in the Princeton University
library with the provocative title, *A Life for a Life*. It was written by Sir
Ernest Gowers, who had just completed several years as chairman of the
British Royal Commission on Capital Punishment. I thought that this was
just exactly the thing I ought to read. So I took the book home and I read it
at one sitting. Gowers, in that book, tells the story of how he became
converted from being uninterested in the death penalty and more or less a
believer in it, to being against it, based upon his study of the matter.
Something of the same sort happened to me.

How did you come to write your first book?

I learned that it was very hard to get information, up to date or any
other kind, about the death penalty. So I started assembling things here
and there. This was in the fifties, before the days of photo-copying, so
developing a library of material, even for your own use, was difficult.
It suddenly struck me that one useful thing that I could do would be to
assemble an inexpensive paperback book of materials about the story
of the death penalty in America. So I set myself that task, and finally,
in 1964, *The Death Penalty in America* was published. It immediately
became a standard reference book for everybody interested in the death
penalty in the United States. It was not the only book, but it was the

first book in America, in recent times, to give a really thorough evaluation of all of the evidence, all of the aspects of the death penalty, all of the arguments, pro and con, from the religious, moral, legal and political perspectives. It helped establish me as a scholar in this area. That book is now in its third edition.

You are on record in your essay, "Challenging the Death Penalty," written after the 1972 Furman *decision, as saying, "We will not see another execution in this nation in this century." What is your reaction since the* Gregg *decision and the executions that have ensued?*

Well, of course, I was wrong. I let my optimism get the better of my ability to predict, and I was not alone in 1972 in thinking that we had seen the last execution in the United States. But we had expected a backlash, and indeed there was one. Many state legislatures turned right around and reenacted the death penalty in 1973 and 1974. People were sentenced to death in the dozens and by 1976 in the hundreds. The mood of the country had become increasingly conservative. Violent crime continued to increase. There was a lot of publicity for politicians who wanted to campaign on a law and order platform. So all of that was moving against the grain that we had hoped for when the *Furman* decision came down.

There are two ways of looking at developments since 1976. One way is to say that the glass is half empty. We have still got the death penalty and we have executed people after the moratorium. We have over two thousand people under sentence of death now, and more are added every day. The rate of executions may very well increase considerably into the 1990s. On the other hand, another way to look at it is to say that the glass is half full. Since 1976, we have eliminated the death penalty for rape. We have eliminated the death penalty for kidnapping. Now there was a time, thirty or forty years ago, when people were executed for those crimes. That's history now. Those are two major pluses.

We have eliminated the mandatory death penalty even for inmates who commit a murder in prison. If there was ever a crime that you would think might get the mandatory death penalty, that would be it. But the Supreme Court, just last year, eliminated it. We may be on the threshold of having the Supreme Court restrict the death penalty for crimes committed by juveniles.

All of these are positive developments. But they go hand in hand with the continuation of the death penalty for murder. So, at this point, nearing the end of the twentieth century in the United States, it's very difficult to know which theme or which trend is going to dominate. Is it going to be the trend that continues to hold onto the death penalty for murder, although narrowly and somewhat precariously, with lots of people sentenced and very few executed? Or is it going to be the other trend, the trend to get rid of it entirely?

I don't foresee in this century a straightforward ruling by the United States Supreme Court in effect saying, "We were wrong in *Gregg* and *Jurek* and *Proffitt* in 1976 and we are saying now that the Eighth Amendment and the Fourteenth Amendment make the death penalty, in any form, unconstitutional." But such a ruling may very well come in the next century.

I also think we will see more and more resistance to carrying out executions and to sentencing people when the public increasingly realizes, what all lawyers and judges involved already know, that the death penalty in the United States is absorbing more and more time and money; it is a crazy investment. We are not getting any benefit from it at all.

Yet the time and the money spent is forced on us by our concern for due process and equal protection under the law. Even so, the death sentences and the executions are arbitrary, and everybody who studies the subject knows that. It is a race between the forces that want to keep the death penalty, no matter what, and the forces that say, in effect, "We have tried every strategy, every tactic known to man to try to make the death penalty fair and we can't do it, so let's quit."

Public opinion seems to support the death penalty.

As I view it, the public supports executions only in the illusion that there are quick solutions to the problem of crime. In our folly we take a Rambo-like approach to crime and violence, thereby provoking more violence and brutality. Public opinion will take some time to change to more pacific, more reasonable, more patient methods.

I think lack of leadership, rather than public opinion, is the root of the problem. Bring responsible leadership to the front to attack head on the reasons why people support the death penalty and the public will change its opinion. I have great confidence in that.

Why do you feel the United States is trailing the industrialized Western democracies in terms of the elimination of the capital punishment?

It is a difficult question. You could ask why is it that the crime rate in the United States is five times (per capita) what it is in any European country. Why is it that the average American household has one or more handguns, whereas the average European household has no handguns?

I think crime, the use of handguns, and the use of instruments of violence like the death penalty are part of a connected pattern of domestic violence in our lives that also connects with our terrible heritage of slavery, Jim Crow and the slaughter of Native Americans. We are quick to attack South Africa for the problem of apartheid, but we forget that we avoided the problem of apartheid by genocide.

Americans never lived through the Nazi era in the way that Europe did. We never saw the abuse of the death penalty by torturers and murderers and genocidal brutes the way the Danes, the French, the Germans, the Italians did under the Nazis. We never learned to see so clearly the abuses to which this punishment can be put. We have seen it only in the form of the normal instrument of criminal justice, rather than in the hands of obvious tyrants and murderers. I think this experience taught the Europeans, certainly of the World War II generation, a lesson that they will never forget. It is those who remember the war that are against the death penalty in Europe, because younger people who don't have that experience tend to support executions. Even in Europe, the public supports the death penalty. It's the politicians, the statesmen, the people with memories, the people who understand the progress of civilization in this century who have set their hand against the death penalty in Europe. It is not the general public.

So the death penalty is always going to be a threat to us, at least for the next couple of centuries in the West, and I suspect in the East and the Third World as well, the danger of the death penalty will never be very far away.

All the more reason why the United States should get in tune with the European countries, from which it draws its heritage, and abolish the death penalty and restrict it and eliminate it, along with torture, along with corporal punishment.

Do you predict an eventual change in public opinion and a move toward abolition?

It is hard to say. Public opinion certainly is more widely in favor of the death penalty today than it was fifteen years ago. And that is true all across the board, academics, non-academics, men, women, white, non-white, college-educated, not college-educated, it doesn't matter. The incoming college freshmen support the death penalty by about three to one, which is extraordinary. Historically, twenty, thirty, forty years ago it was the young who, by and large, were opposed to capital punishment. Not now. So there have been changes in public support. It is something of a mystery what causes these changes and how strong the death penalty attitudes are.

For those who favor it, it is a reassuring symbol of power, of ultimate and final authority in society's endless war against crime. But for those of us who oppose it, in the light of the facts of its actual history and use, it is a very different symbol indeed. It symbolizes arbitrary power, and God-like authority without God-like wisdom. It is mute testimony to society's lack of imagination and incapacity for self-criticism when dealing with the dangerous and lethal conduct of a small minority. Worse still, in a country such as the United States, where the killings that capital punishment involves are all done, ultimately, with the full authority and consent of the people, its violence and futility soils each of us. Each execution figuratively bloodies my hands, and yours, too.

THE COLLECTION

" ' I can do nothing,' said the governor, and a mile
away in Charleston, a shoemaker and a fish-peddler
were as good as dead."

—John Sanford,
A Very Good Land to Fall With, 1987

*During these death penalty interviews, two names came up over and
over again: Sacco and Vanzetti. The story of two innocent Italian immigrants who were executed, in reality, just for being foreigners. Their
deaths became a rallying point for the social injustice that was so
rampant in the twenties. The nation became divided. Foreign governments censured the United States.*

*Sara Ehrmann, one of the great names in the abolitionist movement,
founder and chairperson of the Massachusetts Council to Abolish the
Death Penalty from 1928 to 1968, lives in Brookline, Massachusetts.
The Council was an offshoot of the Sacco and Vanzetti Defense Committee and Mrs. Ehrmann's husband, Herbert, was one of the defense
attorneys in the famous case. The Sara R. Ehrmann Capital Punishment Collection is one of the largest collections of archival materials
in this country relating to capital punishment and over the years Mrs.
Ehrmann has kept records of thousands of people interested in abolition. These records are housed at Northeastern University.*

*The house on Irving Street in Brookline village is a superb example
of 19th century double fronted house. The white painted wooden building has three symmetrical dormer windows set in the roof. Two double
fronted windows grace both the first and second floors and in the*

231

center of the home is a heavy lacquered front door with a brass bell.

Sara Ehrmann, a sprightly ninety-three-year old, has lived here for well over half a century, during which period the house has remained virtually unchanged.

Brookline, Massachusetts
Thursday, March 3, 1988, 3:30 p.m.

Sara Ehrmann

I was born in 1895 in Bowling Green, Kentucky, but I lived my early life in Rochester, New York, until I met, and then married, Herbert Ehrmann in Boston. I have lived here ever since.

So it was in Boston that you got involved in the abolitionist movement?

Coming here, to Boston, really put me in touch with a most learned and humane man. A person who really understood the treatment of offenders, E. Roy Calvert (*The Case Against Capital Punishment*, 1927).

Capital punishment is, as I'm sure you've become aware, almost a completely political matter. So what E. Roy Calvert did for me was to set up a system of running an organization so that it would accomplish a purpose, a purpose which is political. You have to get to the legislature to abolish capital punishment.

What was the climate in America when the Sacco and Vanzetti trial was going on?

It was such a horrible case, with such a miserable judge. These were Italians. You know it was just after the Great War; immigrants were coming into the country, and they were not wanted. The country was very hostile to immigrants. These two Italians were anarchists, idealists, and it just happened in this kind of background of hatred, two innocent people fell into the "justice" system. They had a very unfair trial.

All the National Attorney General wanted to do was send all the immigrants back to where they came from, and when they arrived here in boats, he didn't even let them land. He pushed them out into the ocean again. The whole government was against immigrants. Basically, that was what "Sacco and Vanzetti" was all about.

When were they executed?

In 1927. The murder they were accused of committing was in 1922. My husband had graduated from Harvard Law School. While Herbert was still in law school he and an older close friend, Reginald Heber Smith, set up what became the "Legal Aid Society."

There had been no such organization before then and so they started assisting people who did not have funds. Then Herbert and Reginald were asked by Harvard Law School to take part in the first survey of criminal justice ever made in this country, a national survey. That meant going to live in Cleveland, which we did. We lived there about three years. I have a copy of that survey here, today.

When we returned from Cleveland the Sacco and Vanzetti case was on. All we knew was that what they called a "couple of Wops," that meant Italians, were going to be put to death. Herbert and Reg Smith were asked to take their case.

Sacco and Vanzetti had had very poor legal representation, almost none. They desperately needed help. The judge was utterly prejudiced, he came from Dartmouth College, he had been on the faculty there. He hated foreigners, hated immigrants. He was just as unfair as he could possibly be. You couldn't believe it. So Herbert and Reg took it over. It was an almost impossible task at that time.

Did they take over at the appeals stage?

No. The judge wouldn't give them an appeal! (Herbert and Reg were the ones who later drew up our law and had it passed in Massachusetts providing the *necessity* for an appeal.) At that time you could go to one court, one crazy district court judge, [could] find you guilty and then sentence you to death. Since then, we have had endless books about the case, and the whole world has become involved. My husband wrote two books *[The Untried Case* and *The Case That Will Not Die]* and a lot of articles on the death penalty, and Sacco and Vanzetti.

They were given a posthumous pardon by Governor Dukakis relatively recently, were they not?

In 1977, he proclaimed that they had not had a fair trial. He ordered August 22nd of that year to be proclaimed, "Sacco and Vanzetti" day, and he has never been willing to have an execution in Massachusetts.

There have been many unfair trials in this country in the past. Why do you think the Sacco and Vanzetti case has become so celebrated?

It was because this case was taken up all over the world. It did become very, very famous all over the world. Vanzetti came from a good family, he was highly educated, in contrast to Sacco, who came from a very modest background. They were anarchists and anarchism and communism were spreading around the world at that time, and the world was very alarmed.

The politicians were very much opposed to finding Sacco and Vanzetti innocent. To say that the great state of Massachusetts put two innocent people to death, well that was unheard of! So politically, any opposition, any suggestion that they may be innocent was very unpopular.

The police took it up. Sacco and Vanzetti had been politically active, so after their deaths the case divided the whole state because, literally, the educated people were on one side and the police department on the other. The police force marched on one demonstration at the state house, and broke it up.

At that time our governor, Fuller, learned that he had a very good chance of becoming elected President, if he would just follow the lead of Calvin Coolidge, who had been President shortly before that. The political deal makers told him to get rid of the Sacco and Vanzetti case, so they did everything politically possible to hurt them. So Mr. William Thompson (Head of the Boston Bar Association), the senior lawyer, and Herbert asked Massachusetts for a stay of execution and he acted as though he might consider it. But it was then that Governor Fuller found his name proposed to run for President, and that decided him not to grant a stay of execution.

I will take it from my point of view, my perspective. There had been a great possibility that they would be found innocent. There was a confession by another prisoner, Medeiros, that he was with the criminals at the murder and that Sacco and Vanzetti were innocent. If the court had permitted the trial to go on Sacco and Vanzetti could have proved their innocence. However, the execution date was coming. Governor Fuller then said that if Sacco and Vanzetti would plead "guilty" he would *postpone* the execution and change their convictions to *second* degree murder, with life imprisonment.

Now, Vanzetti said he would plead guilty, because he knew that if he had *time* they could prove their innocence. However, Sacco would not do it. He had a wife and one child and she was pregnant with another. Sacco said that *he was innocent* and would not plead guilty. Herbert and Mr. Thompson pleaded with Sacco, to give them the time to get new evidence, but he refused.

Two days before the execution they asked me to go to the prison to see and talk to Sacco, who was a darling little man, so I went to the old Charleston prison. A group of Boston women had been taking care of the Sacco family. Sacco saw me, alone. We talked in the corridor, and I said to him, "Nick, for the sake of your family, why don't you plead guilty? Then you will live and be proved innocent." He put his hand on my arm and he said, "Mrs. Ehrmann, dear, I am innocent. I cannot be true to my family if I am not first true to myself."

These were amazing people. Vanzetti was highly educated, Nick Sacco was a fine little fellow. The only evidence against them at all was the fact that they each had a gun. There was a perfectly good explanation for it. Nick was a nightwatchman at a large shoe company out near where they lived and so he was given a gun, and he always carried it. Vanzetti had a number of jobs, and this was Christmas time; the night before Christmas the Italians eat some sort of fish or eels. Anyway he became a fish peddler at holiday times, and he actually had ordered his whole supply of fish for Christmas Eve.

The night before the execution, if I am not mistaken, Herbert got into the fish store records in Boston and found the order, proving that Vanzetti was selling eels at the time the crime was committed. But it was too late, the courts would not hear this.

You said there was enormous international interest and outcry at that time?

This hurt the reputation of America a great deal. Other countries were disgusted with us and so it became very, very unpopular the whole thing.

You just had to say "Sacco and Vanzetti" and that was enough to get your head blown off. It was even questionable whether you could work for the abolition of the death penalty or not when our group was organized. But we ran the organizations [The Massachusetts Council for the Abolition of the Death Penalty and The American League for the Abolition of Capital Punishment] and became active, and I must say the number of executions went down.

You were five years old at the dawn of the twentieth century, and witnessed at first hand the Sacco and Vanzetti affair. How do you see the future of capital punishment in the United States?

When I was growing up in Rochester, New York, the local police took care of us. We would go to our policeman and he would take care of it. They were among the very best people I knew. The worst thing that happened was that the police organized in the 40's, after a very sensational murder in California.

When police became "law enforcement officers" and formed "law enforcement associations," they worked to abolish the "abolition of capital punishment"; lobbied endlessly for the death penalty, and it seemed to herald the end of the "friendly policeman."

Things are getting worse and worse. Now the gun lobby prevails. Crime and murder are unbearable. Everything is killing, and having government getting into that business is not going to solve anything.

The following is an excerpt from John Sandford's book, A Very

Good Land to Fall With *(Rosina Sacco and Luigia Vanzetti), and tells
the poignant story of two women pleading in vain for the lives of their
loved ones.*

The evening was well along when the two women were brought
to his chambers in the State House. On being shown into his
presence, they kneeled at the Governor's feet to beg him in Italian
for the lives of their men, the brother of one of them and the
husband of the other. Speaking through an interpreter, they im-
plored him for more than an hour to spare the condemned from
death, awaiting them now in the next square of the calendar.

Did he sit or stand for their pleas and prayers, did he share their
anguish and agonize too, or did his mind stray from the sallow
women to the sheen of his Gainsboroughs, did he preen himself
on his clubs, the Brookline Country and the Union Boat, did he
gloat over his forty millions, his summer place, his Back Bay
stack on Beacon?

Through an hour or more of supplication in two languages, was
he ever once moved, did he doubt his ground however briefly, or
did the sound he heard make him languorous, as if the water were
running for his bath? Would the women still be here for the voltaic
moment, he may have wondered, would Luigia be calling on him
softly, would Rosina be telling her beads? In the end, he had to
end it, and he said, "I can do nothing," and a mile away in
Charleston, a shoemaker and a fish-peddler were as good as dead.

At one minute before midnight, the Governor left the building
and betook himself—where? to his summer place in New Hamp-
shire, to one of his clubs (the Essex County, the Algonquin), to a
card game, a whorehouse, a saloon? He did not see the two
women on the steps, he did not hear their weeping.

A BAD CALL

"It is better that ten guilty persons escape than one
innocent suffer."

—Sir William Blackstone, 1723–1780

*Aaron Lee Owens, age forty-three, spent almost ten of his years
locked behind bars in California's toughest prisons. He did this for a
crime that he did not commit; for a brutal, double murder he did not
commit.*

*At the time of his conviction the death penalty did not exist in the
United States due to the 1972* Furman *ruling (Furman v. Georgia). The
crime for which Aaron Owens was accused and convicted would have
certainly carried a capital sentence, being heinous, premeditated, and
involving multiple victims.*

*The criminal justice system has served Aaron Owens poorly. Yet, this
was a case where the evidence against him looked very convincing.
This was not a malicious prosecution but just another example of the
fallibility of the system.*

*Aaron Owens is an athletic, muscular man with mutton chop side-
burns and a short Afro. He lives in a neat, clapboard, terraced house
in the Hunters Point suburb of San Francisco, a home he shares with
his fiancée, Betty.*

The following is an account of the crime:

*Two killers, a tall man named Glenn Bailey and a shorter, unnamed
man, forced their way into the Piedmont home of Sue Ann Cooke. They
held her while they waited for ex-convict and former state boxing
champion Stan Bryant, who was expected to return to the house. Some-*

thing bad had gone down in a drug deal and these men were about to exact the ultimate price.

  Things began to go wrong for the killers when Bryant arrived with three other people: Johnson, Forest Brown, and Brown's four-year-old son. Santone Johnson managed to get away, but the assailants clubbed Bryant, dragged him indoors, and ordered Brown and his son at gunpoint to follow them.

  Inside the house Bailey told Forest Brown to "get the hell out," but the shorter man said that they all would have to die—no witnesses. Bailey wouldn't stand for this and let Brown and his son go. Brown and his little boy ran out, hid behind a car, and heard two shots from inside the house. Both Sue Ann Cooke and Stan Bryant were killed, execution style, shot with a .38 revolver and a sawed-off shotgun.

  Aaron Owens was convicted of this horrific crime, but later, in a strange quirk of fate, was released through the efforts of the very man who had prosecuted him at his trial.

San Francisco, California
Wednesday, July 15, 1987, 2:35 p.m.

Aaron Lee Owens

Can you tell us about your arrest for the murders?

I was arrested and charged. I was very, very confident that nothing serious was going to happen. I also had an existing drug charge to deal with and I was far more concerned about that than the murder charges. There I was, spending almost every dime on that, because I knew there was nothing to the murder charge 'cause I didn't do it.

I was taken over to the courthouse in Oakland and they brought another guy up in the elevator and he said, "So you must be Owens." I said, "You must be Bailey." And that's where we met, my co-defendant and me. We met on the elevator in jail.

In court my attorney told me, "I don't think they'll be charging you with these murders this morning—they might throw it out, they don't have very much evidence against you." That's what I figured anyway, right?

I was taken back into the holding cell where they had Bailey. We started talking and he assured me they had him wrong too, which I believed. If they could have me wrong I knew they surely didn't know what they were talking about, so I figured they probably had him wrong also. Anyway they called me back and they did, in fact, formally charge me with the murders.

Later, I found out that Stan Bryant and Bailey had done a crime together. It was a pharmaceutical cocaine-type of robbery, after which Stan Bryant and Sue Ann Cooke had turned the gun on him. I thought that stuff only happened in the movies, but they turned the gun on Bailey and said they wanted it all.

I mean jeez, that greedy!

So Bailey then went and got this shorter man who was supposed to be an experienced killer.

How were you identified as the shorter man?

Forest Brown had waited behind a car. Then he called the police and gave them the first story, saying that he didn't know who the men were, that both men wore masks. He couldn't identify them but said the shorter man had a sawed-off shot gun taped to his hand.

The homicide officers called Brown back later and threatened him. He was on some sort of parole, or something like that—he shouldn't have been around at Bryant's in the first place. Seems they met with him on three different occasions. On the third occasion they met in a car and showed him, I think, twelve photos. Remember this is a pharmaceutical cocaine-type of thing, so most of the photos were of men who were trafficking largely in cocaine or someone they thought would purchase that amount of cocaine.

That's why they suspected you?

Yeah. Also they put in some photos of other people [suspected drug dealers] who might know him [Bryant]. My photo was picked out as being the shorter man. At the preliminary hearing they had asked Brown whether he saw the man in the courtroom who killed Bryant and Cooke. He took a fifteen-second pause and then he looked at me—"That's the man."

Did you have an alibi?

In the trial that followed I saw myself being completely outclassed. My attorney, who is now a judge, was clearly outclassed by John Taylor, the DA [see John Taylor interview]. He was so cunning. I love the

man, he's a beautiful man, although on this day *(laughs)* I didn't think
he was so beautiful!

This man [Taylor] opened up and right off the bat said, "I'm not
going to offer a rebuttal to Aaron Owens's alibi."

You see, the witnesses that were put on [the stand] were my
family. This crime took place the day before Mother's Day and I'm
a very, very sentimental man. If they would have asked me where
were you on *any* day other than that day, I probably couldn't have
told them, but when they said it was the day before Mother's Day, I
thought, "I got you now 'cause I know where I was." You see, the
year before I had had a problem with my mother-in-law and my
mother. They were griping because I gave them different kinds of
flowers. I decided this year it was going to be *all* yellow chrysanthemums. *Everybody* gets chrysanthemums and I won't have to deal
with that.

Well, the first florist—I bought them out. So they directed me to
shop on San Pablo Avenue, where I got the rest of the yellow chrysanthemums. All those people, they remembered everything. I had them
there [at the trial], I had my mother there, her story was exactly the
same as my mother-in-law's; but, this is all family, remember. So John
Taylor checked the stories out and the stories did all pan true, all the
way down to this certain TV program that was on at a certain time. He
even called the networks and stuff like that. He said, "It's the truth,
what they're saying."

But this is what killed my alibi. He said it was nothing but family
that I had as witnesses. *(Laughs)* You can't use family—right? John
Taylor goes on and says what they got wrong was the *time*. Then he
goes into this scenario. "It's the bottom of the ninth inning, it's two
outs. Campinaris is on second and Reggie Jackson is at bat. The
pitch comes and Reggie Jackson hits a ball through the middle.
Campinaris runs around and everyone sees this is going to be a close
call and he slides into home. The throw is a perfect throw and the
slide is a perfect slide. There is a cloud of dust—everybody in the
stands gets up and says, 'He's safe!'" . . . Now this guy, John Taylor,
was on the floor! . . . He's wearing a seven-hundred-dollar suit and
he's sliding on the floor! I mean this guy's far out!

When he stood up he said, "There's a cloud of dust and no one
can see anything . . . but everybody in the stands thinks he's safe.
But, when the dust clears, the umpire is standing there with his
thumb in the air saying he's out! Now nobody in that arena, no one
in the coliseum was closer to the player than that umpire. Some of
the people all the way in the bleachers say he's safe. But the reason

they were saying that he was safe was because that was the home team, and the home crowd wants to see the home team score safe." Now wanting to see him safe they refused to see through the umpire's eyes, which were closer.

This was the same man who would one day get you out of prison?

The same, but right now he was putting me there. You see what he was showing them was, "Sure, he brought those flowers ... but it could have been nine o'clock in the morning, it could have been eight o'clock in the morning when he brought those flowers. If the crime took place at twelve-thirty, you can believe that she would see her son there at twelve-thirty. Not with an intentional lie but that's what she would have *believed*. Her son was the home team."

How did you feel when you heard this? Were you worried?

As the trial drew on, I saw myself getting a little more worried and I'm seeing what is unfolding before my eyes. Awesome. If I was a juror, I would be thinking this man could be guilty.

You see, they had a preponderance of evidence on Bailey, bringing it up for hours on end, and they would use evidence on him and try and stick it on me. Like they would say, "These are the gloves, the *bloody* gloves that were found in Bailey's room ... *like* the gloves that Aaron Owens had on. This is a simulated sawed-off shotgun—*like* the one Aaron Owens had taped to his arm. He [John Taylor] made the witness—the eyewitness—use my name. He would say, "When you say the shorter man, you are in fact talking about Aaron Owens." The witness said, "Yes," so Taylor says, "From now on I want you to say, instead of the shorter man, say Aaron Owens."

Aaron Owens continued his story of how each witness was maneuvered by Taylor into placing him at the scene of the crime. Of how the testimony of key witness Santone Johnson, who had taken the Fifth Amendment, was skillfully used against Owens. Of how the presence in court of a member of the Richmond police department, who had arrested Owens on three separate occasions, one involving a sawed-off shotgun (not Owens's), had prevented Owens from taking the stand in his own defense. He talked about how the assistant DA would befriend the jury, each day picking on a different member, always smiling and addressing that person by name until at the end of the trial he was their best friend. Taylor had, by this time, created a weight of circumstantial evidence against Owens.

Co-defendant Bailey took the stand and said that Aaron was not his

accomplice, but then he said he wasn't at the scene of the crime either,
so that didn't help too much.
   But it was the final piece of evidence that would sway the jury.
   Aaron Owens continued:

In Forest Brown's testimony he said that he would never forget
the eyes of the man that wanted to murder his little boy. That really
got the jury. Later on I got to thinking . . . eyes? No way! The one
thing about me is my buck teeth—hell, what's in a pair of brown
eyes?
   Didn't you say Brown had testified that the men wore masks?
   Yeah—he did, but he changed that story. He kept changing his
story, to the police that is—not the jury. Anyway, they found me
guilty.
   What was the sentence?
   The maximum. More really. They gave me two life sentences with
two five-to-life sentences to be run consecutively.
   Of course at this time, in 1973, there was no death penalty in Cali-
fornia.
   Which I would have gotten for sure; remember this was a horren-
dous crime. A cold-blooded, premeditated, execution-style murder. Instead, I was sent to Folsom Prison.
   You were in prison. You were innocent. What was your next move?
   I knew that I had to get hold of Bailey. He knew who the other man
was. Only he could get me off. Anyhow, they'd split us up. Sent him
to San Quentin. But I was allowed to correspond with him under the
appeal procedure, as a co-defendant, that is.
   Did that help?
   He couldn't tell me stuff I really needed to know by letter. I had to
get myself transferred to San Quentin.
   How?
   Well, I spent every day in the library, studying the law, trying to see
how I could get myself out of this mess, and I found out that any two
wardens could, if they were to agree among themselves, exchange or
move prisoners from one prison to another. I was getting into therapy,
too, I'm a therapy freak by the way. And during this I developed good
terms with the warden's secretary. Anyhow, the warden was on *real*
good terms with her. It also turns out that Bailey is the barber of the
warden at San Quentin. So I tell her my story and she talks to the
warden and I get moved.
   That sounds straight out of the movies.

(Laughs) It is! HBO says they want to do it. Not only that, they put me in the cell next to Bailey.

Did he tell you who the other man was?

He did, but that wasn't no use to me. Bailey would have to be the one to tell the judge, and there was another problem that under the rule of appeal I had to provide new evidence.

But Bailey had told you the name of the "shorter man."

Bailey's word wasn't evidence. As far as the law was concerned, we were partners in crime.

I was also getting into trouble with my parole board. They said I wasn't showing any remorse, that I was unrepentant. Every time my review came up, they would bring in John Taylor and he'd tell them that I was the worst kind of vicious criminal and that my lack of remorse proved it.

I was getting fed up. I was serving time in one of the toughest places in the world, I'd been stabbed, beaten, and everything. I told them, "You can throw me in the hole, beat me, but I'm innocent and that's the way it is." As the board was finishing, John Taylor said that he was leaving the prosecutor's office and wouldn't be around at any more of my hearings. When he walked past me at the door, I said, "Don't you sometimes think that you did your job a little too well?" He looked kind of surprised and said he didn't understand. I said to him, "I always assumed you knew I was innocent, you were just doing your job, getting convictions for the state. Anyway, if it's of interest, I know who the murderer is."

From the look on his face I knew, just knew for sure, that I would get out of there.

Aaron's instinctive reaction to John Taylor proved to be well founded. The ex-prosecutor worked tirelessly for his release. Following up on information supplied by Bailey, reexamining witnesses, and tracking down a key witness who had driven the getaway car, Taylor discovered that the man he had sent to jail was innocent. One day Taylor made a special visit to San Quentin.

Aaron Owens continued:

I was called in [to the interview room in prison] one day. John Taylor was there holding a five-by-eight glossy photo. He threw it across the table. He said, "Do you recognize that guy?" And as the picture was spinning, I just turned my head and said with a smile, "It's me." Then I took a second look and realized it wasn't me. We had the same kind of hair. We were the same height, same weight, same build. But if you look close, we were ways apart.

Then he told that he was sure this was the guy, but that didn't mean I was gettin' out. He asked a few more questions and left—anyhow he came back one day and he said, "I have good and bad news, which do you want first?" I said, "Give me the bad news first!" and he said, "Well, you won't be getting out today." "And the good news?" I asked. "You will be getting out," he said.

Wow!

Yeah, wow! Doggone, man, I must have jumped through the ceiling, it was such a beautiful feeling. I mean, it must have been close to ten years now.

So it was over?

Absolutely not. They tried all kinds of tactics to keep me in. The judge refused to take the case. All the district attorneys in the Oakland department told John Taylor that he was being conned, that he was a fool and to "let the nigger rot. If he didn't do that [the murders] he did something else." All kinds of things like this.

In fact, they tried to rush a special hearing through on me, which John Taylor had asked specifically that they *not* do, to give me a tentative release date in 1999 or some such time. I was able to get word via my morning visitor to John Taylor to get here fast before they started to railroad me.

Again?

Again. I was scheduled for the board at ten o'clock. They had me going through the board when John Taylor got there. He came in screaming and hollering and stopped it. He persuaded Ruth Russian, the head of Corrections at the time, to get the judge to vacate the sentence and set it aside. When I got into court, they started raking through my past. I'd had hassles with the Richmond police department; there was this one guy that had me arrested three times and beat up once. I had three or four aliases. And they started asking, "Were you once known as this name? Did you ever go under the alias of that name?" I got mad and said, "What's that got to do with this case?" They said they wanted it for the record, and I said, "I don't!" I told them they were just trying to look good, which they couldn't, and they should just let me go now, "I don't want to be here another minute, I've been here ten years too long already." My mother is looking at me like, "Don't say anything, don't do anything, don't upset the Man." Anyway, the judge says, "We are going to release you," and holds out his hand. I turned away. This man had refused to take my case until ordered to do so. He couldn't just clear my name, maybe apologize? He had to go through all this, "Anyone could have made a little mistake like convicting the wrong man" type of thing.

Owens told us that he and Taylor are friends. Owens says that

Taylor worries he may go back to his old ways. It appeared from the interview that the adversary system of the courts works even better at the cops-and-robbers stage. The philosophy of law enforcement is all too often, if you get a crook in jail, keep him there. Or, as the DAs in Oakland had told John Taylor, "Let the nigger rot."

Aaron Owens was released ten years, almost to the day, after he was first convicted. If the death penalty had been in force, his family might have been mourning the anniversary of his death at the hands of the state of California.

DOWNHILL RACER

"My object all sublime
I shall achieve in time
To let the punishment fit the crime."
                    —Sir W. S. Gilbert, *The Mikado,* 1885

*John Taylor was the district attorney who had prosecuted Aaron
Owens and then, ten years later, proved him innocent. The ex-assistant
district attorney now has a law practice in the prosperous Bay area
suburb of Walnut Creek, California.*

*Aaron Owens had described him as a man who slid across a court-
room floor wearing a seven-hundred-dollar suit. For our interview,
John Taylor wore a beard, a deep tan, several bruises, and a black
eye.*

*"Skiing," he said, pointing to the eye with one hand. "When I ski, I
really ski. I hit a clump of frozen snow. My skis flew off, I did a half
flip and bounced all the way down the slopes on my knees and ribs."
He touched his side to indicate the area. When asked if the paramedics
had carried him off the slopes, he replied. "Heck, no. I made my way
to a first-aid station and had them put a butterfly bandage over the cut.
Spent the rest of the day skiing."*

*This was clearly a man of action. Nothing deters John Taylor from
his set course—winning. Be it on the ski slopes or the courtroom floor,
victory is everything to this counselor. The word "overachiever"
springs to mind, but this would be an oversimplification. He is driven
by a strong moral conviction about what is right and what is wrong,
not always an asset in the DA's office, as he pointed out on more than a
couple of occasions. It was this sense of justice and plain tenacity that*

*at first slammed the jail door shut on Aaron Owens and ten years later
sprung it open.*

   *John Taylor lives with his wife Joanne, a Municipal Court judge for
the Oakland-Piedmont-Emeryville Judicial District, and sons Derek,
twenty-one, a junior at UCLA, and Timothy, nineteen, a senior in high
school.*

   *The John Taylor/Aaron Owens story is an extraordinary tale of how
in a criminal prosecution, even when everything looks so right—everything can be dead wrong.*

Walnut Creek, California
Tuesday, February 2, 1988, 3:00 p.m.

John Taylor

Tell us about the Aaron Owens case.

I was an Alameda County deputy district attorney from 1966
through 1980, about thirteen years. In 1972 two people were killed in
Oakland in a drug-related, execution-style murder. They were killed by
two men, a little guy and a big guy. The latter was immediately identified as Glenn Bailey and it was crystal clear that he was involved. The
evidence on the smaller man was only that he was a black man of a
certain physical description.

Aaron Owens and Glenn Bailey ended up being co-defendants prosecuted by the Alameda County District Attorney's Office. As prosecutor, I was convinced it was a righteous prosecution and that they were
both responsible for the murders.

I had a *lot* of evidence.

For a start, Aaron Owens had a history of drug dealing, and he knew
many of the people among the group, of which two were the murder
victims. Next, the police traced Glenn Bailey to a motel in Oakland,
where he'd stayed on the night of the killings. There, they found he'd
made a phone call to Aaron Owens's house, to a number registered to
Aaron and Barbara Owens. And, to top it off, there was an eyewitness
who, with his four-year-old son, had stumbled onto the scene of the
murders. He said later in court, "I'll never forget the eyes of the man

who wanted to kill my baby." Pretty damning for Aaron in terms of eyewitness testimony.

Prior to the trial, the witness picked out Aaron's mug shot from one of thirteen that the police had put together. There was no racial differential that might mar the identification. Aaron and the witness are both black. In addition, there was plenty of corroboration as to the physical characteristics of the killer: his size, mutton chop sideburns, length of hair, darkness of skin.

What really happened, we found out ten years later, was that the phone call from the motel was made by Glenn Bailey's girlfriend. She knew a girlfriend of Aaron's wife, who lived in Richmond. There were four phone calls made from the motel, three to Richmond and one to Aaron Owens's house. When Bailey's girlfriend called her girlfriend in Richmond, she was told to try her at Barbara's house. That's why the phone call was made to the Owens home. But, at the time, it looked pretty incriminating. So, there wasn't simple eyewitness identification.

There was corroboration in terms of the business he was in, dope dealing, as well as his physical size and more.

I had another break in court. I'd called the motel clerk as a witness, hoping he could identify Glenn Bailey, but he looked around and said, "I recognize him, he's been in my place." He was talking about Aaron Owens, not Glenn Bailey!

I later found out this was a transient motel and, yes, Aaron had been there many times, but not the night of the murders. But as you can see I was getting all the right answers to nail shut the prosecution case.

Aaron Owens was convicted in 1973. I had tried weaker cases than that. It was not a case I was uncomfortable about. I felt very comfortable about the way it was done; it was certainly done fairly and I thought the result was appropriate.

I often went to parole hearings of murderers I had personally prosecuted, and so eventually I went to Aaron Owens's parole hearing at San Quentin. While we were waiting for the parole board to get their act together, Aaron and I had a chance to talk.

I have never felt any hostility, anger, or any particular negative feelings toward people I prosecute. Unlike some prosecutors, I wasn't overly righteous. I felt good about what I was doing, but I thought it was a truth-seeking process and if done fairly and ethically it works out pretty well.

When I look at these people charged with crimes, I often thought, "There but for the grace of God go I." Many people who find themselves in those kinds of positions couldn't tell you how they got there. At any rate I never got on this hate thing, even if the people were charged with some of the more violent crimes.

I had kidded with Aaron during the trial all the time. I had a purpose in doing it; I wanted feedback from him in case he took the stand. I would know more about him, know what buttons could be pushed most effectively. I would come over to him during a recess when the defense lawyer had stepped out and I'd say, "Well, how do you think I'm doing?" and he'd say, "You ain't got nothing on me. You can't get me," and I'd say, "Oh, I don't know, look at that jury. I think maybe you're in some trouble here." It was sort of a friendly, competitive verbal intercourse.

When he saw me at the parole hearing, he starts telling me about how he knew the guy who really did the murders. He had met him in Folsom Prison. I listened a bit and said, "Hey, look, pal, who do you think you're talking to? I am not one of the other cons in the joint who hasn't done a thing. Nobody in jail has ever done anything. We all know that. Right? You're talkin' to the guy who prosecuted you! I saw the evidence. I know you're guilty. You are wasting your time telling me about meeting the guy who really did it and everything."

"You really think I did it, don't you?" Aaron said.

"Of course I think you did it! You know, that's another myth you people have out on the streets that we go around prosecuting people who didn't do it."

Aaron had beaten a number of dope cases on search issues. He had always thought that the prosecution worked such that if we couldn't get him for what he did, we got him for what he didn't do; that we were just balancing the books. He didn't spend any time during the trial trying to convince me of his innocence, because he thought I *knew* he was innocent.

One thing you learn by doing trial work is to become quite accomplished at determining credibility, because you are constantly working on people in cross-examination and comparing testimony, and something was gnawing away at my viscera, so I said, "Hey, who is the guy who did it, then?" and he says, "I can't tell you that." Code of the prison and all. So I said, "That's fine, you want to do time on a double murder for somebody else . . . well." I told him the only vehicle to his proving his innocence would be proving to me who really did do it. "Until you can name that guy, you ain't going nowhere," I told him.

I was leaving the DA's office and moving to Tahoe, so I told him it would be easy to get ahold of me, he'd just have to call the DA's office, and if he ever wanted to tell me who did it, I said I'd be glad to sit and listen.

Now I'm driving back from San Quentin and something is really bothering me. I mean, I can picture it very, very clearly, because when you leave San Quentin—I don't know if you've ever been over there

—you've got to open your trunk, you know, and there was somethin' really, really eating at me. As I'm driving across the Richmond Bridge, it finally dawns on me that a few moments ago, in that room in San Quentin, was the first time, in all of those years, that Aaron realized that I thought he was really guilty. I saw it in his face and in his eyes and in his reaction. An innocent person would not waste time thinking that I thought he was guilty. He would think that I am "balancing the books," and I really knew he was innocent. If I believed that his reaction was genuine, it could only be consistent with an innocent man. It was not consistent with a guilty man.

I have learned since then to trust my intuition. I was trained as a lawyer and therefore I used to believe the only way to approach a problem was to think it out. I had a pretty strong feeling about this case. My wife—she was a deputy district attorney at the time—saw me lost in thought and she said, "What's eating you?" and I said, "You know, Goddammit, I think that guy is innocent" *(laughs)* and I told her why, as I explained to you. Of course there was no way I could go to the system and say, "*My intuition* tells me that I prosecuted an innocent man so you will have to trust me on this one."

Anyway, I went to Lowell Jenson, who was then the district attorney of Alameda County. Now this is on January 3, 1980, my last day was January 5, and I said, "Look, I'm leaving this place, but I want to tell you about something that happened over at San Quentin and I think there is a substantial possibility that this guy didn't do it. Now I know there is nothing that can be done at this point, but if there ever comes a time when another person is named, or there is a basis for investigation, I want you to hear this from me now, while I am a deputy district attorney, before I go out into private practice. Because, you know, sometimes people leave the DA's office and feel some guilt over prosecuting people or something like that."

I left the DA's office on January 5. Well, a year later I am up in Tahoe just having a good time, and Glenn Bailey comes up for, I think, his second parole hearing, and he writes a letter to the DA's office and says, "Well, I did it, but Aaron Owens didn't do it and I want to talk to somebody." Originally he had said he was innocent, that he was across town eatin' chili burgers—had some alibi that he maintained after he was convicted. But he always said Aaron Owens had nothing to do with it, that they had met for the first time in the holding cell after they were both arrested for the murders.

One of the prejudices you get as a prosecutor is that such stories are fabrications, because most often they are. And there certainly is selective perception in law enforcement. The police and prosecution focus on a suspect, and even if you try not to, human nature is such that you are going to focus on convicting that person, rather than keeping your mind open and believing that you could be wrong. You waste a lot of time when you do that. Statistically, most often you will be right, in the overwhelming majority of the cases a situation like Aaron Owens is going to be a guilty guy.

So they called me and asked if I would be interested in going to the parole hearing, and I said, "Sure I'll volunteer." So I went over to see Bailey and he gave me the name of the other guy. I returned to the DA's office and said, "Hey, remember me *(laughs)*, the time has come. There ought to be an investigation. We have a name."

Now this other guy had a record of violence in addition to drug violations. Aaron really didn't have any record other than drugs. And if you want to talk about phone calls corroborating the identity of the other guy, we found all kinds of phone calls between Glenn Bailey and this suspect before the murders occurred. Lots of contact. So essentially they assigned an investigator, a former policeman, now investigator for the district attorney, to work the case with me. I volunteered my time and they paid the expenses.

We went to Los Angeles, we went to Seattle, and we found a witness that Glenn Bailey had identified as being present at the time of the murders.

We talked to a woman who had testified at the trial and had tried to give Glenn Bailey an alibi. She denied being at the murder scene herself, but we sort of felt she was the driver of the getaway car. She now admitted being the driver and said, "I'm glad you're here because this has been bothering me for the longest time and Glenn did it but the other guy didn't."

Aaron Owens told us in his interview that no one in the district attorney's office was interested in new evidence; that the attitude was "Let the nigger rot." Is this true?

They may have said, "Let the nigger rot," but not exactly in so many words. Now many of my social friends were involved with the district attorney's office and I heard that there is this guy going around telling everybody that I am on a wild goose chase. That Aaron Owens is as guilty as the day is long and I am wasting my time, I've gone soft, I've done a Jerry Brown *[former California Governor Brown was in a seminary before taking office]*. Allright? Now, he's a persuasive and somewhat important figure in our little legal world. Then I heard that he'd talked to the judge in the case, the subject of Aaron Owens had come up, and he had told the judge, "Taylor is all wet."

The thing that really bothered me was that he was influential in the community and people would think that he had some inside knowledge and that I was wrong.

One day I collared him, said, "Hey, listen, you've been going around telling everybody that I am full of it and that I don't know what I am doing and I am makin' a big mistake in trying to get this guilty guy off." He admitted that was basically true and I said, "Well, could you please tell me what information you have that would support that conclusion, because I think that I should make that part of my investigation?" And he points to his stomach and he says, "Gut. Gut reaction." I just exploded and I said, "You mean you're going around saying these things, involving people's lives, based on a—a gut reaction! How can you be that irresponsible?" He didn't even know what I was talking about.

However, I was assigned a police officer as an investigator, to keep me on track. The officer also thought I was having some sort of psychological crisis and he was going to have to straighten me out.

The man went into the case believing that nobody could slip through the cracks, be innocent and get convicted. At the end of the investigation, he wrote the same report as I did, which said, "Aaron Owens was innocent and we ought to get him out of prison."

The eyewitness [Forest Brown], the father of the four-year-old boy, still thinks that Aaron was guilty—which brings up the whole question of eyewitnesses—anyway, the process came about and Aaron was released. There was no death penalty in California then, and that was the *only* reason that this was not a death penalty case.

Would you have asked for the death penalty?

Oh yeah, I would have done my job. I was prepared to. If *Furman v. Georgia* had not come down, I would have gone for it, I would have had to, or else not take the case to begin with. What I am saying is that it wasn't a fun thing, I mean, I didn't like doing it, but I didn't have a strong anti-death penalty feeling that would have prevented me from doing it. Most of the cases that I tried would have resulted in that if there had been a death penalty statute. I feel fortunate in that. I am happy now that I never did get involved in putting anybody on death row. I mean, anybody who is pro-death penalty, if there is such a thing, or at least can accept the death penalty as a punishment, doesn't want to be the one pulling the lever. "Yeah, let somebody else to it."

Well, somebody has to collect the garbage—I don't want to do that either.

What is it like in the DA's office?

One of the handiest weapons for a prosecutor is *righteousness*. Because it is so available, you feel so *just*. It is the way you argue to the jury. They like you. You come in and you represent the community, trying to get this bad person put away, whatever. They want to like you and it isn't very hard to get them to like you. "Incompetence is the worst form of corruption," I believe the saying goes, and I think that is where you run into problems. I include the inability of management in a district attorney's office to see that their office has a high level of incompetence. Incompetence includes people who really follow policies and don't use any individual judgment. Most district attorney's offices want their policies followed, they are afraid of independence. For instance, in this county, right here in Contra Costa County, I happen to know that they hire ex-soldiers and they look for men with service records—they do not want people with independent judgment.

I know that I was one of the best prosecutors, certainly in this area, and I know that I could get convictions that other people couldn't, and my motivation was my ego. You can show no fear in the face of the enemy. It's a hard thing to do under normal circumstances because it is a fact that some people fear the battle. It is a tremendous emotional experience to go through a trial, because you are on the line every day, you embarrass yourself if you do poorly. Winning and losing is all there is to it. Winning is very, very important and losing is the end of the earth.

I wanted to win. I wanted to continue building a legend.

Are you for or against capital punishment?

We make decisions all the time in this country; political decisions, governmental decisions, and executive decisions that cause people's death. Whether it be one dialysis machine for five applicants—the doctor makes the decision who gets it and who dies. Or we think a war in Vietnam is a good thing and therefore we will send fifty thousand people to their deaths. It makes much more sense to me to execute somebody who has maliciously and wantonly taken a life. But in a land in which I were king there would be no death penalty.

VIRGINIA IS FOR LOVERS

"The world itself is but a large prison, out of which some are daily led to execution."

—Sir Walter Raleigh, 1552–1618

Historically, from the abolitionist point of view, Virginia has a bad record. It was the first permanent settlement in North America and has the first recorded execution. In 1608, one George Kendall was shot to death (see Watt Espy interview). Virginia has also had more judicial killings than any other state in the Union and, despite its reduced size (it once included both Carolinas and more), it continues to have a healthy appetite for executions.

The man who gave the territory its name was merchant-adventurer Sir Walter Raleigh, in honor of his patron, the "Virgin Queen," Elizabeth I. Ironically, the founder of this very pro-death penalty state met his end at the hands of the executioner. He was beheaded at the ripe old age of sixty-six.

Paul Keve, Professor Emeritus in the Department of Administration of Justice and Public Policy, has his campus office in an attractive, period house at Virginia Commonwealth University.

Bookshelves line one side of the professor's room, diplomas hang from the walls, and a musty smell of learning fills the air, a model of sparse academia reminiscent of childhood visits to the principal's office. The seventy-four-year-old, gray-haired, slightly balding professor, in a gray wool worsted suit, completes the picture of a stern headmaster, but his smile is reassuring and warm.

Paul Keve started his corrections career in the Federal Bureau of Prisons in Washington, D.C., in 1941. He worked for nine years in the

Virginia Corrections system in probation and parole and also with juvenile delinquents. He then moved to Minnesota to accept the appointment of chief probation officer in Minneapolis, a position he held for fifteen years. He went on to become Commissioner of Corrections from 1967 to 1971. He resigned to join a think tank on criminal justice in Washington, D.C., for a number of years, then returned to public service again as Commissioner of Corrections in Delaware, which he describes as "a very different experience and not a happy one, very political and a terrible contrast to Minnesota."

After three years in Delaware he moved to Virginia and became a professor in corrections and criminal justice at Richmond University.

Paul Keve is the author of eight books, mostly to do with corrections methods. His most recent work, a history of corrections in Virginia, focuses on the legacy of slavery and the death penalty in Virginia.

**Richmond, Virginia
Tuesday, February 23, 1988, 11:00 a.m.**

Professor Paul Keve

As a former prison administrator, what is your opinion of life imprisonment as an alternative to death? Are the prisons capable of dealing with that?

The prison system is capable of dealing with life imprisonment, as it should be. I am in favor of life imprisonment, but I am not an advocate of this idea of life in prison without the possibility of parole.

The public constantly kids itself about the death penalty and life imprisonment. It likes to believe what it likes to believe, and so politicians cater to that, and their speechifying on the subject adds to the public's conviction that the death penalty is a good idea. I think that's one of the reasons you have got so much support for it.

The person running for the state legislature makes speeches saying, "Vote for me. I'm hardnosed on crime and we are going to have more death penalty cases. We are going to get tough on crime." That helps to feed that public thirst for the death penalty, so the public keeps hearing this and thinks there must be something to it.

But you know there is a fascinating contrast between death penalty states, like Virginia, and an abolitionist state like Minnesota. You don't hear that rhetoric in Minnesota, and so there isn't the expressed and felt need for it there. I had nineteen years in Minnesota and I have had a good many years in Virginia and three years in Delaware, and I can appreciate the contrast. In Virginia when somebody is sentenced to death, there is that constant feeling, "Let's get on with it. Let's get him burned."

There is a sadistic need to "get it done" and the feeling that justice isn't served until he's been executed. In Minnesota, there isn't any of that. Nobody there, presently alive, has had the experience of expecting anybody to be executed. The last execution occurred in 1911, so there isn't the demand for it at all. It is just a much more civilized sort of thing.

What were your experiences in Minnesota with recidivism?

Oh, it depends on which researcher you read. But all my reading on the subject indicates that states like Minnesota have no more crime and sometimes less of the type of crime the death penalty is supposed to deter. I am convinced from my reading and my personal experience that the death penalty not only does not deter a would-be murderer. It can even aggravate the homicide rate.

Can you give us an example?

Sure. One of my very first cases, a case that I worked on closely, was a professional woman, a nurse. She held a high management position in the Red Cross in Alexandria during World War II. She was an office type and although she had a young child, she didn't like home-making. Her husband was sent off to war and she discovered she was pregnant again, a little bit late in childbearing age, forty or so. Sometimes you get this post-puerperal depression or psychosis following a pregnancy at that age and, with her husband off to war, she had to deal with all the problems of home on her own.

After the birth of that second child, stuck at home instead of at work in her beloved office, she fell into an unnatural and deep depression. The idea that went on in her mind, to oversimplify it, was that she would kill herself, but she couldn't reconcile herself to leaving these two children. So she decided that she would kill the children and then the state would do her suicide for her, through an execution. She ran a bathtub full of water and carefully immersed the two children in it until they were dead, dried off the bodies, laid them out on the bed, and then ran next door to the neighbor and asked her to call the sheriff.

The idea was now that the state would take care of her suicide. Well it didn't. It put her in a mental hospital for study and diagnosis and within a month or so she had worked through this depression and she was a more normal person. That is to say, *relatively* normal, as she was now devastated by the reality of her crime. She had to live with the fact that she had murdered her children. I have no doubt that those two children would still be alive if there had not been a death penalty in Virginia.

Delaware abolished the death penalty during the 1950s. The state hit an uncharacteristic liberal point in its history for some reason or another and they abolished the death penalty. But it is a very small state and anything that happens anywhere in the state is almost like it was in the family; everybody knows about it. Anyway, in a couple of years there were one or two horrible murders committed of the type that naturally gets people uptight: dramatic, tragic, and brutal murders committed by strangers. So a new bill was introduced to restore the death penalty. There was a great deal of feeling about it and so the bill was rushed through. Those people who did not want it to be rushed through demanded that there be public hearings, and there were. One of the people who testified at a public hearing was a long-time police officer and detective named Mulrine. Detective Mulrine came to the hearing and made the usual highly rhetorical speech, "We have got to have the death penalty to protect our people and deter crime." All of that sort of thing. Well, not because of his testimony, but because the mood was there anyway, they restored the death penalty.

Within a couple of weeks after the bill was passed, the first capital crime occurred and the person who committed that murder was Detective Mulrine. He took his pistol and deliberately shot and killed his wife. Nobody in the state could have been any more aware that the state was now ready to execute people. Where's the deterrent?

The first execution that occurred after our moratorium *[Furman v. Georgia]* was Gary Gilmore. I think he suckered the state of Utah into doing his suicide for him when he couldn't quite get up the nerve to do it himself. There is no doubt about it; I could give you dozens of examples.

I have known so many people who were guilty of capital murder and you look at them and get acquainted with them, and you just know that the threat of the death penalty didn't touch the situation at all. These are frustrated and unhappy people who were just not skillful in meeting life's problems—and the threat of the death penalty would not have had a thing to do with the prevention of murder.

You say Delaware hit an uncharacteristic liberal point. Is it particularly conservative?

The pillory, which I think of as a colonial punishment, persisted into this century in Delaware. It was abolished in 1905, but the whipping post was not abolished until about 1952. They whipped a number of people right up to then. They used a leather strap on a wooden handle and there was a whipping post in each of the three counties. Each sheriff had the responsibility of carrying it out in his county and it was always public. The person would be stripped to the waist and his hands handcuffed around a rather large post.

The sheriff would post his whipping schedule in the paper so that anyone from the general public could show up in the jail yard and cheer him on. The court would prescribe the number of lashes. Typically, the court would give a combined sentence. Sixty days in jail and thirty lashes, for instance. The sheriff was free to give the whipping at any time during the man's jail sentence. He might give him all his lashes at once or he might take pity on him and spread it out during a period of time; five or ten lashes a day and so on.

The public actually turned out to see this?

Heck, yes, it was one of the things to do. Another thing about that, women were whipped too. Eventually, a hundred years or so ago, Delawarians got a little bit self-conscious about the public whipping of women stripped to the waist. I think it was in the 1880s that some liberal in the legislature in Delaware put in a bill to abolish the whipping of white women. Some even more liberal legislator offered an amendment to strike out the word "white," which would have abolished it for all women, but that was too much for them, they couldn't go for that. So they continued whipping women for a few more years. But there haven't been any women whipped in Delaware in this century; only men, but lots of them.

You have worked with juveniles. Are they deterred at all by the death penalty?

I have known quite a number of kids who have committed murder. Generally, they do not think about the consequences. You get family situations where there is rejection and coldness and lack of understanding; kids get caught in this situation and can find no way out of it. They are all abused, if you use the word in a very broad context. You won't always see bruises on them. Sometimes it's physical, sometimes badly so, but a child growing up and developing his personality needs love and support and acceptance, and these kids don't get it. Their parents have problems of their own, or they have foster parents. What they get is gross rejection and lack of understanding. The youngster doesn't know what his rights are, doesn't know the avenues available to him for correcting the problem, and one day he just boils over and kills somebody and it's likely to be a parent. I almost have never known a child murderer to have killed some unrelated victim. They are usually close-at-hand people who become the objects of their frustration.

What do you see as the alternative to the death penalty?

Human long-term storage. I don't know what else. There are some people we just don't know what else to do with. But at least we can make long-term storage humane. I don't think there is any need for this life-without-parole sort of thing. We cannot command the next generation and we shouldn't. We don't want the previous generation commanding us. We want to be free to do what we want to do.

What about the question of victims' rights?

Victims' rights are certainly important, but the death penalty doesn't help the victims; it doesn't restore anybody to life. There is a supposition that you are not respecting the rights and feelings of the victim or his or her family unless you execute the offender, and many victims seem to feel the same way. But all I have learned and heard is that the family of the victims who clamor for the offender to be executed still do not feel peace afterwards. So I have no patience with killing people just to be courteous to the suffering family. It has no real restorative effect.

What about the cost of execution as opposed to the cost of keeping someone in prison for a long period of time?

Ah, there is another way the public kids itself. We hear people say, "Let's execute them. Why should the taxpayer feed these killers?" But it doesn't work like that.

The costs of running a prison are *fixed* costs. You can take several people out of it and you don't change the cost to run the prison two cents. You still have to turn on all the lights, employ all the staff, and pay all the salaries. The cook won't put any less food on the table unless the population drops substantially; the cook can't be concerned about variations from day to day. You do not reduce the cost of running a prison by taking inmates out of it, unless you take so many inmates out that you can close down one cell block and turn off the lights and the water, reduce the amount of food appreciably, and lay off several staff members. Otherwise you don't make any cost reduction at all.

So if you closed down death row and put them in the general prison population, you would actually save money?

It would, because the death penalty is expensive. Some people think the cost of an execution is just the additional electric bill you get from turning on the electricity to the chair, but the costs of prosecution are tremendous. The cost of pushing one execution all the way through the courts is well over a million dollars. Just think how many lawyers there must be in the Attorney General's Office and how much computer time, getting the right attorney into the right courtroom, at the right time, with all the right papers, and on and on. It boggles the mind.

What do you think the death penalty does to the society when it condones execution?

I think it keeps the public more accepting and a little more callous about the taking of life.

I was doing some studies a few years ago on the French Revolution, and you see a momentum building up over the course of that revolution as they executed people. The more they executed, the more freedom they felt to execute, and the more of a bloodbath it became. If you really do a thorough study of the French Revolution, you see in it a growing callousness toward human life.

You know we have about two thousand people waiting on death row right now. Let's suppose we were to double the rate that we execute each year, say up to fifty a year. It would take more than forty years to go through the present supply without adding any more. I just keep wishing that people would understand that. When I hear these politicians beating the drums for the death penalty, I wish I could tell them to stop kidding us. We are not doing it. We are just pretending we are doing it and we can't do it. Forty years just to get through the present backlog, and you know that all those people are not going to get executed; we are just pretending.

But when it finally comes down to it, the reason I am opposed to the death penalty isn't the cost, isn't the statistics, isn't the possibility that we will execute an innocent person. Instead, my thinking is that when people murder, it demonstrates an inadequate respect for the value of human life. So what we have got to do is try to encourage greater respect for human life. But—it defies all logic to suppose that you can encourage the respect for human life through the device of taking human life. It's as simple as that.

IT'S NOT ALL RIGHT

"When constabulary duty's to be done,
The policeman's lot is not a happy one."
—Sir W. S. Gilbert,
The Pirates of Penzance, 1879

Officer Ronald E. Hampton, Badge #3286 of the Washington, D.C., Police Department, has a commanding 6 foot 4 inch presence, but his sense of humor is displayed, for all to see, on a button pinned on an orange windcheater over his uniform. It reads: "I must be a mushroom. Everyone keeps me in the dark and feeds me bullshit." The forty-three-year-old, salt-and-pepper-bearded community relations officer does not agree with the majority of policemen who share the overall public view that the only good killer is a dead killer. Officer Ron Hampton is a declared and dedicated abolitionist.

Washington, D.C.
Friday, February 26, 1988, 9:45 a.m.

Ronald E. Hampton

Between 1984 and 1986 I was the chairman of the National Black Policemen's Association. I was born and raised in Washington, D.C., and I have been a police officer for sixteen years.

I graduated from American University and was in the Air Force for four years. I guess I am still involved to some extent in going to school, because I am working on my Master's degree. My original degree was in the administration of justice.

There is a very large black population in Washington. What percentage of the officers are black?

About 54 percent, but the increase to that level only happened in the last six or seven years. Prior to that the black percentage was 36 percent or 37 percent. Like you say, in the city there is about a 70 percent black population.

Is there a difference in the attitude of black police officers?

Oh yes. There is a distinct difference. There is a positive attitude about whom you work for. I don't think we work for ourselves, I think we work for the community, and that's who we are supposed to serve. But the average police officer doesn't think like that and, unfortunately, I don't think all black police officers think like that, because they come into a system where there is a very strong propensity for you to act and be like your white counterparts. So they want to be accepted into the fold and also they want to make it in the system. So they change roles. They just totally change their personality, and a lot of times some black officers are more brutal and more insensitive to blacks than whites are.

But there are also black officers who have decided not to do that, and instead fight for our communities. We struggle within the system because our behavior is totally different. We are also able to gain the support of the community, and that's what prevents the system from doing anything about us because we do have support in the community.

Do the police treat blacks differently from whites?

Oh yeah, yeah. Definitely. I mean even in a minor traffic thing, the way a police officer will approach a white person differs from the way he will approach a black person. You see the same kind of behavior from black officers because of the pressure to conform to norms of the police institution. The institution is a white, powerful institution and there is definitely a difference in the way minorities are approached. Even to the point that, if you happened to be stopped by a police officer and you act like you know the law, you act like you know what he can and cannot do, there may be a resentment from the officer that you know his job, but it will also call to his attention that he can't do anything to you because he knows that you know what he can and can't do. Plus you have *access*. That's something different, you see. Whites have access and always have had access to the criminal justice system. The poor, downtrodden, not necessarily black folks, but any minority, they lack access. Powerful people in the system can take advantage of the people who don't have access. The police department represents those kind of things when they go into these poor communities.

How did you become involved in the anti-death penalty issue?

Well, last year we were invited to come to Atlanta to participate in a Death Penalty Awareness Day. Before that, I was personally quite aware of some of the statistics about blacks on death row. Even more particularly, I was aware the role of the race of the victims in determining the punishment. I mean, when you look at the application of the death penalty, you can see there is something wrong and racist. So, as black police officers, being a part of the criminal justice system, being there and seeing how these things go down, it was our place to take a position. I participated in the Atlanta conference and we made a statement in support of abolishing the death penalty. We also made a statement about the adverse impact that the death penalty has on the black community, and that we would be willing to work with any organization that was interested in abolishing it and bringing it to the forefront, particularly in discriminatory application. We don't only represent ourselves, we represent all minorities—period.

What do you say when people bring up deterrence as an argument?

There is no deterrent value to the death penalty. Also, having been a police officer for sixteen years, I think that our present correctional system, if that's what you want to call it, has no deterrent effect on crime. The things that motivate crime in this country are altogether different.

To a great degree, the dollar is the most valuable thing in America. The people in power have made money the only measuring stick. If you don't have money, then you don't have anything. So how can you fault someone who simply wants to mirror America's goals? To make money, get money, or acquire money and a whole lot of it? That's how a lot of the powerful people in America got to be powerful . . . taking it from somebody else.

So crime is thought to be a behavior done only by people at the bottom of the pile. But all they are doing is the same kind of behavior that goes on at the top of the ladder, they're just doing it in a different way. The way the rich do it is concealed and covered up. Unfortunately, when it is done at the bottom of the ladder, it is done mostly against other poor folks. So the people who don't have anything take from people who also don't have anything. In those instances in society where the "have nots" take from the "haves," the punishments are more severe. It is then that law enforcement brings out the tanks and everything else to capture and prosecute those people. That's what is so lopsided about the whole thing.

Many policemen say we need capital punishment to protect police officers. Would you feel safer with the death penalty when going into a dangerous situation?

Not at all. I don't think that has anything to do with it. Usually when an officer loses his life it is due to circumstantial factors, not premeditation. Usually the person you encounter who may be a threat to your life generally has done something to start off with that has nothing to do with you. The fact that you have to carry out your job is what threatens your life. If you have been properly trained, if you are aware and conscious of the kinds of things that you have to do as a police officer—you are going to take the necessary precautions to prevent being injured. Of course, there will always be situations where you are at risk, but I don't believe that police officers are any safer with the death penalty. It won't stop anyone.

If the death penalty was not racially biased, what would your attitude be?

It would be the same, I would not support it. I just can't see the value in it. When someone takes someone's life, I don't believe we have the right to do the same. I don't believe in that. That's not going to bring that individual back, and I don't believe our system has the God-given right to up and do that. Even if there was a way to do it equitably, I couldn't support it.

There are people who have been falsely imprisoned for years; how can we repay them for the time they spend in prison? There is no amount that can, especially if he's on death row. At the snap of a finger you cannot bring back all that they lost. It ain't no "put on a smilin' face" when you have suffered like that. You couldn't give me a million dollars a day for every day I was in prison that would pay me back for putting me in prison for something I didn't do. It would hurt me for the rest of my life. And suppose an innocent person is executed, the idea of repayment is, of course, silly.

Congress has voted to introduce the death penalty for drug-dealing-related murders. Would you care to comment?

Like the guy they busted for selling marijuana in Virginia and want to execute? The police department can take the kid pushing on the corner, go arrest him any time it wants, but how many times do they go into the suites and the boardrooms, into the halls of the Fortune 500 companies where the drugs are being used? You think the drug barons make their money selling crack to kids? It's the white-collar trade that keeps Colombia in business. There's a snowstorm going on in the financial districts of our large cities! But who do you think is gonna be executed?

What do you think capital punishment does to the society that condones it?

Well, I guess I don't think very much of the way we run our country, because the people who run it and the people who are in control live by a different standard than those who live at a lower level. You can talk about equality and those kinds of things, but that's not true, and I don't live under those kinds of illusions. It reminds me of a situation where there are police officers who use drugs and then they go out and lock people up for using drugs. I think there is something wrong with that. It's a hypocrisy, especially in a country that preaches humanity, for us to turn around and terminate people's lives. It is totally wrong and hypocritical. I have very little respect, if any, for the people who support it and are involved in it.

THE VIRGINIAN

"Never, never will we desist, till we have wiped away this scandal from the Christian name."

—William Wilberforce, 1759–1833,
address to Parliament on slavery

William Styron has been an enormous help to us on this project. In March 1987, Ian met with Bill and his wife, Rose, in Los Angeles, and asked advice on a proposed book. A book that Amnesty had asked us to write—this book. Our initial idea was that the work would include essays and opinions from world leaders and artists in every field of human achievement, lavishly illustrated with "art" photographs.

Both Bill and Rose were very supportive of this fledgling idea but suggested, without being specific, that we should seek a different approach—an approach that resulted in a formal interview with the Pulitzer Prize-winning author.

William Styron was born in Newport News, Virginia, in the Tidewater region—not far from Southampton County where the Nat Turner Revolt took place. He served almost three years in the Marine Corps in World War II, and after the war returned to complete his studies at Duke University.

His works include: Lie Down in Darkness *(1951);* The Long March *(1962);* Set This House on Fire *(1960);* The Confessions of Nat Turner *(1967, Pulitzer Prize winner);* The Clap Shack *(1973); and* Sophie's Choice *(1976).*

William Styron

You were born in Virginia near where the Nat Turner Revolt took place in 1831. Did you grow up hearing stories of the uprising?

Yes, it was always in the background, but at the time I only had a vague conception of what it all meant. It meant something to me, but in a very remote and subliminal way. When I was a kid, I heard this almost mythological story about Nat Turner and it occurred to me that it was an absolutely extraordinary thing to have happened. I didn't quite know what to make of it then, but as I grew older the significance of this long-ago revolt became more and more understandable. About the time I got into college it had really engaged my attention and I resolved that someday I would write about it.

Can you tell us a little about your background and family?

The society in which I grew up was completely closed. There was complete segregation all over the region, as there was throughout all of the Southern states. In many ways, it was very similar to South Africa today. So I was living a schizophrenic life, as most white people were, with everything totally segregated.

My father was really a son of the old South. My grandmother, as a little girl, had slaves. This was around the time of the Civil War. Somehow, my father miraculously escaped some of the bigotry that afflicted most of his generation. He was born in 1889 in a very small town in a remote area of eastern North Carolina. It was very backward and I am sure very racist at that time. For a man of his background, he emerged, I thought heroically, to be what I guess you would call a liberal. He was an engineer in a shipyard in Newport News, which was, and still is, one of the largest shipyards in the world. He had rather strange ambivalences about race and culture. I remember he was very proud to be the president of a chapter of an organization called the Sons of the American Revolution, which, like the Daughters of the American Revolution, is an organization that, paradoxically, is made up of very conservative people despite its name. He became president of the state chapter in the early 1950s, but it was a measure of this kind of duality in the man that when the Sons of the American Revolution declared their solidarity behind Joe McCarthy, my father quit in a rage. So he really was a man who had liberal leanings.

You narrated The Confessions *of Nat Turner* in the first person. *What was it like getting into the soul, as it were, of a black man?*

From the outset I was determined to write from the first person. I felt this had never really been done before by a white man. It offered a challenge and I wanted to rise to it. It seemed to me that by doing this I could more readily, and perhaps more penetratingly, get into the mind of a black man.

Nat Turner was a minister. Are you religious?

I don't think I am. I don't know what the word "religious" means really. I am certainly not in the traditional sense. I loathe most of the clergy and the people who make up the infrastructure of Christianity. I despise them with a passion, but I certainly don't have anything against Christianity itself. I have a great respect for the gospels and for what Jesus, if he were listened to, could teach us.

Do you feel that Americans still have not addressed the all too recent history of slavery and its legacy?

Plainly we have not yet gotten out from under the legacy of slavery. Every time we commit an injustice against a black person in this country, which we continually do, we are more or less reacting to the heritage of slavery.

For all intents and purposes, millions of black people in this country live under a system of informal slavery. Racism is an inevitable offshoot. There is no doubt about it. It is a national tragedy that black people in this country seem to be in a state of almost perpetual deprivation. It's a dilemma—the title "The American Dilemma" used by Gunnar Myrdal in 1944 still applies.

You testified against the confirmation of Judge[Robert] Bork to the Supreme Court at the congressional hearings in 1987. How did this come about?

Well, I belong, like many writers, to the writers' organizaton, PEN. The organization which asked me to be their spokesman. I was willing to speak for them provided I was not the sole author of the statement that I made. I felt totally beyond my depth in terms of the legal aspects of the thing. Floyd Abrams, the famous First Amendment lawyer, was the architect of the opening statement, but after that I was pretty much on my own.

Bork was rejected. The Supreme Court, however, handed down one of its most controversial civil rights decisions by denying the petition of

Georgia death row inmate Warren McCleskey in 1987. What is your reaction?

It was appalling. It was one of the most outrageously, blatantly bigoted decisions ever made by the Supreme Court. There was a hollow, casualistic sort of buffoonery behind the decision that made no sense in terms of logic. It is a disgrace as far as I can tell and an out-and-out piece of racism.

As far as the death penalty is concerned, do you think we can kiss the Supreme Court goodbye for the time being?

Oh, I think so. At the moment they are examining an aspect of the death penalty having to do with juveniles. The chances are, I imagine, that they will say that juveniles should not be subjected to the death penalty. That should have been made clear many years ago, and I don't think it takes an especially liberal or humane court to make that kind of judgment. It takes a far more liberal and humane court to make a fair judgment having to do with racism in death sentencing.

Since it seems that the abolitionist cause will have to be carried to the legislature, how do you think the issue will be received there?

Given the nature of the Congress, it would seem close to impossible to push an abolitionist measure through. Legislators, senators, and members of Congress are rarely moral leaders. Most are cowards. They are usually sheeplike and follow the passions of their constituents. They will do anything for the votes of their constituency, who have this primitive view about the death penalty—namely, that it is good.

Very, very rarely is a politician given to saying, "I am against the death penalty." Two obvious exceptions are Mario Cuomo and Michael Dukakis, both of whom have been brave enough to take a stand. But as far as the Congress goes, the only possible way I can see change is if an abolitionist were to be elected President. After he or she got a lot of the other things out of the way, presidential leadership could be exerted on this issue. It would plainly not be high on the agenda and I don't know what a president can do, other than offer moral guidance and leadership, but that is very important.

You are a World War II veteran. How do you feel about Vietnam veterans who have been executed, even though they suffered from PTSD [Post Traumatic Stress Disorder]?

It would seem to me that any person who has endured the horrors of war is very fragile indeed. Like any other human being who commits a violent crime under stress, a veteran should not be sent to death row any more than any other person who is judged to be incompetent and is given leniency because of that.

There are many men on death row who have been executed despite insanity. It is appalling to me whenever anything like this does happen, and it calls into question that whole area of the law that deals with mental incompetence. The public in general is not very likely to be particularly tolerant of the insanity plea. A person has to be a cartoon freak or a total loony before the public will listen to an insanity plea. So these poor guys who have been to Vietnam, some of whom have mental problems because of it, are the unfortunate victims of the inability of this society to accept that people really are mentally ill and are not responsible for many acts of violence.

Your wife, Rose, is a tireless worker on behalf of human rights issues and has been actively involved with Amnesty in anti-death penalty work.

I think she has done a great job, but she's fighting an uphill battle. I saw Joan Baez last summer, here on the Vineyard, and she referred to the anti-death penalty cause as the "Leper" cause. She told me that once she was in Atlanta and thought she had a wonderful audience which was responding so beautifully to her; however, when she brought up the death penalty, they began to boo. I have often thought of that since, as an example of what Rose has had to put up with, because it is simply not a cause that people in this country want to think about.

What do you feel the death penalty does to a society that condones it?

Well, it brutalizes the society in a very subtle way. I don't think people realize that the continuing existence of the death penalty is a wound from which we suffer morally every time it is inflicted. It is a moral blight that spreads, and it has far more implications than one might imagine because it is, in effect, allowing the state, of which we are a part, to commit murder. The death penalty continues to degrade and makes us far more callous and violent.

We are brought up in a very vengeful, judgmental society to believe that the death penalty is a quite ordinary and natural thing. We are conditioned to believe that it is right and proper.

I didn't give it much thought until I was in my thirties, or even later, but when I began to puzzle it out, I came to realize that the death penalty was an immoral and evil act. Education is extremely important, as most Americans form their opinions from brute passion, not national thought. But attitudes can be changed. I have had the experience of talking to several people, on a one-to-one basis, who have changed their point of view forever. I hate the missionary role but I have personally converted people with conversation, which is an indication of how easy it should be, theoretically, to break down this barrier of ignorance.

HAND IN HAND

"With malice toward none: with charity for all:
with firmness in the right, as God gives us to see
the right, let us strive on to finish the work we are
in."

—Abraham Lincoln, March 4, 1865

Our appointment on this clear bright New York day was with Tanya Coke, director of research for the Capital Punishment Project of the NAACP Legal Defense and Educational Fund. We arrived at their headquarters, which are located at 99 Hudson Street in the shadow of the two giant columns of the World Trade Center that dominate SoHo.

We took the elevator to the 16th floor where we were greeted by Ms. Coke, a beautiful young woman in her mid-twenties.

There were several meetings going on in the LDF offices but we eventually found an empty room with spectacular views of just about all of Manhattan, and Tanya began to tell us a little about herself.

Tanya E. Coke was born in Jamaica but brought up in America (Columbus, Ohio). Like ourselves, she is a resident alien. She graduated from college in 1986 with a degree in Latin American studies and joined the Capital Punishment Project of the NAACP in June of that year.

276 TANYA COKE

New York, N.Y.
Tuesday, March 1, 1988, 11:00 a.m.

Tanya Coke

Why is the NAACP involved in the death penalty?

Well, back in the 1940s, when the Legal Defense Fund was first founded by the NAACP, we were called in on certain cases in the South involving black defendants accused of crimes against whites where there was little, if any, prospect of a fair trial. In many of those individual cases, the LDF would go down and defend or coordinate the defense of those men. Over the years we saw that while racism worked evil in all walks of American life, it seemed especially pernicious in the area of the death penalty. It was a systematic and rampant racism that sent hundreds of blacks, some of them innocent, to their deaths.

In the late sixties we commissioned a study by Professor Marvin Wolfgang, a well-known criminologist, to examine the effect of racism in death sentencing for rape. What he found was quite amazing. He found that out of the 455 executions for rape which took place between the years 1930 and 1967, 405 involved black defendants. It seemed the death penalty for rape in this country was a criminal sanction essentially reserved for blacks. It was really that study which confirmed for us the need for programmatic involvement by a race advocacy organization like the Legal Defense Fund.

What LDF recognized was that the death penalty has historically been used as a means of social control over black people beyond its ostensible justification as a criminal sanction.

The Wolfgang study was used by LDF staff attorneys in a 1970 case called *Maxwell v. Bishop*. *Maxwell* was a challenge in the Supreme Court to the states' use of the death penalty for rape, on Eighth Amendment grounds, arguing that the punishment was cruel and excessive in proportion to the crime. *Maxwell* failed. While clearly there was no dispute about the fact that race played a role in death sentencing here, the Court simply was not ready to let go of it.

We see no little precedent in *Maxwell v. Bishop* for where we are with the *McCleskey [McCleskey v. Kemp*, 1987] litigation today. There are some clear parallels to be drawn. Sixteen years after *Furman v. Georgia*, we have clear evidence that race still plays a powerful role in determining who shall be sentenced to death and who shall be sentenced to life imprisonment. But the courts are again showing themselves unwilling to deal with that reality. However, the Court finally did see the light on the rape question in 1977 and in *Coker v. Georgia* they disposed of the penalty for sexual offenses.

We heard that many older black inmates had a rape conviction on their record which was almost as commonplace for them then as getting a parking ticket.

We have good reason to seriously question many of those convictions. It is likely that many of the black men convicted and death-sentenced for rape during the earlier part of this century were entirely innocent. All a white woman had to do until fairly recently in this country was scream rape, point to a black animal that did it, and a death sentence was ensured. I also think that that whole phenomenon —this sensationalism around interracial crimes—is still quite prevalent in criminal prosecutions today. It is typically the white victim cases that get the most press attention—particularly when the defendant is black and the white victim is female. Those are the cases which capture the headlines, those are the cases that generate the intense public interest coverage and, correspondingly, the most vigorous prosecution.

I am utterly convinced that in ten, fifteen, or fifty years we will look back on the *McCleskey* litigation and see in it the same sort of light that we now recognize in *Maxwell v. Bishop*. Unfortunately, this kind of historical reflection on race issues at present is extremely difficult.

The McCleskey *decision seemed to say very clearly that even though the Court agreed racism was present, they didn't have the courage to do anything about it.*

I believe that *McCleskey* may well be the most cynical civil rights decision issued by the Court in the twentieth century. The 1954 ruling in *Brown v. Board of Education* had engendered a federal judiciary willing to act, if you will, as the guardian of minority rights and willing, for the most part, to enforce various sanctions against racial discrimination. But in *McCleskey* we see the Court's very pointed declination to do just that. For the first time since the 1857 *Dred Scott* case *[a famous case contributing to the Civil War, in which the Court acknowledged that slaves were property, even if the slave owner took them to a free state]*, the Court has acknowledged that racial bias exists in an area of public life, and that it exists in a terribly debilitating way. Still, it is not willing to remedy it. *McCleskey* was a decision that was not only wholly out of step with constitutional precedent, but also wholly consistent with the political times. We now have a majority of the Court which is no longer willing to restrict the states' ability to inflict the death penalty, no matter how wide or persistent the racial disparities are in its application.

What is the answer to that decision? Do you feel the Racial Justice Act will be successful?

Well, the Racial Justice Act is a legislative remedy which the Court itself suggested. In *McCleskey* they say clearly that the evidence of racism is troubling, but they are only judges on a court: courts do not make law, and the propriety of capital punishment and whether racism will be tolerated are issues for the states to decide for themselves. The Racial Justice Act would prohibit states from imposing the death penalty in a clearly discriminatory manner such as we are seeing now.

We understand the bill asks that the states keep records and really puts the ball in their court?

Precisely, in the same way that the Voting Rights Act in the 1960s created federal oversight over voting practices in the South, and required that states keep detailed records of how they administered their systems. This act would do the same thing. It would require a state to justify how and why it prosecuted certain cases and thereby explain any substantial racial disparities produced by the system. The act would also restore to defendants the right to challenge racially discriminatory sentences.

Passing this legislation cannot, and should not, be an effort of abolitionists alone. We think that it's an important step in getting the government to realize that its responsibility is to administer the criminal justice system in a fair manner. It is not one that can be compromised to the prevailing political sentiment of the moment. We really think that racial fairness is not much to ask, or at least should not be too much to ask.

Is the Legal Defense Fund also helping minors and mentally retarded persons on death row cases, which cut across racial barriers?

Sure. With the closure of litigation over the race issue, we really are faced with a new era in capital defense. There do not appear to be any great constitutional issues that will soon convince the Court that the whole business of execution is ghastly and not worth doing. It is unrealistic to think that the prohibition of executions for juveniles or the mentally retarded—constitutional issues on which we are making some progress—will bring the whole system to its knees within the next two or three years. What I do think is that the abolitionist movement is becoming far more savvy about public education and the need for popular local dissatisfaction with executions. The retardation and juvenile issues very much tap into a widespread ambivalence about our ability to apply the penalty in a consistently rational way.

We see a sense of great uneasiness among Americans about executing children and people who are not mentally competent. What we are trying to make the American public see now is that the system is still as arbitrary as it ever was as we tell the stories of the Clarence Brandleys in Texas [see interview with Steve and Lisa Haberman] and the Edward Earl Johnsons in Mississippi [see interview with Clive Stafford Smith], of the Jerome Bowdens [a mentally retarded man executed in Georgia in 1986]. These are people who have been completely disserved by the criminal justice system, the ones who have fallen through the cracks, as it were.

It seems that it is in the initial trial stage that the inadequate representation occurs?

Precisely. The task of skillful appellate lawyers is to go back and piece together the story of how this individual came to commit this crime, why it was that a jury saw fit to sentence him to death, and, ultimately, why it is that he nevertheless deserves to live. Today, instead of focusing on abstract and broad legal theories, we are beginning to investigate each and every case, one by one. We need to do that in order to save people's lives. We must also do this in order to document and indict a system that just doesn't work, a system that singles out poor, mentally ill, and/or black people who were consigned to the society's garbage heap from the very beginning. Ultimately, we must ask ourselves whether this is the policy that we want to engage in.

Is it also a regional problem?

You know it's a very tenacious phenomenon of parochialism. We find there are counties where juries never impose death penalties and counties where juries always do. There are districts where prosecutors always seek the death penalty and districts where they don't. There are hanging judges and lenient judges and judges whose judgment as a whole is riddled with arbitrariness. I suppose some philosophers or constitutional scholars would consider that fact as one of the great failings of the American legal system, but I think that it is just a testament to human imperfection.

Unfortunately, a majority of the public officials of this country are still willing to focus all of our resources and collective fire on the wrong end of the horse. Instead of examining why it is that we are so terribly plagued by these homicide rates, or remedying our historic inattention to the poor and mentally ill who commit these crimes, we have opted for a hopelessly futile policy of extermination.

We have been talking mainly about the Southern states. Does the same hold true in other states?

In virtually every state you look at, whether it is Illinois or Alabama, death sentences are sought far more often for white victim homicides than for black victim homicides. Really, when you look at race of victim and race of defendant combinations in California, it doesn't differ too markedly from states like Tennessee, Georgia, or Mississippi. It is quite surprising. While the legal representation afforded a criminal defendant in a Northern state is generally superior to that found in the South, in every area one experiences the same disturbing problem with prosecutorial discretion as to which kinds of cases are considered the most serious by the public and by the officials in the criminal justice system. The same phenomenon works across the country.

However, it is really not a matter of seeking and destroying some virulently racist core of prosecutors or sheriffs in the Deep South. The problem rarely presents itself in so blatant a fashion anymore. What we are seeing instead are lingering, deeply held biases that almost all Americans hold about which kind of crimes are bad and which kinds of defendants are culpable and which ones are absolutely the worst. Those sorts of prejudices are ultimately reflected in our criminal sentencing. The phenomenon is an endemic one—it cuts across all American communities, be they Northern or Southern.

Could you offer any optimistic outlook for the future?

(*Laughs*) Absolutely, it's hard to do this work without one! I would like to think that Americans will one day find it within themselves to dispense with this horribly brutal policy as a matter of moral decency. But, in truth, I think that before that day dawns, we will see capital punishment dismantled simply because it can no longer be cast as an effective or affordable policy. There is already little question that the legal system is straining at all sides under the weight of these two thousand death cases, overwhelmed by legal appeals and drained financially because of the cost of keeping a death penalty system. Therefore, eventually, the states will very much cut back on the use of the death penalty and dismantle the whole system.

The public seems to see the death penalty as a matter of security.

They do, but the penalty has little, if anything, to do with the touted goals of criminal justice. You don't have to be a historian to observe that policy making is cyclical and we now find ourselves in an extremely conservative time where these "tough on crime" symbols are very important to people, despite their inefficiency. I think eventually we will move beyond that and assess the death penalty as a social policy in a more objective light. Hopefully, in that more enlightened time, states like Florida and California, that can in fact afford a death penalty, will see it as a sanction that is not necessary but only degrading and wasteful. Abolition will then become a real prospect.

I think, however, we are going to see a disturbing number of executions before that day dawns. I wonder if the American public can countenance the systematic execution of two thousand people plus the three hundred odd who we add to death row each year. I think that a country like the United States, which sees itself as a standard bearer of human rights, will have a very difficult time sanctioning that kind of mass extermination.

Do you think Americans see themselves in the same company as Iran, South Africa, China, and all the other human rights abusers on the death penalty question?

I think many Americans don't realize the kind of company we keep in the death penalty area. One big beef I have is that public schools no longer teach geography as they once did. Our ignorance of international affairs has some very clear consequences on the way in which we formulate our world view. We should see that we are way out of line with other Western industrialized democracies and that our use of capital punishment makes us comparable to countries whose human rights records we regularly condemn. These are the sorts of points that need to be brought home.

A "Sexy" Issue

"Justice is such a fine thing that we cannot pay too dearly for it."

—Alain René Lesage, 1668–1747

Footsteps echo down the corridors of power of the Rayburn House Office Building on Independence Avenue, Washington, D.C. On either side of the marble aisles, floor-to-ceiling mahogany doors bear gold-leaf signs naming states—California, Mississippi, Virginia, Michigan.

Detroit, Michigan, is the home of Congressman John Conyers, Jr., a Democrat who represents the 1st District.

Congressman Conyers is chairman of the House Criminal Justice Subcommittee. His committee assignments also include Civil and Constitutional Rights, Human Resources and Intergovernmental Relations, Legislation and National Security, Procurement, and Innovation and Minority Development. He is also active in the Democratic Study Group, Congressional Black Caucus, Arms Control and Foreign Policy Caucus, Congressional Caucus for Women's Issues, Congressional Arts Caucus, Energy and Environment Study Conference, and is an honorary member of the Congressional Hispanic Caucus.

The congressman, whose home is in Detroit, was born on May 16, 1929, educated at Wayne State University, and is an attorney.

It is difficult to believe John Conyers is two years shy of sixty. He is a slim man, 5 feet 11 inches, 160 pounds, with smiling eyes framed behind gold-rimmed glasses. He wears a well-cut suit with style and taste.

After McCleskey v. Kemp *(1987), when the Supreme Court acknowledged the overwhelming evidence that racial bias influenced cap-*

ital sentencing but said that this issue was best addressed by the legislature, John Conyers responded by drafting the Racial Justice Act and submitting it to Congress. This act would create a right to have death sentences imposed only under procedures that are free of the effects of racial bias.

To balance this weighty issue, the congressman, a jazz buff, introduced a resolution that designated jazz music a rare and valuable national American treasure. The House of Representatives passed his resolution on September 23, 1987.

Washington, D.C.
Wednesday, February 24, 1988, 4:00 p.m.

Congressman John Conyers

You are well known for your views on the death penalty. What drew you to this area?

Once you get into the death penalty, it gets to be awfully exciting. I remember during the hearings on the death penalty, last year, one of my colleagues, I will not give you any indication who he is by mentioning the state that he's from, came into the hearing room. It was late in the day and we were the only two there. As he got up to leave he said, "Let's face it John, these hearings are not very 'sexy.'" That hit me like a thunderbolt. Here we are talking about life and death, I mean directly, we are not talking about it indirectly through the commission of war. Here we sit in a room determining what the law will be that will govern the United States taking the lives of its people . . . and that is not "sexy"!

To me, this is more sexy than examining whether the Wall Street people are using illegal methods in mergers. It's more sexy than whether the labor laws are being violated. To me, the rules governing life and death are very sexy. I mean, it's an exciting area when you talk about being able to give a person life that he would not otherwise have. It's an awesome subject.

When we reinforce our association with the society of decent people doing human rights work who understand that this is not a matter of law and order, not some abstract legal principle or that vengeance is not an acceptable public motive, it can be very satisfying—personally.

If I weren't in government, there would be nothing more exciting than trying to frame death penalty cases for relitigation and appeal to the Supreme Court. I mean, when you win one of these, you are talking about life and death. What can be "sexier" than life and death?

How does racial bias operate in death penalty decisions?

We have a system that is trying to come out of a history of racism, that has come out of the most obscene system of slavery ever. First of all, when slavery was intact, there was a law for blacks and a law for whites—the Black Codes. This made any attempt to educate or alter the condition of servitude of blacks a crime. This applied not only for blacks but for any white who might aid or abet.

Today, the descendants of these slaves live in a system with this racial bias. When we look at death row, this lottery, where three hundred or so get the death penalty out of the more than twenty thousand murders annually, you can see certain patterns. If you are a poor, black defendant and the victim was white and you live in the South and you had a court-appointed attorney, the odds that you will be one of those few selected for execution each year goes up very dramatically —astronomically.

We have a flawed criminal justice system, of which this is an outstanding example.

The McCleskey *decision seems to back up what you are saying.*

What made *McCleskey* frightening is that Justice [Lewis F.] Powell rationalized the racially discriminatory character of the death penalty that, we said, should preclude its use. In other words Powell said, in effect, "Even if there is a little discrimination . . . what can I tell you? . . . there is a little discrimination in everything. As long as it's not a lot."

What are your plans to counter this decision?

We are now moving the legislature to correct *McCleskey* by permitting the use of statistical information to show a racially disproportionate sentencing pattern. *McCleskey* said statistical proof of discrimination did not constitute proof; evidence of discrimination had to come from each individual case. We want to put the burden on states to show the death penalty is not being applied in a discriminatory manner.

There were two things that happened. In addition to the Court saying a little discrimination may not be correctable in these kinds of capital questions, it also said that statistical data, showing that death penalty cases are racially skewed, would not be accepted in the same way that such data is allowed in other discrimination cases. "You now have to show us that the prosecutor was racist, or the police, or whatever." The general statistical patterns were not enough.

We are going to introduce legislation on the anniversary of *McCleskey* in April to correct this problem.

And the name of the bill?

The Racial Justice Act. We expect to have some good hearings because the *McCleskey* decision was defective in at least those two respects. We think that this is a good place to bring the legislature back into the picture.

It's like every other struggle you get into. Like civil rights, you start doing what you think is right even though you haven't the foggiest idea of how you are going to overcome, and then things start happening.

In the end this will have to come up for a vote, so you have to build up a constituency, in and out of the Congress, to get a majority. Right now we start from a very slim base, but we figure that this is what we are here for, this being an awfully important part of American jurisprudence.

How about the Supreme Court and the death penalty?

Here's the real tragedy from a purely legal point of view. In the 1972 *Furman* case, the Court said, "It's arbitrary and capricious and this system has got to go." It was a landmark decision. But they left the door open for the states to correct it.

In *Gregg* [1976] it was determined that there must be bifurcated proceedings to determine whether there were mitigating or aggravating circumstances. These are mere trappings that have not changed the problem that was raised in *Furman*. We are still doing the same thing. All they did was say, "Okay, after we find guilt and before we rush to the death penalty, we will have a separate hearing." This whole sanitized version of procedure has not changed the substance that underpinned *Furman* in 1972.

The jury says, "Guilty."

"Okay, any mitigating circumstances?"—Not a one.

"Any aggravating circumstances?"—Plenty!

"Counsel, have you got anything to say before we pass sentence? And make it quick. None? Okay, the Court is familiar with *Furman* and *Gregg* and we've complied with the procedure."

Then Bam! It's off to the chair.

That's why I am saying that the constitutional question is enormous here.

So you did not think that it was all over when the Furman *decision came down?*

I guess I assumed that we won a victory, but the language in the decision allowed the states to work out an acceptable means to proceed with more executions.

If you had won the McCleskey *case, do you believe that would have swung the tide again?*

No, I think the composition of the court has become so politicized that you can now frequently predict the outcome of a case based upon the philosophy of the judiciary. Judges are ordinary people, endowed with no more particular gifts, intellectual or moral, than most anybody else. What they bring with them, in terms of their views about people of a particular skin coloration, their views about class, their views about family, their views about sexual orientation, their views about enemies from without that may descend upon this country, are all baggage that everybody else has. They are expected to suspend it as they sit as impartial arbiters of these questions that come before them. But what does this mean in practice? It means that, within the very limited range of discretion that exists in the legal system, you can literally arrive at any decision you want.

I don't mean to lodge an incredible attack upon our judicial system and I am not saying that every judge does this, but I think you have to be sensitive to the fact that a judge who came out of a racially discriminatory background could find it very easy to rationalize any decision that he or she wanted to, moving backwards rather than forwards.

In addition, is there a diffusion of responsibility in death penalty cases, to the point where it is so watered down that no one is accountable?

Exactly. It is diffused remarkably across the system, from the arresting police officer to the Chief Justice of the United States Supreme Court who refuses to hear the writ of *Habeas Corpus*.

You seem to dismiss the defense.

Here's the other part that is tagged onto it. We don't have enough good public defenders, lawyers, or assistants to even begin to review the constitutional basis of convictions of people on death row. The American Bar Association is begging lawyers to come in and pick up these cases on a pro bono basis.

Would you say the phrase "judicial lynching" is too strong?

No. Except that it's more than judicial, it's systemic. I prefer the term "systemic lynching" because it really starts off with the arresting officer, the coroner, the prosecuting attorneys—it's larger than the judge. If it was just the judge, we could stop some of this stuff, although the judge is by far the most important link in it.

The result is that some very interesting things have been happening in the last few years. Just as the growing fear of crime and criminals is leading to a reinstitution of the death penalty, there is, at the same time, fortunately, growing sentiment against the death penalty. These two phenomena, both contradictory, are occurring in our society.

What about your own state?

The only thing that stops Michigan from imposing the death penalty is that it is not already on the books. There has been fanatic activity, frenzied activity, to have a referendum and get this back on the books, and we are fighting tooth and nail. Fortunately, the groups that are anxious for a referendum ballot that would allow for the law to be changed are a little sloppy and not very tidy technically. We have held them at bay, but they're anxious and eager.

Even though Michigan abolished the death penalty as far back as 1847?

What we are finding is that people are becoming more and more accustomed to this horrible exercise [executions]. You hear casual radio debates about whether injection is less cruel than gas. They were talking about one guy they had to electrocute a couple of times because after they turned the juice off he was still alive. Then they had to turn it back on and fry him again. You occasionally read a description of what it's like to witness a person's life being taken by these exceedingly crude methods. You find there is an element of inhumanity here, which leads me back to the constitutional question. I would suggest we have such serious problems that even if you could say that, under certain circumstances, a life ought to be taken, there are so many constitutional defects in the system that it should not be implemented.

Under which amendment do you see the penalty as unconstitutional, the Eighth or the Fourteenth?

Well, both of them, because the constitutional defects are from the Fourteenth Amendment and the practical defects are from the Eighth Amendment.

Right now I would like the Supreme Court to go back in, as any reasonable set of jurists would if they looked at this fairly, and say, "Yes, in 1972 these penalties were arbitrary, but we haven't corrected them, and this new approval in 1976 that reopened the death penalty has not overcome the arbitrariness."

Can we look toward Congress for changes to be made?

We realize that that's all that's left. That's why, as I said before, we are now moving the legislature into this. In many curious spots of our lawmaking, whenever the legislature cannot do it, we have always deferred to the courts. Civil rights law was literally shaped by the Supreme Court making decisions about old laws and existing circumstances that had been taken for granted, even revisiting their own decisions and just updating them.

If it hadn't been for the courts there would have been no way to move the country forward, out of the long history of legally accepted segregation with the *Brown [v. Board of Education]* case in 1954. Then in the sixties came the first timid activity on the part of the legislature. With President Kennedy we passed the Civil Rights Act of 1964 [enacted after his death], and with President Johnson we passed the Voter Rights Act of 1965. The first Civil Rights and Voter Rights acts were improved upon as they came up before the Congress for reauthorization. They were very modest instruments and were enacted with great difficulty.

Ironically, Martin Luther King Jr., a murder victim, had a great deal to do with the legislative development of these civil rights laws, and the fact is his widow, who has been victimized by murders in her family, still carries the philosophy that Martin had about the value of life being so high that the government cannot teach against violence and employ violence at the same time.

How are you going to communicate the message that not only is the death penalty no deterrent and will not help rid us of violence, but also that it is very expensive?

There is an irrationality. Most people don't know that it may cost in excess of a million dollars to exhaust a person's legal rights before they are finally executed. The cost is astronomical and, of course, the average murderer is a person who has committed only that crime and has a much different profile than the one who is generally ginned up for popular media consumption: the vicious, horrible, inhumane character, who, it would seem, the nicest thing that could ever happen would be that he be executed or destroyed in any way possible. I was looking at this genre of movies . . . who's this guy who is always going out and avenging?

Charles Bronson in the Death Wish *series?*

Yeah, Bronson. I saw a movie of his on television. In this one the police let him out and gave him his gun back and said, "Be careful, it's a new world now, these guys are more vicious than when before you were in the slammer." They were letting him out and authorizing him to take care of whomever he could and they would look the other way. The prosecutor personally engineered his release and, of course, the first afternoon he's out he has to save this girl who is being attacked by these awful guys. This goes into the popular ethos of our time; the notion of a rugged macho decision maker is very much a part of Americana.

We are now caught between these sociological forces and this romanticized history of the gun slinger and also a romanticization of the Robin Hood criminal.

When you put all these sociological forces into the backdrop when we are busily passing laws and rearguing morality, the death sentence becomes a perfectly logical instrument of public vengeance. It makes our work as opponents of capital punishment more difficult because you have to reject a machoism. You have to identify with the wimps. You know, there is a perception of a certain wimpishness about being against the death penalty. I mean, some of my colleagues say to me, "Fry these vermin, John. What's the problem, man? Why do they deserve to eat up taxpayers' money in a prison for the rest of their lives?" So, when you approach the death penalty, you are addressing internalized impressions that have been collected throughout the length and breadth of our society, and that's what makes this exciting and difficult to argue.

On the other side of the coin, what is being done for the victims' families?

We have a Victims of Crime Act before the committee, in which we are trying desperately to send federal funding to local law enforcement agencies so that people who come in contact with the criminal justice process won't be treated just as witnesses and appendages to a trial, and so that the emotional part of being a victim is given some consideration.

In conclusion, what would you say that the death penalty does to a civilized society?

Most citizens of developed countries have come to realize that the death penalty is a dehumanizing tool of the government. The United States and South Africa are the only Western industrial countries that haven't reached that conclusion. I have, however, every confidence that as a nation we will reject capital punishment, and in the not too distant future. Remember not all the states execute—Michigan doesn't!

STATUTES OF LIBERTY

"You can fool all the people some of the time and some of the people all the time but you cannot fool all of the people all of the time."

—Abraham Lincoln,
Speech, November 19, 1863

The metal sign—ACLU—over the doorway of 132 West 43rd Street, New York, is a familiar sight to TV news watchers. Over the years, reporters have been filmed in front of these doors as news-breaking stories of the legal battles and debates participated in by the ACLU are described.

The American Civil Liberties Union has been a protector of the rights of liberty and quality of life. Their work was the subject of several slippery attacks by President Bush in his 1988 campaign.

The sixty-two-year-old director of the ACLU Capital Punishment Project, Mr. Henry Schwarzschild, was born in Germany. He came to this country in 1939 and obtained a degree in political theory from Columbia University. He followed this with service in U.S. Counter Intelligence during World War II.

He is the founder and first director of the National Coalition to Abolish the Death Penalty and continues to serve on the executive committee of that group. From 1972 until 1976, Mr. Schwarzschild was director of the ACLU's Project on Amnesty for Vietnam War resisters. Before that, he had been a staff associate with the Field Foundation and a fellow of the Metropolitan Applied Research Center, headed by Dr. Kenneth Clark. From 1964 until 1969, he was the executive director of the Lawyers Constitutional Defense Committee, a civil rights lawyers group active in Alabama, Mississippi, and Louisiana. He participated in the early desegregation sit-ins in 1960 and Freedom Rides in 1961. He worked closely with Dr. Martin Luther King, Jr., and the other leaders of the civil-rights movement.

Mr. Schwarzschild has served as research project director for the U.S. Department of State, as educational director of the Rand School of Social Science, as public relations director of the International Rescue Committee, and as national publications director of the Anti-Defamation League of B'nai B'rith.

The director's most obvious features are his bushy eyebrows and his awesome command of the English language.

New York, N.Y.
Monday, March 7, 1988, Noon

Henry Schwarzschild

What is the ACLU's position on the death penalty?

We oppose the death penalty. We believe that in an enlightened, humane, and civilized society, which thinks of itself as a bearer of standards of human rights, the Constitution ought to be read as prohibiting the death penalty. Oddly enough, the ACLU came to this issue rather late. We have been around since 1919. It did not take a formal position on the death penalty until the late 1960s.

In this century, governments have shed endless rivers of blood—in wars, in revolutions and counterrevolutions, in enforced labor camps and extermination camps, and by police actions. Governments always say to the rest of the society that "Killing some will be good for the rest of us." We should have learned by now that governments are extremely inappropriate institutions to decide who lives and who dies. I do not mean to conjure up spectacles of mass extermination on the walls of American culture and history, but it is dangerous to let governments kill.

I don't minimize the horrendousness of violent crime; to the very contrary. We abolitionists are, after all, the only people in the society who think that killing human beings under all circumstances is destructive and appalling. We would not have private people do that when it's called murder, we wouldn't have the state do it when it's called an execution.

What about the argument that society has the right to defend itself, that the death penalty would deter would-be offenders?

Deterrence cannot be the only criterion. If somebody came along now and said, "Look, in any jurisdiction in this country, in any given year, there are more burglaries than murders. The present criminal punishment simply isn't sufficient. Why don't we go to the legislature and make the penalty for burglary cutting off the burglar's right arm?" —that is certainly a more severe penalty, likely to have a greater deterrent effect on burglary.

The legislature would say, "This is not the Middle Ages. We are not going to put maiming back in the American criminal code. It's barbaric, it's crazy, it is an Eighth Amendment violation, and the federal Constitution wouldn't permit it, it is not acceptable."

That which is acceptable—this argument brings us to lethal injection, does it not?

A line written by a drama critic in the 1930s in connection with a play was, "The worst sin of all is to do something well that should not be done at all." This could be said about lethal injection.

Lethal injection is somehow aesthetically more acceptable than the grisliness of a gas chamber, the electric chair, the gallows, or even the firing squad. But most electrocutions have gone well. Some few have misfired. Most lethal injections go well. Some have already misfired. The horror of that, puncturing somebody forty times before they can find a vein and blood all over the ceiling is, of course, precisely as appalling as hangings that misfire with the sheriff pulling on the guy's legs. It is all very unappetizing indeed.

In any event, it is precisely in the measure in which lethal injection is seen by almost everybody as relatively less horrendous than some other methods of execution that it is more objectionable, because the entire point of the operation is to make execution more *acceptable*. That's the only point.

I have avoided testifying on lethal injection bills in state legislatures. If I say, "No, I don't want you to enact lethal injection," and they will answer, "That means you want us to keep the electric chair?" and I say, "No, no, I don't mean that at all. I want you to abolish the whole thing," they will tell me, "Mr. Schwarzschild, you are here under false pretenses. We are not talking about abolition of the death penalty, we are here to talk about the method of execution. What are you doing here?"

I don't have any vested interest in *how* the state kills people. If they want to sneak into the guy's cell in the middle of the night with a baseball bat and beat his brains out, I think it would be just as good and just as bad as lethal injection or the electric chair.

The issue is really whether it *ought* to be done, not *how* it is going to be done. Lethal injection is offensive because it is used to calm people's stomachs and nerves and to give killing the appearance of being more humane, using medical technology. I think it's all totally contemptible.

Do you have any insights as to what happens in the Supreme Court in a death penalty decision?

Not insights that are particularly private to me. If you read the Woodward and Armstrong book *The Brethren,* there are long stories both about the *Furman* decision in 1972 and the *Gregg* decision in 1976. The death penalty provokes a terribly divisive, passionate argument inside the Supreme Court, and has done ever since the whole issue moved to center stage in the late sixties and early seventies.

Look at *McCleskey. McCleskey* was a 5–4 decision written by Justice Powell, now retired. The case came a lot closer than I thought it would. For Powell to go some other way would have required him to write another *Furman* decision, effectively abolishing capital punishment, and they all knew that. For all intents and purposes it would have struck down the working of the entire death penalty as the Court had done sixteen years before. At the very least, state legislatures would have been forced to rewrite their death penalty statutes once again, as they did after 1972.

The Supreme Court's business is, of course, to interpret the law. The Eighth Amendment says that "neither cruel nor unusual punishment shall be imposed." Obviously that is very vague language. Who is to say what is cruel and unusual? In the seventies, the Court said, "We will look at American society to see what this culture now considers cruel and unusual." They no doubt considered torture to be cruel and usual, burning at the stake, or any other medieval sanction, but they went all the way and struck down as unconstitutional the then existing death penalty statutes in 1972 because of the irrational and discriminatory fashion in which they were applied.

In four short years, thirty-four states responded against that decision by reframing the laws so that they would be constitutional, so that they could kill people within the framework of the law. The states had put over six hundred people on death row by 1976, and public opinion polls showed that 70 to 75 percent of the American people were in favor of it.

The Court thought they should not "suck the meaning of the Eighth

Amendment out of their thumb." They believed they were *not* here to enact their own private preference into the Constitution but to interpret the Constitution with values that arise out of the developing legal system and culture. They said, "It does not strike us as though America had come to the judgment as a society, as a culture, that the death penalty ought to be considered cruel and unusual punishment."

I wish they *had* read it the other way because I think a lot of things the Supreme Court did in the sixties and seventies were also not based on the consent of the majority. If one had subjected *Brown v. Board of Education* in 1954 to referendum, it would have fared very badly. I dare say these days we could not get majority support for the First Amendment very easily.

But the legal system does require a certain integrity of its own. In many comparable situations we would not want the Supreme Court to enact its own personal judgments, but rather to deal with the Constitution and how the society views those matters.

In the McCleskey *case, did it not say in the last paragraph of Justice Powell's opinion that even though he recognized that discrimination existed, it should still be taken to the legislature?*

He did suggest explicitly, "If you have a problem, take it to the legislature," but I don't think he meant to do us any favors there. He was evasive and the suggestion was hostile. Powell has not been particularly friendly to us on this issue. The Court was not going to strike down all the death penalty laws in this country, not with two thousand people on death row, not in the context of the politics of the society.

There isn't a single legislature in the country today, except maybe Alaska, in which abolition is a realistic political possibility. If you tried to push an abolition bill through the two houses of the Oklahoma Legislature, for example, you would get a vote reaffirming the death penalty by a margin of perhaps ten to one.

Whenever the issue of the death penalty comes up, most Americans feel very strongly one way or another. Somehow people intuitively know that there is something terribly important at stake here. It's much more important than a mere two thousand cutthroats on death row.

The Court reads that mood correctly. I think it was Justice John Paul Stevens who in 1976 said, "As a thoughtful person I would like the death penalty abolished. I think I would vote against it if I was in the state legislature but I am not on the U.S. Supreme Court to enact statutes; I am here to interpret the Constitution. I see no grounds on which I could read the United States Constitution, at this stage of the game, to prohibit it. We leave it to the states to make those judgments."

How about the future? Do you think we will still be executing in the year 2000?

Yes. I think it is going to last another generation. I think the reason that there is so much public and institutional support for the death penalty—legislative, judicial, and the like—is that there is an enormous amount of crime and violence in this country. Over twenty thousand murders in this country in a year is a pretty horrendous number by the standards of any Western country, even if one allows for the population differences. People are afraid for their lives and for the lives of their family, for their property and the like. People are very angry at a criminal justice system which doesn't seem to work very well. It doesn't deal effectively with crime. The popular conception continues to be that people who commit murder will be out on the street again in seven years.

Today, we live very much in a post-Vietnam era. American self-esteem rode high from the end of World War II to the Vietnam War. It was the century of America. We were the richest, most powerful, most industrialized, most sophisticated, most effective country in the world. That was very much the sense that America had of itself. The Vietnam War, the longest war we had ever fought, was historically and culturally divisive. This immensely powerful country got beaten by a bunch of backward mountain folks in a country twelve thousand miles away that nobody could nor can find on a map. That was an immense, unacknowledged trauma to American self-esteem. There was also the oil crisis and the hostage crisis in Tehran.

This culture is now dominated by a kind of macho reaction. *Toughness* is the universal solvent to every problem that America faces abroad or at home, whether it is Grenada or Tripoli, Florida or Texas. A tough response proves to ourselves, proves to all these people who try to damage our national and social interests, that we will come down on them like the wolf on the fold. We are going to demonstrate that we are tough. We are going to show people that Vietnam was idiosyncratic. The Reagan image, you know, sitting tall in the saddle, being very tough, then flexing our large masculine muscles. There is an overwhelming desire for Americans to demonstrate, to themselves and to everybody else, that we are very tough people. The death penalty is a symbolic demonstration of toughness.

The death penalty may diminish murder, Americans think. But, at bottom, they don't really care. They are retributive out of a desire to be tough. That's what the death penalty is all about.

I never believed, in contrast to some of my colleagues, that support for the death penalty was possible only because of the absence of executions and that once people were confronted with the stark reality of executions their stomachs would heave. I do not believe that for a moment. We executed 199 people in 1935, which was the high point in modern times. We are now sentencing people to death at a rate higher than that. We are not executing as many, but even if we got to three hundred executions, which after all, means one every working day, I don't think that would produce a revulsion. There may be a point at which revulsion might begin to set in maybe if we executed fifty people a day, but I don't think that is in the foreseeable future. Nor do I believe, as some of my colleagues used to believe and still may, that if we only got one or two dramatically innocent people executed people would rethink their support for the death penalty.

Ultimately, a generation down the pike, we will abolish this lingering throwback, this ghastly reminder of unenlightened times.

THE WRITE STUFF

"Criminals do not die by the hands of the law.
They die by the hands of other men."

—George Bernard Shaw, 1903

Some of the most interesting and articulate essays on the subject of the death penalty are the work of an Oakland-based free-lance writer, Michael A. Kroll, who specializes in criminal justice issues.

Michael is an activist, totally committed to non-violent protest. Forty-five years old, he is far from middle-aged. Piercing blue-gray eyes are set above high cheekbones, his hair a graying mane barely under control. Around his neck hangs a St. Christopher medal, given to him by Bobby Harris, prisoner on death row, who received it from Mother Theresa when she visited San Quentin.

Oakland, California
Monday, May 16, 1988, 10:30 a.m.

Michael Kroll

Can you give us some background on yourself and tell us how you became involved in death penalty work?

First of all, I grew up in a household that was concerned with social justice, and so we talked about a lot of issues that were political and that had a social justice angle. I also grew up in California, where the death penalty was a very regular feature of our justice system. We talked about the real thing: "Caryl Chessman was executed today." It was a dinner-table conversation.

I went to Berkeley in 1961, got involved in the Free Speech movement, and got arrested. You know who prosecuted us? One Edwin Meese, who was then the DA.

How did you get involved in prison work?

I became the director for the ACLU prison project in Louisiana. Once I saw the inside of our prisons, my social consciousness had a real focus.

You go into an American prison and you can't be the same person. I got the job as coordinator for the National Moratorium on Prison Construction, an organization I had dealt with many times in my prison work. Brian Willson [the peace activist] conceived the idea and wrote a piece called "Designs for a Caged Society." Americans have this insatiable appetite for institutional solutions to all their problems, so according to his theory, maybe if we blocked this avenue of escape—built no more prisons—we would force people to face the problem, not shove it under the rug. The Unitarians funded it. I also wrote and edited a national newsletter called *Jericho,* which was really well respected in the criminal justice field.

While I was there, one of the major campaigns was Stop the Olympic Prison campaign; it was news in Europe but was not well reported in this country, although it did get an editorial in *The New York Times.* The government was building housing for the Winter Olympics at Lake Placid in 1980, a job they turned over to the Federal Bureau of Prisons, which built a prison. It was first occupied by white ice skaters from

Sweden, and is now occupied by black and brown inner-city kids from New York. A very long way from the city. I was sent to make a pitch before the Human Rights Commission in Geneva and they accepted it as a human rights violation.

Can you give us a journalist's viewpoint of how California's Supreme Court has changed since the ouster of the Bird Court?

We have a governor, George Deukmejian, who started off his career as a DA and Attorney General, with the death penalty as his focus. He is a very pro-death, law and order politician, who understood early on in the game that there were "votes in them thar bills." He proposed many of them, lengthened prison sentences, and in 1977 the California Legislature passed his bill for resuming the death penalty. The following year, in 1978, the electorate was asked to vote on a ballot initiative which called for a wider application of the death penalty than even Deukmejian had called for. It was called the Briggs Initiative.

The irony for the pro-death lobby was that if the Briggs Initiative, named after State Representative John Briggs, its creator, had never gotten on the ballot or never been passed into law, by now executions may very well have started again in California. The Deukmejian bill was virtually constitutionally perfect. It was modeled after other laws that had been approved. It satisfied *Furman* and *Gregg,* but the new Briggs Initiative violated those models in many ways—in terms of jury instructions, in terms of who it might apply to, in terms of its automatic application in some cases. It is very interesting that in the Bird Court, only three of sixty or so cases were affirmed. All three were pre-Briggs cases, Deukmejian cases, but as the people sentenced under the Briggs Initiative came up, there were challenges to the law, challenges to jury instructions, and all of those challenges were successful.

Rather than simply take the [Supreme Court Justices] Marshall/Brennan approach that the death penalty cannot be applied constitutionally, the California court, led by Rose Bird, took the position that they had *no legal scruples against the death penalty or constitutional opposition to it per se but they had to apply this law in each case and each time.*

The Bird Court has been portrayed as frustrating the will of the people?

Precisely. It didn't take the politicians long to realize they had something major going here, so they started using the California Supreme Court as their whipping boy—or maybe whipping girl.

Any other court would have given the same rulings. There were no differences between the interpretations of the Bird Court and the courts in Mississippi or Florida. When Deukmejian and another key player in this issue, [Conservative State Representative] H. L. Richardson, saw people being executed in Florida, they wanted some of the action, and the easiest way of saying the people of California are not getting "justice" was because of obstructions from the Bird Court.

The California Supreme Court is appointed by the governor with the approval of the voters every twelve years. The death lobby had long realized the way to gain power was to unseat the Court, and they had already come very close to it. This time they were determined.

The politicians then used—I believe grossly overused—the victims as their mouthpiece. They organized the victims, the survivors of murder, and put them on the tube, saying, "My little Jennie was brutally murdered and they let her murderer read books in San Quentin and he talks to his family which my little daughter will never. . . ." All true but hardly related to the [California Supreme] Court. They whipped up this fury. They were saying absurd things. I wrote a piece about the Court. I had just returned from China where a judge gave a rapist/murderer a life sentence in the morning. The "will" of the people was made known that afternoon, and that afternoon he changed the man's sentence to death, and that evening it was carried out. I wrote: "Is this the kind of society you want, where the people make their will known in a courthouse?"

There was a lot of speculation whether Rose Bird should have resigned and saved her colleagues, or whether or not she should have given a sacrificial victim to the gas chamber so the people would have their blood lust sated.

What about the deterrent effect of the death penalty?

(Michael Kroll raises his eyebrows) You know, one of the things about being against the death penalty is that you are always on the defensive. There are no statistics to show that the death penalty is a deterrent—none! Conversely, I can show the death penalty *actually increases* the murder rate. I wrote an article about it.

Europe, from where we inherited this nasty practice, now gets along fine without the death penalty. Domestically, thirteen states have no death penalty laws, and many states that do have a death penalty have an informal moratorium on executions. So who's doing the killing? Texas, Louisiana, and Florida for the most part. States with above-average murder rates.

When John Spenkelink was put to death in the chair, the murder rate in Florida rose 14 percent in the year following the execution. In 1980, two sociologists, William Bowers and Glenn Pierce, did a study going right back to 1907. They found that in New York within a thirty-day period following every execution, between 1907 and 1963, there were two or three murders over and above the expected rate.

After [John] Hinckley shot Reagan, there was a dramatic increase in the number of arrests for threats against public officials. Why?

I call it the "Tylenol effect."

Within days of the discovery of the poisoned capsules, product tampering had become a near epidemic. One killer, one lunatic, put deadly cyanide into Tylenol, and immediately other maniacs followed, who needed only the authority of example to put their murderous impulses into effect. Copycat killers.

There are many examples. There was the razor blade in the Halloween apple and all the bloody copycat trick-or-treaters. You know that firefighters dread the first arson-inspired forest fire because it will be followed by a spate of others. Hijacking, hostage taking, etc.

Whatever its intended purpose, a real execution is an example set by the highest authority in the land, the government itself. It is by example we learn, and executions are an invitation to twisted minds, drawn perhaps by the notoriety that will turn them from nobodies into somebodies.

So, not only is the death penalty bad morality, it's even worse law enforcement. Every time we pull the electric switch or drop the cyanide pellets, all our lives are in that much more danger.

There is a great deal of gang-related crime and juvenile crime in California. What do you see as the cause?

I just sold a story to *California Magazine* about our kiddie prisons in California. Prisons for kids. The California Youth Authority. There are nine thousand California youngsters in prisons, as opposed to Utah or Massachusetts with sixty. Now in California, we are allowed to keep them until the age of twenty-five, so we have them from age twelve to twenty-five within the same institutions, but the majority are sixteen, seventeen, and eighteen.

I did this odyssey. I went into a dozen of these institutions and met the wardens, and the kids, and the line staff, and the administration, and the governor's representatives. What became crystal clear to me is the political rhetoric. Everyone working with the kids sounded like Jesse Jackson. They were all saying, "This is a total waste, this is a Band-Aid, this is making things worse; unless we do something at the front end, unless we do something about the conditions, we are going to keep having trouble."

It is chicken and egg time. You are nobody, as far as your peer culture is concerned, until you have gone through this system. I interviewed kids in the institutions who absolutely support that contention. This one kid I spoke with said, "You know, I immediately figured out the gig and I went right to the top. I was the role model, negative, to be sure," he said, "but I was it. I lied, I cheated, I manipulated, I extorted, I was number one—the American way." And in many ways the drug thing is the American way, private enterprise to a T, where there is virtually no other enterprise.

I say in my piece: while we discuss the future, the future is being hatched in these cells; these nine thousand kids are hatcheries. They told me, "These people don't give a damn about me. When I get out of here, I'm going to rip some faces off." All of which is true. Nothing has been done to address their sense of responsibility, the world, or human relationships.

I have written about Jerry Miller, who pioneered the deinstitutionalization of kids. He was the head of the correctional department for kids in Massachusetts and later of Pennsylvania and Illinois. As someone right in the thick of it, Jerry realized that no matter what he did, he kept seeing these kids come back, and getting worse and worse. So finally he said he was locking the door of these state training schools.

What sort of things can be done?

I talked to the authorities about parenting. Everywhere I went I asked, "Is there anything that addresses the problems of being a parent? We are a very abusive culture, we abuse our children, we don't like them, and we pay the price." Well, they say, "Parenting? What do you mean?" They didn't know parenting themselves, so how were they going to teach parenting?

A group here in Oakland, called Allied Fellowship, proposed to the California Youth Authority that they set up a group home for pregnant girls in custody. First they were told, "We don't have that problem." But the group kept at it, and they realized that of the four hundred girls they have in custody on any given day, about 15 percent are pregnant. So they said, "Well, I guess we do have that problem." For a year they tried to get them to approve a group home. They finally got approval because Deukmejian saw some political value in this—girls, pregnant girls. A month ago they got the approval—for a locked facility. No great shakes except it is more homelike. Rooms for three—count that, one, two, three—girls!

They were transported to their new "home" in total shackles, shackled to the waist, their legs, and their arms. A seven-hour drive in a prison van. All of them were in very advanced stages of pregnancy.

Shackled, pregnant, and sixteen years old.

They wanted to stop to go to the bathroom. Here are three pregnant young girls trying to say, "I guess you don't understand what it is to be pregnant. We got to stop. We got to pee. STOP." Finally they agreed to stop and undid one cuff to let them go to the bathroom. One girl gave birth four days later. It's a nightmare.

I asked the people in Sacramento about parenting, and one parole officer says, "I have learned a lot about parenting in the last year; we are going to teach these women parenting." I said, "I'm glad to hear that, but you have four hundred women and nine thousand boys." He said, "What do you mean, boys? It only takes five seconds for a boy to become a parent!"

In Sacramento area you get quoted, "The governor believes in protection for the public. We need to put people in prison and keep them there longer. This is the policy of the administration."

There is, in this country, a need for a class of despised people. An economic need for both an unemployed group who do not compete for jobs and a group to care for them. A kind of socialized system where the guards and, to an extent, the police are really the recipients of a social welfare program.

What do you think it does to a society that condones the death penalty?

In some ways you have to pull yourself back from America and see it for what it is, and it is an extraordinarily violent place. Cowboy, macho, it started even before the Puritans. I mean, we come from violence; we had a revolution. I am not sure that in having the Revolution we didn't lose everything right there. We pursued a genocidal war against the indigenous population, enslaved a race of people—stole them from their country and shipped them away to build our country.

Then we put the whole thing behind us, like Iran-contra. "Yes, we acknowledge this isn't right, but let's not dwell on the past, let's put it behind us." We have this whole history of death and destruction which we keep putting behind us so that we can pretend to be innocent and blunder through Vietnam and blunder through the world—innocently. All this in a very short time. Which is why I say, I hate the hypocrisy almost as much as the actual killing. This pretense of innocence!

You know when I saw Oliver North on television, I should have known that Americans would invite fascism into their living rooms if it had a smile and perfectly timed quaver in its voice. But one must never underestimate the depth of America's shallowness, so he is quickly yesterday's deodorant.

I worry about what appears to me to be our pleasure in punishment, in hurting people. I think there is something sexual at the root of it that has to do with the way we raise little boys to be soldiers, and that our sense of what is acceptable or not acceptable gets perverted.

Most of the grossest criminals are white males. In this category are not only killers, but those who hurt others. Pain, torture. I feel that in a subliminal, internal way the majority of people also get pleasure in the pain. It's a brutal fact of life that, as a white man, you have to be just a little worse to end up on death row.

CALIFORNIA DREAMING

"'If the law supposes that,' said Mr. Bumble, 'the law is an ass, an idiot.'"
—Charles Dickens, *Oliver Twist*, 1837–1839

In the beautiful city of San Francisco, at an address within aria distance of the Opera House, is an unimposing Victorian-style building that has been converted into the law offices of the California Appellate Project, a state-funded facility, the desperate last hope for many of the over two hundred inmates of San Quentin's death row.

We met the director, Michael Millman, forty-eight years old, a tall, youthful-looking, bespectacled redhead. Mr. Millman holds an impressive clutch of degrees, including a Bachelor's in physics from Harvard and a Master's in physics from Berkeley.

Inspired by the movement lawyers in the sixties and tired of research in the basement of Birch Hall, Berkeley, he moved from the lab bench to the bar after obtaining yet another degree, this time from Yale Law School.

San Francisco, California
Monday, May 16, 1988, 5:30 p.m.

Michael Millman

Can you tell us about the California Appellate Project?
The California Appellate Project (CAP) is an outgrowth of a cut in the state Public Defender budget in July 1983 by the then newly-elected governor, George Deukmejian.

Everyone, including the Supreme Court, urged him not to do it, but he went ahead and cut the budget by 50 percent anyway. Chief Justice Rose Bird then went to the state bar and said, in essence, if the state Public Defender is going to do less, then obviously the private bar will have to do more. We were already having difficulty finding lawyers to do these appeals. So the state bar passed a resolution to create a small office, CAP, to find private attorneys to do these appeals and then to assist them by providing them with technical expertise.

What kind of lawyers do you look for? How do you go about finding them?
(Michael Millman laughs) Well, every day at noon I stand out in front of City Hall—I've got a little bell. . . .

You must have about as much luck as a leper?
Ah yes, but I keep going.

Actually, we go around in every forum we can find, encouraging qualified people to take on a case. The ideal person is someone like a former state public defender; a person with extensive criminal appellate experience who is known to do high-quality work. The problem is, there just aren't enough of those folks around.

You can understand why if we look at the way new lawyers in this country in effect become apprentices. When they come out of law school, many go to the DA's office or a Public Defender Office, as I did, and they learn how to become trial lawyers. If you do that day in and day out for two, three, four years, you learn your way around a trial court. When those people leave and get into private practice, they become a part of the trial bar. Unfortunately, there isn't an appellate bar comparable to the trial bar. Traditionally, when people came out of law school, a justice from the Court of Appeal makes a pitch to them at their swearing in: "By the way, we've got all these indigent appeals, and we would sure be appreciative if you young lawyers would volunteer to take one of them." So you took one, and usually it was not a very satisfying experience. You didn't know what the hell you were doing, and nobody gave you any help. They paid you something incredibly small, and when it was over, most people thought to themselves, "Thanks, but I'm never going to do this again." So there never developed a group of people who knew how to do appellate work. Then the state Public Defender Office was established, and it began to create a cadre of appellate lawyers who were recruited, trained, and supervised, and who, as a result, developed appellate expertise. If there were more of those folks around, we wouldn't have so much problem finding attorneys now.

It's interesting to figure out what kind of lawyer to look for. If you take criminal trial lawyers, who know lots of criminal law but do not do appellate work regularly, they generally don't do particularly well at death penalty appeals. They have been, on the average, less successful than attorneys with well-honed appellate skills who have some basic familiarity with the criminal process, even though they don't practice criminal law regularly. We are trying to draw those people into the system, and when we do, we provide them with resources and technical expertise—manuals, newsletters, and advice—in order to help them do first-rate appellate work.

After judgment of death has been pronounced, to do the appeal alone, you have to figure something on the order of one thousand attorney hours for an "average" case.

How much compensation do they get?

California is remarkably generous compared to the other states. The attorneys are paid $60 per hour and are compensated for many of their expenses, including their investigative and expert witness expenses.

What about the big, rich law firms that do pro bono work; are you getting any help from them?

Some, but so far not from as many as we would like. That's a major potential source that we are trying to tap. The large firms attract some of the finest legal minds in the land, people who can bring a different perspective to bear on the problem.

When you get involved in this process, when you realize that this is your client whom they are trying to kill, it changes you. It is a very sobering thought which sinks in over time. You may start out just handling a case, reading transcripts and writing briefs, and then, as the years go by and you keep getting closer and closer to an execution, you think, "Holy mackerel, they really want to kill this guy!" As that reality sets in, you start to think, "Well, this is really wrong, because I

310 MICHAEL MILLMAN

have come to know him over several years. I know he did something terrible, and he probably shouldn't be out in society, but we are not talking about an extended prison sentence, or even life without the possibility of parole, we are talking about *killing* him." Suddenly you really don't want *this* person, *your* client, to be killed. That realization transforms many people.

What kind of people undertake death penalty work? For the most part, "liberal do-gooders" are the ones you'd expect to defend the men on the row. The involvement of partners in the large law firms, who are personally well known to the judges and respected by them and who move in the same circles, can be very important. If it's *their* client who is going to be executed, they will, I think, feel very differently than they might about the abstract question of capital punishment. In a sense, each lawyer becomes an advocate against the death penalty on behalf of his or her individual client.

Can you tell us why so many sentences were overturned in the California Supreme Court? Is it true that it was because of the Briggs Initiative?

California is a good example of what can happen when badly drafted laws are enacted. A former capital punishment law was invalidated in 1976 as a result of the decisions of the United States Supreme Court. A new law was passed, drafted by experienced prosecutors, who tried to come in as close as they could to the statutes of Florida, Georgia, and Texas that were approved by the United States Supreme Court. They produced a relatively tight bill that was reasonably likely to be constitutional. Barely a year later along comes Briggs, who was a legislator trying to get the Republican nomination for governor and using the death penalty as his platform. Basically Briggs said, "To hell with all this narrowing language. We want a broad death penalty that will catch as many first-degree murderers as possible." That's where much of the tension was created. The more narrow you make a statute, the more likely it is to protect constitutional rights and, therefore, the more likely it is to be upheld. On the other hand, the broader the statute, the more categories of first-degree murders are included, the more diminished are its procedural protections. It then becomes more likely that some court will say, "Wait a minute. This law is not fair. It doesn't satisfy the Supreme Court's concerns in *Furman* or *Gregg*." For example, one of the provisions Briggs added said that in capital cases, the jury should be told that they are supposed to decide between two penalties, one death and the other life without the possibility of parole, and that in every case the governor has the power to commute life without the possibility of parole to life.

This provision was widely attacked by informed lawyers. The California Supreme Court had filed a decision a decade earlier which essentially said that such a provision was impermissible under California law. But Briggs went ahead, his proposal was enacted into law, and eventually the California Supreme Court said it was unconstitutional. Then the United States Supreme Court, in a 5–4 decision, held that it did not violate the federal Constitution. The California Supreme Court finally came back and said it violated the state Constitution. About twenty capital cases have been or will be reversed because of this instruction.

The other example has to do with "intent to kill"—whether accidental killings committed during the course of a felony also qualify for the death penalty. Briggs took out the Deukmejian provision, which said you had to have a "premeditated killing in the course of a felony," and replaced it with no requirement of intent at all.

So in a sense Briggs was a loose cannon when he put this to the electorate. How were the people to decide that issue in terms of extremely complicated constitutional law? What they were told instead was to vote for this proposition because it expanded the death penalty. They voted for it, and in doing so they inadvertently messed up the law.

It was not that the Bird Court picked esoteric provisions of the Briggs Initiative to quibble with, but rather that they pointed out the flaws in the law which should have been obvious to everyone.

So these cases were reversed on major constitutional questions, not nitpicking points of law on the part of the Bird Court?

Yes, that's true. We are talking about substantial errors. However, the [Chief Justice Malcom M.] Lucas Court appears to be much less troubled by the presence of error in the trial proceedings than the Bird Court was. The same errors that would have concerned the Bird Court are much less important to the current Court.

As a result, it is only a matter of time before there will be executions in California. The real question is, how many executions do people really want? How many executions do they need? How many executions can they afford?

Politically or economically?

Economically. How much money do they want to spend on this one aspect of the criminal justice system? What is the death penalty's utility? Extremists who argue that we should execute every first-degree murderer are not dealing with reality. There is absolutely no historical precedent in this country for executing all first-degree murderers. It is inconceivable. What we know is that, historically, we are going to execute between 0.5 and 2 percent of those in this country who have been convicted of intentional homicides. If you execute 0.5 percent, the system can probably afford it, in the sense that there are enough qualified lawyers to represent the defendants and the courts can handle the cases without getting overloaded. When you get up to 2 percent, you are severely overloading the system. In actual numbers, if you have forty death judgments a year in California, as we had in the early 1980s, we are pushing the system to its limits. If we ever get to sixty a year, which is 2 percent of the intentional homicides, we will have a real crisis on our hands. People talk about returning to "the good old days" when we had lots of executions, but what were the good old days? How many executions did we actually have in the peak years, the 1930s? In California, the largest number of executions per year in this century was in 1935 and 1936, when there were seventeen executions each year. That's the high point. There were very few years in which the number per year was more than ten, and the average for the century is less than six. So, if we are already sentencing thirty people to death each year and have more than two hundred people on the row, why are people trying to spend more and more money to tie up the system even further?

What will be gained by executing more than ten people a year, assuming that anything is gained by executions at all? All we are ever going to do is perform a "symbolic ritual," through which a minuscule percentage of society's murderers are executed. Even if you really believe, in the face of all the evidence to the contrary, that the death penalty is a deterrent, the marginal gain in deterrence you would achieve by executing forty people a year instead of twenty is negligible, but the marginal cost to the system will be enormous.

It seems that the prosecutors want to go for the death penalty more than ever. Would you say the system is out of control?

It is out of control in the sense that it has so many independent components. There are the individual prosecutors, making choices county by county, case by case. There is the legislature, which makes its choice in terms of the statutes. Then there is the Court having to make individual decisions in cases which come before it on appeal. Obviously, they don't all sit down together and coordinate each other's activities. Everybody goes about on their own course, and this can create enormous damage to the whole system because nobody is thinking through the systemic consequences. A prosecutor may think, "I get more notches on my gun if I push through these cases as capital." If you have a lot of prosecutors around the state doing that, without thinking about the whole picture, you will soon have a system in total overload.

What do you feel the death penalty does to the society that condones it?

I am not convinced about the actual impact. I know that the popular perspective is that it does something very profound, one way or the other. Either it's the greatest thing since sliced bread, because it is going to get everybody in line and stop crime and all that sort of stuff, which I certainly do not believe, or there is an apocalyptic vision in which it's going to destroy the moral fiber of our society and we will all turn into barbarians and go down the tubes.

I don't share either of these views.

I have much more of a sense that this is a terrible waste; an irrelevancy. Its harm is more subtle than first appears. As long as we think that killing this tiny handful of people is going to solve our problem with violent crime, we are unlikely to deal meaningfully with the real causes of crime and take useful preventive measures that will actually make us safer.

As long as we perceive capital punishment as the remedy for the problem, as long as we keep buying the political hype telling us that this brand of snake oil will cure violent crime, we are not likely to address the problem intelligently. We spend a lot of money on the death penalty with very little return on our investment, money which could much better be used to prevent crime or to compensate its victims. It is this illusional aspect of the death penalty that may be its greatest liability, because it actually deflects us from more productive efforts to address what is a very serious problem.

THE DEFENDER

"Are you going to hang him anyhow—and try him
afterward?"

—Mark Twain, *Innocents Abroad*, 1869

*He wears a well-cut dark blue suit, but Robert Bryan's conservative
appearance is deceptive.*

*His ore-mine red hair and mustache, freckled face, piercing blue
eyes, and almost hypnotic voice laced with slight Southern tones give
the immediate impression of a senior partner in a prosperous and established law firm. But behind bright scarlet suspenders and a hand-
made shirt beats the heart of a radical people's advocate; a man who
takes on only the most difficult, unpopular, and challenging cases.*

*In his twenty-year career, this attorney has acted for the defense in
over a hundred murder trials, most of them capital. His record of
acquittals is phenomenal.*

*Robert R. Bryan was born in Tennessee in 1943. He was raised in
Birmingham, Alabama, where he graduated from Cumberland Law
School. He won his first murder case at the age of twenty-six. Since
then, he has tried over a hundred murder cases.*

*A California jury recently returned a verdict of acquittal in his most
recent, capital murder trial, an infamous case that was considered
impossible to defend.*

*Robert R. Bryan is a dedicated runner, vegetarian, and abolitionist,
who finds time in his crammed agenda to be the chairman of the National Coalition to Abolish the Death Penalty as well as co-chair of the
Northern California Coalition to Abolish the Death Penalty.*

We interviewed him in his San Francisco offices on fashionable

Union Street. It is an old-fashioned place; the decor ranges from late Dickens to early Conan Doyle. Leatherbound books abound. Over a cast-iron fireplace and pine mantel hang blown-up photographs of trials and executions. Suspended in one corner of the room is a human skeleton, sporting a black hat and a T-shirt bearing the legend: "Support Your Local Gas Chamber." A macabre reminder of why we were there.

San Francisco, California
Friday, July 8, 1988, 3:30 p.m.

Robert R. Bryan

We have read that you are very critical of lawyers who are provided by the court. Is it mainly because they are inexperienced or because they are badly prepared?

I don't think experience is necessarily a criterion. I think it's important, but when I defended my first case I was only twenty-six and did not have very much experience. It's more a matter of attitude. A lawyer has to be totally committed to the welfare of his client. For instance, a surgeon operating on a patient bleeding to death would consider it unthinkable to hesitate in attempting to save that person. The doctor has an obligation to stop that person from bleeding to death and do everything possible to save the person's life.

As an attorney, I am trying to prevent people from legally bleeding to death. That's a reality I deal with every day. I do not go to see horror pictures where people get cut up with chain saws, because it's all very real to me. I do not enjoy violence.

One of the mistakes that lawyers make is they often do not attempt to humanize their clients at the guilt/innocence stage. It is a mistake to wait until the penalty stage before the jury sees that the client is just like the rest of us—a person and not a monster. They are going to know right at the trial stage that my client is not a freak.

You made the national press recently when you pleaded and lost the Hauptmann case, some fifty years after his death. Are you still convinced that Richard Hauptmann was innocent?

The man was totally innocent. I can show you doc
were in the prosecution files at the time of the "Trial of th
1935 that would have destroyed the entire case against Ri
mann.

The case is still recognized as the biggest trial in American history.

I have the fingerprints of the actual kidnapper which, of course, don't match Richard Hauptmann's. The prosecution and the state fingerprint expert lied about that at the trial. The state police finally admitted privately to the FBI that they had the real kidnapper's prints. But none of this ever came out publicly. I can give you probably about 150 examples of that sort of cover-up in this case.

Mr. Hauptmann was offered a commutation from death to life if he admitted he was involved in the kidnapping of the Lindbergh baby, but he turned it down, saying he would rather die than live with a lie. He was very courageous.

Here you had an overzealous and corrupt prosecutor, and a tremendous amount of pressure to solve the "Crime of the Century." It was unsolved for two and a half years, until they linked part of the ransom money to Mr. Hauptmann, which had innocently come into his possession. From then on, the end justified the means. The authorities fraudulently staged evidence to frame him.

I can establish that Charles Lindbergh lied on the witness stand when he identified the voice of Richard Hauptmann. He had heard two words, "Hey, Doctor," from 150 yards away in the cemetery where the ransom was being paid years earlier by the go-between, Dr. John F. Condon. But before the trial Lindbergh had testified, in secret, before a grand jury, that he could not identify the voice as that of Richard Hauptmann. But the jury at the trial never knew that.

The press took a poll of the jury after the trial. The jurors all said that once Lindbergh testified, they needed to hear nothing else in the case; it was as if God had spoken. Lindbergh was a living legend. The jury knew after Lindbergh spoke that the right and patriotic thing to do was to kill Richard Hauptmann.

I have seen this end-justifies-the-means type of philosophy in other murder cases. Innocent people have died, as in the Hauptmann case and as, I think, in the Willie Darden case. That is what is frightening. Also, because of the Hauptmann case, we got the Little Lindbergh Law under which more people died in execution chambers for non-homicidal crimes.

We receive mail from around the world, and in this country— mostly from the Northeast and the Midwest—all supportive of our efforts to exonerate Mr. Hauptmann. I only run into resistance when I get into the power structure.

When I go to New Jersey to deal with the officials, you would think that the case happened last year instead of back in the thirties. My office was torched, in 1982, over that case. People have followed me when I am in the East working on the case. Once when we were holding a press conference in New Jersey, the tires on my rental car were ice-picked. And of course there are the threats. When I get telephone threats, they don't come from "nuts" or John Q. Public, but rather from the police. Only cops talk that way. "Cop talk."

It may seem very juvenile and pranksterish but it shows just the mentality of these people. They are incredibly defensive about this whole thing.

There is no question about the fact that Richard Hauptmann was innocent, based on governmental documents that have been uncovered. We don't want money, we don't want damages—we just want to clear the official record. I am only asking the authorities to recognize that the "Trial of the Century" was unfair, and that an innocent man was executed. I believe one of the reasons we are getting resistance is because if the officials admit they fouled up the "Trial of the Century," they are conceding that other cases are also suspect. By doing that they would be forced to concede that we should not play God with people's lives, that the death penalty is wrong.

Mistakes can and do happen, because of human error.

Richard Hauptmann was no different than Willie Darden. Darden was black, Hauptmann was German; both were victims of prejudice, executed for who they were rather than what they allegedly did. There was strong anti-German feeling in New Jersey when Richard Hauptmann was tried. He had a thick German accent and was a poor man who could not afford good counsel. The hucksters arranged for the Hearst papers to bring in Edward J. Reilly as the defense attorney, who was known as "Death House Reilly." The man was intoxicated during most of the trial. He was a buffoon. He did crazy things at the trial. Incidentally, he was put in a mental hospital a year or so later.

When Mrs. Hauptmann was approached, she didn't know what the Hearst papers were; she didn't know who Reilly was. All she knew was that she was poor and these people were being very nice and were offering to pay the fees for this big-time lawyer. Mrs. Hauptmann had contacted Clarence Darrow in Chicago, but he was just too ill to handle a case of that magnitude at that time. What a difference there would have been had Mr. Hauptmann had good representation. Likewise, a significant number of the two thousand people in this country on death row today would not be there if they had received good representation at trial.

I am sorry to say things have not changed that much since the era of the Hauptmann trial. We see in case, after case, after case, people whose representation is a bad joke.

It seems in five of the most famous executions of this century—Sacco and Vanzetti, Ethel and Julius Rosenberg, and Richard Hauptmann— there are grave questions as to whether justice was served.

I think the Rosenbergs' case is a blot on this country. Prosecutor Roy Cohn advising the judge on the death sentencing and so forth—Disgraceful and tragic!

The Rosenbergs did not kill anybody. They were victims of the Cold War era, the bomb scare, blatant prejudice. If it hadn't been them, it would have been somebody else. Then you look at the Sacco and Vanzetti case. What happened was so terrible.

Since the Hauptmann case, our legal system has changed very little. Lawyers still make opening and closing statements; you still have prosecutors; you still have defense attorneys; you still have judges. Some say, "Well, it couldn't happen today." But miscarriages of justice do continue to occur. People are convicted and sentenced to death because of bad lawyers, politics, corruption, prejudice, and overzealous prosecutors motivated more by ambition than a sense of justice. Capital defendants are like mere pawns in a chess game. It's a fight all the way to save the damned.

In our interviews, child abuse comes up over and over again. What is your experience?

It is a common denominator in nearly all the cases. I have not had a case where someone was capitally charged, in which he or she was not abused in some way. Of all the people on death row whom I have helped, all have been victims of abuse in some form.

Can you give us a recent example of an innocent man sentenced to death?

Yes. I'll give you one that was resolved only a couple of months ago; the Bigelow case.

Jerry Bigelow had made ten confessions that he was at the homicide scene. For the prosecution, this was an open and shut case—how could they lose? Jerry was convicted and sentenced to death. Yet, at the retrial in 1988 the jury came back and said, "Not guilty!"

This was an especially horrible murder, an execution-style killing where a man picked up some hitchhikers. In the middle of the countryside they forced him to get out of the car. He was taken to a cornfield, made to kneel down, and then a gun was put to the side of his head and his brains were literally blown out. Jerry was arrested a few weeks later driving the man's car in Arizona.

During the first six months of representing Jerry, we believed that he was guilty. Our whole defense was based not on what he did, but why he did it.

One night it hit me. I thought, "Why am I believing my client? I should certainly listen to what he says, but since when have I let anybody dictate my cases?" So I decided to go back to the beginning and investigate the case from scratch, as if I had no information at all. He had bragged to the press about having committed this execution-style killing and that he wanted to see what it felt like to kill somebody, and that he didn't want to leave any witnesses.

Amazingly, we uncovered evidence that the kid was innocent. The murder was committed by somebody else.

Now, the way most lawyers think, Jerry would by now be back on death row in San Quentin.

You asked earlier about child abuse. Well, Jerry was a horribly abused child, to the point that whatever his father accused him of, Jerry would admit to—to stop the pain and the beatings. A pattern developed of Jerry admitting to things he did not do. I established that, after he was convicted the first time and on death row, years before I became his lawyer, he regularly made detailed confessions to crimes. How does he stop the pain, living day in and day out, looking at the gas chamber? He dies. He says, "I did it. Let's get it over with."

He filed motions and petitions to have himself executed, and twice attempted suicide. When the case was reversed by the California Supreme Court, Jerry filed a motion asking that the reversal be set aside so he could be executed.

We brought all this out to the jury. I placed in evidence all the petitions he filed asking to be executed.

The jury knew he was on the run and that he had committed a series of robberies unrelated to the murder. The prosecution brought all these people in to testify against him, even an elderly lady he had robbed when he was seventeen.

It wasn't a lot of fun dealing with that.

I asked the jury, "Why did Jerry commit these series of robberies?"

I recreated the beatings that he received when he was no higher than a table. His father beat him with a leather strap so severely that the family would run outside in the snow to get away from his screams and moans.

It is still very real to me.

At one point, when the trial was in recess, one of my aides went into the rest room and saw a jury member crying her eyes out. I put the jurors in Jerry's shoes.

If we had gone the way most lawyers go and not delved into his mental state, it would have been a very different outcome. We were not afraid to go into Jerry's mental state at trial. If it had been tried with just "the facts," like Joe Friday, "Gimme the facts, ma'am, just gimme the facts," then the jury would never have known about the beatings and the horrors of Jerry's childhood.

There are some people who should never even go to trial because they are mentally incompetent. Yet, many today are sitting on death rows across the land.

The whole psychology of death row is a world of insanity. It's like *Alice in Wonderland,* where everything is backwards and reversed. You feel as if you are in a madhouse. It is a place where the norm is not normal.

I will give you an example. In two of the death cases which I am appealing, I am trying to undo the damage done by other lawyers at the trial level. There is no question about the insanity of the clients. They are really sick in very different ways. One is a coprophiliac; last year he was found licking out the inside of the toilet bowl. Toilet bowls are nasty, but can you imagine how bad they are in prison? In the area where the death row inmates take baths, he would be down on the ground sucking up the dirty water. He has done incredibly brutal things to himself. He has tried to kill himself. He tried to set his cell on fire, with himself in it. He has thrown excrement on the walls and smeared it on himself. He vacillates and is apparently quite bright, which makes it even more pathetic.

It took me forever to get the authorities here to recognize that he was nuts, and this is in enlightened California where things are better than most states. He was finally sent to the California Medical Facility at Vacaville. But guess what? He was sent back to death row at San Quentin! Just as nutty as he was the day he got involved in the homicide. Now he is back at Vacaville, since he continues to play with feces and hallucinate. The officials do not want to recognize that he's insane because if they do, and they get to the stage of strapping him in the gas chamber, that might present a real problem. So they pretend he's normal. That is insane!

It is so warped it goes against everything that is moral, everything that normal people consider ethical in society. When horror becomes the norm—anything is possible.

Is the death penalty good for law enforcement?

Violence breeds violence. We are setting up a terrible example telling young people that they should obey the law and be good and yet we deal with violence by treating those who do violence in a very violent manner. We are saying one thing, but we are doing another. It goes back to the cavemen, the Neanderthals—Who has the biggest club? Might is right!—Well, might is not right!

We have been killing people for millions of years in the name of law, order, and God, and it hasn't put a dent in the crime or homicide rate. It has increased. Brutality is not the answer.

To sum up, how do you feel state sanctioned killing affects society as a whole?

No person on death row today or in the history of this country has ever committed as premeditated a murder as is committed in the name of the laws of the United States of America. The whole process of government being in the business of slaughtering human beings is wrong, and benefits no one.

A person is placed on death row and told that he or she will be killed. The authorities plan it, there is a ceremony and procedure, and the damned sits there, year after year, continually reminded that "We are going to kill you—but not yet. This is how we are going to kill you—but not yet. We are going to electrocute you, or gas you, or give you a lethal injection—but not yet."

It is the ultimate torture and barbaric treatment of a fellow human being.

I think it is the ultimate hypocrisy for the American government to talk about peace and freedom, to get involved in other parts of the world as the supposed keepers of peace, freedom, and democracy, when we treat our fellow citizens in such a horrible way.

We go through an elaborate appellate process so we can say we gave the person all these benefits before we will kill them. It is like the Old West where they gave a person a trial before the lynching. What is the difference between setting up a quick court in a bar room and going through the whole charade of trial and appeals courts before we kill somebody? You cannot respect a system like that. It is damn hypocritical.

You know, if Christ were here today, I cannot imagine Him strapping someone into the electric chair.

BEYOND PERADVENTURE

"As a justice it is also important that before we allow human lives to be snuffed out, we be sure— emphatically sure—that we act within the law. If we are not sure, there will be lingering doubts to plague the conscience after the event."

—Justice William Douglas, 1953

Former Governor of California Edmund G. "Pat" Brown has offices on the Miracle Mile section of Wilshire Boulevard, east of the La Brea Tar Pits, but west of the smog that hangs over downtown Los Angeles.

The vital eighty-one-year-old lawyer governed California for two terms, from 1959 to 1967. His son, Jerry, later held that office.

There is a sadness when he talks about the "duty" he had to perform when in office regarding decisions he made on the lives of condemned men. "Nobody should be forced to do that. What did the good Lord give me that I should have the right to determine whether even the most abject, horrible character lives or dies? I don't think that anyone has that right."

Los Angeles, California
Tuesday, August 25, 1987, 11:30 a.m.

Governor Edmund "Pat" Brown

How many death penalty cases did you have when you were governor of California?

I had sixty-two during the years in which I was governor and I commuted twenty-two, I think. I may be wrong about that, but it was within that range, and two of them committed suicide in prison after I commuted them. I changed their sentences to life, some without the possibility of parole, you see. I didn't let any of them out, but I let forty die—even though, even then, I didn't believe in capital punishment. But that was the law of the state and I didn't feel that I could take the abolition of the death penalty into my own hands, so I enforced it. But wherever I found what I felt was a case for mercy—I'm not talking about wrongful conviction here—I used clemency.

Take for example the first case I had—a man named Crooker. He went out and got a knife and killed the woman he was living with because she wouldn't come back to him. Now, if he'd been waiting for her with a gun, I wouldn't have commuted the sentence, because if he'd had the weapon *with* him it would have indicated to me that he was a premeditated murderer, that he had planned it. That is the best example of the distinction that I tried to make, in my own mind, before granting clemency or reducing the penalty. But if a person took a loaded gun and went to do a robbery and murdered somebody, they indicated that they were prepared to kill if they didn't get what they wanted. Then I let them die.

Do you believe that there is a deterrent value in the penalty?

I don't think the evidence shows any deterrent value in the death penalty, but that's the way the people felt about it. They voted for it. There's a legal basis for it . . . Whether there's any moral basis . . . each one has to make up his or her own mind as to the situation.

After my eight years as governor, public opinion was almost even stephen on the abolition of the death penalty. There's only been one execution since I left the governor's office; that was under Ronald Reagan. There were none under my son Jerry, and none so far under Deukmejian.

Both Reagan and Deukmejian believe in the death penalty and would have let them die, but the courts held it up, you see.

Have you ever witnessed an execution?

No I never did; although during my first term as D.A. in San Francisco, I was invited to attend an execution at San Quentin. I told a couple of homicide detectives about this and they urged me not to attend. I asked them why not, and these are hard boiled cops, and they told me that if I did, I would never be able to ask a jury for a death sentence again.

How do you feel the present administration is going to handle the backlog of people on death row?

If you mean practically speaking, this is what they'll do. On a Friday. They execute on a Friday. They'll take the first one at eight o'clock in the morning and they'll gas him or her. Then it takes about four hours to clear the gas, then they'll take the next one at twelve, the next one at four, and the last at eight o'clock. That's the way they'll do it. Then, between you and me and the lamp post, by the time they get to the eighth week of this execution spree, I think the people of California will begin to regurgitate.

Then you believe there will be a public outcry at this kind of bloodbath?

I don't know whether there will be a public outcry, but there will certainly be a very strong reaction against the death penalty.

So you believe that it is in the cards that executions will begin again in California?

Oh, I believe beyond peradventure! You have Deukmejian, who made his career asking for the death penalty. I debated him, when he was a young assemblyman, down in Long Beach, and that's all he talked about then . . . the death penalty . . . and gassing them. There's a sadistic streak, in my opinion, in this man.

Were you always against the death penalty?

No. When I was District Attorney in San Francisco, I was for it.

You are on record as saying that the death penalty is fundamentally and morally wrong. What brought you to this conclusion?

When, as governor, I read the record of the cases, and studied the backgrounds of the individuals, the life that they lead, the circumstances of the killings. The cold-blooded bringing of a human being, a live human being, to a death cell and holding him for twenty-four hours before taking him out and gassing him, no matter what the crime was—I came to the conclusion that it was morally wrong. I just concluded that, although the state had the right to do it, it was morally wrong. . . . It wasn't even serving its purpose. If by gassing somebody you could save the life of a human being, or by gassing twenty people you could save the life of one human being, then maybe it would be justified. I don't know. But I didn't feel that there was any evidence to sustain it, and in view of the fact that there wasn't any evidence to sustain it, then we had no right to take life. That was the conclusion I came to.

You have said that no one man should have to make that life or death decision. Can you describe the kind of anguish this must have caused you?

Why, if you can just think of sitting in the governor's office, all alone, and you said, "thumbs up they live, thumbs down they die." And then you picture that person on death row in San Quentin and if you say "thumbs down" . . . he dies. . . . Nobody should be forced to do that. What did the good Lord give me that I should have the right to determine whether even the most abject, horrible character lives or dies? I don't think that anyone has that right.

How do you think America looks when compared with other Western democracies in this area?

They've abolished the death penalty in all European countries and there is less homicide there than in the places where they execute. The states that execute the most have the *highest* crime rate.

What we should do, and it *would* cut down the murder rate, is abolish handguns. The only purpose of a handgun is to kill somebody. There's no other purpose on God's green earth. I gave five thousand dollars of my hard-earned money to an initiative to do this here in California. But it didn't do any good because people are afraid. Now, if they want to go shooting a handgun, they can shoot targets at a rifle range. Don't think the American citizens who vote for handguns are mean people—they are actually afraid and they think that handguns will protect them. It's the most ridiculous thing in the world. You and I know that it doesn't. The freedom to buy a gun even for people who are desperate, out of work, or mentally ill, is an indication that murder will continue. The possession of a handgun is almost a challenge. It's a vicious tool and a major contributing cause to homicides in the United States. I'm not talking about the long gun—people who go out and hunt deer or duck are usually good people. You don't find anyone going into a bank, holding it up with a long gun!

Who ends up on death row?

Mostly minorities and underprivileged people. Young people drop out of school, they have nothing to do. Inevitably, they'll get into trouble. You've got to get these kids doing something until they are at least eighteen. We've got to tackle the root cause, the education system. Forty-seven percent of the blacks and 35 percent of the Hispanics drop out of school. They're going to commit crimes.

What is the effect of the abnormally long periods of time the condemned spent on death row?

The long delay between the conviction and the execution itself diminishes any deterrent value that it has. The way it is now, where it goes on five and six and seven and eight years . . . by the time he's executed, everybody forgot what he did and, of course, the fact that they forget what he did is also evidence of the fact that it has no deterrent value. Most violent crime is either done by mental cases or on the spur of the moment.

Was homicide the only type of capital case you dealt with?

Well, rape is not a capital offense in California any longer. But here was the case of Eddie Wein, he raped at least ten women, but they charged him with kidnapping, which used to carry the death penalty. Wein was the "Want-Ad Rapist." What he'd do was go to a house in answer to an ad of a person selling a sewing machine or a piano. He would say his wife couldn't come with him, then he'd drop something on the floor and say, "Gee, my eyes are bad, I can't see to pick it up," then he'd grab the woman, take a knife, and rape her. They got him on kidnapping because he moved the women from the living room to the bedroom and then he also stole. He was sentenced to death.

I commuted the sentence.

Then there was the Chessman case.

He died. . . . I couldn't commute him. I mean, the feeling against him was so great. I did give him a sixty-day stay, you know. I tried to get the legislature to give a moratorium on the death penalty; they turned me down. Then I asked the Supreme Court for permission to commute his sentence, from death to life, and they turned me down. The whole episode was nightmare and I was in a no win situation, but the fact was the law mandated the death penalty. I had to let him go.

Do you feel that the death penalty demeans society?

I very definitely do. If you look at the world and see what's happening in France, Germany, and Canada, and you look at the United States and you look at the crime rate in the United States and compare it to those other places, we are way out of line.

THE LAST RESORT

"Crime is only the retail department of what, in wholesale, we call penal law."

—George Bernard Shaw, 1905

Alan M. Dershowitz has a spacious office overlooking a courtyard outside Griswald Hall, in the center of the Harvard Law School. In legal circles, Professor Dershowitz has been both praised and criticized for allowing himself to be so readily available to the media, which constantly court his opinions on every legal controversy.

As a weekly columnist, his writings have been syndicated in the daily newspapers in most of the fifty states. His book Reversal of Fortune: Inside the Von Bulow Case, *was described by the* New York Review of Books *as "a remarkable story . . . great skill and a novelist's flair." The Boston* Globe *called his previous best-selling book,* Best Defense, *"an astounding legal memoir."*

Others have been less flattering. Pinned to his office door is his "fan mail": letters from those who disagree with the professor's views. The writing is less eloquent than the East Coast reviewer's but is, nonetheless, descriptive. One of the more restrained missives reads: "You shyster commie pinko lawyer. . . . They should take you out and string you up with your scum bag clients. . . . Yours, A hundred percent American."

The professor's hair, receding in the front, seems to have a will of its own, the mustache turns down in the style of a sixties radical—not the appearance that one would expect of a man who has defended some of the most controversial figures in this century, including John Delorean, Claus von Bulow, and Patricia Hearst.

Cambridge, Massachusetts
Wednesday, March 2, 1988, Noon

Professor Alan M. Dershowitz

Do you believe the death penalty to be unconstitutional?

I participated in the beginning of the judicial campaign against capital punishment. I was Justice [Arthur J.] Goldberg's law clerk in the summer of 1963. He had recently been appointed to the Supreme Court and we spent the month of August just talking about what it was he wanted to do during that year. I had just come off a clerkship with Judge David Bazelon, who was the great liberal reformer of his day, and we had thought about trying to mount an attack on capital punishment on racial grounds, but we didn't really have the right case. Well, Justice Goldberg suggested it first, but we were both thinking about it. We decided that we were going to try to open up the issue of the unconstitutionality of the death penalty. I spent the entire summer writing up a memo on why the death penalty is unconstitutional.

This had never been suggested by a judge or a scholar before, so it was really a novel issue. Just a few years earlier Chief Justice [Earl] Warren, the great liberal Justice, had said, "Of course the death penalty is constitutional, the Framers intended it, they talk about it five times in the Constitution. Of course they also intended it for adultery and burglary. Everything was punishable by death at the time, everything was a capital offense until around 1820, when the Quaker movement in Pennsylvania started reducing the levels of murder."

So we introduced the memo and circulated it to all the Justices. Justice Warren was appalled. He was furious. Remember, *Brown v. Board of Education* was just then taking effect, and the idea that we would then allow blacks killing whites to be saved from the death penalty was too much for a politically sensitive Justice like Warren to accept.

So we went public, by writing a dissenting opinion in *Rudolph v. Alabama*. Justice Goldberg persuaded Justice Brennan and, interestingly enough, Justice Douglas, who was not very strongly in favor of this issue. The three of them filed a dissenting opinion from the denial of review. It was a paradigm case of a black man sentenced to death for raping a white woman, and we thought the Supreme Court should have reviewed the case.

We had done a study and had found four hundred or so cases in which people were sentenced to death for rape. It was always a black man sentenced to death for raping a white woman. So we took that case to ask if the Court would simply like to consider the question. We also invited lawyers in future cases to address the question of whether the death penalty is unconstitutional. Of course I sent copies of the dissenting opinion to every lawyer in America who I knew, including Tony Amsterdam, who became, appropriately and properly, the hero of this whole thing.

Tony picked up the ball and ran with it and started the campaign against the death penalty, which culminated in *Furman [Furman v. Georgia]*.

The villain of the piece, of course, is Warren Burger, who was adamant against having his term seen as a tenure which involved undoing the death penalty. He ran for Chief Justice on a "law and order and kill 'em" program. So in his dissent in *Furman,* he tells the states how to circumvent the *Furman* decision. It is a remarkable dictum for a judge who believes in judicial restraint. He says, "Here's the way you do it. Write statutes that don't have too much discretion." Then the Ping-Pong match began. So they started mandatory death sentences and the Supreme Court said mandatory was no good. They went back and forth.

Then the states came up with this middle ground called "channeled discretion" which is a fraud. It doesn't work. If you look at those who get executed today under "channeled discretion," and if you did a scientific study, you would find little difference between the randomness of execution today and the randomness of execution pre-*Furman*.

Legal rules do not determine who gets executed. What determines who gets executed is race of the victim—that's the single most important factor—the quality of the lawyer and the wealth of the client.

There is another thing we haven't looked at systematically yet, but that I am convinced has an effect. That is, the locale. That is, whether the defendant and victim comes from the town in which the trial is occurring. You find a tremendous disparity when the victim comes from the town in which the jury is sitting but the defendant does not. It is really like the white/black thing because the white/black thing is simply a metaphor for something else. It's a metaphor for how we value human life.

We value the life most of those who we are most like. If you look at judges and juries, you see the pattern is: if we were the victims, if our daughter or our son were the victims.

An example of how we don't value women's lives, in the criminal context, is, I believe, in the area of rape. You know rape is primarily against the man, not against the woman, going back to biblical times. It was a crime against the man who *possessed* the woman. Therefore, if you raped the daughter of somebody, you raped the father. If you raped the wife, you raped the husband.

How do you see reversing the trend toward more death sentences and executions?

Today in the United States there is no way of reversing the trend by theoretical arguments, or by arguing against the constitutionality of the death penalty, by asking for broad steps. It seems to me we have to take little tiny steps.

Do you believe that executing an innocent man would have any effect on public opinion?

Totally innocent is not enough. It would take executing an innocent, *decent* man.

Supposing the victim turns up alive?

I have such a case. Fortunately, we stopped the death penalty on that one before it happened. I was involved with the Joe Hunt case for a short period of time. I was consulting; I never formally entered the case. Joe Hunt is the famous Billionaire's Boy's Club defendant convicted of murdering a man who may very well be alive. We firmly believe that this guy may, someday, slither up from under a rock in Mexico or somewhere and thumb his nose and say, "Ha, ha, ha."

How do you see America's standing in the eyes of the rest of the world vis-à-vis the death penalty?

I don't think Americans care about that. Eighty-six percent in the last opinion poll seem to favor the death penalty. These polls are phony. As Justice Marshall suggested in the *Furman* decision, if you sit down with most decent Americans and you really explain how the death penalty works, aside from the rhetoric and the propaganda, most would end up opposing capital punishment. My mother would probably vote in favor of the death penalty on a poll, but she wouldn't vote in favor of the death penalty in any case if she knew the facts.

How America stands in the world? I mean, we are very self-righteous about this stuff; we think we have a better system of justice than most other countries in the world and yet we have the death penalty. On the other hand, a lot of Americans think we don't have the death penalty. A lot of Americans think we have it in theory but not in practice. I mean, in the last dozen years there have not been a lot of people executed, and if anything there is a call for more death sentences for the first time in many years.

One thing that happens when you organize formally against the death penalty is that you also incite people to organize in favor of it. For example, in Canada, just two years ago people organized to prosecute Nazi war criminals. For the first time in history some members of the Ukrainian and other eastern European communities *[in Canada]* got together and formed organizations, in effect, in support of the Nazi war criminals. It was the first time these communities had gotten together, and they said, "Hey, it wasn't so bad what happened. Let's forget it. Let bygones, etc." When you organize in favor, you get organizations against. We are getting, for the first time, major organized forces in favor of the death penalty. We have Capital Legal Foundation and other conservative forces that are filing amicus briefs in every death penalty case.

Have you run into Joe Freeman Britt, a prosecutor from North Carolina, who lectures all over the country, urging people to speed up executions?

Do you think executions will begin again in states like California where there have been no executions in over twenty years?

I think one of the most dangerous developments in places like California is that there is a liberal backlash in favor of the death penalty. There is a liberal backlash in the black community, in the gay community, in the Hispanic community, in Chinese and other Oriental communities. The feeling is that the streets are not safe. There is a new trend with liberal politicians. The liberals say, "Don't give the conservatives the crime issues, we are entitled to quality in our lives and safety in our streets." I suspect in the coming years we are going to see a trend toward more liberals supporting the death penalty. I see it right here at Harvard Law School amongst some of my colleagues. I see it most dramatically in the black community where liberal black politicians, who on every other issue are terrific, are saying, "Let's remember who the victims are here." The real fact that it is more likely to be a black executed for killing a white victim is ignored. Their answer is not to do away with the death penalty, it is to increase the number of executions among whites who kill blacks.

The point is this. How we define the crime of murder also involves a large amount of discretion. Murder does not, for example, include drunken driving cases. Drunken driving cases are white middle class and the punishments for that tend to be trivial. Those are crimes where, if you did get a little tough, it would seem to me you could have an enormous impact.

I could reduce the homicide rate in this country dramatically if you just gave me the ability to tamper a little bit with prison sentences. Abolish the death penalty and increase, substantially, prison terms for the kinds of deaths that are really preventable. White-collar deaths. Crimes caused by environmental polluters, caused by drunken driving, caused by people who make rational decisions to do wrong, and where calculated decisions are made to kill hundreds of people for money.

I think one way of helping to abolish the death penalty would be to argue for an increase in prison terms for murderers, and liberals don't want to do that. They are caught in that one. Do we really want life imprisonment to mean life imprisonment? One of the problems is that when you escape the death penalty, it is so easy to get out early in certain states. Often the issue for many Americans is not death versus life imprisonment, it means death versus letting them out pretty well immediately. That is a dilemma for many liberals.

How about the death penalty as a prosecutorial tool? A bargaining chip?

It's the major bargaining chip that results in guilty pleas in murder. I do believe that is one argument the death penalty advocates do have empirically. In states where the death penalty is not available, I think it is much harder to get a plea to second-degree murder or first-degree murder with no possibility of a parole. Because the difference between a twenty-year sentence and a twelve-year sentence doesn't seem that great to a person who has to give up his rights to litigate, whereas the threat of death has an enormous impact.

So the death penalty does deter. What it deters is your constitutional right to go to trial. That, for some, is an argument in favor of the death penalty. For me and others, it's an argument against it.

Do you believe capital punishment to be cruel and unusual, bearing in mind the torture of the long waiting on death row that is mandatory given the length of time for due process?

I think it is always going to be cruel and unusual. But we do a lot of cruel and unusual things in a society. I think it was [Justice] Holmes who once said, "The very essence of a society is to decide who dies and who lives." We do cruel things; when we have wars, we do cruel things. I think if I were writing the Eighth Amendment, I would have talked about "cruel and *unnecessary*." I think it is cruelest when it is done without purpose or reason, and that is the way it is done today. It is really just the muscle flex to make it *seem* as if our justice system is working. But it is not working.

One instance where capital punishment worked wonderfully was during the last days of the Nazi occupation in Denmark. The Nazis asked everybody to comply with blackout laws, so that no lights were on and the Allied bombers couldn't bomb the city. Of course almost everyone was in favor of the Allies and so they were leaving the lights on. The punishment in those days was twenty years in prison, pretty strict punishment for violating blackout laws, and everyone was violating them, for obvious reasons—twenty years punishment meant thirty days punishment, because the Allies were soon going to liberate the country. The Nazis then imposed the death penalty for violating the blackout law and it worked 100 percent. Nobody violated the blackout laws because the choice then was not between death and life imprisonment. It meant instant death. You could see whose light was on and take them out and shoot them. There was no due process, nothing like that. No cruel and unusual delays or anything.

The death penalty can work . . . if you have an authoritarian regime that doesn't have to worry about due process.

So a death penalty could never work in a democratic country like the United States?

No, I don't believe so. I think you are right when you say that. If we were ever to make a death penalty work efficiently, it would be at the cost of justice.

THE FILMMAKER

"Every human being that believes in capital pun-
ishment loves killing."
—Clarence Darrow, in debate with
Judge Alfred J. Talley, 1924

*The American Film Institute in Washington's Kennedy Center is a
film fan's dream come true. A short elevator ride from foyer to the
third floor reveals what at first appears to be the entrance to a store-
room, but after a couple of turns the visitor finds himself or herself
surrounded by blow-ups of movie stills from landmark movies of the
American film industry. But this is no museum. This is an active, working environment. Film editors in white cotton gloves sit at work
benches feeding celluloid into the teeth of movieolas. Librarians scan
computer lists of thousands of film titles. We walked to the end of the
room that appears to terminate in a mirror but that in fact turns into
the executive offices, and there we were greeted by producer-film-
maker George Stevens, Jr., who produced the 1987 NBC mini series,
"The Murder of Mary Phagan."*

*The movie tells the story of the 1913 conviction of Atlanta business-
man Leo Frank of Ms. Phagan's murder, his condemnation, the commutation of his sentence, and his subsequent lynching. Frank received
a posthumous pardon in 1986 because of due process in his case.*

George Stevens, Jr.

What made you decide to produce "The Murder of Mary Phagan"?

It is really one of the extraordinary stories in American history. It is often compared to the Dreyfus Affair in France. What interests me about the possibilities of film and television is that sometimes you can find a fascinating story that is also able to open people's eyes and minds, without preaching; I really don't enjoy films that talk at me.

In fact, I was talking to someone yesterday who said how much they appreciated and how engaged they were by the film because they did not feel they were being pushed around by the filmmakers. I think it is awfully important when you are telling a story that involves issues to let the audience come to their own conclusions rather than, from the first moment, being aggressively assaulted by the author's point of view.

How did you happen to pick this particular project?

One of my collaborators was the director, Billy Hale, who was born in Rome, Georgia. This was a story he was familiar with since childhood. It is a story they talk about in Georgia and they sing about it, "The Ballad of Mary Phagan." We were talking about what would be an interesting project and we landed on this idea. We were interested in it because of the combination of the famous Leo Frank case and the lesser known aspect of the governor of Georgia, John M. Slaton, sacrificing his political career by taking himself out of politics as a result of it.

When did you start?

Actually we started on this . . . well, these things are always difficult to do . . . *(laughs)* in 1982. That was when we first proposed it to NBC and then worked on the script with Larry McMurtry for a two-hour film. But by the time we were ready with the script there was new management at NBC, and the new fellow said that the country was not interested in history, so they were going to do the John Lennon and Yoko Ono story instead.

He said ours was one of the best scripts they ever had but audiences weren't interested in history.

So the project was put aside and I moved on to making *A Film Makers Journey [a motion picture on director George Stevens, George Stevens, Jr.'s, father]*. Then two years later I got back to this. By that time there was yet another group of people at NBC and they were interested in doing the Mary Phagan story as a mini series, which was good, because this form provided more time for the story.

How did the ratings go? Was the public interested in history?

Yes. It was very well watched. It was the tenth-rated show of the week. It led its time period on each night. It was a big success from that standpoint. And thank heavens it was successful, because otherwise it would have been a long winter in hell before they would tackle another subject like that.

It seemed that the janitor was the obvious suspect from day one.

I think one angle on this story is that it had the black janitor, as a star witness and prime suspect, but then attention turned from him to Leo Frank. Lynchings of blacks were quite common in those days, and I believe that to simply convict a black person was not sufficient compensation for this tragedy that had so infuriated the good people of Atlanta. And I say the "good people" of Atlanta not with any ironic intent. These were hardworking people, living through tough times. Many had been forced to leave their farms and go to work in the new industrial cities—there were over a hundred young girls working in this factory for twelve cents an hour. It was, obviously, among other things, wounding to the pride of the men in the community that they had to send their daughters off to work twelve-hour days for that kind of money. So, when Leo Frank behaved strangely and gave some reason for people to think that he might have been involved in the crime and the press reported this, it became more and more a celebrated case. They called him "the silent man in the tower." People's attention turned to the outsider, the Northerner, the industrialist, the Jew.

That became, in the minds of many, a much more worthy sacrifice for the memory of Mary Phagan than a "mere" Negro janitor.

The governor was a very courageous man considering the political climate of the day.

Yes. Before the case was considered for clemency, the U.S. Supreme Court had upheld a federal District Court's decision to deny relief, thus giving the people of Georgia the entitlement to say that Frank had been convicted by a jury of his peers, and that the conviction has passed the Supreme Court's scrutiny. "Don't stand in the way of justice, let justice be done." So it took a very courageous person to go against the tide. The words in the film are the true words of Governor John Slaton. His own words are probably a little more flowery than we might have dared write for a character when he said, "I cannot abide the companionship of an accusing conscience."

There was a very dramatic part in the film where they crushed the umbrella in the elevator; did that really happen?

No. That was a dramatic license we took. There was a corresponding element in the case. There was something in the elevator shaft that had not been crushed by the elevator, and this evidence countered the testimony of the janitor, Jim Conley. It was known at the time as the "shit in the shaft" theory. Conley had relieved his bowels in the elevator shaft, and when the police took all the notes on the girl's death they had noted this and the fact that the feces were uncrushed, a vital clue. Mary Phagan had a yellow umbrella, so we made that dramatic adjustment.

We were told that that case actually brought into being both the Ku Klux Klan and the B'nai B'rith in Georgia.

In a way. The Anti-Defamation League of B'nai B'rith grew out of this case. The Ku Klux Klan preceded the Frank case by many years, but it had become dormant. The Frank case triggered a revival of the Klan.

What was the response of viewers?

It has interested me. I sometimes wonder how people can stay with something through all those commercials and still have their concentration, but many have said that it was an experience that stayed with them long after they had seen it. That there are images and aspects to it that remain with them is pleasing to me. That is why we make films.

One image in the film that stayed with us is of the people outside looking through the courtroom window. The lust for death.

Yes. One of the more compelling things about the Leo Frank case with respect to the death penalty is that although it was complicated because he was lynched, the commutation that Slaton gave Frank would provide time for evidence to emerge and a later opportunity for a full pardon. Frank's lawyers did not ask for a pardon at the time, only for a commutation. This brings us to the great problem with the death penalty. It removes the opportunity for new evidence to emerge and for opinion to be swayed. It stops the clock for later judicial or executive relief.

What do you feel the death penalty does to a society?

I oppose the death penalty. Our society has existed for two hundred years, most of which have been with the death penalty in force, and the appetite for vengeance is one of those aspects of human nature that is very persistent. People don't want to give it up easily. I think when there are difficult times that appetite is greater. Of equal or greater concern to me is our country's preoccupation with the right to bear arms. The unchecked license to carry guns is responsible for even more deaths than the death penalty.

SPANNER IN THE WORKS

"... To die; to sleep;
No more; and by a sleep to say we end
The heart-ache and the thousand natural shocks
That flesh is heir to, 'tis a consummation
Devoutly to be wished. To die, to sleep;
To sleep: perchance to dream;
Ay there's the rub
For in that sleep of death what dreams
    may come..."

—William Shakespeare, *Hamlet*

David Kendall is a forty-five-year-old Washington attorney who modestly proclaims himself "antediluvian" on the subject of death penalty work. However, during the crucial ten years from 1972 to 1982 he made a considerable impact on the scene when he was at the forefront of much of the major capital litigation in this country.

David, a Hoosier, was born of Quaker parents in 1944 and is married to a psychologist; he has three children aged thirteen, eleven, and seven. Now living in Washington, he practices as a media defense attorney, representing such diverse publications as The Washington Post *and the* National Enquirer. *He recently represented the movie* Missing *when it was sued by three American officials. He also teaches a course at Georgetown University.*

David Kendall

How did you get into death penalty work?

I had been active in civil rights work at college (Wabash College, Indiana). I'd spent two summers in Mississippi trying to register voters in 1964 and 1965 and managed to build up quite an impressive arrest record.

We were all getting arrested, right and left. That was during the period when the Voting Rights Act was being formulated and passed.

I then went to graduate school at Worcester College, Oxford University, and returned home two years later to go to law school. After I passed the bar I was full of expectations, and I had this notion that someone was going to offer me a job—a job which combined, in equal parts, being Ralph Nader, Edward Bennett Williams, Tony Amsterdam, and Clarence Darrow. Surprisingly enough, those jobs were not on the immediate horizon.

I clerked with Justice [Byron] White for a year at the Supreme Court. This was 1972, the same year that the Court decided *Furman v. Georgia*. After my stint of clerking and looking around at various job possibilities, I finally decided to work for the NAACP Legal Defense and Education Fund [LDF], which of course has a long history of civil rights litigation.

I had no particular desire to do *only* death penalty work, but I certainly wanted to get involved in it. However, it turned out that I worked almost exclusively on capital punishment cases.

The atmosphere must have been highly charged when it became clear that the states were determined that executions were to become, once again, a reality?

We were surprised at the explosion of work which resulted when the states returned so very quickly and enthusiastically to the death penalty.

It became a symbolic issue.

Even as the crime rate was falling, the public felt less secure and pushed to have death penalty statutes enacted.

I experienced a sort of hydraulic pressure and that pushed other kinds of civil rights cases off our docket. Representing people under sentence of death was a demanding, time-consuming job, and I spent more and more time trying to develop cases to test the statutes.

Tony Amsterdam was involved in every case, planning, advising, identifying issues, and trying to shape the way new statutes were interpreted by the state courts. We sought to represent the first defendants sentenced under those post-*Furman* laws. I therefore did a lot of "ambulance chasing" to get cases—except, in these cases, it was "hearse chasing." Usually it was pretty easy to obtain these row clients, because the state lawyers were paid peanuts, and usually when we offered to do a brief or a legal memo they were delighted to have free help. In fact, the process was such a success that once we got into the business, people began throwing cases at us.

While at the Legal Defense Fund you represented the first non-volunteer to be executed, John Spenkelink, in Florida. Would you tell us about that?

I had represented John on his first petition to the Supreme Court, back in 1975. The Court ultimately denied review. John's case was a relatively simple one factually and legally, but Florida set an early execution date for him after the Supreme Court's pro-death decisions of 1976. Another consideration for the state, in my view, was the fact that he was a white defendant and Florida had such a terrible, discriminatory history of executing blacks.

I was active in the efforts to try and avert that execution, first through both state and federal *Habeas Corpus*. We were able to secure a stay of execution in the summer of 1977 and litigated the case up through the Court of Appeals. It was about that time, in 1978, when our last effort at seeking Supreme Court review failed, that I left the LDF to go into private law practice.

I liked John, so when I left I said I'd be happy to take on his representation for the clemency hearings. In clemency, for all sorts of legal and practical reasons, you can really only represent one person, and the LDF was representing many other defendants on Florida's death row.

Even before the Supreme Court denied review in March 1979, I had begun putting together a clemency case for John by contacting witnesses, developing facts, and trying to collect evidence. In Florida the system is such that it takes the governor and three cabinet members to grant clemency. The governor of Florida in 1977 was Bob Graham, who is now a U.S. senator.

John was raised in Iowa. The name is Dutch, and Spenkelink is spelled many different ways in many court records; the officials didn't even bother to spell it right. John lived on a farm for a period, then went to California where he got into trouble. At the age of eighteen, in a single night when he was high on drugs, he robbed six or seven convenience stores. He was then sentenced to prison under California's indeterminate sentencing procedure and spent a few years in California prisons. He walked away from a medium-security prison in 1972. He had been at large for a while when he hooked up with another former prisoner, an older guy named Szymankiewicz, who had a worse record than John's. They traveled around together. Eventually there was a struggle over a pistol, and John shot the guy. John admitted the shooting: the state's theory was that John had shot him while he was asleep; John claimed self-defense.

Wasn't there evidence that Szymankiewicz had forced John to play Russian roulette, sodomized him, and stole his money?

Yes, all this came out at the trial. John's defense was based upon his fear of Szymankiewicz; the fight occurred when John tried to leave. There was a co-defendant named Frank Brumm, who was indicted for the murder along with John. His fingerprints were found on a glass in the motel room, but because John testified that the guy wasn't in the room at the time of the murder, he was acquitted. Brumm just walked out of the courtroom to freedom, while John, subsequently, was sentenced to die. It was a crap shoot, and John lost.

Wasn't Spenkelink offered a plea of second-degree murder?

This was another one of the great ironies of the case. John's fate, I'm convinced, resembled Eddie Slovik's execution in World War II for treason. The Florida prosecutor in John's case thought of it as a killing of one ex-con by another and felt it merited a prison sentence, but not—in his heart of hearts—the electric chair. So, they offered John a plea of second-degree murder, before the trial began, literally on the courthouse steps. John declined because he insisted that he wasn't guilty of premeditated murder, as the killing had happened during a struggle. So he elected to gamble, and he lost.

But why the death penalty?

Because he was an escaped prisoner, because of his record, because he came from out of state, because both he and the victim had strange foreign names.

Also you have to remember that when his death penalty was imposed, back in 1973, there had been a de facto moratorium on executions since June of 1967. I don't think anybody connected with the trial ever thought that he would, in fact, *actually* be executed. It was just another one of the ironies of the case. I am convinced that if the jurors, the prosecutors, and even the judge had believed that he would really be electrocuted because of their decisions, they'd have all made different decisions.

I was talking to John the very day, in 1977, that the de facto moratorium on executions was broken. I was representing him at his initial clemency hearing, and it was the same day that Gary Gilmore was shot, in January 1977. I remember vividly a guard listening to the radio quietly and then yelling over to another guard so that we could hear, "They just shot old Gilmore." Neither of us said anything—there was nothing to be said—and we just continued to try to prepare for his clemency hearing that afternoon.

Later, in 1979, John's mother and sister came out from California for the final clemency hearing. We got affidavits from the warden at Starke, from other officials in the prison, and from guards saying John was an exemplary prison inmate.

In my judgment this was an appropriate case for commutation of sentence. Commutation does not pin a medal on anybody. It just says you are the kind of first-degree murderer that we sentence to life imprisonment, which means in Florida serving a minimum of twenty-five years without the possibility of parole.

But Florida wanted to get the grisly machine going again, and because John's case became a symbol, its appropriateness for clemency was never fairly considered.

Why was Furman v. Georgia *chosen as a test case to put before the Supreme Court?*

The Eighth Amendment argument in *Furman* was the last card in the hand of the anti-death penalty lawyers in 1971, and it was not a card that anyone had much confidence in. The Supreme Court had just rejected what they all thought were stronger due process issues relating to the lack of requirements for the bifurcation of trials and death-sentencing standards. The Eighth Amendment's ban on cruel and unusual punishments was deemed to be a relatively weak argument for judicial abolition. There was simply not much case law there.

William Furman was a burglar whose pistol had gone off while he was fleeing; the bullet went through a screen and killed the home owner. His death sentence was almost totally capricious, a symbol of the arbitrariness of the death penalty. Justice White likened it to being struck by lightning. That was the basis of the Court's decision, the only ground on which the five Justices could agree, the only common denominator in the Court's ruling: that a system of death sentencing so totally irrational and capricious constituted cruel and unusual punishment for those who lost out in the "ghastly, brainless lottery."

Isn't the Supreme Court supposed to look at evolving standards of decency which may not necessarily reflect the will of the majority?

The Eighth Amendment does indeed mandate that the Court look to society's "evolving standards of decency." The Bill of Rights, for example, says that you are not to be put in jeopardy of "life or limb." Now that phrase, of course, comes from the 18th-century corporal punishment—chopping off digits, branding, and whipping. Now all those punishments have been repudiated and are long gone. "Limb" has no meaning anymore because of society's evolving standards of decency. The Supreme Court is not supposed to look at popular will; that's expressed through the legislature. Mere statutes can be repealed or enacted at the will of the majority. Rights put into the Constitution are placed beyond the reach of the legislature; they are there so that a transient majority *can't* take them away from even a single despised citizen.

In a 1977 case, *Coker v. Georgia,* the Supreme Court finally was persuaded that the death penalty for rape was excessive under the Eighth Amendment. In *Furman* and *Coker,* the Supreme Court agreed. It is that analysis that someday will cause the Supreme Court to do with the death penalty for murder what it did for the death penalty for rape. Just as our society has abandoned the pillory, the whip, and the branding iron, so will we, at some point, abandon the shooting, suffocation, poisoning, and electrocution of humans.

Were you in private practice when you mounted an attack on lethal injection?

Yes. We developed a case arguing that lethal injection is illegal—not unconstitutional, but illegal under the various federal regulatory statues. We argued that because the drugs had not been tested, nobody really knew what they were going to do, and that this was therefore in violation of the federal Food, Drug and Cosmetics Act.

Would you give us some background on this case?

Actually it goes back to a press conference that Ronald Reagan gave when he was governor of California, in about 1973. He was talking about proposed death penalty legislation in California. When Reagan was asked about the death penalty, he casually remarked, "I don't see why we can't do it like we do with animals on the ranch. Just give them a shot." Cartoonists at the time had a field day because it seemed so bizarre.

In the next two years some consideration was given to a more "humane" means of execution. In the mid-1970s a number of states enacted lethal injection procedures to replace electrocution or asphyxiation. The arguments were invariably couched in quasi-medical and "humanitarian" terms, but in my view it boiled down to an issue of aesthetics. It was just unaesthetic to execute people by frying and suf-

focating them. A lot of people who were squeamish about those forms
of execution wanted something more psychologically pleasant, a kind
of a medical termination. Lethal injection looked terrific—the very
name was therapeutic. Euphemism City!

Shortly after I came to Washington I was at a cocktail party—this is
the only useful thing that has ever happened to me at a Washington
cocktail party—and I was talking to a drug lawyer who did technical
work for pharmaceutical companies. He was complaining about the
Food and Drug Administration taking his animal euthanasia product,
which I believe was called something like "Doggy Doze," off the mar-
ket. I asked him what the problem was and he told me that it hadn't
been tested. All I knew about the Food, Drug and Cosmetics Act was
that drugs had to be "safe and effective" before they could be marketed. Of course there were a lot of regulations defining those two
terms, but I couldn't see how a euthanasia drug could be labeled "safe
and effective" by the FDA. It seemed to me that it either produced
death quickly or it didn't, but this morose and bibulous lawyer impa-
tiently told me that in fact you have to demonstrate to the FDA that the
drug was reliable and would produce a "quick and painless" death.
"Safe and effective" meant, in the euthanasia context, "quick and painless."

A light bulb went on in my mind. I began to do legal and factual
research. I found that the pharmaceutical companies whose drugs were
being used by the states to execute prisoners were very uneasy about it.
They wouldn't talk to us, but they also wouldn't do anything to help
the state's efforts, because they manufactured and marketed medicines
for doctors and they didn't want them stigmatized as execution drugs.

I was certain that there was no evidence which could be used to
demonstrate with the scientific rigor demanded by the FDA that these
drugs reliably produced "quick" and "painless" death. So another lawyer and I began developing legal arguments. We didn't want to choose
cases where the defendants were near execution, because we were
afraid that our arguments would be perceived as frivolous, so we selected inmates from Texas and Oklahoma who were in the early stages
of their appeals and who had only recently been sentenced to death by
lethal injection. We developed information on them and sent a lengthy
letter to the FDA requesting a hearing on whether these human execution drugs met the standards set by the Food, Drug and Cosmetics Act
for "Doggy Doze" and other animal euthanasia drugs. Our petition got
thrown out by the FDA, so we filed a lawsuit, on behalf of the inmates,
against the FDA. We purposely didn't involve the states, since it was
the FDA's responsibility to regulate drugs used by the states.

We lost in the trial court. The judge invoked the doctrine of prosecutorial discretion; that ordinarily a court cannot tell a federal agency who to investigate and who to prosecute. Our argument was that we simply wanted a *hearing* because the FDA had completely abrogated its jurisdiction.

We appealed and won by a 2–1 decision. The one judge against us was Judge [Antonin] Scalia, who eventually became a United States Supreme Court Justice. He wrote a lengthy and strident dissent. We didn't deny that the FDA had prosecutorial discretion, but we argued they couldn't simply ignore the statute. The Court of Appeals agreed with us, but the government sought and obtained review in the Supreme Court, and we lost there unanimously.

I had thought, as had the Court of Appeals, that our legal arguments were sound, and that if we could establish that the procedure was illegal, it would throw an enormous monkey wrench into the execution machinery. At the Legal Defense Fund I came to the belief that time is literally life; that the system didn't, in fact, care so much about *really* executing people. The whole system is totally capricious and arbitrary, and so if you could derail a state's execution procedures by a well-founded legal argument, you could get more life for your clients and hopefully allow a body of evidence to build up, on which someday the Supreme Court would declare the death penalty unconstitutional. I believe that will happen. It is only a question of when and how many people are arbitrarily executed before that time.

Do you believe the legislators are plain cynical and use the death penalty as a political tool?

They are both cynical and gutless; being for the death penalty is a very popular political position. You cannot be against the death penalty without being aware that you differ from two thirds to three quarters of your constituents. Now, that's not to say that two thirds to three quarters of your constituents are *really* for the death penalty, but they will tell pollsters that they are. When you reach them at a deeper level, in some kind of detailed poll, you don't get so much popular acceptance. But the politicians who have come out against the death penalty, in my view, ought to get a medal for political heroism. Such a leadership stand takes extraordinary political courage, because it will certainly lose votes and hand an advantage to one's opponent.

However, everyone connected with the Corrections system knows that the death penalty doesn't work. Law enforcement people know that the death penalty doesn't work and that it is counterproductive; that it's cost-inefficient and is lousing up the whole system.

How does having the death penalty affect the society?

I think it brutalizes a society in ways we don't fully appreciate. It expands the frontier of what we can do to people. It makes us accept things, particularly in the prison system, that I think we would not otherwise accept. After all, if the state can kill its citizens, it can do anything to them.

I think, ironically, it influences our attitudes toward the victims of crime because it trivializes the consequences of crime, by in some way suggesting these survivors are getting retribution. They're not. But it allows our legislators to create the false impression that, through the death penalty, they are doing something to help these families.

I think that the death penalty is in fact an atavism. If you suggested that the federal criminal code should be amended to include whipping, lopping off of ears, slitting of nostrils, people would look at you as if you were from another planet. Those punishments were quite common two hundred years ago. The death penalty is really the last one of that group. It has a significance that is, in large part, symbolic, so it hangs on.

Somehow, people believe, in an almost religious sense, that they are safer because of the death penalty. Yet all the empirical evidence is that they are not. There are many better ways to spend the enormous sums we now commit to executing people. There are things that can be done to make people marginally more protected against crime, but we don't do them because we waste our money on executions.

I think that the position of feminist groups to the rape issue back in 1976–1977 is instructive. In the *Coker* case, we got an amicus brief from a number of women's rights organizations. These groups were certainly not soft on or sympathetic to rapists. They well knew that the death penalty for rape was a joke when it came to protecting the victims. They went in on our side with a hard-hitting brief that said, "Look, let's not kid ourselves, we do speak for the victims, we speak for aggressive and effective prosecution, and the death penalty has nothing to do with that. It's an archaism." The Court didn't focus directly on those arguments, but my own belief is that it was moved by them.

ISLAND OF THE DAMNED

"DON'T MESS WITH TEXAS"

—Bumper Sticker

Steve and Lisa Haberman are two young high school teachers, aged thirty-three and twenty-nine respectively, who decided to take a couple of years out to do some full-time volunteer work. They joined the Mennonite Volunteer Program, to become coordinators for the Dallas Coalition to Abolish the Death Penalty. In doing so they moved from the sanity of Milwaukee, Wisconsin, a non-executing jurisdiction, to the lone star state of Texas, which continues its legacy of killing wrongdoers.

The Habermans came to Texas to try to halt, or at least slow down, the death machine that executes more people than any other democratic jurisdiction in the world.

Everything is big in Texas.

It is the largest state in the continental Union, at 267,369 square miles. Its plains, mountains, and rivers occupy two time zones, stretching almost 900 miles from its northwest tip, at the border of Oklahoma, to the southeast edge of the Gulf of Mexico. A landmass twenty-two times larger than Rhode Island and four and a half times the size of England, it has had the greatest number of executions in the United States since the Furman decision in 1972. In 1988, it executed its twenty-seventh prisoner, one for each U.S. congressman representing Texas. More have been executed since.

Steve and Lisa moved from Dallas to Houston, where in 1988 we found them heading the Justice and Mercy Project. They moved, they told us, because "Houston is much closer to the prison at [Huntsville] where the men on death row wait and is also much more central to the whole issue of crime and the prison system in Texas."

Steve and Lisa Haberman

Why did you pick on Texas to do death penalty work?

It was partly because nobody else was doing it. The Dallas Coalition Against the Death Penalty had been looking for a director for almost two years before we took the position, and some of its members were the only abolitionists in the state at that time. This state needed work, and lots of it.

We moved to Dallas and became full-time volunteer directors for the Dallas Coalition. We stayed there for a little over a year, and then decided that if we were really going to get involved in this work, we should be in Houston. Most of the people who are on death row in Texas come out of Houston.

We always felt strongly about the death penalty from our moral ideals, but when we got here we saw it from other perspectives—crime, deterrence, cost, justice—everything. From every perspective the death penalty is wrong. There is not one thing the death penalty serves except, possibly, the Texas legacy of "do or die."

The violence that is so ingrained in the culture here is aggravated by the economic crisis that has hit the state so very hard. There is also the cry of desperation and vengeance that is so much a part of Texas.

Was much work being done by abolitionists when you arrived?

Texas was considered the "Island of the Damned" by abolitionists in the United States; ideologically a lost cause. Even the National Coalition to Abolish the Death Penalty didn't know what to do. Nobody would touch it.

It is incredibly enormous, sixth in population, and in sheer physical size. So, it's really hard to deal with.

There is also the legacy that has allowed Texas to not only become the number-one executioner among the states, but also to have one of the biggest death rows in the country. This, coupled with the over-whelming crime and legal crisis, demoralizes a lot of people.

We understand that Texas has the highest rate of killings by police in the country?

That's true. Also the most handgun accidents.

Why is that?

Dallas and Houston, the two main metropolitan areas, exploded during the boomtown oil years. As a result, a lot of money and a lot of people came here very quickly. When it started to thin out, it created a real economic crisis, and the various subcultures had a hard time mixing.

It created a real tension and a fever zone which has affected the whole state. Quick answers just weren't there and the death penalty is a good example of trying to have a quick fix to clear the air of violent crime. These, and other things like handgun accidents and police brutality, just added gasoline to the fire. In times of economic hardship, attitudes usually become more hardened.

The death penalty machinery here has been oiled pretty slick since 1982.

You mentioned a legal crisis, can you elaborate on that?

Texas has the largest death row in the country, but until recently it was one of the few executing states that didn't have any procedure set up to guarantee legal representation for people on death row.

Florida has a state-funded program. Louisiana has a privately funded program; but Texas didn't have anything. We had a death row that had, basically, a couple of hundred unrepresented people—inmates who didn't have the money to hire an attorney. There weren't enough volunteer attorneys to go around. However, thankfully, that problem is finally being addressed.

About a year ago, the Capital Punishment Clinic was established in Austin. They have made a tremendous difference. They are supported by a number of different groups. Amnesty International in West Germany has been part of the support to the clinic, which now has three full-time lawyers, Robert McGlasson, Scott Howe, and Eden Harrington.

There have been a number of cases in Texas where not only innocent people ended up on death row, but also where people were not afforded anything close to decent representation during their trials or during their appeals.

Texas has a rather unique death penalty statute. Can you tell us about it?

The Texas statue is different from any other state statute in that it doesn't allow the jury in deciding whether or not to impose a death sentence to consider mitigating or aggravating evidence about the person convicted of capital murder. Rather, it asks two questions: "Was the crime deliberately done?"—which is a moot question considering the man has been found guilty of intentional first-degree murder already—and: "Is there a probability that the defendant will commit a criminal act of violence in the future that will constitute a threat to society?" Now, anybody who has committed one capital crime is someone who would be suspected of having the probability of acting out a threat, even in prison, in the future.

Texas's infamous "future dangerousness." How is it determined?

Testimony is given by a psychiatrist and other expert witnesses. There is one psychiatrist in particular, Dr. James Grigson, otherwise known as "Dr. Death," *[see William Geimer interview]* who is in private practice but is hired by the state in capital trials. Basically, he is a hired gun for the prosecution.

He has no problem in labeling a man a "sociopath," which is not a disease; it is not curable; it is not a sickness, it has no culpable mitigation. This he does after a forty-five-minute interview with the accused. Basically he tells the jury, "This man is evil."

The American Psychiatric Association has said that this kind of diagnosis is completely invalid in any kind of scientific or medical sense. Predicting "future dangerousness" is something that even the most competent psychiatrist would not attempt. However, it seems Dr. Grigson has no problem going around, in a very homesy way, convincing juries that the convicted man is an anti-social person who deserves no pity, cannot be treated, is more dangerous than Hitler, Jack the Ripper, and Charlie Manson combined and the only thing to do with him is put him to death.

Grigson has made a living for himself across the state doing this, so much so that in some cases the defense will buy his services, just to keep him from being hired by the prosecution. He is a hired gun that sometimes is hired *not* to fire.

There's another weird law, the law of parties. Could you explain this to us?

There is a "law of parties" in Texas that says when two people are involved in a crime, they are both equally responsible. Doyle Skillern [executed 1/16/1985] is a tragic example. He was sitting outside in his car when the murder took place. During litigation, the actual killer plea-bargained with the prosecutors. Doyle was executed and the actual killer was given a prison term.

Because Skillern had a past record, he was considered more easily condemnable under the Texas statute given its question about "future dangerousness." What we just described, in other words, made it easier for the jury to sentence Skillern as a lost cause or as a threat, regardless of his minor role in the crime. For that reason he was the one who got the death penalty.

It was a deadly combination of the law of parties and future dangerousness.

Are you saying that what is happening in Texas is not constitutional?
The Texas statute will be challenged again and again because it certainly is unconstitutional.

The U.S. Supreme Court, at this time, is very cowardly. It does not want to look at states' rights more closely and they certainly consider the death penalty to be one of the states' sovereign rights.

They don't want to get involved.

There was a decision recently in the *Franklin* case [*Franklin v. Lynaugh,* 1988] that said that while the Supreme Court won't pretend that there are no problems in the Texas statute as far as the constitution is concerned, they don't want to be involved in making any blatant decision about it.

The U.S. Supreme Court had upheld the Texas statute in 1976 *[Jurek v. Texas].* So for them to change their minds now would take a lot of courage.

Using the *Jurek* ruling, Texas has already killed twenty-seven men since 1982, and every month between four to five more are scheduled for execution. It would be tough for the Supreme Court to now admit that these men were executed under an unconstitutional statute.

We always thought of Texas as being the cradle of American macho and manhood. Isn't lethal injection a bit "limp wristed" for such a frontier state?

Texans like to think of themselves as progressive, and lethal injection gives the appearance of not being brutal.

They are always very nice to the condemned man at the end. He is given a last meal of his choice and is spoken to in soft tones. Prison officials go out of their way on the last evening of the person's life to show how "civilized" they are. But, no matter how clinical you make it, killing someone in cold blood is still premeditated murder: it is wasteful and foolish. It is callous and we don't want to look callous, so we try to make it look nicer, medical almost, with all the tubes, needles, and drugs.

This humane approach isn't for the benefit of the guy strapped down on the gurney, whom we have already characterized as an animal, a person not even deserving to live in the zoo of a penitentiary we have in Texas.

Execution by lethal injection is for the witnesses and for society. It is something carried out so often that we can't afford it to be gruesome.

We have to try to veil the inhumanity of it in some way and what better way than the nice "doctor curing the patient" approach?

Can you tell us about the Streetman case?

Robert Streetman was executed on January 7, 1988. His situation was very bizarre. There were many unanswered questions in his case, even as to his actual involvement in the crime, and many questions about his mental stability.

Nearing his execution date he wanted to give up all his appeals—he'd had enough. He could have had a retrial, but his own actions in the courtroom blew it. Basically, he told the court he didn't want any help, he didn't want any appeals, he didn't want any more hearings.

One district judge took him seriously and said, "Okay, we won't." Then Streetman's sister helped persuade him to fight for his life. Robert McGlasson, one of the clinic's attorneys, came in at that time, just days before the execution.

The U.S. Supreme Court had voted to hear the Streetman case, but on the day of the scheduled execution, the Court had only eight members and reached a tie vote on whether or not to stay the execution. They had enough votes to hear the case, but not enough votes to stop the execution.

Robert Streetman was due to be executed at midnight. He was put on the [execution] gurney and a couple of hours later he was taken off it. Then, at 3:30 a.m. he was put back on the gurney because the Attorney General of Texas decided not to recognize that there was pending litigation.

They let the execution go through.

Ten minutes before the execution started, McGlasson made a phone call to the governor's office and to the Attorney General. He was put on hold for ten minutes, and by the time the phone was picked up again the execution had already started. There was nothing they could do about it.

We also heard from a very reliable source that Governor [William P.] Clements himself called the death house at about the time the execution had started. He was told that the needle had already been inserted. Later he said the only reason he called was to see what was going on, but it is highly unlikely that a governor, with that kind of power, is going to ring the death house minutes before an execution for a chat—it's like the call to the death house in the movies when the guy is in the electric chair. My feeling is that perhaps Clements, in that moment, realized how completely insane and unjust the situation was. Maybe, just maybe, he was considering stopping it until he heard the executioners had already inserted the final needle.

Some people are calling it death by default. Other people have really criticized the Attorney General for not making sure that all litigation was completed before we put a man to death. The Supreme Court said they voted to hear the case but didn't have enough votes to stop the execution.

It was a tie and Robert Streetman lost.

It was a horrific scene. We put a man through three hours on a cross before we killed him. Crucifixion on a gurney.

Is racism a factor in prosecutions in Texas?

Are you familiar with the case of Clarence Brandley? Here is a classic example of the good ol' boy network at work, especially the racist good ol' boy network.

Clarence Brandley *[see Tanya Coke interview]* was a black janitor working at a school, in a small town in Texas, where a white girl was found murdered. There were also four other white janitors working with Brandley that same day.

Clarence was arrested, tried, and sentenced to death for the crime. At the time, there were a lot of questionable things going on. Evidence was lost that would have shown him to be innocent. That was eight years ago. Last fall he finally got an evidentiary hearing to prove his innocence, and at that time many people came forward, including witnesses who had testified against him at his original trial, saying that they had been pressured into lying by the local police, Texas Rangers, and the sheriff's department, telling how they had basically been given a story to tell on the stand.

According to testimony, there was collusion between the prosecutor and the judge, they were having meetings each morning before the trial. The judge's secretary testified that the judge who set an execution date for Brandley had set it to coincide with her birthday, saying, "Now we can celebrate both of these things together."

Even at the time of the crime, the story went around that a police officer came into a room where there were three of the four janitors and said, "Well, one of you is going to hang for this. Since you're the nigger," pointing to Brandley, "you're elected."

The two men who probably did the murder not only have not been prosecuted, but it appears that the judge and the law enforcement people of Montgomery County have gone to great lengths to destroy evidence that would have shown their guilt. There have been allegations they even supplied them with the alibis that got them off the firing line.

The collusion between the whole network of the powerful white racists in Conroe just railroaded Clarence Brandley into not only being tried twice, but also into coming within a couple of days of being executed.

Clarence is still on death row, even though the evidentiary hearing really blew the entire case wide open. National media are all aware of it. He will remain on death row until the Texas Court of Criminal Appeals makes their final ruling on whether or not he should be granted a new trial.

Somewhere down the line he will have to be released.

We heard that the Texas Attorney General was bemoaning the fact that no one seems to be aware of executions in Texas anymore. But wasn't there a time when cheerleaders would be at the gates?

In the early eighties executions used to draw big crowds, both protesting and encouraging. But now, after twenty-seven executions, it's become commonplace. Not even the media bothers to turn up in big numbers anymore. Usually, nobody is there. We go, not so much to get coverage, but simply because we don't want someone to die without anyone being there. One time the press reported that no protesters were there, so we made a commitment that we wouldn't let an execution happen without someone being there to say, "No!"

Recently, Utah had their third execution: their first was Gary Gilmore's in 1977. This one drew a lot of protesters. In Texas, it is the antithesis of that. The more you execute, the more people get used to it.

How do you feel executions by the state affect the society in general?

Not only is it morally wrong and offensive to human rights but it is also suicidal to society. It is killing *us* every time we inject a condemned man. It is poisoning *us*. It is not only making us more violent but also more callous. It is almost as if we are trying to cover up the terrible cancer that we have. The death penalty is certainly one of the major tumors of the cancer that has riddled our society.

"To hell with the prisoners"—if that's what you want to say—but for our *own* sake, for our *own* dignity and the dignity of *our* laws; for practical as well as idealistic moral reasons, we cannot afford to use the death penalty if we are serious about enlightening our society or making it safe, or making our laws work.

That's something that is very difficult for some people to hear, because when you are in the business of killing, you don't want to hear criticisms. The people we know who are most closed to criticisms are the ones who are most involved with the condemnation of their fellow human beings. I am speaking now of prosecutors in capital cases, whose job it is not only to get the guy off the streets and punish him in the most severe way, but also to convince a jury that this man doesn't deserve to live. Those are the people who really rankle when anyone raises questions about the death penalty or about what value there is in putting a man to death. These are the politically ambitious men who, if they get a death sentence, see it as a step toward getting into the legislature or some senior office.

The death penalty, for them, is a stepping stone to a bigger and brighter career.

THROUGH THE LOOKING GLASS

"The calculated killing of a human being by the
state involves, by its very nature, an absolute denial
of the executed person's humanity. The most vile
murder does not, in my view, release the state from
constitutional restraints on the destruction of
human dignity."

—Justice William Brennan, 1986

*Franklin E. Zimring is Professor of Law and director of the Earl
Warren Legal Institute, Boalt Hall, Berkeley.*

*In his early forties, Professor Zimring is one of the most brilliant
academics writing and teaching in the field of crime and punishment.
He was born and raised in Southern California, attended the University of Chicago where he graduated with a law degree in 1967, and
ever since has been doing empirical, legal research. Most of this research has been on criminal behavior and the responsiveness to the
criminal justice system. He spent eighteen years in Chicago, where he
was director of the Center for Studies of Criminal Justice at the University of Chicago, and a professor at that law school.*

*Other work includes research on deterrence, firearms, juvenile jus-
tice and crime, the criminal justice system, major empirical research
of violent attacks in Chicago relating to homicide and non-lethal assault, and more recently on the death penalty.*

He is the author of several books, the most recent being Capital

PROFESSOR FRANKLIN E. ZIMRING

Punishment and the American Agenda *(1986) written with Gordon Hawkins, former director of the Institute of Criminology at Sydney University, Australia. The book takes an optimistic view of the future of death penalty legislation in the United States and is a masterpiece.*

In 1985 Franklin Zimring moved to Berkeley to take up his current post.

Berkeley, California
Friday, September 25, 1987, 9:30 a.m.

Professor Franklin E. Zimring

Why is the United States out of step with other Western democracies in the area of capital punishment?

If you take the long-term view, I think that the answer is that the United States is not out of step. What you're looking at now is really quite consistent with what is going on in the rest of the Western world: a country in the process of abolishing the death penalty. From 1967 through 1977, there were no executions in the United States and all objective measures looked like America was right on the verge of accomplishing what western Europe had done in the seventies and eighties.

However, there have been over a hundred executions in the United States since 1977, and California, the state in which you teach, is gearing up.

I see this as kind of a last gasp of execution policy, concentrated in the Southern states. It is not inconsistent with long-range trends toward abolition, but does reflect two or three peculiarly American traits. One of them is a devotion to states' rights.

When the Supreme Court strongly hinted in *Furman v. Georgia* in 1972 that as a matter of federal constitutional law the death penalty was out, the most violent reaction wasn't on the part of crime victims but was in the tradition of states' rights. This same tradition gave us the Civil War. People said those folks, those pointy-headed liberals in Washington, can't tell us what to do in Alabama, or more to the point in Georgia, Louisiana, Texas, and Florida. So, strong public reaction to the possibility of the death penalty being taken away was added to a long tradition of states' rights and resentment of federal authority, and what you're looking at is a kind of rebellion.

But I think it's a rebellion against the forces of history. I think it's very difficult to imagine a United States of America fifty years down the line in which execution is part of an otherwise modern and liberal and humane society. While it's difficult to figure this out, given the present set of political circumstances, I think there's a certain amount of historical necessity for abolition in the pretty near future.

What would it mean then if non-Southern states with large death row populations such as California or Illinois were to start executing again?

If the bellwether states start executing in earnest—that is to say, if there's a real transition so that events call the bluff of the almost thirty states which have capital punishment laws and death row populations but no executions—what will happen will never have happened in this country before. It will be unprecedented.

There is nobody who has a plan about how this would or should happen, so it will come as a surprise to everyone. We have been averaging about twenty-five executions a year in the last two or three years in the United States. The death row population now exceeds two thousand, and if you were talking about only the execution of one in ten [200 executions], you are talking about more executions in the United States each year than the peak number of 199 in 1935; more than in any *other* year in this century.

If this should happen, do you believe it would change public opinion?

I think that one would get a very substantial change in public opinion; it would become more deeply divided. I think that right now, for most of the country, the issue of capital punishment is one of an abstraction. Should we have a law? Should there be a possibility for execution?

But most of the population is still pro-death penalty.

The majority of the population was always for locking up criminals, and the average American, who says he's for the death penalty, means he likes to have the possibility there, in the same sense he likes to have missiles in silos aimed at the Russians. . . . that doesn't mean he wants to push the button now.

Many states have adopted lethal injection as the official form of execution. You devote one of the chapters in your book Capital Punishment and the American Agenda *to this. Can you tell us about it?*

What we argue in the chapter is that the whole question of lethal injection simply exposes the contradictions in American character when approaching the question of executions. As recently as twelve years ago there wasn't a state in the United States that was even discussing lethal injection.

There is a wonderful Ronald Reagan quote, when he was governor of California, in which he says as a former horse raiser, he knew what it is like to try to eliminate an injured animal by shooting him. "What you do is call the veterinarian, who gives him a shot and the horse goes to sleep. . . . so why don't we do that with prisoners, adopt a more humane method?" Now, one of the problems with this is that Reagan neglects to make one distinction between animal euthanasia and a human execution. He forgot that the horse doesn't know the shot is coming! But he neatly summed up the genesis of the enthusiasm for lethal injection. "Wouldn't it be a wonderful idea . . . now maybe those pointy-headed liberals won't object to execution."

Why anyone would have such a fantasy is a question I want to put aside for a minute, because let's see what happens to the idea. It takes off like wildfire between 1977 and 1979. It is now the most authorized form of execution in the United States. You get the first execution— you actually have to execute somebody. Very soon, thereafter, you get all of the enthusiasm for lethal injection as a cure-all disappearing. Nobody is sending medical observers from other states to the first lethal injections. Nobody is talking about how nice lethal injection is after the first execution. When you talk about whether lethal injection could have solved the problem, you have to ask "what was the problem?" Suppose you say to someone who wishes to move a factory to Dallas, "It's a very modern place, we've got opera and symphony and lasers and hi-tech and an electric chair . . . or gas chambers. . . . or gallows!" They didn't want execution to look like a throw-back. What they wanted was hi-tech, something consistent with progress. They had to find a way that appeared to be modern. Well, lethal injection sounded good as an abstraction. The law says you should use "an ultra-fast-acting barbiturate"—that sounds like a commercial for a pain pill! The idea was that it should look modern. Then you see one of these executions. They wheel somebody in strapped to a gurney and it doesn't look modern at all—and the bubble's burst. I don't expect that that will come back. Once that fantasy is penetrated, it's gone for good. I do expect somebody to come out with the idea that they ought to try lasers. Something that makes it look like it's compatible with being progressive and modern and scientific. Which of course it isn't.

Where does that place members of the medical profession?

Well, the medical profession is between a rock and a hard place. They said this is a terrible idea and you can't use doctors to do it. But the terrible idea, as far as they were concerned, was using medical parlance and medical personnel, not capital punishment. So that while the doctors were upset, they tended to get upset about an issue that was almost superficial, rather than take a fundamental moral stand that you would think would come from their own rhetoric.

Wasn't lethal injection suggested as a form of execution as far back as the invention of the electric chair and rejected as inhumane then?

Just about the time they came up with the electric chair they came up with the idea of lethal injection with poison, but dismissed it because they thought the electric chair was more humane.

Now this, given our experience with the electric chair, tells you something about how good we are about acknowledging levels of humanity in the execution process. When you talk about more or less humane, nothing is much more humane than anything else. When you schedule an execution and tell a feeling human being, with capacities for cognition, that you will put him or her to death at 7:00 a.m. next Tuesday—what could be more inhumane than that?

Mutilation would never get past the American public. They would be outraged and horrified, but somehow execution is acceptable.

The notion that murderers "be dead" is fine. The means of execution—that's a point of detail on which the American population is divided. If you can do it in a progressive and sanitary way—and that was the appeal of lethal injection as a theory—then maybe that would be a *nice* way. The instant it was adopted, the instant it was used, everybody knew it wasn't a nice way at all. It's absolutely astonishing that states that hadn't used the procedure, but who'd passed laws calling for it, didn't send observers to see how it worked. They didn't want to find out what they already knew. But lethal injection was not merely a fraud, it was a fantasy.

What do you feel about the "holding" situation on death row, the warehousing of human beings for years and years?

It is not the case that death by natural causes is the leading cause of death on death row, but it comes in second. You ask what sort of designed legal policy would produce the two thousand or so people who are backed up on death row? It is a surprise . . . to everybody. The people who wanted capital punishment certainly weren't wanting this. So there is no serious planning that has been done. The people who are on death row would rather be there than be executed, they are not going to file a writ of mandamus demanding their own execution. The people who are managing these huge populations see absolutely no way out. Nobody who's read the statistics has a plausible solution to this problem other than to call the practice of execution to a stop.

Let me give you an example from Florida, the second leading executor in the United States since 1979. The Florida Department of Corrections issued a report that, at current rates of executions, they expected a death row of eight hundred in that one state alone by the year 2000!

They'd certainly have to build new facilities.

Well, all prison officials love to build. I even remember one time being told of plans for a new prison geriatric center in Ohio!

But here is a state authority saying with a straight face that we're going to have eight hundred people ready for execution by the year 2000. And you can't turn around and say, "Well, if they'd only get serious about executions". . . . They *are* serious about executions!

So it's another one of those wonderful instances where not only haven't we planned for these circumstances—nobody thought about it—and we *continue* not to plan for them. No one that I know of in American government, and this again is federalism, has just sat down to think about five years from now. How many will you have to execute if you want to keep a steady state, nationwide, of just the nineteen hundred on death row? Nobody seems to be doing that sort of analysis. This is left to the individual states. There is no national policy analysis going on.

What would you say to those who question Amnesty's anti-death penalty stand, particularly when three quarters of the American population voice support for capital punishment?

This stand must be made because execution is so accurate a symptom of the larger problem of human rights. After all, more people are going to be killed on Rhode Island highways than are going to be killed by execution in the United States. Why is it such a big issue? I think the reason is that it is expressive of the same fundamental problem, a problem of the abrogation of absolute power to political ends by the state. The problem of the non-recognition of the value of individual human existence. We have come to recognize how much of the seamless web this aspect of the state powers is in many different contexts.

Could you summarize your views for us?

The historical argument that we try to make in our book is that what's going on in the United States now is a "blip." Historians of future times will not much notice that early in the next century executions will have ceased in the United States, just as they will forget that France stopped ten years later than Britain. It will be an accomplished fact in the Western world very soon. A non-controversial policy. And we will join it.

Interestingly enough, at the level of national government in the United States we do have de facto abolition of the death penalty. There hasn't been a [federal] execution since 1963, and you have, in Ronald Reagan, the most conservative President we are ever likely to have in this country. . . . a big fan of capital punishment. I think the best thing that can be said about late-20th-century execution is that it is a temporary condition.

We don't advocate the abolition of capital punishment so that America can become a better place. It already is a better place. The way in which we educate our schoolchildren, and feed the poor, and the way in which there is concern for human welfare are the fundamental traditions of democracy. These are all elements of a social and political order which are inconsistent with capital punishment. So abolition can be seen as a process of American society catching up with itself.

Now American culture lives with its inconsistencies for a longer period of time than other societies. . . . but not indefinitely. And I think that it is not simply rose-colored glasses but some sense of the historical linkages between capital punishment and very basic social judgments about the worth of an individual that leads me to be an optimist. I must say that since our book has come out, many people have come to regard Hawkins and myself as kind of the Shirley MacLaines of criminology. Yet I think in fifteen or twenty years the death penalty will go. I guess one reason this view is not widely shared is that Americans are also usually allergic to taking the long view. Yet if you take that long view, and obviously it already takes into account the activities of groups such as Amnesty, then history is really on the side of decency on this issue. That is not uniformly the case in terms of history, but in respect to this penalty, and certainly in the industrial West, I think the strong forces of developing history are also on the right side.

KEEPER OF THE FLAME

"We have it somehow in our nature, to perform horrendous acts which we would never dream of as individuals, and think if they are done in the name of some larger group, a state, a company or a team, that these vile acts are somehow magically transformed and become praiseworthy."

—Leo Nikolayevich Tolstoy

Our mentor and friend, a former priest, now executive director of Amnesty International U.S.A., John Gabriel Healey (known to all as Jack), doesn't look like the director of a 290,000-member organization with an $15 million budget. Healey, with his round Irish face, receding hair, and frameless glasses perched precariously on his nose, also seems an unlikely candidate to organize and direct the largest international rock 'n roll extravaganza in history, the 1988 "Human Rights Now" world tour.

In a triumph of hard-rock packaging he managed to place superstars Bruce Springsteen, Sting, Peter Gabriel, Tracy Chapman, and others before audiences who otherwise could never have dreamed of experiencing such talents in live concert.

After only a few minutes in his company, Healey's offbeat humor, infectious enthusiasm, and strength of purpose are contagious. He may have left the priesthood but there's a lot of priest left in Jack.

Healey was born fifty-one years ago, the youngest of eleven children, into an Irish Catholic family in Pittsburgh, Pennsylvania. At the age of thirteen he entered seminary school in a small town north of

Pittsburgh, switched to the monastery at age twenty, and was ordained at age twenty-six. He left the priesthood at age thirty.

Why? "I was bored," he says. "Absolutely bored."

Influenced by the Priest Worker movement in France, his first job out of the seminary was as director of the "Walks for Development," where he raised about $10–$12 million for development projects both in the United States and developing countries. From there he helped build a hospital in Mexico, then worked for the Center for Community Change.

"Bored" with Washington, Healey then looked for an overseas assignment. A directorship in the Peace Corps, in Lasutu, southern Africa, fitted the bill. The day he landed at the Jan Smuts Airport in South Africa was the day Steve Biko was buried.

Five years later he returned to the States, appalled at the way so many Western relief organizations worked. "Looking at these guys with their $90,000 tax-free salaries riding around in Mercedes, I figured this was not the way to work with the Third World. It's hard to understand problems from a Mercedes. It's a little too high off the ground."

Now as Amnesty's United States director he brings his enthusiasm, exuberance, and candor to bear on exposing the worst horrors that human beings impose on one another.

Los Angeles, California
Monday, December 12, 1988, 5:30 p.m.

John G. Healey

What does Amnesty International stand for?

I think its goals are to represent all the people of the world, equally well, on three key issues:

No one should be picked up without being given a fair and speedy trial.

No one should be thrown in jail because of their race, color, or creed.

No one should be killed or tortured for *any* reason.

I think it is a very radical message, because United States foreign and domestic policy does not contain a straightforward single principle on human rights.

For example, if you have a series of human rights problems in the Soviet Union, Poland, and Romania on one side, and you have a series of problems in the Philippines, Israel, and South Korea on the other, the volume of letters, interest, yelling and screaming about the Eastern bloc from Congress would be profound. There would be an awful lot less about the friends of the United States. Incredibly different.

What Amnesty argues is that there is no *lesser* person in this world. United States foreign policy has determined that there *are* lesser persons. As long as you can make someone *less,* you can kill them, torture them, wipe them out, call them a name.

Amnesty International is against capital punishment, but some of your own members are for it. Why are you bringing this controversial issue out at this particular time when you risk losing membership?

There are those who are apprehensive because they feel that it detracts from our overall work, but they are a small minority. It's a matter of education; once people are given the facts, they tend to see that our position is not a contradiction—indeed, that it is crystal clear that our demands for abolition are right.

I don't think the death penalty is a controversial issue. I think among civilized people it is not controversial. Among the uncivilized, the uncouth, it is a controversial issue. I think that among the people who really think about life, death, justice, and equality, it is not controversial at all.

In the West in general, it is not controversial. The United States is out of sync. The United States is there along with Turkey . . . and even Turkey hasn't actually executed anyone in nearly five years. South Africa and the United States are the only "Western" nations that continue to kill their own people. South Africa is not exactly the kind of company we want to keep with respect to human rights.

We have a leftover cowboy philosophy in this country with regard to the death penalty. The American people are for it, but they are misinformed or uninformed. For example, most American people don't know that we regularly kill retarded people. We kill our children, which very few countries in the world do. It's an embarrassment.

Everyone in the human rights movement has to make a stand against the death penalty because if you don't understand the pernicious nature of state-sanctioned death, you don't understand the basic fight for human rights—the need to drive governments out of the business of destroying citizens and push them back into the business of protecting them. That is basically what we are all about. We aren't just about giving fair trials and stopping torture and then hiding this other part of the mandate. That part has always been there. And rightfully, because if you can't protect the people against their governments by keeping those governments out of the killing business, the rest of it is undoable. It is only when they stop that you have a chance of providing some equality.

The basic obligation of governments is to protect people, not to destroy them. Governments whose business is to kill are violating the basic reasons of why they are there.

If a state can kill its citizens, it can do anything else to its citizens. And we know, from Amnesty's records, what they do. So what you must do to protect the fabric of society is keep governments out of the business of killing their citizens.

The majority of the American public would say that statement is true in Third-World countries, that the argument is valid for mad mullahs and banana republics, but that this is America, and America is different because of due process guarantees. Aren't you just running a red flag up the pole and being an alarmist?

Not if you are serious about a justice system; seriously dedicated to equality and human rights. There is no equality in the death penalty.

If you said to an American that this is what is happening in this country and that's what the Pinochets and Khomeinis and others do around the world, they would say, "Oh, no, no! We are not in that company. No! No! No! We are the West. We are freedom lovers. We are Democrats. We are Republicans. That's not us!" But it is exactly what we do here and nobody wants to own up.

Who do we kill? A poor person. The next person is black. The next poor. The next both. But Americans somehow cannot afford honesty when we reflect on our own behavior.

We all know that nobody who is rich has ever been on death row, or will ever be on death row. It is by definition a poor people's process. The executions are of the poor—mainly black but always poor—American citizens. A whole segment of society will never get the death penalty. That alone should be enough reason to wipe out capital punishment.

It is not equal justice under the law—never has been and never could be.

The "haves" have another justice system from the "have nots." The justice system for the "have nots" includes the death penalty. The "haves" do not have the death penalty in their justice system. It looks like the same building when you go into the court. . . . but it isn't. There are two courts. Physically there is one court, but psychically there are two courts. The rich have the "rich only" courts, and then there are the "poor only" courts. The "poor only" can go to the death chamber. The "rich only" don't go and never will go.

Since we can't seem to get the relationships between black and white people right, and the rich never get to death row, you don't have a real justice system. So, we need to take away the finality of killing people. It would be a symbol of fairness to the poor and to the black that the government is serious about fairness. It may not offer the fairness but it would offer the symbol of fairness. That would mean something.

The killing of black persons by white people in the United States, both by lynching and by legal methods, is a horrendous embarrassment. The white man has been a mean person to the black person throughout our whole history, and that continues to be true. What they are saying is that these people are *lesser persons*.

The pro-death penalty leaders and politicians in this country say they are reflecting the will of the people.

The politicians who say they want the death penalty often lie, because they really don't want to kill in earnest. They really want to pretend that they kill, or can kill fairly, and that's it intrinsically.

The system has to prove to itself that it is involved with death. So they put up a death row to *prove* that they *want* to kill people. Even if they *don't* kill them very often.

It is no deterrent. The idea that the death penalty is a deterrent is a joke, a sick joke on the American public which is so profound and so persuasive that it is really embarrassing at its base.

Here you come along with twenty thousand murders each year in the United States. They can't build jails fast enough. Nobody bothers to examine the society to see what's wrong that promotes all this violence. Take a look at this swampland of the courts all bogged up, jails are filled, everything is wrong, crack dealers running around, drug dealers running around, violence, robberies, kids are into it, and the politicians say, "I am going to use the death penalty!" The people think that this is going to correct all the problems that I just named. It is such a insult to the constituency and a total abuse of rhetoric.

It is the equivalent of having a cockroach spray in a building infested with cockroaches and you yell out the window, "You watch, I am going to reduce the cockroach population in this building!" You take the can and "shoooooooooosh" you hit *one* cockroach and it falls over and dies, right? (Little later he probably wakes up anyway and says, "Thanks, I needed that," and walks off.) You don't rid yourself of the cockroaches in the building by killing *one* of them.

The politicians are really saying, "Let's execute a cockroach." Then everybody is cheerin', "Yeah they killed a cockroach in that building." But go ask the other people in the building about the cockroaches.

It is the same with crime. Go ask the people about crime on the streets the day after they killed Willie Darden in Florida. Did it lower the crime rate? Do you feel safer? People would crack up. "Who? Willie who? Who died? We didn't know anybody died." Nobody knew they killed him. And if they did know, they sure didn't care!

Now if you really want to have a deterrent, really want to lower the crime rate, the only way to do it is to kill the way Khomeini killed after his revolution. Immediately and frequently. You must blow their brains out immediately and do it so often that *everybody* thinks they are going to the death chamber, and that you are lucky if you don't go in. You will probably have to kill somewhere in the neighborhood of fifty thousand to a quarter of a million people a year to get that kind of terror in our society. But I think that you might lower the crime rate.

If they fuel the death penalty enough so it really addresses the problem in the United States, we would have to execute so many citizens, especially from our poor and black communities, that it could never be done. That's the truth behind deterrence. But politicians will not own up to the truth of the present system.

If they make it work the way Meese, Bush, and all those people who are for the death penalty tell their constituents, if they really reach into the society at the rate they say they are going to, there would be so many people dying that this country would have to stop the death penalty overnight.

Can you imagine what ten or twenty thousand people on death row would say to our own society? We who turn to the world and say we are the "freedom lovers," we are the "leaders of the West. Follow us." And we are killing ten to twenty thousand at home? The politicians won't do that . . . they won't own up to their own rhetoric. Even if they succeed at the ballot box by saying, "Vote for me, I'm the death penalty guy," when he gets into office he won't use it. . . . He is lying again. He lied saying it would lower the crime rate. He lied after he gets in. He is *afraid* to use the death penalty.

But at its root it is even more cynical than that; with the death penalty, the politicians can have their cake and eat it too. Executions have settled down to about ten or twelve a year—nobody knows who the executed are or what they did, but that doesn't matter—The politicians say, "We have the death penalty, we are punishing criminals, and justice is being done. Of course we'd execute more, but those damned liberals are tying up the courts with their nit-picking points of law."

The reality, however, is that it is the *pro-death penalty* lobby who are jamming up the works, by hanging onto a policy that is morally bankrupt, constitutionally unworkable and blatantly unequal. In a certain sense though, you have to hand it to them; it's a brilliant political strategy.

Then why do you think they do this?

Because society always demands a cultural scapegoat for its sins. This is as ancient as eating, there is a need for blood and cultural scapegoats.

They want that symbolic cockroach dead. And that's a poor person and that's a black person. Society has had enough of that crap. *Symbolizing.* Using your poor and your black as scapegoats.

Isn't it considered to be "wimpy" and soft on crime to be an abolitionist?

I think that is the perception, and that is why I believe the argument should be made that you have to protect everybody's rights equally. We need to take on society across the board to make civil rights human rights. The truth is they will never use the strength of their position. They will never ever do what they threaten, so they are lying again. So we are not wimps. In fact, to my mind, we are strong and they are liars. I think it is barbaric. Killing people is barbaric. And that's not wimpy. It's wimpy *not* to shout out at such gross injustice.

Do you see lethal injection as a way of making it more acceptable?

Lethal injection is like the new hotels. You've got the mirrors, elevators you can see through; you go in and you feel good because these are *new* hotels. You feel bad when you are in enclosed cranky old elevators where there's some old guy running it because that is the old way. Well, the same goes for lethal injection—you are supposed to feel good about this person getting killed, because they are using lethal injection, it's new, it's hi-tech, it's merciful. But the prisoners are still dead. They keep hunting for ways of killing people that are humane. It is intrinsically contradictory. It has been and will be forever. I think this method is how we keep escalating our instinct to cover up the killing. It is proof that they want to hide this business. It is cultural proof that they hide death by pretending that they are doing it nicely.

Once, in Utah, I was arguing with some guy, I think he was number two in the justice department, about the death penalty. He was talking about a recent execution and said, "Well, they only made one mistake. We had to walk through the chamber where the prisoner was on the gurney." I asked why that was a mistake and he said, "Well, we had to be *near* the prisoner." I said, "You mean, you can watch someone die and not feel you are near him? The mistake is that you killed him in the first place. You might as well have picked up a gun and blown his brains out. Have the guts to do it, if that's what you want." But they don't. They want to have the feeling that he is just slipping away and all that other bull is to make you feel good. So this guy goes on to say, "You know, the next person wants to die, he is volunteering, and that makes us feel better." And I said, "I was a Catholic priest and I used to

be a counselor for young people. Suppose I met your daughter on the
street and she tells me she wants to commit suicide, and I say to her,
'Hey, that's great—you volunteering for death, we'd really like to
thank you. What kind of flowers would you like? What kind of coffin?
And the best part of it is I'm a priest, I can perform the burial service.'"

He said, "Well, that's ridiculous," and I said, "Yes it is. If someone
volunteers for death, you tell them there is something wrong. And you
counsel them out of wanting to die. There is something sick about it.
Why do you think it's healthy? Because you have an intrinsic need to
feel good that you are killing somebody? Stop it!" And he really got
shook up. He was a nice boy; I mean, I don't know if it changed him,
but it shook him.

What you do is uncover that societal need to pretend that this is all
very *nice*. Microwave execution is coming soon. I swear that'll be the
next one.

When do you think the death penalty issue will be over?

I think we are going to turn this thing around in four to five years.
You see, you can't ask a populous base to get this story correct. In
legislators it's appropriate to expect reform because they are educated
and elected to oversee governance, and if governance is not fair they
should change it. Other Western governments changed their governance to protect their citizens, and that's what we should do. That's
what our Congress ought to do—they ought to eliminate the death
penalty. And they will. We will.

*Amnesty International historically has not tackled problems within
the borders of its own country, yet the United States section is doing
this with reference to the death penalty. Why?*

Amnesty members are not supposed to work on issues regarding
political prisoners, unfair trials, and torture in their own country. But
the reason for Amnesty International is to stop human rights abuses. So
if you find out you can't stop the death penalty from working outside
the country, you have got to work inside the country. You pragmati-
cally do that. You've just got to be effective at what you do. There is
no sense in having an institution that is built on a paper tiger that can't
bite, and I think we have discovered the only way to bite and stop this
business of killing citizens by government is to work in this country.
So we do. What we are built to do is to stop human rights abuses. And
that's what we do. That's why I like this battle.

It is particularly poignant that some of our uninformed members,
who feel they are in the human rights movement, want to walk away
from the issue of the death penalty. They are intrinsically contradictory
and do not belong in the human rights movement. They do not philo-

sophically understand the concepts of human rights. That *everybody is equal*. If everybody is equal, and you can't kill fairly, then you can't kill at all. That's the game.

So what we have asked our members to do is take a look, philosophically, at what Amnesty International is really for. Amnesty is not for societal endorsement. Amnesty is built to be a societal challenge to the wrongs of what's going on. The day we start looking for endorsement we are gone, then we should get off the mountain and go home.

THE MANDATE

AMNESTY INTERNATIONAL is a worldwide movement which is independent of any government, political grouping, ideology, economic interest or religious creed. It plays a specific role within the overall spectrum of human rights work. The activities of the organization focus strictly on prisoners.

It seeks the release of men and women detained anywhere for their beliefs, color, sex, ethnic origin, language or religion, provided they have not used or advocated violence. These are termed *prisoners of conscience*.

It advocates fair and early trials for all political prisoners and works on behalf of such persons detained without charge or without trial.

It opposes the *death penalty* and *torture* or other cruel, inhuman or degrading treatment or punishment of all prisoners without reservation.

Amnesty International acts on the basis of the Universal Declaration of Human Rights and other international covenants. Amnesty International is convinced of the indivisibility and mutual dependence of all human rights. Through the practical work for prisoners within its mandate, Amnesty International participates in the wider promotion and protection of human rights in the civil, political, economic, social and cultural spheres.

Amnesty International does not oppose or support any government or political system. Its members around the world include supporters of differing systems who agree on the defense of all people in all countries against imprisonment for their beliefs, and against torture and execution.

BIBLIOGRAPHY

Amnesty International. *The Death Penalty*. London: Amnesty International Publications, 1979.

———*United States of America: The Death Penalty*. London: Amnesty International Publications, 1987.

———*When the State Kills . . . The Death Penalty: A Human Rights Issue*. London: Amnesty International Publications, 1989.

Baldus, David C.; Charles A. Pulaski, Jr.; and George Woodworth. "Arbitrariness and Discrimination in the Administration of the Death Penalty: A Challenge to State Supreme Courts." *Stetson Law Review 15* (1986): 133–261.

Bedau, Hugo Adam (ed.). *The Death Penalty in America*. 3rd Edition. New York: Oxford University Press, 1982.

———*The Case Against the Death Penalty*. New York: American Civil Liberties Union (132 W 43rd St., New York, NY 10036), 1984.

———*Death Is Different: Studies in the Morality, Law and Politics of Capital Punishment*. Boston: Northeastern University Press, 1987.

Bedau, Hugo Adam; and Michael L. Radelet. "Miscarriages of Justice in Potentially Capital Cases." *Stanford Law Review 40* (1987): 21–179.

Black, Charles L., Jr. *Capital Punishment: The Inevitability of Caprice and Mistake*. 2nd Edition. New York: W.W. Norton and Co., 1981.

Blume, John; and David Bruck. "Sentencing the Mentally Retarded to Death: An Eighth Amendment Analysis." *Arkansas Law Review 41* (1988): 725–764.

Bowers, William J.; with Glenn L. Pierce and John F. McDevitt. *Legal Homicide: Death As Punishment in America, 1864–1982*. Boston: Northeastern University Press, 1984.

Brown, Edmund G. ("Pat"); with Dick Adler. *Public Justice and Private Mercy: A Governor's Education on Death Row.* Weidenfeld and Nicholson, 1988.

Calvert, E. Roy. *Capital Punishment in the Twentieth Century.* 5th Edition. London: G. Putnam's Sons, 1936.

Camus, Albert. "Reflections on the Guillotine." Pp. 173–234 in Albert Camus, *Resistance, Rebellion, and Death.* New York: Alfred A. Knopf, 1966.

Duffy, Clinton T. *88 Men and Two Women.* New York: Doubleday, 1962.

Ehrmann, Herbert B. *The Case That Will Not Die: Commonwealth vs. Sacco and Vanzetti.* Boston: Little Brown, 1969.

———*The Untried Case: The Sacco-Vanzetti Case and the Morelli Gang.* New York: Vanguard Press.

Ehrmann, Sara R. "For Whom the Chair Waits." *Federal Probation 26* (1962): 14–25.

Eshelman, Byron. *Death Row Chaplain.* Englewood Cliffs, NJ: Prentice Hall, 1962.

Espy, M. Watt, Jr. "Capital Punishment and Deterrence: What the Statistics Cannot Show." *Crime and Delinquency 26* (1980): 537–44.

Geimer, William S.; and Jonathan Amsterdam. "Why Jurors Vote Life or Death: Operative Factors in Ten Florida Death Penalty Cases." *American Journal of Criminal Law 15* (1987–88): 1–54.

Gross, Samuel R.; and Robert Mauro. *Death and Discrimination: Racial Disparities in Capital Sentencing.* Boston: Northeastern University Press, 1989.

Haas, Kenneth C.; and James A. Inciardi (eds.). *Challenging Capital Punishment: Legal and Social Science Approaches.* Newbury Park, CA: Sage, 1988.

Kennedy, Ludovic. *The Airman and the Carpenter: The Lindbergh Kidnapping and the Framing of Richard Hauptmann.* New York: Viking, 1985.

Lempert, Richard O. "The Effect of Executions on Homicides: A New Look in an Old Light." *Crime and Delinquency 29* (1983): 88–115.

Pierrepoint, Albert. *Executioner: Pierrepoint*. Sevenoaks, Kent: Hodder and Stoughton, 1974.

Radelet, Michael L. (ed.). *Facing the Death Penalty: Essays on a Cruel and Unusual Punishment*. Philadelphia: Temple University Press, 1989.

Radelet, Michael L.; and Margaret Vandiver. *Capital Punishment in America: An Annotated Bibliography*. New York: Garland Publishing Co., 1988.

Streib, Victor. *Death Penalty for Juveniles*. Bloomington: Indiana University Press, 1987.

Turnbull, Colin. "Death by Decree." *Natural History 87* (1978): 51–66.

Zimring, Franklin E.; and Gordon Hawkins. *Capital Punishment and the American Agenda*. New York: Cambridge University Press, 1986.

For More Information, Write to:

Amnesty International
322 Eighth Avenue
New York, NY 10001

American Civil Liberties Union
132 W. 43rd Street
New York, NY 10036

National Coalition to Abolish the Death Penalty
1419 V Street N.W.
Washington, DC 20009

NAACP Legal Defense and Educational Fund, Inc.
99 Hudson Street
New York, NY 10013